The Persecution of the Templars

Scandal, Torture, Trial

Alain Demurger

translated from the French by

Teresa Lavender Fagan

PROFILE BOOKS

First published in Great Britain in 2018 by
PROFILE BOOKS LTD
3 Holford Yard
Bevin Way
London WC1X 9HD
www.profilebooks.com

First published in French as *La Persécution des templiers: journal (1305–1314)*
by Éditions Payot & Rivages, Paris, 2015
Copyright © Alain Demurger 2015, 2018
Translation © Teresa Lavender Fagan 2018

This book is supported by the Institut français (Royaume-Uni) as part of the Burgess programme.

INSTITUT
FRANÇAIS
ROYAUME-UNI

1 3 5 7 9 10 8 6 4 2

A CIP catalogue record for this book is available from the British Library.

ISBN 978 1 78125 785 2
eISBN 978 1 78283 329 1

Typeset in Fournier by MacGuru Ltd

Printed and bound in Great Britain by Clays, Elcograf S.p.A

FSC
www.fsc.org
MIX
Paper from
responsible sources
FSC® C018072

I can easily rank among the plots against a whole society the ordeal of the Knights Templar. This barbarity was even more atrocious because it was committed through the judicial system. This was not at all one of those furies that sudden revenge or the necessity of self-defence might seem to justify; it was a deliberate project to exterminate a whole order which was too proud and too rich. I can well imagine there were young members whose debauched behaviour merited some punishment, but I will never believe that a grand master and numerous knights, including princes, all venerable by their age and their services rendered, could be guilty of the absurd and pointless villainies of which they were accused. I will never believe that a whole religious order in Europe could have renounced the Christian religion, for which it fought in Asia, in Africa, and for which many still languished in the chains of the Turks and Arabs, preferring to die in their dungeons than to abjure their religion.

Indeed I can easily believe in more than eighty knights, who, dying, swore to God their innocence. Let us not hesitate to rank their proscription among the grievous effects of a time of ignorance and barbarity.

Voltaire, *Concerning Conspiracies against Peoples, or Proscriptions*, 1766[1]

CONTENTS

ABBREVIATIONS

AD	Archives départementales
AN	Archives nationales de France
BnF	Bibliothèque nationale de France
CTHS	Comité des travaux historiques et scientifiques
HLF	*Histoire littéraire de la France*
Michelet	Jules Michelet, *Le Procès des templiers*, Collections des documents inédits sur l'Histoire de France, 1841–51; new edn, Paris, CTHS, 1987
RHGF	*Recueil des historiens des Gaules et de la France*, 21 vols
SHF	Société de l'Histoire de France

TABLES AND MAPS

Tables

Maps

TRANSLATOR'S NOTE

The reader will notice that some elements of the names of some of the individuals and places discussed in the text and listed in the index are given in *italics*. The author explains this as follows:

The trial unfolded in the Middle Ages, and the notaries and scribes who recorded the interrogations of the Templars wrote in Latin, while the Templars mostly spoke in French. And so all the names of individuals and places were given in French, and were then translated more or less accurately into Latin. Not all were translated fully, however, and so we see various spellings of the same name: Oiselay, which becomes Oyselier, Oyselaer and so on. It is common practice among historians of the Middle Ages to use roman type for the names of people and places for which we are confident of the French rendering (or at least if the words sound French), and to use italics for those that are in Latin, and whose French equivalent cannot be determined. For example, Jean de *Alneto* is italicised because we can't be sure of the French equivalent: Aunet, Alnet or perhaps Aunay. In any event, 'Alneto' is clearly not French, and writing it in roman type would indicate that it is. Sometimes, when there is a significant difference between the Latin name and its French spelling, I have included both, with the Latin name in italic in parentheses, for example: Herbley (*Arreblayo*).

Such conventions are not merely the whims of historians but reflect the reality of the fourteenth century and the challenges of communication that arose in an affair, such as that of the Templars, which brought together a large number of men who spoke only the vernacular and men of the Church who spoke only in Latin. Entire sessions of the trial were devoted to translating from Latin into French (and in the English trial, from Latin into English), the texts of the indictments.

INTRODUCTION

The trial of the Templars, sometimes known as the 'Templar Affair', continues to intrigue through its sheer magnitude: here was a religious order with a military vocation – powerful, international, protected by the pope – being accused of heresy by the king of France, Philip IV the Fair. On 13 October 1307 the Templars in the kingdom of France were arrested and imprisoned, and their possessions seized and impounded on the orders of the king. Tortured and interrogated in the months of October and November 1307, they confessed to appalling acts: when knights entered the Order, they renounced Christ, trampled or spat on the cross and engaged in sodomy and other lewd acts; their priests didn't consecrate the host during the Mass; and they held their chapter meetings at night, in secret.

This is how the Templar Affair began.

The Order of the Temple (1120–1307)

The Order began with a handful of knights who offered to defend the Holy Land of Jerusalem, the city of Christ and the Latin states that had been established following the First Crusade (1095–9): the Latin kingdom of Jerusalem, the County of Tripoli, the Principality of Antioch and the County of Edessa, which soon disappeared. These states needed men, weapons and money to defend themselves against the Muslim kingdoms of the region, which, having survived the shock of the First Crusade, were regrouping and attempting to regain the territories they had lost. Help came regularly from the West in the form of the constant Crusading expeditions during the twelfth and thirteenth centuries, but it also came from the resources of the states themselves, which had feudal-type armies similar to those in the West. This was not enough. A few Christian knights, led by Hugues de Payns, a knight from the Champagne region, began to assist the canons of the Holy Sepulchre. The knights felt that their talents were being wasted, and sought to establish themselves as a religious order, subject to a Rule and to religious vows of obedience, chastity and poverty, under the direction of a master. In 1120 they received permission from the king of Jerusalem, Baldwin II, and from the patriarch of the holy city. They just needed the recognition of the Roman Church and the pope. This wasn't a fore-gone conclusion, because their proposal was novel, indeed almost revolutionary: they would be a new religious order whose vocation was not, like Benedictine monasticism and its Cistercian variant, meditation and contemplation but action – and furthermore military action. Their proposal was thus violent, involving the possibility of killing and of being killed.

This official recognition was, however, granted, in January 1129 during a council assembled in Troyes under the direction of a papal legate and in the pres-ence of Bernard, the Cistercian abbot of Clairvaux (the future Saint Bernard). The new religious-military Order very quickly found supporters among the lower and mid-level aristocracy, and attracted the interest of the powerful. There was an increase in recruits and donations, ensuring the new Order the human and economic means necessary to carry out its dual mission on the 'front': the protection of pilgrims who were going to Jerusalem and the defence of the Latin states.

On the Iberian Peninsula, the Aragonese, Castilian and Portuguese rulers, who were actively involved in the Reconquest of the small Muslim kingdoms that had emerged from the dismemberment of the Caliphate of Córdoba, quickly understood the importance of the Order of the Temple. They increased their donations of castles and territories to the Order, in exchange for the Templars' protection, but also to glorify these holdings and encourage people to live there.

The Order derived its name from the location of its headquarters in Jerusa-lem, in what was believed to be the ancient temple of Solomon. It was, in fact, the site of the palace of King Solomon, on which the victorious Arab Muslims had constructed the al-Aqsa mosque. The Order's full, official name was: *pau-perum commilitonum Christi Templique Salomonici* (Poor Fellow-Soldiers of Christ and of the Temple of Solomon), which was shortened to the Order of the Temple. By the 1130s the Order had grown considerably, and needed stricter organisation.

A Templar lived in a 'house' (*domus*); houses were grouped together in com-manderies or preceptories, which were in turn grouped in provinces: France,

Provence, Poitou-Aquitaine, Auvergne, England, Germany, Italy, Sicily, Aragon, Castile and Portugal. At the top of the hierarchy the Order was governed by a Master or General Master (although modern historians tend to refer to 'Grand Masters') and a dozen or so dignitaries (marshal, grand commander, draper, turcopolier and others).

The Order comprised three categories of brothers: knights, the only ones who wore the white mantle bearing the red cross; sergeant brothers; and priests or chaplains. The many sergeants were subdivided into sergeants-at-arms, who fought, and brothers with skills, whose duties involved daily labour, farming the estates and working in trade.

Borrowing the Templar model, other religious-military orders were created in the Holy Land and in the European regions where Christians were threatened by Muslim 'infidels' (Spain) and pagan hordes (Slavs and Prussians from the Baltic regions): these were the Iberian Orders of Calatrava, Alcántara, Aviz and Santiago, and German Orders on the borders of Prussian territories. The Teutonic Order, established in the Holy Land at the end of the twelfth century, quickly took root in Prussia and in the Livonian region. The Order of the Hospital of Saint John of Jerusalem was an order apart: at the beginning of, and even before, the First Crusade a hospital was founded in Jerusalem to lodge, feed and, if necessary, take care of ill or wounded pilgrims. With the success of the Crusade it became the leading Order in a network of houses in the West. Recognised as an order of hospitallers, it became militarised during the twelfth century and became the equal of the Temple, its partner and rival.

In the Holy Land, with their energy and effective military strategy, the Latin states were initially successful in containing their Muslim adversaries, who were, in any case, quite divided among themselves. Around 1160, although the County of Edessa had disappeared, the three other Latin states enjoyed their largest territorial expansion. But the Muslims joined forces: Nur al-Din (who died in 1176) united northern Syria and Damascus; his successor, Saladin, continued his efforts and became the ruler of Egypt. In 1187 the Latins were defeated at Hattin and were forced to abandon Jerusalem. The kingdom was reduced to a few scattered territories, including Tyre. And it was from this port that the Latins set off to besiege Acre. With the support of the Third Crusade, led by Richard the Lionheart, they gradually reconquered the coastline and rebuilt a new kingdom of Jerusalem, reduced to a long coastal strip, of which Acre became the capital: in fact, Jerusalem itself remained in the hands of Saladin and his successors in the Ayyubid dynasty. The county of Tripoli and the principality of Antioch, although damaged, survived.

The balance of power between the Latins and the Muslims was eventually completely reversed. Once this happened, the religious-military orders, thanks to the means at their disposal, played an increasingly important military and political role and became the true masters of the Latin Orient. As guardians of imposing fortresses, which they alone were able to maintain and secure (the Hospitallers' Krak des Chevaliers or the Templars' Castle Pilgrim, for example), they became responsible for the defence and survival of the Latin states. These states endured until 1250, when their demise began with the rise of the Mamluks, an army corps originally made up of Turkish slaves, who seized power in Egypt and conquered Muslim Syria.[1] The Mamluk offensives, sometimes slowed by the hostile advances of the Mongols from Persia, gradually consumed the Latin territories, and the fortresses fell one by one. In 1291 the fall of Acre forced the Latins to abandon the last of their coastal retreats; they fled to Cyprus, where they hoped to join forces with the Mongols in order to take back the Holy Land. Despite the fact that both the Templars and the Hospitallers transferred their 'convents' – their central headquarters and military apparatus – to the island, they never abandoned the hope of one day reconquering Jerusalem.

At the end of 1306 Jacques de Molay, Grand Master of the Temple, and Foulques de Villaret, his Hospitaller counterpart, set off from Cyprus for France to meet with Pope Clement V, who had summoned them expressly to discuss preparations for a new crusade and plans to combine their two Orders.

De Molay was never to return.

The trial of the Templars (1307–1314)

My intention in this book is not to write a new history of the trial of the Templars. There are many such histories, and I refer the reader to Malcolm Barber's work, the most comprehensive of them all.[2] My goal is different: to reveal what must have been the actual everyday lives of the Templars of the kingdom of France during an affair that spanned five years, from the arrests in 1307 to the suppression of the Order at the Council of Vienne in 1312. (The affair did, however, continue another two years for the dignitaries of the Order, until the execution of Jacques de Molay and Geoffroy de Charney in March 1314.) Nor will I attempt to explain the reasons for the trial, or to continue the distorted debate on the guilt or innocence of the Templars, or to retrace once again the confrontation between the pope and the king of France, which was central to the affair. However, to provide context for what follows, I will present an overview of some of the most important elements of the affair. A brief presentation of the available documentary sources will be helpful before discussing the contradictory positions historians have taken.

The trial records

There are abundant documentary sources for the affair, in the Vatican Archives and in the Royal Archives of France and elsewhere. Of these sources, the records of the interrogations of the Templars during the various proceedings are essential, but difficult to interpret. Many historiographical debates revolve around the question of the reliability of sources of this kind. I will present the sources here in sequence, according to the chronological development of events.

The first period (October/November 1307) involves only France. The Templars of the kingdom were arrested on 13 October and interrogated by royal agents and inquisitors. We have records for Paris, Caen, Cahors, Carcassonne and Nîmes. It should be noted that only a very small number of Templar depositions have been found.

The pope had not been informed of the king of France's intentions or of the actions he took in October. The pope protested, and, to emphasise the authority of the Church throughout Christendom, he reacted on 22 November 1307 by ordering the arrest of Templars throughout the West and in Cyprus. In doing so he believed he was regaining the upper hand in the matter. Afterwards, and at the cost of a harsh confrontation with Philip the Fair and his advisers, the pope was allowed to interrogate seventy-two Templars (some of whose testimonies have been preserved), and in July/August 1308 he was able to initiate dual proceedings, against individual Templars and against the Order as a whole. The first would be carried out on the diocese level by episcopal commissions which also included inquisitors; the second would be on the state level, by papal commissions set up by the pope. This first, investigatory phase would be followed by one of judgement, which would occur on the provincial (archbishopric) level, in provincial councils for individuals and in an ecumenical council for the Order. The French Archives contain the diocesan investigations of Clermont (June 1309) and Nîmes (August 1310 and 1311); a further document is truncated in such a way that it can neither be dated nor placed – it is probable, however, that it involves the Dauphiné and a part of Provence (regions that at the time were not part of the kingdom of France); and I am not including that of the diocese of Elne in Roussillon, which at the time belonged to the kingdom of Majorca.

Outside France the two sets of proceedings were often carried out in parallel, and we have more or less complete records of the interrogations held in Cyprus, England, Italy, the Iberian kingdoms and Germany. The proceedings did not begin until 1310 or even 1311.

In France the proceedings against the Order got off to a difficult start in November 1309 and continued, with a hiatus of several months, until May 1311. Known to us thanks to two manuscripts (one in the Bibliothèque nationale de France in Paris, the other in the Vatican Archives in Rome), the depositions given by the Templars in the trial are by far the most detailed and the most specific that we have: in addition to the interrogations of 224 Templars and six non-Templar witnesses, they contain a great deal of valuable information about issues tangential to the sessions and about the attempts at resistance by Templars in the kingdom of France in the spring of 1310.[3]

Before addressing the question of the reliability of these depositions, some facts need to be pointed out. First, torture was systematically used to obtain confessions from the Templars. Second, although the interrogations carried out by the papal commission of Paris involved 224 Templars, there were more than 650 Templars who appeared before the commission to defend the Order; they did so in an increasingly confident manner and often collectively, presenting the commissioners with well-argued 'memoranda'. This resistance was swiftly suppressed by a forceful takeover by the archbishop of Sens (under whose domain the bishopric of Paris fell), who on 11 May 1310 assembled the council of his ecclesiastical province to pass judgement against the individual Templars of his province: the following day, 12 May, 54 Templars were burned for relapsing into heresy. On 19 May, 44 Templars (out of more than 600) withdrew their support for the Order. Some of them appear among the 224 Templars whose depositions we have, but not all of them. And so we must be careful not to argue only from the depositions we possess, because that would be to ignore a (probable) majority of Templars whose positions we are unable to know.

While bearing these points in mind, we will now look, first, at the reliability of the Templars' depositions and, second, at the reasons for and the causes of the Templar Affair.

Can we believe the Templars' confessions?

There are three possible responses to this question: 1) yes, they represent the truth; 2) no, they are pure and simple fabrications; 3) maybe; they don't justify the trial brought against the Templars, but they do contain an element of truth.

In other words, to the question: 'Were the Templars guilty?' the historian might respond: 'Yes,' 'No' or 'No, but …'.

For those who answer 'yes', the accusations are true: the Templars who were interrogated were unable to hide their scandalous practices, and we must take their confessions seriously. There are only differences of nuance, at best, between someone like Pierre Dupuy, a seventeenth-century author and loyal royalist for whom the motives of the king of France were beyond question, and Jean Favier or Joseph R. Strayer, recent historians of Philip the Fair, who admit that, although the affair may not have involved heresy, there was a lot of laxity in the Order and its unpopularity was not without reason. Philip the Fair didn't have to expend much effort in constructing his accusations. As for torture, it was a common practice at the time, and no one thought to question its use (which isn't entirely true, as we will see).[4]

The idea that the practices denounced by the prosecution were the result of the corruption of the brothers and the negligence of their leaders fits perfectly with the idea of the unpopularity of the Order that is proposed by many historians (and which distorts historical reality): the Temple was no longer fighting, it was overseeing its banking network; it was no longer involved with the Holy Land and had transferred its headquarters from Cyprus to Paris; its members, at loose ends, were behaving like delinquents, frequenting taverns and brothels. Jonathan Riley-Smith uses these arguments and essentially answers in the affirmative to the direct question that serves as the title of one of his articles: 'Were the Templars Guilty?'[5] Riley-Smith, an eminent historian of the Crusades and of the Order of the Hospitallers of Saint John of Jerusalem, contrasts the disorder reigning in the Temple to the good governance of the Hospital during the same period. The same comparison, unfavourable to the Temple, is used by another great historian of the Hospital, Anthony Luttrell, who does not even mention the trial.[6] Here we find the theme, widespread among historians of the Hospital, though never fully debated or verified, of the contrast between the blinkered and unintelligent Master of the Temple, Jacques de Molay, and the brilliant and astute Master of the Hospital, Foulques de Villaret. This is meant to explain in part the misfortunes of the Temple in 1307, but it is a somewhat simplistic explanation.

According to those who would answer 'no, but . . .', the trial was fabricated by the king and his counsellors. The accusations of heresy contained in the arrest order and repeated in the proceedings issued by the pope were drawn from a manual that had been gradually developed by the inquisitors in the thirteenth century. That manual was also used for other trials initiated by Philip the Fair against Pope Boniface VIII and the bishops Bernard Saisset and Guichard de Troyes; the use of torture was expressly recommended in such manuals, and it was used on the Templars to obtain confessions that matched the accusations.

This is all true. But didn't the Templars invite criticism and defamation by allowing stupid and tasteless practices to take root in their Order, practices resembling initiation ceremonies, which in themselves weren't heretical but which could provide the king of France with enough evidence to merit an accusation which, though completely fabricated, would then appear true?

Many historians of the Temple – and I was one of them – albeit with some slight differences of opinion, have adopted this argument: the renunciation of Christ, spitting or trampling on the cross, 'obscene kissing', being encouraged to engage in sodomy, may all have taken place. Moreover, almost all the Templars admitted to these acts: yes, they renounced their faith, but from their mouths, not their hearts; yes, they spat, but next to the cross, not on it; the encouragement to engage in sodomy, yes, that happened, but the encouragement was not acted on.[7] Anne-Marie Chagny-Sève rejects as unfounded the stories about worshipping a cat, the omission of the words used to consecrate the host, the encouragement to homosexuality, and sacrificing to idols, but adds: 'Nonetheless, the renunciation and the spitting on the cross are a problem.'[8]

Were these isolated individual events or collective practices based on the statutes of the Order, as some Templars maintained in their defence? Nothing along these lines has been found in the statutes, which has led Barbara Frale to suggest the existence of a *codice ombra* (initiation code), discreet if not secret, introduced as an adjunct to the perfectly orthodox admission ritual, which was meant to test the new recruit upon his entrance into the Temple. The existence of this ritual, which was never performed outside the admission ceremony, might thus have co-existed alongside beliefs and religious practices in keeping with the Catholic faith.

I will admit that this argument seduced me and that, abandoning the caution I showed in *Vie et mort de l'ordre du Temple*, I adopted it in both *The Last Templar* (2002) and *Les Templiers* (2005).

This 'no, but ...' leaves certain questions unanswered, though. The secrecy of the Temple's internal deliberations (chapter meetings, the admission ceremony) was standard and not at all unique to the Order. If blasphemous rites such as renouncing Christ and spitting on the cross were general practices, surely this would have been known about outside the Order, given that many Templars, for example, admitted that, in the days following their admission ceremony, they had confessed to priests of the Order and also to secular preachers or brothers of the mendicant Orders, Franciscans or Dominicans, or even to the pope? Alan Forey has legitimately raised the question (and answered it in the negative): is it possible for all of this to have gone on in secret for decades without being discovered?[9] Still examining the 'no, but ...' position, this side-steps the question of torture. The geography of the confessions corresponds exactly to that of the use of torture; no one denies this. In France, where torture was used routinely from the beginning of the proceedings, the use of torture was not meant to elicit *the* truth from the Templars regarding practices they wished to hide but was intended to obtain confessions from them that conformed to *a* truth that had been established in advance by their accusers.

Outside France, where torture was not used, there were no confessions: how is this compatible with a generalised implementation of a *codice ombra*? I originally explained this discrepancy by suggesting that the Templars outside France, knowing what was going on in the Capetian kingdom, would simply have avoided making trouble for themselves by denying the existence of an 'initiation code' (especially since there was no torture). On reflection, this explanation now seems to me a bit feeble.

The 'no, but ...' or, to borrow a phrase from Julien Théry, 'I know, but even so' doesn't hold up.

And so it must be 'no': there is no truth in the confessions. As Théry writes, 'it is impossible to attempt to separate truth from falsehood' in the reports, and 'nothing, beyond the arrests and forced confessions, leads us to believe that the Templars were guilty'.[10] For Sean Field, who analyses the case of the Templar Mathieu de Cressonessart, 'however closely they may read testimony such as that, historians will never find anything but a predetermined "truth," forcefully imposed through royal imperatives.'[11]

This categorical 'no' isn't new. The same position was held by a certain number of nineteenth-century historians (not including Michelet), whose arguments were supported with the publication of sources from the trial. The position is also shared by many current historians of the Temple who have based it on solid research and documentation: Malcolm Barber, Helen Nicholson, Alan Forey, Julien Théry and others. I consider myself part of this group, and in the pages that follow I hope to provide additional material, not derived from the trial records, which further supports our position.

How can the Templar Affair be explained?

Everyone knows the saying 'There's no smoke without fire'. When one runs out of proof for something, it is very useful. Historians sometimes fall back on it, forgetting to ask the essential question, 'Who lit the fire?'

In this case, the response is clear: the king of France and his counsellors. It is not in the history of the Temple, in its real or assumed weaknesses, that we will find the reasons for its demise. To quote Julien Théry again:

> The fate of the Temple was sealed within the logic of a story that was not its own, but rather that of the French monarchy: the story of the confrontation between Philip the Fair and the pope; the story of privileged ties formed on that occasion between God, France and its 'Most Christian King'.[12]

In view of this, there is no need to return to what I argued in *Les Templiers*: 'It is through an analysis of the king's reasons that we can find a plausible explanation for the Templar Affair.'[13] We must exclude financial motives (the expected gains from the collapse of the Temple were just a side-effect) and see the actions against the Temple in the context of the confrontation between the king and the papacy under the pontificate of Boniface VIII (1295–1303) and its aftermath. The king of France went so far as to accuse the pope of heresy and wanted to have him deposed and judged by a council. Boniface VIII was attacked and held prisoner for a time in his residence in Anagni shortly before his death in 1303. The Templar Affair had not been premeditated for very long; the king merely seized an opportunity that was offered to him to put pressure on Pope Clement V (1305–1314) to condemn the memory of Boniface VIII and thereby justify his action and the violence perpetuated against Boniface in Anagni. I use the word 'opportunity' because, as we will see, the king did not initiate the rumour against the Templars; he simply took advantage of it to create the affair. It is important to highlight the difference: the rumour was a reality, but what it contained was a lie. Throughout the Templar Affair, the condemnation of the memory of Boniface VIII remained the king's chief preoccupation and, because of that, the chief occupation of Pope Clement as well, who, of course, refused to countenance it.

To erase the Anagni incident and its aftermath was, however, only one of the reasons for the king of France's attack against the Temple. There were others, which related to faith, beliefs, the mystical leanings of the king and of his closest advisers. I have analysed those causes previously, with the help of the work of Robert-Henri Bautier and Malcolm Barber. Bautier's study focuses on the king's personality; Barber attempts to uncover Philip the Fair's 'world view'.[14]

The mysticism of the Most Christian King made the purification of the kingdom his primary objective; the expulsion of the Jews in 1306 and the destruction of the Order of the Temple in 1307 were his means.[15] The Templar Affair was also intended to make the king of France – the 'angel of God', according to his faithful adviser Guillaume de Nogaret – a 'pope in his kingdom'. By attacking the Temple, Philip the Fair was not simply challenging the authority he felt the pope had over the bishops and the clergy of his kingdom: he was also challenging the pope's right to intervene in matters of faith (here, the 'heresy of the Templars') and to act for the good of all Christendom. In the end, appropriating the model of the Church for himself, he tried to turn the kingdom of France into a mystical body of which he, Philip, would be the head and the Church a limb in the same capacity as any other.

And so, one year after the expulsion of the Jews, the king attacked the Templars, originally housed in the Temple of Solomon, accusing them of crucifying Christ a second time by renouncing him and defiling the cross on which he had been martyred. The Order of the Temple had to be destroyed so that the new alliance between the king, Christ and the people of the kingdom could be formed.

The average Templar knight was quite removed from all this. On 13 October 1307 the sky, and the heaven he believed he deserved through his acts of bravery in the service of the Church and Jerusalem, crashed around his head. It is this man, and the way in which he experienced his persecution on a daily basis, that I will follow in this book.

1

PRELUDE

(1305–1307)

The Agenais rumour

Brother Ponsard de Gizy, originally from Picardy, had entered the Temple before 1298. His uncle was Raoul de Gizy, also a Templar, who had had a long career as royal tax collector in Champagne and Brie.[1] At the time of the Templars' arrest Ponsard was commander of Payns, near Troyes (the town that was home to Hugues de Payns, founder of the Order). Although he was held in the Paris Temple, Ponsard was not one of the Templars interrogated by the inquisitors in October/November 1307, but we know that he appeared before the bishop of Paris after being severely tortured.[2] On 27 November 1309 he appeared in Paris before the papal commission assigned to investigate the Order; he was one of the first Templars to testify before it. He stated that the accusations made against the Temple were false and presented the commissioners with a short memorandum written in his own hand. In it he denounces

> the traitors who have falsely accused members of the Order of the Temple and have attributed disloyal acts to them: the monk Guillaume Robert, who brought them in for questioning; Esquieu de Floyrac de Biterris, prior of Montfaucon; Bernard Pelet, prior of Mas d'Agenais; and Gérard de Boyzol, a knight who came from Gisors.[3]

In presenting this statement, Ponsard de Gizy was using the only means of defence available to the accused in the inquisition procedure: denouncing their accusers as their enemies, who were therefore telling lies against them. For a long time the identities of the four 'traitors' were unknown, but they have now been established.[4] Guillaume Robert was not, as was previously believed, Guillaume de Paris, the inquisitor of France, but a monk from Saint-Martin de Bergerac. Bernard Pelet, from a minor family of knights from the region around Buzet-sur-Baïse, was indeed the prior of the Mas-d'Agenais and adviser to the king of England (who was also the duke of Guyenne). Esquieu de Floyrac, or Floyran, prior of Montfaucon – a dependency of Saint-Martial de Limoges – was not from Béziers, in Languedoc, but from the Agenais.[5] Floyrac is also the name of a district in Agen, where members of Esquieu's family had been canons. Finally, Gérard de Boyzol is believed to have been either Gérard de Lavergne, commander of Andrivaux (Périgueux), who, when interrogated in Cahors, declared he had been threatened with death because he was the first to reveal the secrets of the Temple,[6] or Gérard de Causse, sometimes called de Basoez, because he was the commander of Le Bastit, or Basoez, near Cahors. This latter identification, though tempting, seems to be undermined by two facts. Gérard de Causse appeared before the papal commission for the first time on Saturday 22 November 1309; he appeared rather by chance, as he was there just to observe.[7] On 27 November Ponsard de Gizy appeared and denounced Gérard de Boyzol as a traitor and one of the four men responsible for the misfortunes of the Temple. If Gérard de Boyzol were indeed Gérard de Causse, the commissioners would certainly have had him return to testify, and to challenge the denunciation of Ponsard de Gizy. Furthermore, Gérard de Causse, who had already been interrogated in October 1307 in Paris, had been transferred on 25 January 1308 to Corbeil, where he was held with the Grand Master:[8] the Gérard du Cancer of the document is none other than Gérard de Causse. The same Gérard de Causse co-signed a letter from Jacques de Molay written in Poitiers on 9 June 1307, as commander of Le Bastit.[9]

The four 'traitors' (with the Boyzol case pending for the time being) would thus all have been from the same Aquitaine region, bordering English Guyenne; this was confirmed by the king of England himself. Informed by Bernard Pelet of everything he knew, Edward II wrote to the king of France on 30 October 1307: 'Since it is difficult to believe these things, we have ordered our seneschal from the Agenais, where the rumours originated, to appear before us.'[10] Another text, a lamentation in defence of the Temple written at the beginning of 1308, also situates the origin of the rumour within the confines of Guyenne.[11]

One of the four 'traitors', Esquieu de Floyrac, boasted of having revealed the scandal to the king of France. We know this from information he provided in a letter addressed to James II, king of Aragon, dated 21 January 1308:

To the most serene and mighty prince [...] Lord James, by the grace of God illustrious King of Aragon, Valencia, Sardinia and Corsica, Count of Barcelona, his
devoted Esquin of Floyran [*sic*], servant to the illustrious lord king of France [...]
May it be manifest to your royal Majesty that I am he who exposed the actions of
the Templars to my lord king of France, and may you acknowledge that you were
the first prince in the whole world to whom I exposed their actions at Lerida in the
presence of your confessor, Brother Martin Detecha. In this you were unwilling,
lord, to give full credence to my words at the time, which is why I had recourse
to the lord king of France, who investigated the activities and brought them out
into the daylight, particularly as concerns his kingdom; consequently he has fully
informed the pope about their activities, as well as other princes, namely the king
of Germany, the king of England and King Charles, and other princes.

[...]

My lord, remember what you promised me in your chamber at Lerida when
I departed, that if the activities of the Templars were found to be proved you
would give me 1,000 *livres* in rents and 3,000 *livres* in money from their goods.
And now that has been shown to be the case, think fit to remember that.[12]

Esquieu, bursting with pride, had not lost his business acumen. He doesn't
mention the date of his revelations, but it is conceivable that they occurred
toward the middle of 1305, and that it was his information that caused Philip the
Fair to begin to take interest in the Templars. As we can see from the beginning
of the letter, Esquieu was rewarded, since he calls himself the 'servant' of the
king of France: his letter to the king of Aragon was written in Boulogne-sur-
Mer, where he was performing his duties as valet in the retinue of the king of
France, who had travelled there for the ceremony and festivities of his daughter
Isabelle's marriage to the king of England, Edward II.[13]

Lyon (November 1305)

In fact, it was on the occasion of the coronation of Pope Clement V in Lyon
that the king of France brought up the issue of the Templars for the first time.

Bertrand de Got, archbishop of Bordeaux, had been elected pope on 25 June
1305, at the end of a very long conclave in Perugia. He was now a French pope,
but also a subject of the duke of Guyenne and of the king of England, for whom
in the past he had been the procurator.[14] The conclave was divided between

cardinals who were allies of the king of France and those who aligned themselves with Boniface VIII. Such division explains why the conclave took so long
to make a decision (close to a year) and the choice of an individual from outside
the Sacred College of Cardinals.

In the fourteenth century two Florentine chroniclers, Villani and Agnolo di
Tura, spread the idea in Italy that a plot had been hatched by the king of France
to have a 'French' pope elected against the wishes of the Italians on the side of
Boniface VIII.[15] According to this story, an encounter in Saint-Jean-d'Angély
had sealed the alliance between Philip the Fair and Bertrand de Got. In exchange
for the king's support with the conclave of cardinals he controlled, Bertrand
allegedly agreed to five conditions: 1) the removal of all ecclesiastical sanctions
against the king's partisans implicated in the attack in Anagni; 2) a formal condemnation of the memory of Boniface VIII; 3) the collection of tithes from the
French clergy for five years to finance the war with Flanders; 4) the naming of
new cardinals favourable to the king of France; and 5) a secret request that the
king would unveil at a later date.

Naturally, many historians have interpreted that mysterious request a bit too
hastily as the king's directive to arrest the Templars and to suppress their order;
but in any case this encounter, the date of which isn't specified but which could
have taken place in May 1305, never took place. This was demonstrated in the
nineteenth century: the itineraries of the two protagonists did not coincide. The
records of Archbishop Bertrand de Got's pastoral visits between 17 May 1304
and 22 June 1305 indicate no stop in Saint-Jean d'Angély or elsewhere in the
nearby provinces of Saintonge and Aunis;[16] as for the king of France, he didn't
leave Paris or Île-de-France between January and July 1305. During the summer,
the king left Île-de-France to go to Loches (he was there at the end of August),
then went back to Paris, then to Fontainebleau. He left Fontainebleau at the
beginning of November for Lyon, where he arrived on 8 November.[17] A meeting
between the king and Bertrand de Got during the conclave and before its conclusion could not have taken place.

Bertrand de Got was not Italian. After he became pope, he never went to Rome
and established the papacy in Avignon, where it remained for nearly seventy
years. That alone was enough to irritate the Italians, who had no qualms about
twisting reality and substituting fiction for reality. It is worth noting, however,
that neither Villani nor Agnolo di Tura sought to know what that 'mysterious
request' might have been.

And so Clement V was elected pope out of a compromise between two rival parties in the College of Cardinals. He wasn't the king of France's man; the fact that the king later sought to make him his pope is another story.

At Pope Clement's coronation Philip the Fair told the new pope what he had learned about the Templars and asked him to open an investigation. The pope refers to this fact in a letter of 24 August 1307 in which he informs the French king that, upon the entreaties of the Master of the Temple and his brothers, he has ordered an investigation to be launched: 'We do not believe indeed that it has slipped your memory that at Lyon and Poitiers [...] you spoke to us about the question of the Templars.'[18] And he also recalls the importance of the Lyon encounter in launching the affair in the bull *Faciens misericordiam* of 12 August 1308.[19] Similarly, the king refers to that Lyon conversation in a letter he sent to the king of Aragon on 16 October 1307.[20] The Templar Jean Taylafer de Gène, who did not defend the Order, was interrogated by the papal commissioners on 14 April 1310, and declared that he had heard from various secular sources 'that the aforementioned crimes were divulged in Lyon when the current pope and the king met there'.[21]

Pope Clement took all the rumours with a grain of salt; he listened to the king but at that time was not convinced by the revelations. He was in close contact with the Templars, notably those who served him at his court, such as the *cubicularius* (gentleman of the bedchamber), or those who, such as Hugues de Pairaud, Visitor of France, often had occasion to meet with him. These men would probably have discussed the rumours among themselves, but nothing more.

Guillaume de Nogaret's 'moles'

The king and his counsellors were more proactive. Without having yet decided what they would do with these reports, they added to them by making discreet inquiries into the Order and by placing 'moles' within its ranks. Jean Bourgogne, the king of Aragon's envoy to the Curia in Poitiers, gave his master a detailed report about the meeting of the consistory held by the pope on 29 May 1308. In it he wrote that the king, before the arrest of the Templars, had ordered twelve men in various parts of the kingdom to enter the Order, and 'boldly do what they were told and then leave'; they informed the king that the accusations against the Templars were true. It is probably pointless to try to find any trace of this espionage: like all good policemen, Guillaume de Nogaret protected his 'sources', who would not have been among those arrested in 1307.[22]

However, royal investigators did use the testimony of apostate Templars who had left the Order before the arrests, for good or bad reasons, and of Templars who, while remaining in the Order, had given information to the royal authorities or the bishops – again, before the arrests. Later, in 1310, the four Templars who had volunteered to defend the Order before the papal commission – Pierre de Bologne and Renaud de Provins, both priests, Guillaume de Chambonnet (or Chamborand) and Bertrand de Sartiges, both knights – presented a memorandum rejecting the accusations brought against their Order in which they accused those

> who had suggested these unjust lies to our lord the pope and our most high lord the king; they are false Christians or true heretics [who ...] like very impious sowers of scandal sought out apostates or fugitive brothers who, because of their crimes, had been banished from the Order [...] They seduced them in such a way so that all those who have been discovered, they sought them out, brought them back, reprimanded them, and they compiled a dossier of these lies to bring to our lord the king.[23]

Among the Templars who were interrogated it is possible to identify some of those apostates or lost Templars whose examples may have been useful to royal officials building their case prior to the arrests. Barthélemy *Bocherii*, who entered the Order in 1270, apostatised in 1301, due to the Order's 'frivolity', he first said, before revealing the Order's heretical practices, but he returned to the Order in 1303.[24] Guillaume de Soromina, received in 1303, left the Order the following year, but he was taken back almost immediately and pardoned on the condition that he remained silent.[25] Nothing indicates, however, that either of them had direct contact with the king's agents or 'moles'.

Others, on the other hand, clearly did.

The sergeant brother Jean de Vaubellant (or Valbellant), who entered the Temple in 1291 or 1293, was interrogated on 7 November 1307 by inquisitors, and then on 15 February 1311 by papal commissioners.[26] He didn't say anything specific during his first interrogation; during the second he confessed to having left the Order two years before his arrest, in 1305. When he learned that he had been excommunicated for leaving, he asked to be accepted back again, and he was reinstated during the general chapter in Paris on 24 June 1307. He had to do penance and, in conformity with the Rule, had to eat on the ground, on his mantle, for one year. In the meantime he had denounced the Order's crimes to the inquisitor of Poissy, something he did not tell his brothers when he returned. Whether he was 'groomed' or not while he was on the run doesn't matter: his confession before the inquisitor could be used. Let's note, however, that prior to testifying against the Temple before the papal commissioners in 1311, he had appeared in 1310 to defend the Temple along with five other Templars who were also being held in Paris; he was even the spokesman for the little group.[27]

Another Templar who openly admitted to talking was the chaplain brother Jean de Fouilloy, who was the first to be interrogated, on 19 October 1307. He had entered the Order in 1304, and after having allegedly renounced Christ and spat on the cross against his will, he sought advice from a Paris lawyer, Boniface Lombard, to establish whether he could leave the Order. He mentioned this to the bishop's representative in Paris (the one who was directing the episcopal procedure) and suggested that there was documentation of that meeting bearing an official seal dated the Tuesday after the feast day of Saint Luke, 1304. He confessed to the bishop, who imposed a salutary penance. Nothing more.[28] What can we learn from that testimony? Did it come from one of those unhappy Templars whom the king's 'moles' might have overheard?

The case of Jacques de Troyes reveals a great deal about the incoherence, contradictions and incredibility of the depositions, and the difficulty of distinguishing what was true from what was false in them. He testified against the Order before the papal commission on 9 May 1310. He had been received into the Order three and a half years before the arrests (in fact, only just three years, on All Saints' Day 1304); he had renounced and spat on the cross; he had taken religious vows, including that of chastity, but he added that those vows had been meaningless because he had left the Order a year before the arrests to be with a woman he loved. Then, during his deposition he stated that before entering the Order he had heard many things about the sinful practices that went on in it; they had been introduced by a knight who had returned from Outremer: 'this has been going on for a good five hundred years [sic]'.[29] In concluding, he returned to his apostasy: he had left the Order more out of disgust at its practices than for the love of a woman; indeed, while he was in the Order he could have all the women he wanted; and he added that he believed many others left the Temple because of the abominations that went on in it. Obviously he hadn't believed the rumours;

otherwise he would not have entered the Order in the first place. He doesn't say anything about a possible return to the Order, again before the arrests of 1307.

He is not one of the Templars who were arrested and interrogated in 1307; he appeared before the papal commission dressed as a layman. We can assume that Jacques de Troyes was 'approached' by the king of France's henchmen, who convinced him to testify. It is clear that the royal officials had easy means of putting pressure on this type of individual: the lay powers gave the Church a helping hand in finding apostates and punishing them; in exchange for testimony for the prosecution they would look the other way. But in Jacques de Troyes's case, this is only hypothetical.

However, it is important to cast a critical eye on all these cases of pre-trial apostasy and flight from the Order that are 'revealed' by the Templars in their depositions. It was indeed quite useful to justify one's position by the sinful practices that were going on in the Order; but were they truly the cause? To leave or flee from a religious Order because one didn't feel at home in it was a common occurrence in the medieval monastic world.[30] Granted, some entered the Order out of a vocation, but how many had been obliged and forced into it against their will: by their families, for example? Leaving, though risky, was a tempting way to escape a life one hadn't chosen. And the professed motive, 'going after a woman', was also common. Some men, such as Jacques de Troyes (in part) or Jean Le Bourguignon (Bergonhons), acknowledged that motive: Jean Le Bourguignon appeared before the papal commission in a lay habit with a group from Poitiers; he alone refused to defend the Order because, one year before the arrests, he had apostatised because of a woman.[31]

In short, we know nothing about the 'moles'; we have only the testimony of the disgruntled Templar rank and file, who, because they had a great deal to be pardoned for, were ready to say what the prosecution wanted to hear.

Facts v. hearsay

The image projected by the testimony of most of the Templars interrogated in France is that of an Order that had been completely corrupted and degraded by 'heresy'. It is difficult to believe this dark legend of the Temple which the historian Jonathan Riley-Smith has brought back to life.[32] Looking at the same testimony, we might, on the contrary, find more objective elements that point in a different direction.

Both in 1307, in front of the inquisitors or royal agents, and in 1310–11, in front of the papal commissioners, the Templars first had to respond to a questionnaire regarding their identities: name, diocese of origin, date and place of their entrance into the Order, the names of their receptor and the brothers who attended the ceremony and so forth. Then they were interrogated about the articles of the accusation. There are no valid reasons to challenge the responses to the questionnaire about identity; it contained what can be considered true information even if the rest fell into the realm of fiction. At most we should take into account approximations or lapses of memory that caused names to be forgotten, facts or dates to be confused. Jacques de Troyes, however confused his deposition may appear, was still Jacques, from Troyes, around twenty-four years old. He entered the Order three and a half years before the arrests (in 1303/04), was a sergeant in the Order and seneschal of the house of the Temple of Villers, near Troyes, in 1307.[33] This information, which can be considered objectively true, allows us to sketch an image of the Order at the time it was under attack that is very different from the one conveyed by the historiography.

With all the data compiled, the records of the interrogations of the Templars in France reveal the names of 2,330 Templars, who were divided into two categories: 1,120 living Templars who were involved in one or the other of the proceedings carried out between 1307 and 1311, and 1,210 Templars (some of whom were still alive) whose names were cited. These numbers are precise and were obtained by systematically counting and recording names, the goal of a prosopographical work that has been ongoing for some time and which will no doubt ultimately bear fruit.[34] The first figure of 1,120 Templars involved in one or other of the proceedings is a minimum, because many of the living Templars didn't appear: those who had fled and whose names weren't already recorded, and those who have been forgotten because they weren't interrogated or didn't volunteer to go to Paris to defend the Order in 1310. Another distinction among those 1,120 Templars should be made: there were those who were interrogated and others who were not or, more exactly, for whom we do not have a record of an interrogation, either because there wasn't one or because it was lost. We have 290 interrogations from 1307 (the royal-inquisitorial proceedings), 45 interrogations from 1308 (before the pope in Poitiers and Chinon), 69 interrogations from 1309 (the episcopal proceedings of Clermont) and 224 interrogations from 1310–11 (the proceedings against the Order).[35] That adds up to 628 interrogations. However, we must take into account the fact that some of those Templars were interrogated twice, sometimes three times. Therefore the number of Templars for whom we have a trace of an interrogation is at best around 50 per cent of the total number of Templars who appeared. The great majority of the 659 Templars who defended the Order in February/May 1310 do not appear in the interrogation records.

Only an analysis of the data gleaned from the interrogations allows us to go beyond a simple division between present/deposers and present/non-deposers, and to obtain some information about the Templars' biographies: let's take just as an example the date of their reception into the Order, which is very important for an understanding of one aspect of their recruitment.

By constantly repeating that the Temple had become unpopular, useless, corrupt and interested only in managing its bank accounts, and by not looking into the facts more closely, lazy historiographers ended up believing that mantra, and making others believe it too. As proof, historians pointed to the fact that by the turn of the fourteenth century recruitment was drying up, owing to the bad reputation of the Order, its growing unpopularity and its abandonment of its original purpose: 'The Order of the Temple is dead from having abandoned Jerusalem.'[36] This is incorrect, because the Order continued to fulfil its mission up to the final months of its existence. The records of the interrogations of 1307, like those of 1310–11 in France, contain the testimony of 327 Templars who, with two exceptions, provide the dates of their entrance into the Order.[37] One hundred and twenty-five of these, or 38.4 per cent, joined the Order in 1300 and subsequent years, and thirty-eight of these, or 11.70 per cent, were received in 1305, 1306 and 1307. These are not the most convincing examples of dwindling numbers.

In 1310, seventy-six Templars were interrogated in Cyprus, a very large majority of whom were knights. Thirty-six of them had been received in a French house of the Order. Out of these thirty-six, twenty-five had been received after 1300, with two or three in 1305. Their depositions, as well as sources outside the trials and the Order, show that the Temple, even after the fall of Acre in 1291, did not cease to act on behalf of the Holy Land. Neglected or discounted by a large portion of the historiography, this significant action, launched from Cyprus as part of an alliance formed among all the Latin forces in the East and the Mongols of the Ilkhanate of Persia, was made possible at the turn of the fourteenth century by the arrival in Cyprus of hundreds of fighting brothers, as documented in the records of general chapters of the province of

France in Paris in 1300 and receptions recorded into the Order in Marseille in 1302–3.[38]

Those Templars who were received in France but interrogated in Cyprus admitted and acknowledged nothing. It was in fact torture, meted out in the country where the trial took place, that was the determining factor in Templars' confessions, not the country where a Templar was received.

Poitiers–Paris, 1306–1307: crossed paths

While the king and his counsellors were building their case against the Templars, the pope was working on two projects: preparations for a new crusade and the merging of the two religious-military orders.

A requirement for the new crusade was peace among the princes. Pope Clement was therefore working to resolve conflicts or to prevent any new ones from erupting. The situation in Sicily and Aragon seemed to have settled ever since the peace of Caltabellotta (1302), which ratified the partition of the kingdom of Sicily that had occurred in 1282, during the Sicilian revolt against the Angevin dynasty (the event that came to be known as the Sicilian Vespers). The Angevins kept southern Italy and the title of King of Sicily, while the Aragonese dynasty kept Sicily itself and renamed it the kingdom of Trinacria.

On the borders of Guyenne the war between the king of France and the English king/duke had calmed down. In 1307 Edward I died, and his son Edward II succeeded him. France and England, under the aegis of the pope, committed to a peace process that culminated at the beginning of 1308 in the marriage, celebrated in great pomp in Boulogne, between Edward II and Isabelle, the daughter of Philip the Fair. The other conflict affecting the kingdom of France, the one in Flanders, was also waning. After a bitter defeat in Courtrai in 1302, Philip regained control in June 1305 by concluding the treaty of Athis-sur-Orge in his favour. The peace remained fragile, however, and in any case did not last.[39]

In terms of the Empire, the most important issue was that of the imperial election or, more specifically, the election of the king of the Romans. On 5 September 1299 Philip the Fair and the king of the Romans, Albert of Austria, had concluded a peace between their kingdoms. But Philip the Fair did not relinquish his desire to elect a French prince. In 1308, when Albert died, he promoted – in vain – the candidacy of his brother Charles of Valois.

In short, whatever the future may have held, in 1306–7 Pope Clement could justifiably hope to launch a crusade. On 6 June 1306 he summoned the masters of the two great religious-military orders, the Temple and the Hospital, to return west on All Saints' Day 1306 to discuss his plans. The proposal to merge the two orders would also be dealt with on that occasion. The pope asked the two masters to provide him with memoranda on those subjects.[40]

Jacques de Molay left Cyprus in October 1306, and Foulques de Villaret, the Master of the Hospital, a bit later. In the end, the two masters were unable to arrive on All Saints' Day; they were late, but this had nothing to do with the fact that the pontiff, who had been taken ill, had postponed the meeting to a later date, since they only became aware of this change of plan after they had arrived in France. Jacques de Molay probably arrived in Marseille at the end of December or the beginning of January 1307. The pope was resuming his audiences at that time and arranged a new date for his meeting with the masters of the military Orders, which the king and his advisers would also attend, for May of that year. It is conceivable that upon arriving in France, Jacques de Molay heard the rumours circulating about the Temple and about what the king was asking the pope to do.

In fact, the king didn't go to Poitiers primarily to discuss the crusade or the merging of the orders. It's not that he wasn't interested in those matters; he was in favour of the crusade, especially if he could collect tithes from the clergy, something the pope would surely authorise. As for the merging of the orders, Philip planned to make proposals that would please neither the pope nor the Orders themselves, and even less so the other European princes: a new Order united under the rule of a single master, a king or the son of a king. He mentioned no names. He went to Poitiers to put pressure on Pope Clement finally to force a judgement against the memory of Boniface VIII, and to take action against the Templars.

Jean Bourgogne, the envoy of James II of Aragon to the Roman Curia in Poitiers, and a very valuable informant, apprised his master of the situation in a letter dated 14 May.[41] He informed him of the 'indecent' demands of King Philip: the canonisation of Pope Celestin V, who had abdicated and whom Boniface VIII had succeeded, and the posthumous condemnation of Boniface. But Jean Bourgogne didn't know anything else and says nothing about the latest meeting between the pope and the king on that same 14 May. He writes: 'the Master of the Knights of the Temple is soon to arrive here; he is expected, as is the Master of the Hospital of Saint John of Jerusalem, and the pope, according to strong rumour, is to deal with the union of the two orders and plans to do it with them.'[42] The king, who left Poitiers on 16 May, thus did not meet with the masters of the Orders. However, some of his counsellors stayed, as we learn from Jean Bourgogne in another letter, dated 26 June: Guillaume de Nogaret and Guillaume de Plaisians requested the opening of proceedings against Boniface VIII.[43] Jean Bourgogne says nothing about the Temple or about any demands the king made against it. Clearly he didn't know everything, for that issue was indeed discussed by the king and the pope in Poitiers. We may recall the texts that I cited earlier regarding the 1305 meeting in Lyon: the Temple was discussed in Lyon and in Poitiers, in November 1305 as well as in May 1307.

According to narrative sources close to the French court, the king also asked the pope to arrest the Templars.[44] The pope refused. In the records of the consistory gathered in Poitiers the following year, on 29 May 1308 (again compiled by Jean Bourgogne), the pope, responding to a vitriolic speech by Guillaume de Plaisians, rejected the latter's assertion that 'This affair had progressed with the authority of letters of the lord pope himself.'[45]

Jacques de Molay arrived after 16 May and after the king had left; on 9 June he sent a letter written 'in Poitiers, in the hospital where brother Jacques de Molay was then staying'.[46] He then went to Paris on 24 June for the meeting of the general chapter of the province of France; he returned before 4 August to Poitiers, where he remained for the summer.[47] It is possible that Molay met with the king in the second part of July 1307, and it is possible that on that occasion, when questioned by the king, he may have admitted that some Templar dignitaries, including himself, had absolved brothers in chapters, which only priest brothers of the Order were rightfully allowed to do. According to Guillaume de Plaisians, the Master appeared before the king, and 'he explained some of the statutes of his Order, and among other details said that on occasions when brothers were unwilling to confess their sins because they were afraid of being punished, he himself absolved them in the chapter, despite being a layperson and not having the authority'.[48]

We cannot know exactly what the three protagonists – the Master, the king and the pope – had in mind at that time (July/August 1307). This is the challenge for the historian: there are documents, of course, but above and beyond them?

Since his arrival in Poitiers, Jacques de Molay had met with the pope and with the Templars assigned to the papal court; he also saw Hugues de Pairaud, the

Visitor of the Order in France, who was well informed of the situation in the kingdom; a short time later he also had the opportunity to talk to the king. He probably understood that the situation was more serious than it had seemed and that he had to do something. Quite naturally he would have turned to the pope, the Order's mentor and protector.

The king of France no longer had any doubts: the Templars were heretics and heresy had to be eradicated, so the Temple was to be suppressed. For the time being he was still counting on the pope, because he needed him for the other important affair preoccupying him: the trial against the memory of Boniface VIII. But if necessary, he wouldn't hesitate to act alone. While waiting, Philip continued to put pressure on the pope and sent him emissaries to inform him of any new information he obtained (probably reports provided by the 'moles' introduced into the Order). Thus the pontiff, in his letter of 24 August 1307, cites information provided 'through the prior of your new monastery at Poissy'.[49] Similarly, again in the consistory report of 29 May 1308 prepared by Jean Bourgogne, the pope cites Geoffroy du Plessis, the pope's notary but also a royal cleric, who was sent by the king to discuss the Templars.[50] Du Plessis would play an important role as a mediator between the pope and the king as the affair unfolded.

As for Pope Clement, he was almost certain that the king's accusations against the Templars were false, even if some of the information he received shocked him (he said as much in his letter of 24 August 1307). He expected, however, that the king would continue to apply increasing pressure and that he would use the Temple to obtain the condemnation of Boniface VIII's memory. And that was something the pope would refuse at any cost. This was the trap he found himself in.

No one had blinked yet; everyone knew a move was inevitable, but the first to move risked losing a great deal.

The Saint Bartholomew's Day letter (24 August 1307)

Jacques de Molay was the first to act. Back in Poitiers after his trip to Paris, probably alarmed by his meeting with the king, during which he must have admitted some irregularities within the Order (notably concerning the absolution of sins, which we will look at again later), the Master turned to the pope, as seen in the pope's letter of 24 August 1307, in which he acknowledges and agrees with Molay's request to open an investigation:

Since the Master of the knights of the Temple, and with him several preceptors of the same Order from your kingdom and others, having heard, so they said, how their reputation has suffered repeatedly at your hands and in the eyes of us and some other temporal lords in relation to the already mentioned deed, have sought with great insistence, not just once, but on several occasions that we seek out the truth of the accusations laid against them (unjustly as they said); if they were to be found innocent, as they claimed, we should absolve them, but if they were to be found guilty, which they believed not to be the case, we should condemn them.[51]

Thus in his letter of 24 August 1307 addressed to the king of France, Pope Clement relates the request the Master of the Temple made during that month. In this letter the pope begins by telling the king that, because he needed to begin some serious medical treatment which would continue through September, he would be unable to receive the king's envoys before October. He then reminds Philip of their conversations in Lyon and Poitiers regarding the Templars and his incredulity at that time. But based on the information provided by the king, and on that which he himself had gathered (he mentions strange rumours), he has resolved, not without regrets, to act according to what reason demanded. He then mentions Jacques de Molay's request, which has hastened his decision to begin an investigation.

To explain his decision, the pope gives the same weight to the king's frequent interventions as he does to the Master of the Temple's insistence on an investigation. Philip the Fair would surely have appreciated this. The machinery was thus set in motion, but, given the legal procedure that had to be followed and the delay that the pope's illness would cause, there was little chance of it gathering much speed.

Had the pope obtained information that was more credible than the stories of Esquieu de Floyrac or the accusations spread by the king's emissaries? Jacques de Molay, in Poitiers for the entire summer, was obviously not being targeted. How about Hugues de Pairaud? The Templar Mathieu d'Arras, interrogated on 10 November 1307, reports that

Brother Hugues de Pairaud, going to the Roman court [in Poitiers] the week following the last feast day of Saint Rémi [15 January 1307] had told him that the Order had been slandered with the above-mentioned cases before the pope and

the king and that he [Hugues de Pairaud], if he could, should save his own skin
and should tell others to do the same; and then he [Mathieu d'Arras] asked him
to give him his letters on this subject, because otherwise he wouldn't believe it;
and he answered that he wouldn't do it because it wouldn't please the Master.[52]

Was Hugues de Pairaud the high-ranking Templar whom Pope Clement
mentions on two occasions, without citing his name – first in the bull *Pastoralis
praeminentiae* of 22 November 1307, then in *Faciens misericordiam* of 12 August
1308 – who had told him in confidence about the abuses of the Order? There
is no evidence that Pope Clement was told anything before the arrests, or that
an encounter between him and Hugues de Pairaud was organised by the king
of France and took place in the summer of 1307.[53] Hugues de Pairaud was in
Poitiers with Jacques de Molay in May and June 1307; he attended the general
chapter in Paris with the Master at the end of June. Did he then go back to Poitiers with Jacques de Molay? We have no evidence of that, but he was there in
October: while Jacques de Molay was in the capital of the kingdom to attend the
funeral of Catherine de Courtenay, the wife of Charles de Valois on 12 October,
Hugues de Pairaud stayed with the pope 'because the king had asked him to do
so'; he was, moreover, arrested on 13 October with some fifteen other Templars
and imprisoned in the Château de Loches the next day.[54] And he confessed on 9
November 1307 in Paris.

Pierre Dupuy, the seventeenth-century historian, mentions a Templar chamberlain, Guillaume de Chanteloup, who supposedly confessed to the pope and
revealed the turpitudes of the Order to him. Dupuy was a serious historian,
very anti-Templar, who cites many documents, some of which, including this
one, have since disappeared. It is worth noting, though, that the name of Guillaume de Chanteloup does not appear among the servants of Pope Clement or
among the Templars who were arrested and interrogated during the trial. We
must therefore be on our guard.[55]

However, the affair having been launched and the Templars arrested, Pope
Clement, as we will see, reassured and protected the Templars in his residence.
The pope agreed to conduct an investigation, a thorough one, without haste; he
would then pronounce judgement and, if necessary, order appropriate sentences.

His 'agenda' didn't correspond at all to that of Philip the Fair.

2

THE ARRESTS

(13 October 1307)

Maubuisson (September 1307)

Philip the Fair left Poitiers on 16 May 1307 and took his time travelling to Île-de-France, stopping in Poitou, Loches, the Berry, Montargis, Auxerre and Fontainebleau. He chose not to stay in Paris, opting for other residences nearby: in Crécy-en-Brie, Tremblay and Vincennes. If he met with Jacques de Molay in the second half of July, the meeting would have taken place in one of these locations. In August the king again travelled in the immediate vicinity: to Verberie, Domont, Saint-Germain-en-Laye, Poissy and Saint-Denis. And on 28 August 1307 he arrived for a month's stay in Pontoise at the nearby abbey of Maubuisson. It was perhaps not a coincidence that the crucial decisions that launched the Templar Affair were made in this Cistercian abbey founded by Blanche de Castille; through her, the memory of her husband, Saint Louis, canonised in 1297, was a very vivid presence, and we know the devotion of Philip the Fair for his grandfather. Jean de Joinville, Louis's old Crusade companion, was just finishing his *Life of Saint Louis*, which Philip the Fair's wife, Queen Jeanne de Navarre, who had died in 1305, had commissioned him to write.

In Maubuisson the king was obviously not alone: his family, his court and his counsellors all accompanied him on his travels. Throughout the Middle Ages the government travelled around depending on the king's mood (and on favourable hunting grounds). When the king and his entourage arrived in Maubuisson, Philip the Fair had already received the letter from the pope dated 24 August 1307. When was the decision to arrest the Templars, without the pope's consent, and therefore at the risk of committing a serious illegal act, actually made? We don't know. There was a meeting of the council, debates and consultations. But everything was decided before 14 September. Two texts are dated on that day (the feast of the Exaltation of the Holy Cross – again, this was not by chance), which were immediately placed into circulation; copies of them must already have been made. The first, written in Latin, is the order for the arrests of the Templars in the kingdom of France; the second contained the practical instructions to be followed by those who were to arrange for and carry out the arrests – and this is written in French.[1]

In the arrest order the king first expresses his stupefaction and pain when he learned of the enormities committed by the Templars, who had abandoned God and distanced themselves from Him. Crucifying Christ a second time, these lost souls entered the Order while denying Him, spitting on His cross, carrying out obscene acts and engaging in sodomy. At first incredulous, and doubting the purity of the denouncers' intentions, the king was nevertheless forced to accept the evidence. He spoke to the pope about it, consulted prelates and barons and deliberated with his council. To verify his suspicions he assigned Guillaume de Paris, the inquisitor of heretical perversity, the task of pursuing an investigation into the veracity of this widespread rumour. Given the very strong suspicion resulting from the investigation, the king decided to arrest all the Templars in his kingdom and to confiscate their property. Bailiffs and seneschals were then ordered to arrest the Templars in their districts and seize their property following the instructions attached to the order for their arrests. The text is dated 'from the abbey of Sainte-Marie [i.e., the abbey of Maubuisson, dedicated to the Virgin Mary], near Pontoise, on the Feast of the Exaltation of the Holy Cross, in the year of our Lord 1307'.

This summary, deliberately neutral, masks the grandiloquent rhetoric of the text, of which I will cite two examples. The beginning talks of: 'A bitter thing, a lamentable thing [...] a detestable crime, an execrable evil deed [...] a thing wholly inhuman, furthermore, foreign to all humanity'. Then it says: 'This is why the wrath of God has fallen on these sons of infidelity. This unclean tribe has abandoned the source of living water, has exchanged its glory for the likeness of the Calf and made offerings to idols.'

These statements must be taken seriously. Above and beyond the speeches of Guillaume de Nogaret and Guillaume de Plaisians, the two royal counsellors who would be in charge of the affair and who were probably the authors of the text (there would be even more such rhetoric in Guillaume de Plaisians's speech in Poitiers in 1308), this rhetoric is typical of all the texts produced at the time by the royal chancery in its efforts to exalt the king and the French royalty. These texts are essential in explaining the Templar Affair. They would be disseminated and the ideas they contain reused in the impassioned speeches given on various occasions at every stage of the affair.

The instructions that accompanied the arrest order bring us back down to earth and to the police operations that would enable the king's agents to carry out the announced plan: the simultaneous arrest of all the Templars in the kingdom, without any scruples about the probable innocence of some of them. 'Because of the extreme seriousness of this affair, in which the truth cannot be fully brought out into the light in any other way [...] it is fitting that if there are any innocent ones among them these should be tested in the furnace like gold and cleared by the due process of judicial examination.'

Once they had arrived at their destinations, the royal emissaries delivered the arrest order and instructions to the bailiffs and seneschals, and instructed them to keep everything secret for the time being. They were to make very discreet inquiries into the Templar houses in their districts to learn what they could about what went on in them and what the brothers were up to. If necessary, they were to use the pretext of a forthcoming levy of a tithe on all the property of the clergy; they could cover their tracks by also visiting the houses of other religious orders.

On the appointed day, early in the morning, the bailiff or seneschal[2] would assemble as many *prud'hommes* – men of experience, prudence and wisdom – and sergeants as needed to carry out their orders simultaneously in all the Temple houses, arresting the brothers and seizing their property, an inventory of which would be drawn up immediately. The farmland and vineyards were to be preserved intact and would be overseen by 'good, rich men of the region'. The arrested Templars, held in isolation from each other and under guard, would immediately be interrogated, prior to appearing before the inquisitors. Torture would be used if necessary. They would be told that the pope and the king had been informed of their crimes; they would be pardoned if they acknowledged them and sentenced to death if they did not.

A list of the main accusations was drawn up, and the Templars were expected to acknowledge them: renouncing Christ, spitting on the cross, obscene kissing, engaging in sodomy, wearing a cord that had been in contact with a beloved idol worshipped during chapters, priests of the Order not consecrating the host during the celebration of the Mass and so on. Then the depositions of those who confessed 'the said errors or, in particular, the denial of Our Lord Jesus Christ' would be carefully collected.

Emphasis was placed on the renunciation of Christ, which alone was enough to prove the 'heresy of the Templars'. The aim of torture, which was used almost immediately, was not to obtain the actual truth but to elicit the specific truth that the accusers wanted to hear – it was that truth, or death. There would be interrogations in the hours following the arrests, carried out by royal agents; it was only later that the Templars would be delivered to the inquisitors. Ultimately, only the depositions that conformed to the accusations would be retained.

The texts quoted above contain an important lie: that the pope and the Church were the origins of the king's decision: 'the person sent with the seneschal or the bailiff on the appointed day [...] will choose powerful *prud'hommes* of the region [...] and will inform them of the task under oath of secrecy and of the fact that the king has been informed of it by the pope and the Church.' It was less a matter of convincing the Templars than of convincing those whom the king's agents planned to recruit in order to carry out the arrests in the early hours of 13 October.

The commissioners armed with the arrest order and the instructions immediately left to inform the bailiffs and seneschals of the kingdom. Each of them received a copy addressed to them personally. The archives hold only three copies: those addressed to the bailiff of Amiens, the seneschal of Beaucaire, who at that time was Bertrand Jourdain de l'Isle, and the bailiff of Rouen, Pierre de Hangest.[3] To strengthen his operation further, on 20 September the king wrote a letter from Pontoise to all the prelates and barons of the kingdom to inform them of the arrival of royal emissaries tasked with speaking to them about various matters. Only the letter involving the bailiwick of Amiens has been preserved: Jean de Picquigny, Jean de Varenne and the bailiff of Amiens were expected to transmit this information throughout the bailiwick.[4]

Thus we see the strictly royal side of the launching of the Affair. However, the king and his counsellors were well aware of the need to have their actions legitimised by ecclesiastical authority. This explains their efforts to bring the pope into their decision; but since it was obviously a lie, they could not go too far in that direction. Let's look again at the order for the arrests: apparently, the king had acted in response to the preliminary investigation carried out by Guillaume de Paris, the Inquisitor of France: 'We have agreed to the justifiable requests of the said inquisitor, who has invoked the help of our arm in this

matter.' Guillaume de Paris was a brother in the Order of Preachers (Dominicans), a doctor of theology. He was made Inquisitor of France in 1303, if not
earlier; he had, moreover, been the king's confessor since 15 December 1305. His
position as Inquisitor of France was indeed a papal appointment, and although
he had been named Inquisitor prior to Pope Clement's accession to the pontificate, the pope had to assume some responsibility for the Inquisitor's actions. Was
Guillaume de Paris's authority enough to legitimise the king's actions, and did
it implicate Pope Clement?

The answer is no. In fact, Guillaume de Paris was not assigned specifically
to deal with the Templar Affair. He was 'in general' responsible for rooting
out heresy. To proceed against the Templars he needed an explicit mandate.
He didn't have that mandate, he didn't ask the pope for it, and the pope never
granted it to him. Even on 26 September, Pope Clement was unaware of the
proceedings the king had launched on 14 September; on that day it was, on the
contrary, the pope who asked the king to inform him of any new information he
might have. For the pope there was as yet no Templar Affair, no Templar heresy
and thus no specific heresy to pursue. And so the pope could not have granted a
specific mandate to Guillaume de Paris.

That didn't matter. Guillaume de Paris was the humble servant of Philip the
Fair. On 22 September another meeting of the royal council took place at the
abbey of Maubuisson. Two decisions were taken. First, Guillaume de Nogaret
was made Keeper of the Seals; it has been suggested that he took the post from
Gilles Aycelin, archbishop of Narbonne, who had supposedly expressed his disagreement with the decision to have the Templars arrested, but this is debatable.[5]
Second, the Inquisitor of France wrote to the inquisitors of Toulouse (Bernard
Gui since 16 January 1307[6]) and Carcassonne (Geoffroy d'Ablis since 1303[7])
and asked them to look into and pursue the heresy of the Templars, and to send
the most carefully chosen depositions to the king.[8] The tone and the vocabulary
of this letter resemble almost exactly those of the act of accusation, to such a
degree that it has been suggested that either Guillaume de Nogaret or Guillaume
de Plaisians actually wrote it. It contains the same words of caution: you will
investigate only those who are the objects of vehement suspicion, but not the
Order itself (since only the pope, as guardian of the Order, which was exempt
from all other ecclesiastical authority, could do that). The sole objective of this
letter was to mobilise the inquisitors in the south to aid in the undertaking being
carried out by the king of France.

Throughout the kingdom royal agents and inquisitors would proceed hand in hand.

The early morning of 13 October, in the bailiwick of Caen

Let's look at the continuation of the chronicle of Guillaume de Nangis:

> The Friday after the Feast of Saint Denis, on 13 October, at daybreak, all the
> Templars that we found in the kingdom of France were immediately – and all at
> once – seized and locked up in different prisons, following an order and decree
> by the king. Among them was the Grand Master of the Order, who was taken
> and held prisoner in the house of the Temple in Paris.[9]

Like all his colleagues, Jean de Verretot, the bailiff of Caen, had received the order to arrest the Templars. He was in on the secret operation that was set for Friday 13 October. In accordance with the instructions, he was to proceed discreetly with an investigation of the Templar houses in his bailiwick.[10] Five principal houses serving as commanderies were in his bailiwick: Baugy, Bretteville-le-Rabet, Voismer and Courval, all in the diocese of Bayeux, and Louvagny, a dependency of Frémeaux in the diocese of Sées. On the appointed day the bailiff himself went to the house in Baugy; he was accompanied by a knight, Richard de Bretteville, and five sergeants. For Bretteville, Courval and Voismer he delegated two royal knights to lead the operation: Hugues de Chastel and the viscount of Caen, Gautier de Bois Gilout. These two sent Raoul Gloi and several others to carry out the arrests in Bretteville. For Courval they sent another cleric from the viscounty of Caen, Thomas Alapenne, with a lieutenant of the viscount of Vire, a cleric from the viscounty, two equerries, a royal sergeant and a burgher from Vacy. In Voismer a cleric, Jean du Chastel, and six other men were assigned to lead the operation. In Louvagny, home to only one Templar, the operation was carried out by a royal knight, Enguerrand de Villers.[11]

Thirteen Templars were arrested: one in Louvagny and three in each of the other houses. Of those arrested, Gautier de Bullens was a knight and the twelve others were sergeants. Twenty-four men had been mobilised for the operation. In comparison, the arrest of the Templars in the commandery of Payns, in Champagne, involved forty men under the command of Jean de Villarcel, appointed by the bailiff of Troyes.[12] In the bailiwick of Amiens the bailiff, Denis d'Aubigny, assisted by Renaud de Picquigny, had to proceed – given the large number of Templar houses in his bailiwick – as the bailiff of Caen had done: he assigned the actual arrests to his deputies and had to mobilise a large number of royal sergeants, knights and clerics, as well as other *prud'hommes*.[13]

The bailiff of Caen was not expected simply to arrest the men; he was also responsible for seizing their property, making an inventory of it and assigning managers to oversee it and ensure that it would continue to be profitable. He made the Templars placed under arrest draw up their own inventories. This was perhaps not done everywhere in France. In Baugy the three resident Templars, Aubin Langlois, Raoul de Pérouse and Guillaume Le Raure, were simply present during the inventory. The same thing happened in Bretteville-le-Rabet and in Courval, and probably in Voismer as well, although the records don't mention it. At the end of the inventories of each of the houses there is a list of the names of 'those who live in the house': that is, the people the Templars hired to manage and work the estates. Their roles included cowherd, cattleman, keeper of foals, keeper of pigs, keeper of tack, miller and so on. Twenty-five people are listed for Baugy, twelve for Bretteville-le-Rabet, thirteen for Courval and four for Louvagny. These 'men of the Temple' who, although not Templars, benefited from a portion of the Templars' privileges were allowed to stay in the houses to continue their work on the estates. The bailiff and his assistants sometimes chose one of those employees to be the steward henceforth responsible for the property that had been placed under royal sequestration: in Bretteville-le-Rabet, Richard Mauduit, 'provost of the said Templars', was 'guardian for the king of all aforementioned things and lands by command of said lord Hugues [de Chastel]'. By contrast, in Courval, the equerry Guillaume Canteil and the burgher from Vacy, Pierre de la Baille, who were members of the small group summoned by the bailiff to arrest the Templars, were given the job of guarding the property; in Baugy, 'Bertin du Coisel, sergeant of said place [for the king] was ordered to oversee the guard of the things in the house so that they might be treated well'; he was assisted by four residents of the surrounding area.[14]

These were temporary assignments, made in haste. Later, once the administrative structures responsible for the management of the property under royal sequestration had been put in place, commissioners overseeing the bailiwicks and the seneschalsies would be named. The management of the Templar houses in the bailiwicks of Caen and Cotentin would fall to two commissioners (we know their names for 1309[15]) who would assign stewards for each house.[16]

In Sainte-Eulalie du Larzac, in Rouergue, the castellan of Najac was responsible for the management of property in the seneschalsy of Rouergue; but on
3 January 1308 the seneschal Pierre de Ferrières replaced him with two other
managers, Garnier de Moissac, a royal notary, and Arnaut Durand, who lived
in Sainte-Eulalie. Their assignment included making an inventory of the commandery property, which was completed on 27 January 1308.[17] The official
records of the commandery of Payns for the sequestration period reveal that at
the time of the arrests twenty-seven permanent salaried farmers worked there
(whom the steward, Jean de Hulles, retained); temporary workers were also
being employed.[18]

To my knowledge there are no records pertaining exclusively to the arrests
of Templar brothers in France. In the case of the houses in the Caen bailiwick
we have been dealing with records of inventories of property, and we learn
something about the arrests of the brothers only because they were required to
lend a hand in the undertaking. The records of the inventories of the houses in
Provence, which began in early 1308, are similar. In the inventories drawn up
later the arrests are no longer mentioned. They are, however, alluded to in the
inventory compiled in Toulouse on 27 December 1313 during the transfer of
Templar property to the Hospitallers: in it there is mention of the fact that eight
Templars arrested in 1307 were still being held at that time in the new hall in the
city palace.[19]

We must look at the testimony of the Templars themselves to shed some light
on the places and conditions of their arrest, and to glean the nuggets of information they managed to provide in their depositions.

In Dormelles, in the Gâtinais, the royal provost of Château-Landon carried
out the arrests of Herbert de Colombe, Thibaut de Taverny and Pierre de
Beaumont.[20] The knight brother Guillaume de Verneiges cites Jean de Fonte-
nay, arrested in Issoudun, and Clément de Saint-Hilaire, arrested in La Bruyère,
two houses in the diocese of Bourges.[21] Geoffroy de Thatan was arrested in
Molendines, a dependency of L'Île-Bouchard, in Touraine.[22] According to
Étienne de Nérac, guardian of the house of the Order of Friars Minor in Lyon,
Barthélemy Chevrier, a burgher from Lyon and wine keeper for the lord king
of France, 'having the power and mandate from the lord king to arrest the Templars, called said witness [Étienne de Nérac himself] the day of the arrests, and
among those who were arrested was a secular cleric, whose name he did not
know'. This cleric was carrying sealed letters from the Master of Passage in

Marseille addressed to the Grand Master.[23] The case of Aymeri Chamerlent is unique. He normally lived in the Templar house of Crabannat (in the commune of Féniers, in the Creuse), in the diocese of Limoges, but he was not there at the time of the arrests because, being ill, he was at his parents' home and so was not arrested with the others. Once he learned of the arrests, he went to the Roman Curia in an attempt to seek safety; that is, he went to Poitiers, where the pope and the Curia were residing at the time. There he was arrested; he in fact appeared before the pope at the end of June 1308 with seventy-two other Templars, and he was still being held in that city at the beginning of 1310.[24]

In addition to trial documents, there are other sources we can consult. The minutes of the deliberations of the consuls of Cahors mention in Latin the arrests of 13 October: 'May it be known to all that in the year of our lord 1307 all Templars throughout the world were arrested.' Continuing in French, the minutes note:

> Let it be known that in the year of our lord 1307, the Friday before the Feast of Saint Luke the Evangelist [i.e., 13 October, the feast day being on the 18th], the very illustrious prince Philip, through the grace of God, king of France, and the sovereign pontiff Pope Clement, both reigning, all Templars were arrested and their property seized, and notably master Atho de Salvanhac, knight of the Temple, commander of the house of La Chapelle with his companions of the diocese of Cahors.[25]

The royal police acted only within the royal purview. The duke of Brittany watched over his own prerogatives. All the same, in the absence of archival documents, we don't know what became of the Breton Templars who were arrested in Brittany, for there were indeed some.[26] In Burgundy the seventy-two-year-old Étienne de Dijon, a priest of the house in Dijon, was arrested by the duke of Burgundy's men.[27] On 9 November 1307 Jean, duke of Brabant, wrote to the king of France:

> Very dear Sire, we inform your highness that we have accomplished what you mandated to us in the matter of the Templars. In response to your highness's wishes we have arrested the Templars living in our lands and are holding them in prison, and their property has been seized, just as you have mandated to us.[28]

Finally, let's mention the example of a particularly violent arrest in Arras: the sergeants ordered to carry out the arrests attacked the Temple house and strangled half the brothers; those who survived their assault were imprisoned in Arras.[29] Perhaps the Templars there had attempted to resist.

Prisoners in the Temple of Paris (13 October 1307)

On the very day they were arrested, the Templars were put in prison. Thus the thirteen Templars from the diocese of Caen, after being made to inventory their houses, were locked up in the royal castle of Caen. Five Templars from the house of Saint-Étienne de Renneville, arrested by Pierre de Hangest, the bailiff of Rouen, were imprisoned in Pont-de-l'Arche, where they were joined by brother Thomas, from the house of Sainte-Vaubourg. The commander of that house, Philippe Agate, the former commander of Renneville, was imprisoned in the neighbouring castle of La Roche-d'Orival.[30] A sergeant brother, he had entered the Temple in 1281; he was an important member of the Order, and as the trial progressed he was always associated with the small group of Temple dignitaries. Might this have been the reason for his imprisonment in La Roche-d'Orival, separate from the other Templars of the bailiwick of Rouen?

In Île-de-France the imprisoned Templars were mainly concentrated in the Temple of Paris. It was there, the story went, that in the early hours of 13 October Guillaume de Nogaret himself arrested the Grand Master and the other Templars who were there.[31] Jacques de Molay had been in Paris for a few days; he had left Poitiers to attend the funeral of Catherine de Courtenay on 12 October, and so he was staying at the Temple house in Paris.

But there were other detention sites in Paris: in private residences, for example, as we learn from a valuable document written three or four months after the arrests.[32] In January/February 1308 the royal authorities decided to disperse all the Templars imprisoned in Paris so that only a hundred were left in the Temple house there. I will return later to the details of this document that deal with the transfer, and the reasons for it, but will point out one fact here: the movement occurred in both directions. On the one hand, some Templars were transferred from the Temple to other detention sites outside Paris; on the other, some Templars held in Paris, but not in the Temple, were then transferred there.

And so, on 5 February 1308, 'Monsignor H. de la Selle brought all the Templars who had been in the houses of Barbel [Barbeau] and Pruylli [Preuilly] who numbered fifty-eight and put them in the Paris Temple.' Unfortunately, the names of those Templars are not given. The Barbel and Pruylli houses were two private residences; Pruylli was that of the abbot of Preuilly, in the diocese of Meaux. Similarly, on 12 February 1308 'all the Templars who had been imprisoned in the residence of the bishop of "Chaalonz" were taken to the Paris Temple'. Six sergeants guarded the Templars from the Preuilly house, twelve those of the Barbeau residence and another twelve those of the residence of the bishop of Châlons en Champagne.

The document indirectly provides information about the duration of the Templars' detention in those places and the cost of that detention. The sergeants were paid 10 *deniers tournois* per day; those who guarded the brothers in the Barbeau residence were paid for eighty-eight days, and those of the Preuilly residence for sixty-nine days; if we assume that 4 February, the day before the transfer, was the last day they were paid, this means that those in the Barbeau residence were there from 9 November to 4 February and those in the Preuilly residence from 28 November to 4 February. In that case they would have been arrested not in Paris itself but in other houses in Île-de-France, from which they would have come to the Paris residences on 9 and 28 November. Since their names are not given, we cannot know if they were among the 138 Templars interrogated at the Paris Temple between 19 October and 24 November 1307.

This document now enables us to affirm that in Paris there were more Templars incarcerated than interrogated (or at least for whom we have the record of an interrogation) during that period: they amount to 235, not counting those who were held in the residence of the bishop of Châlons (or Chalon), 137 of whom are listed by name. Among the former, 58 (or 59) are included among the 138 Templars who were interrogated and whose names appear in the records. From this we can deduce that 97 Templars at least (235 minus 138), imprisoned in Paris, either weren't interrogated or weren't mentioned in the record, and that 78 (or 79) interrogated Templars are not among the 137 imprisoned Templars who are named (137 minus 58 or 59); but they may well have been among the 98 others who are not named.

The records of the interrogations from the seneschalsy of Nîmes-Beaucaire involve 66 Templars who were being held variously in Aigues-Mortes (45), in Nîmes (15) and in Alès (6).[33]

Through the depositions given by Templars during their trial we learn of other detention sites: Gisors (where Gillet de *Encreyo* was held), Montreuil-sur-Mer (Jean de Pollencourt, Gilles de Rotangi and several others), Sens (Jean de Couchy [*Cochiaco*], Laurent de Beaune, Simon de Corbone, Gaubert de Silhi, Simon de Lyons en Santerre [*Lechuno in Sanguine Terra*]), Montargis (Pierre de Loison), Mâcon (Guillaume La Gayte, Geoffroy de Montchausit), Niort (Humbert du Puits, Mathieu de l'Étang), Saint-Jean-d'Angély (Guillaume Chandelier, Pierre de Montignac), Saintes (Hugues Raynaud) and Tours (Guillaume de Plessis [*Plexeyo*]).[34]

Jean Quentin says he was held at the abbey of Povomaco and questioned in Sens; this could have been the abbey of Pontigny, but this is only a guess.[35] Six Templars came from the prison in La Rochelle to testify in Paris on 9 March 1311, but it is not clear whether they had been held there since their arrest in October 1307.[36] The same is true for some of the places listed above (La Rochelle, Saintes), because there must have been transfers, dispersals and regroupings like those that occurred in Île-de-France in 1308. The castle of Najac in Rouergue was also used as a prison for Templars from the Midi. There were obviously many others, given the very dense concentration of Temple houses in some regions: Picardy, Champagne, Burgundy, Auvergne and Poitou-Aquitaine. But there are many gaps in the documentation, and we are therefore unable to establish names.

The Treasurer of the Paris Temple (and until then of the king) was arrested in Rouen, where he was on the king's business; it seems he was taken the same day to the Paris Temple.[37] Hugues de Pairaud, the Visitor of the Order, who was arrested in Poitiers, was first taken to the royal fortress of Loches before being transferred to Paris.[38] Like the fortress in Loches, there were probably other temporary prisons: Geoffroy de Thatan, arrested near L'Île-Bouchard, was imprisoned in Loudun before being taken to Chinon, to be interrogated there by the bailiff of Touraine.[39]

Occasionally, the royal administration's well-oiled machine malfunctioned: after his arrest the knight brother Giraud Béraud, from the diocese of Limoges, was taken from place to place in a cart, his hands tied together.[40]

On the run

How many Templars avoided arrest? Not very many, it would seem. A document issued from the royal chancery gives 'the names of brothers who fled'.[41] The first to be named were brothers from Burgundy, Richard de Moncler and Clairambaud de Conflans, both of whom 'repaired [i.e., returned to their country] to the march of Germany and to the county of Montbéliart', and then there were Renaud de la Folie, Guillaume de Lins (or Lurs), commander of Villemoison (in the *département* of the Yonne),[42] and Hugues de Chalon, commander of Épailly. Also cited are Hugues Daray, brother Baraus, commander of Puy,[43] Géraudon, 'son of Monseignor Geraut de Chatiaunuef returning to Grusignan near the county of Veneci',[44] Adam de Vallencourt[45] and Pierre de Bouche (or Boucli), 'who fled to the march of Germany'.[46] There were two other important dignitaries of the Order: Humbert Blanc, commander of Auvergne, who was in England at the time of the arrests (he was arrested there later), and Gérard de Villiers, Master of France, who fled with forty other brothers.

Thus there were twelve names cited, to which we must add the forty anonymous brothers who left with the Master of France.

The information gleaned from the trial depositions enables us to add another twenty-two names to the list (see the following table). And so there were thirty-four Templars listed by name who avoided arrest. However, eight were captured: Renaud de La Folie, Humbert Blanc, Adam de Vallencourt, Pierre de Bouche or Boucli, Renaud Beaupoil, Jean de Chali, Pierre de Modies and Pierre de Sornay.

The cases of Pierre de Sornay and Renaud de la Folie are better documented than the others. Pierre, interrogated on 22 November 1309 by the papal commission responsible for investigating the Order, had been received in the Temple three months before the arrests and had fled from it fifteen days before they happened. As we will soon see, he was captured shortly before 22 November 1309.[47] As for Renaud de la Folie, he was not captured until 1312, after the Council of Vienne, and we will later see under what circumstances.[48]

And so it appears that not all the Templars who fled were successful, and that those who did succeed took refuge in their lands (their '*repaire*') just beyond the kingdom. They may have been aided by their families or friends: for example, Pierre de Modies, Foulques de Milly and Hugues de Chalon may all have been related, and Jean de Milly fled with Pierre de Modies. Malcolm Barber suggests the escape had been planned.[49]

There were undoubtedly many other fugitives, many Templars who hid, as shown by documents concerning the summoning of the Templars of the diocese of Clermont before the diocesan commission in May/June 1309: on 28 May the summons to appear was addressed to the brothers who had fled, were hiding or were absent.[50]

Table 1 Templars who fled, as mentioned in interrogations

Guy d'Arzac	Michelet, vol. II, pp. 123, 222
Jean Atger	Michelet, vol. II, p. 147
Renaud Beaupoil	Michelet, vol. II, p. 267*
Bertrand, de *Belda* in Périgord	Michelet, vol. II, p. 180**
Bernard de Bort	Michelet, vol. II, p. 159
Humbert de *Cayneyo*	Michelet, vol. I, pp. 575, 628
Jean de Chali	Michelet, vol. II, pp. 263, 265***
Humbert de Charnier	Michelet, vol. II, p. 241
Robert de Charnier	Michelet, vol. II, pp. 136–40
Renaud de Dompierre	Michelet, vol. II, pp. 32–4
Guillaume Gatz	Michelet, vol. I, p. 509
Aymeri George	Michelet, vol. II, pp. 143–6
Déodat Hugo	Michelet, vol. II, p. 157
Pierre de Lagny	Michelet, vol. I, p. 362; vol. II, p. 1
Hugues de *Lata Petra* (de la Depère)	Michelet, vol. II, p. 179
Gérard de Laon	Michelet, vol. I, p. 250
Foulques de Milly	Michelet, vol. II, p. 266****
Pierre de Modies	Michelet, vol. II, p. 266*****
Pierre de Sornay	Michelet, vol. I, p. 30
Humbert Valhant	Michelet, vol. II, p. 114

Two Templars should be added; according to Jean de Chali, they would not have been arrested, although they were not fugitives: Janserandus, priest and curate of Bure, and Hugues de Frey, sergeant, about whom the witness thinks 'that they are alive and have not been arrested' (Michelet, vol. II, p. 264).

* Remained hidden in the Lorraine house of Villencourt after the others were arrested.

** Escaped prison.

*** Fled when the others were arrested but was captured 'a year ago' (i.e., 1310), according to Pierre de Modies, and was interrogated in May 1311.

**** Fled at the time of the arrests.

***** Arrested with Jean de Chali, having fled when the others were arrested.

The fates of the dignitaries of the Order who escaped arrest varied. It seems that Humbert Blanc was not trying to escape when he went to England: he was arrested there. Gérard de Villiers, who left with forty other brothers, had been forewarned and planned his escape. 'Fantasy History' latched on to his case, and was, moreover, supported by the testimony of the Templar Jean, from Châlons-en-Champagne, who had heard that Gérard de Villiers, taking fifty horses, set sail on eighteen ships.[51] That is a lot. It has been suggested that he was in Italy, in Genoa, where, during the summer of 1308, he had attempted to spearhead a plan for a maritime expedition to free the Templars from the kingdom of Cyprus, but the chronicle of Amadi, which is cited in support of this assertion, says nothing on the subject.[52] Again, according to the information gleaned from the list of fugitives provided by the royal chancery, Gérard de Villiers's nephew Hugues de Chalon-sur-Saône and Richard de Moncler, also listed as having fled, had supposedly planned to kill the king with accomplices from the sect of the Temple.[53] Where, when, how? We will probably never know. And finally, still regarding Hugues de Chalon, we further learn from the same Jean de Châlons that, when they fled, Hugues and company took valuables from Hugues de Pairaud with them. Here too there is an error or some confusion: Hugues de Pairaud did indeed have some valuables, but Hugues de Chalon had nothing to do with them.

Before focusing on this point, let's mention one last time Jean de Châlons, who says something very interesting – 'The powerful of the Order, foreseeing the confusion that was reigning, took flight' – before talking about Gérard de Villiers and Hugues de Chalon. If Hugues had fled with Hugues de Pairaud's property, it was indeed a sign that, in the mind of our witness, the Visitor of France suspected something and had told his nephew to save what he could. It is true that Hugues de Pairaud tried to hide some items of value, but they did not actually amount to much, as we will see in the final chapter of this book.[54]

If Hugues de Pairaud suspected something, Jacques de Molay must also have had his suspicions, and I will address this question in detail in a later chapter, and notably the question of whether he could have escaped the trap.[55] Probably neither of them had imagined the brutal form the king's plans were going to take.

The Templars' leaders had indeed caught wind of the king of France's threat against the Order of the Temple, which was looming during the summer of 1307. Jacques de Molay's request for an investigation is evidence of this. So too are the various initiatives taken, such as Hugues de Pairaud hiding his valuables or Gérard de Villiers and Hugues de Chalon preparing their escape (because this was not improvised on the morning of 13 October) or the attitude of Jacques de Molay, who, confident of his lawful rights, perhaps stepped right into the lion's den in Paris. However, the way in which the threat materialised in the early hours of 13 October caught the Templars off guard, as it did their rightful protector, the pope.

3

THE KING AND THE INQUISITION

(October–November 1307)

For the king of France 'the heresy of the Templars' was obvious; there was nothing to prove, and the Templars simply had to acknowledge their crimes. Everything was to be carried out swiftly and would result in the suppression of the Order. Beginning the day after the arrests, the means that the inquisition had been using since the middle of the thirteenth century to deal with heresy were used on the Templars: most notably, torture.

The instructions sent to the bailiffs and seneschals and then passed on to all those who were to carry out the arrests invited them to interrogate the Templars on the very day they were arrested, then to hand them over to the inquisitors. There are no archival documents that describe what today we might call the 'police custody' of the Templars, which involved threats, pressure and torture.

Troyes (15 and 18 October 1307)

The first interrogations we know of took place in Troyes: three Templars, Jean de Genèfle, Nicolas de Serre and Raoul de Gizy, appeared on 15 and 18 October.[1] On the 15th, the Sunday after the Feast of Saint Denis, the first two were interrogated in Isle-Aumont, near Troyes, by Jean de l'Isle, prior of the Preachers', or Dominican, convent in Troyes, who was delegated by the Inquisitor of France, Guillaume de Paris. Jean de Genèfle was from the diocese of Liège and Nicolas de Serre from the diocese of Troyes; Jean was arrested in Serre-les-Monceaux and Nicolas in Villiers-les-Verrières, two Templar houses in the diocese of Troyes. They both admitted that they had renounced Christ and spat on the cross, had performed or received obscene kisses and had been advised to have carnal relations with other brothers if asked to do so. Both had been received into the

Order by Raoul de Gizy: in the case of Nicolas de Serre, just four months earlier. The interrogation took place in the presence of another Dominican brother and ten other men, including Guy de Villars-Montroyer, a royal knight and former bailiff from Chaumont. He oversaw all the tasks involved in the arrests in the bailiwick of Troyes as instructed by the bailiff, Pierre le Jumeau.

Three days later the two Templars appeared before Guy again in the Petit Boulancourt residence, which belonged to the Cistercians of the abbey of Boulancourt. The records reproduce in the same terms but more briefly their confessions of 15 October. On the same day, still in Troyes but in the tower, the inquisitor interrogated Raoul de Gizy, who acknowledged the same crimes as the first two. Three other Dominican brothers as well as Guy de Villars-Montroyer and his cleric were present.

The reasons for these three interrogations are not very clear. On the one hand, many other Templars were arrested in the bailiwick of Troyes, and some were even interrogated on the spot: Lambert de Cormelles, in his deposition given on 5 March 1311 before the papal commission, says he had been interrogated by the prior of the convent of the Preachers of Troyes (Jean de l'Isle), commissioner of Guillaume de Paris, Inquisitor of France,[2] and yet there is no record of this. On the other hand, those three Templars were transferred to Paris in the days that followed to appear again before the inquisitors, and on that occasion even Jean de l'Isle came to Paris and participated in the sessions. In both cases, in Troyes as well as in Paris, the same questions were asked by the inquisitors, so why this repetition of the process? The connection between the three men must be emphasised: Raoul de Gizy had received the two others, and he was not any old Templar. To obtain a confession from him quickly could prove beneficial as the affair unfolded. It is important to note, however, that neither Jean de Tour, the Treasurer of the Temple of Paris arrested in Rouen, nor Hugues de Pairaud, the Visitor arrested in Poitiers, was subjected, as far as we know, to an interrogation at the time of their arrest; their interrogations in Paris occurred rather belatedly, during the month of November. So we are left without an answer to the question above.

In addition to those that were carried out in Troyes, we have documented records of the following interrogations:

Place	Number of Templars	Date
Pont-de-l'Arche and Roche-d'Orival	7	18 October
Paris	138	19 Oct.–24 Nov.
Caen[3]	13	28–9 Oct.
Cahors	44	31 Oct.–27 Nov.
Cahors	7	2–3 Jan. 1308
Carcassonne	7	8–13 Nov.
Aigues-Mortes	43/45[4]	8–11 Nov.
Nîmes	15	16 Nov.
Bigorre	6	21 Dec.

In addition, two German Templars travelling back to Germany were arrested and interrogated in Chaumont before being released.[5]

Paris (19 October–24 November 1307)

The inquisitors interrogated 138 brothers, with almost no representatives of the royal administration present. The commission held sessions in the Temple of Paris, except on 23 October, when it moved to the house of the Preacher brothers (Dominicans); it held its sessions in the chamber of the Inquisitor of France, Guillaume de Paris, who was a Dominican.[6] Guillaume presided in person on 19–27 October and then on 7, 10 and 17 November. When he was not there, he most often delegated responsibility for the questioning to Nicolas d'Ennezat (fourteen times) but also to Guillaume de Saint-Euverce, prior of the convent of Preachers of Paris, Durand de Saint-Pourçain or Laurent de Nantes, who were also Preachers. Four or five others assisted the one presiding; they were clerics and, the overwhelming majority of them, brothers of the Preachers' convent in Paris. In all, thirty-two Dominican brothers participated in at least one session, seven in at least three sessions. Most of them came from the convent in Paris or were students. Jean de l'Isle, prior of the convent of Troyes, was present twice, along with another brother from the same convent, Felix de Fayo. Seven Augustinian brothers (another mendicant order) also attended at least once; there were five canons, including Renaud d'Aubigny, canon of Bourges, who

attended seven times. A burgher from Paris, Guillaume de Choques, who had
ties to the king's entourage, attended ten sessions; Hugues de la Celle, a royal
knight, was there three times; and two royal officers each attended once: Renaud
de Royat, treasurer, and Simon de Montigny, bailiff of Orléans. The interrogation of a few 'stars' of the Temple mobilised the 'upper crust' of the Dominican
Order. When Geoffroy de Gonneville, Master of Aquitaine, was interrogated,
Guillaume de Paris, Nicolas d'Ennezat, Laurent de Nantes and Durand de Saint-
Pourçain were all present.[7]

The canons and brothers of the Order of Saint Augustine attended only
the first interrogations. No Minor (Franciscan) brothers attended the sessions.
The 'king's men' were essentially absent, with the exception of Guillaume de
Choques, the burgher from Paris, who was involved in the management of the
Temple's property.

The commission held sessions on twenty-one days during this period, including the Sundays of 22 October and 12 and 19 November; it suspended its hearings
for the period of All Saints' Day, from the evening of 27 October to the morning
of 2 November. The number of Templars interrogated each day varied from
one (twice) to twenty-one (the day before the All Saints' Day break), although
the reasons for such irregularity are unknown. Ten sessions involved the testimony of five to eight Templars; seven other sessions involved four Templars or
fewer; and finally there were four sessions when there were more than ten witnesses. The records of each interrogation are short; they are a bit longer when
they involve notable Templars such as Jacques de Molay, Hugues de Pairaud,
Geoffroy de Gonneville, Raoul de Gizy and others. The questioners followed
the royal instructions: after a short series of questions about identity (name, age,
position, place and date of reception into the Order, witnesses), the accused was
interrogated about renouncing Christ, spitting on the cross, obscene kissing and
sodomy, as well as the existence and veneration of an idol. Rainier de Larchant
and Guillaume d'Herblay admitted they had seen an idol in the shape of a head;[8]
Raoul de Gizy, who hadn't mentioned one at all when he was interrogated in
Troyes, this time admitted he had seen one.[9]

One hundred and thirty-four Templars, including all the dignitaries of the
Order, acknowledged all or some of these crimes. Only four Templars did not
admit to anything: Jean de Châteauvillars, Henri de Harcigny, Jean *dit* de Paris
and Lambert de Thoisy. The records of the interrogations of these four brothers are particularly brief: they weren't of interest because they didn't admit to

anything. Were they tortured before appearing, and did they resist the torture? That is the most likely explanation. And they were not asked the question that was asked of all the others: were they subjected to 'torment' so they would tell the truth?

Jean de Châteauvillars, aged thirty, had been received in Mormant, in the diocese of Langres, in 1303.[10] He subsequently did not appear again in the various proceedings carried out up to 1311–12. The same is not true of the three others.

Henri de Harcigny, from the diocese of Laon, aged forty, had just entered the Order, as he had been received in Seraincourt on 2 February 1307;[11] he was known by other names and spellings: Li Abès, Antinhi, Archeim, Hintengentis and others. He appeared as a defender of the Order on 10 February 1310, and we can follow him until 1312, as I will soon show.

Jean dit de Paris, son of an Isabelle d'Orléans, was twenty-four when he was admitted into the Order in Paris on 29 June 1299 during a general Chapter;[12] years later, he was detained with Henri de Harcigny and went to Paris with him to defend the Order on 10 February 1310 – they were moreover held together in the house of Penne Vayrié. We then lose all trace of him.

Lastly, Lambert de Thoisy, aged forty, had entered the Order in 1294, in Uncey-le-Franc in the diocese of Autun; his uncle Renaud de Thoisy, a Templar since 1286, had attended the ceremony. On 5 February 1308 he was transferred from the Temple of Paris to Conflans (a residence close to Vincennes, not the place called Conflans-Sainte-Honorine, at the confluence of the Seine and the Oise rivers), then to Montlhéry, because it was from there that he was taken to testify on behalf of the Order on 10 February 1310.[13] We have no more information about him after that.

Having admitted nothing in 1307, did those four Templars persevere in the years that followed? We don't know about Jean de Châteauvillars; the answer is yes for Henri de Harcigny; and we can assume so for Jean de Paris and Lambert de Thoisy. Other Templars, held in the Temple or elsewhere, who were not interrogated or whose records we don't have, probably refused to confess in Paris in October and November 1307. Thibaud de Plomion, for example, held in Senlis in January 1312 with Henri de Harcigny, and not reconciled to the Church as Henri was, was imprisoned in the Temple but not interrogated; he too appeared to defend the Temple in 1310.[14] Perhaps he wasn't interrogated because the inquisitors knew (since their torture had been used on him without producing the anticipated results) that they would not obtain his confession?

Those four 'negative' interrogations (from the prosecution's perspective) obviously could not make up for the disastrous effect of the 134 others. This is probably why the prosecution avoided taking the risk of increasing the 'negative' numbers by presenting before the inquisitors Templars who had not admitted anything under the torture carried out following their arrests. This could explain why not all the Templars being held in Paris were interrogated.

Seneschalsy of Nîmes-Beaucaire (8–15 November 1307)

In this district the king assigned Oudard de Maubuisson, a royal knight, and Guillaume de Saint-Just, lieutenant-general of the seneschal Bertrand Jourdain de l'Isle, to carry out the operation. Guillaume, along with another royal knight, Hugues de la Celle, had proceeded to arrest the Templars in the seneschalsy.[15]

The two commissioners first went to Aigues-Mortes, where forty-five brothers were imprisoned. They were joined by Pierre Jean, a royal lawyer in the seneschalsy, Barthélemy de Clusel, a judge in Aigues-Mortes, the nobleman Guillaume de *Limeriis*, castellan and provost there, Adam de Montreno, royal knight and provost of Bagnols, and Mathieu de Mantina, royal procurator in the seneschalsy.[16] There were only royal agents in the seneschalsy, except – and this was by design and specified in the text – for the pope's inquisitors.[17] The interrogations took place over four days, from 8 to 11 November, in the residence of the royal treasurer in Aigues-Mortes.[18] The commissioners assisting Oudard de Maubuisson whom I cited above were joined on 9 November by the under-provost of Nîmes, Pierre d'Auriac, then by two Minor brothers and, on the 11th, the knight Hugues de *Scosia*, the lieutenant of the bailiff of Velay (subordinate to the seneschal of Beaucaire) in Villeneuve-de-Berg and the castellan of *Mota*. Forty-four Templars, not forty-five, were present, but only forty-three depositions were taken. The scribe responsible for recording the proceedings reproduced in detail only the first deposition, that of Bertrand Arnaud, indicating later only the name of the witness and a few items on his c.v.: the Templar house where he had been received into the Order, his function, his position. The response Bertrand Arnaud gave provided the template; only additional, new pieces of information were recorded from other witnesses: this is the case for nine of the depositions. By 12 November the interrogations had been completed, and Oudard de Maubuisson gathered together the Templars who had been questioned and asked them to confirm their statements, which they all did;

they henceforth intended to persevere in the faith of the Holy Roman Church. A public instrument was drawn up by a notary.

Then, still in the treasurer's residence, Oudard de Maubuisson summoned Déodat Catalan and Pierre Fabre, respectively prior and lector from the convent of Preachers in Nîmes, inquisitors appointed by Guillaume de Paris in the diocese of Nîmes (the letter of appointment dated 22 September from the Inquisitor of France is included in the records) and had the 'forty-five' Templars brought back. Their depositions were then read back to them in their own languages.[19] They confirmed them in front of the inquisitors, who admonished them and invited them under the threat of ecclesiastical sanctions to reveal within the next eight days any errors or omissions they might have made. A monk from the convent of Psalmodi and two Minor brothers were added to the other witnesses in this new public instrument.

On 16 November, Oudard de Maubuisson and Guillaume de Saint-Just went to the king's residence in Nîmes to interrogate the fifteen Templars imprisoned in that city. The first eight, all connected to the convent of Saint-Gilles, were interrogated the same day in the presence of Pierre Jean and Mathieu de Mantina, who had already been in Aigues-Mortes, and Guillaume de Romans, a jurist, Jaquet de *Mosderio* and, this is important, Pons *Plancuti*, a Templar who had recently been interrogated in Aigues-Mortes. Naturally, all the brothers adopted the confession of the first of them, Pons de Castelbon. Guillaume de Saint-Just was unable to be there, and Oudard de Maubuisson waited for his return to interrogate the seven other Templars connected to the convent of Puy (five) and to that of Jalès (two). The next day, 17 November, the royal commissioners repeated the process that had been carried out in Aigues-Mortes, summoning the fifteen Templars and the inquisitors. The inquisitors delivered the same speech to the Templars.[20]

The six Templars held in Alès were not interrogated at that time, for reasons we cannot explain.

In Aigues-Mortes, as in Nîmes, all the Templars admitted to renouncing Christ, spitting on the cross, obscene kissing and sodomy (which had been encouraged but not practised). The meetings took place in secret, the brothers wore cords over their shirts, but they had never heard about an idol and thus never imagined that the cords had been in contact with one, as was supposed to have happened. In Aigues-Mortes, as in Nîmes, the inquisitors' role was reduced to that of a subordinate to the royal agents.

Nîmes and Paris thus represent two different situations. In Nîmes the royal agents presented the inquisitors with Templars who had already made complete confessions; in Paris they presented the inquisitors with Templars who had been put in a condition to make those confessions. The difference was of form, not substance, and the common element was, as we will see, the threat and use of torture.

Elsewhere in France

Identical scenes were played out in Normandy, and elsewhere in southern France. In Pont-de-l'Arche the six Templars of Renneville were interrogated on 18 October by the bailiff of Rouen, Pierre de Hangest, assisted by five knights (the lord of Oisneval, Guillaume d'Oisneval, Jean de Tonneville, Raoul du Plessis and Guillaume de Houdetot), by the viscount of Pont-de-l'Arche, by Jean Larchevêque, royal valet, and several others. The first of the accused, Thomas Quentin, confessed to renouncing Christ, spitting on the cross, obscene kissing and sodomy; he 'believed that a cord that he wore on his chemise had been touched by an image he had previously been shown'. The same day, the bailiff and Robert d'Oisneval, Jean de Tonneville and Raoul du Plessis went to the castle of La Roche-d'Orival to interrogate Philippe Agate, who confessed to the same offences. No cleric or inquisitor is mentioned.[21]

In Caen, on 28 and 29 October, the interrogations took place in the hall of the small castle; they were carried out by inquisitors and royal commissioners. The under-prior and the lector of the Dominican convent of Caen were appointed by the Inquisitor of France; the royal commissioners were Hugues de Châtel and Enguerrand de Villers. Witnesses, clerics and royal officers, eight of whose names are mentioned, were also present. The thirteen Templars held in Caen were interrogated on the articles contained in the royal instructions. The royal interrogators had to try three times to get them to admit what they wanted them to admit:

And because we were unable to get the said Templars to tell the truth about the errors contained in said articles [the act of accusation] although they had sworn twice and were interrogated with the greatest of diligence, we [...] because the said Templars had denied everything, showed them [...] how they could save their souls.[22]

Twelve of them were persuaded and then confessed, but the last, Jean Pesnée, gave in only under torture, as we will see later in this chapter.

In Cahors the interrogations were carried out in two phases: forty-four Templars appeared before the interrogators from 30 October to 27 November, and seven others on 2 and 3 January 1308. In both cases the commission held sessions in the house of Raymond La Barda, the royal *bayle* (a local officer, in the southern seneschalses) in Cahors. In the first round the under-prior of the Preachers of Cahors, Barthélemy Gandeire, took the oaths of the accused. Present with him, in addition to three other Dominican inquisitors, were the seneschal of Quercy and Perigord, Jean d'Arrabloy, and the *bayle* of Cahors, just mentioned, as well as the prior of Montfaucon in the diocese of Perigueux.[23] On some days the royal castellan of Lauzerte or a relative of the *bayle*, Pierre La Barda, attended the sessions.[24] On 2 and 3 January the seneschal, Jean d'Arrabloy, led the interrogations assisted by a royal cleric; the *juge mage* (high judge) of the seneschalsy, Hugues Magon; the provost of *Fagia* (in the diocese of Limoges), Guillaume de Vassinhac; and Hugues Morel, the prior of Montfaucon; there were no inquisitors.[25] Everyone confessed.

In Carcassonne we have the interrogations of only six Templars, although there were many more brothers held there: in 1310 the group of Templars who came from Carcassonne to defend the Order included twenty-eight names.[26] On 8 November, in the royal castle of the walled city of Carcassonne, the seneschal of Carcassonne and Béziers, Jean de *Alneto* (1305–9), and two Preaching brothers assigned by the inquisitor of Carcassonne, Geoffroy d'Ablis, directed the questioning; they were assisted by four clerics and Pierre Peytavin (or le Poitevin), the *juge mage* of the seneschalsy. The following days, on 9, 12 and 13 November, other men joined the seneschal: his lieutenant-general, Lambert de Thury, the royal judge of Saulx, Aimeri du Cros, and the castellan of Cabaret, Jean le Boc. The inquisitors are mentioned in the records only as witnesses. The six accused men were interrogated on the usual points but also, and this is what makes their testimony unique, on the idol, which they admit to having seen.[27]

A comparison of these interrogations with those carried out in Paris and Nîmes does not reveal any unusual characteristics. For all the investigations but one, the inquisitors were still associated with royal representatives, as in Paris; only the investigation in Renneville and Sainte-Vaubourg was conducted without inquisitors present, as was true for the one in Nîmes. All the Templars who were interrogated confessed, with the exception of the four in Paris; there was resistance only in Caen.

The investigations of 1307 were not limited to just the places where the records of interrogations have been preserved; others are mentioned in the testimonies of Templars who made depositions before the papal commission in 1310–11. There were interrogations in Amiens, where Baudouin de Saint-Just said he was questioned by Preacher brothers shortly after his arrest and was tortured,[28] and in Troyes, where, in addition to the very first interrogations of 15–18 October, others must have occurred since Lambert de Cormelles, from the diocese of Soissons, states that he had been interrogated by the prior of the Preachers of Troyes (Jean de l'Isle).[29] Again let's mention Mâcon, where the bailiff ordered the torture of Gérard de Passage, and Sens, where Gautier de Bure was questioned by the bailiff.[30] Geoffroy de Thatan, who had been arrested in the Temple house of Molendines and imprisoned in Loudun, was transferred to Chinon to be interrogated by the bailiff of Touraine.[31] Jean de Janville, a royal knight, one of the two men responsible for guarding the Templars in northern France, and the seneschal of Poitou investigated – and tortured – Jean Bertaud in Saint-Maixent and Humbert du Puits at the *Bovini* monastery of Poitiers.[32] These same investigators were also present in Lusignan, where they obtained the confession of Humbert de Comborn, commander of the Limousin commandery of Paulhac; they were assisted there by two Preacher brothers. The witness first confessed spontaneously, then retracted his confession; but when he was subjected to torture, he returned to his initial confession.[33] Adémar d'Esparre, taken to Poitiers to testify before the pope, had been interrogated earlier in Toulouse by inquisitors and/or royal officers.[34] There are two other testimonies for which we are unable to identify the place where the interrogations were held: Jean de Villiers-le-Duc was interrogated and subjected to multiple forms of torture by Guillaume de Marcilly and Hugues de la Celle, royal knights; and Humbaud de la Boyssade, from the diocese of Limoges, who was questioned by Preacher brothers, perhaps in Limoges.[35]

Torture

Nineteenth- and twentieth-century historians of the Templar trial often had a rather casual attitude toward the use of torture: it was awful, of course, but that was the Middle Ages, so it was normal. And they were surprised that the 'heroic

Templars' gave in so easily to this torture. Henry C. Lea's monumental *A History of the Inquisition of the Middle Ages* in part takes issue with this attitude, but there is still the suggestion that if the Templars had been completely innocent they would have said so loudly and clearly.[36] Today we view the question differently, and the historical approach to the trial has been greatly modified.

Let's look again at this passage from the record of the interrogations in Caen:

> And because we were unable to get said Templars to tell the truth about the errors contained in said articles although they had sworn twice and were interrogated with the greatest of diligence, [...] because the said Templars had denied everything ...

In other words, the accusers wanted to obtain confessions that conformed on every point to the articles of accusation in the arrest order of 14 September. If that didn't happen, it meant the witness was lying.

The Templars in Caen at first refused to acknowledge these accusations, on two occasions. And so the interrogators took them aside, highlighted the advantages of admitting to the *a priori* true facts, because many other Templars had already acknowledged them, and the disadvantages of not doing so. Torture? It is not mentioned, because it had not been necessary to use it, at least on twelve of the thirteen Templars interrogated. The thirteenth, however, had been tougher. Jean Pesnée had 'sworn two times and had been thoroughly interrogated on the aforementioned articles, but he had denied; he was put to torture the following Saturday but would confess nothing. He returned the next day and was again interrogated and questioned on said articles, he confessed the errors in the same manner they had been confessed by the others.' The admonishment had not been enough to convince him to say what was expected of him. So he was tortured, but he still would not admit anything. It was Saturday 28 October. He appeared again the next day, Sunday, but this time he toed the line and 'confessed the errors in the same manner they had been confessed by the others'. It is not difficult to imagine what had happened: on Saturday evening the torturers advised him to think hard and, if he still refused to confess, they would begin again. Jean Pesnée gave in. Can we blame him? By telling the truth he fell victim to the torturers; by lying – that is, by acknowledging the truth of his torturers – he thought he would save his skin.

The instructions attached to the arrest order anticipated the use of torture:

the commissioners of the Inquisitor 'will determine the truth carefully, with the aid of torture if necessary', and 'they will be promised a pardon if they confess the truth [...] otherwise they will be condemned to death'.[37]

The use of torture in the pursuit of heretics had been accepted since the *Ad extirpanda* proclamation fulminated by Innocent IV on 15 May 1252. Torture was authorised *citra membris diminutionem et mortes periculum* (if mutilation and death were avoided); its use was confirmed in 1259 by Pope Alexander IV.[38] It was used more commonly in lay courts of justice, and this is linked, as in the jurisdictions of the Church, to the development of the inquisitorial procedure. This procedure made the admission (the *confessio*) the 'queen of proof' of guilt.[39] There were, however, strict conditions for the use of torture: there had to be 'vehement' presumptions against the accused that made the suspect's guilt almost certain; torture was only applicable for capital crimes liable to corporal punishment; finally, torture should be used in moderation and leave no permanent marks on the body (in principle this prohibited the use of fire).

In the case of heresy, torture was to be carried out under the direction of the inquisitors themselves. It was used a great deal during the trial of the Templars, but this was unusual and, according to Jean-Marie Carbasse, not representative of normal practices.[40]

In launching the Templar Affair, Philip the Fair knew he was taking a risk. He took advantage of the cover afforded by the Inquisition, but without the pope's support it was worthless. And so the king had to obtain confessions from the Templars as quickly as possible to justify his actions and silence his critics. The 'vehement suspicions' expressed in the arrest order were almost certain proof of their guilt, and torture was used only to confirm it.

In Paris the Templars were pressured to acknowledge that they had confessed without any coercion: 'Asked to tell if he had, through fear of torture or prison or for any other cause, said falsities or included falsities in his deposition, he said no.' This was a pure formality, and we are not even sure that the question had really been put to them: the Templars did not review and sign the records.[41] Such precautions were of little concern in Caen, where the records give a more realistic picture of events.

The use of torture was eventually denounced by the Templars, but only later and not before the royal courts; rather, denunciations occurred before the pope in Poitiers in 1308 and before the papal commission in Paris in 1310–11. Gillet de *Encreyo* (or Ecci) says nothing about it in his deposition before the inquisitors on

10 November 1307, but on 8 May 1310, before the papal commissioners, he says
he had been interrogated by inquisitors and tortured shortly after his arrest.[42] We
can thus count some thirty testimonies in the depositions of 1310–11 that mention
the use of torture. In 1308, before the pope, out of the forty-two Templars whose
interrogations have been conserved, eight say they had been tortured and four
that they gave in before being subjected to it; three others describe the harsh
conditions of their incarceration.[43] Guillaume de Limoges was not tortured, but
he says that some of his friends were.[44]

Let's focus on two of these testimonies. Jean de Cugy declares that Pierre,
commander of the Temple in Paris, had ordered him, eight days before the
arrests, not to speak, but he had not been able to endure the torture and admitted
everything. Was the witness mistaken about the timeline, or was his deposition
proof that there had been escape attempts before 13 October 1307?[45] Itier de
Rochefort was tortured several times even though he had admitted everything
during the first round of torture, but he was subjected to it again because his
torturers wanted him to admit things he knew nothing about, such as the worshipping of the idol.[46] This is a good example of the goal of the accusers: not to
stop with what the accused knew, but to force him also to say what the torturers
wanted to hear.

Some Templars downplayed the impact of the torture they endured: Déodat
Jafet was tortured but did not confess; it was later, inspired by God, that he
acknowledged the facts.[47]

I've mentioned the Limousin knight Humbert de Comborn, whose journey
was somewhat 'tortuous': taken to Lusignan (in Poitou), he spontaneously and
without torture acknowledged the facts before revoking his confession. He was
then tortured, and returned to his initial confession.[48]

To summarise what we've seen: in 1308, before the pope, fifteen Templars
(out of forty-two) mentioned torture; they probably thought that in front of him
they risked nothing by informing him about it. In 1310, before the papal commission, some Templars (before and after the extreme actions of the archbishop
of Sens on 11–12 May that year) again took the risk of saying that they had
confessed under torture: twelve before that date, fourteen after. We should add
to the former group the seventeen Templars who came from Périgueux who, *en
bloc*, asserted that they had been tortured. Torture seems to have been employed
mainly during two key moments of the proceedings: shortly after the arrests and
before the interrogations in the autumn of 1307, and before the Templars were

presented to the bishops, although it is still not possible to give a precise date: 1308 or 1309? In the latter case, it would have involved the episcopal procedure against individuals ordered by the pope in Poitiers.[49]

Aside from torture, the witnesses' statements also provide information about the harsh treatment they had received and the conditions of their incarceration. Many brothers spent weeks on bread and water, in the cold, sometimes shackled or with their hands tied: Aymon de Barbone, who had his hands tied behind his back so tightly that they bled; Jean de Bar, tortured three times and given bread and water for twelve weeks; Consolin de Saint-Joire, Raymond de Vassignac and Humbert du Puits.[50]

Lastly, a few witnesses describe briefly the torture that was inflicted on them. Gérard de Passage had to endure weights hung from his testicles and limbs until he passed out; Bernard de *Vado*, from Toulouse, was subjected to such cruelty and such horrible torture by fire that the skin on his feet was burned off and the bones of his heels fell off in the days that followed – he held out two of his bones to the commissioners; Aymon de Barbone was subjected to water torture;[51] Jean de Cormele had four teeth broken; and Jean du Four was crippled for a year from the torture he endured.[52] According to Jean de Sacy, twenty-five Templars died from torture and its aftermath, and Robert Vigier cites three brothers he knew who died from the torture they endured.[53]

The continuation of the chronicle of Guillaume de Nangis provides a sort of synthesis in the form of a survey of the interrogations of 1307. After mentioning the confessions of Jacques de Molay, confirmed before the masters of the university, it says:

> It happened that some, crying, by themselves admitted a large part or all of these crimes. Some, led, so it appeared, by repentance, others questioned through the use of various torture, or frightened by the threats or the prospect of torment, others led or attracted by engaging promises, finally others tormented and forced by the lack of food in their prison, or forced in many other ways, admitted the truth of the accusations. But a large number absolutely denied everything and several who had first confessed later denied and persevered to the end in their denials; some of those perished while they were being tortured.[54]

The final sentence is very revealing. It probably explains why we don't have the interrogations of all the arrested Templars. The royal counsellors wanted confessions, not denials. And if we believe the chronicler, there were many denials, many brothers who did not confess or who recanted their confessions. This paints a very different picture of what really happened during the trial of the Templars in France.

4

AT NOTRE-DAME DE PARIS (?)

(24 or 26 December 1307)

At this point in the narrative we should take a look at the way in which the Grand Master of the Temple, Jacques de Molay, responded to events in the latter part of 1307. We will also look at how the king conducted the affair, as well as the reactions of Pope Clement.

The confession of Jacques de Molay

As we may recall, in August 1307 Jacques de Molay wrote to the pope, requesting that he undertake an investigation. Like other Temple dignitaries, at that time he suspected that the king of France was plotting something against the Order. To go from that to imagining the coup of 13 October was perhaps a mental leap that they could not make. Did the Grand Master, arrested at dawn on 13 October at the Temple in Paris, have the means and, if so, the intention of escaping? The answer is found in a letter dated November 1307 that an anonymous member of the Papal Court (in Poitiers), probably a Templar, sent to the commander of Ascó in Aragon; he cites another anonymous informant, an officer from Paris. According to this second- or third-hand information, the Master had 'strong and very harsh words' with the king, and was advised to flee by his fellow detainees: 'Because you, my lord, you can escape, go seek counsel with the pope and the cardinals.' Jacques de Molay replied:

> It is not my intention to do that because we all know that we will be proved right. And so I tell you that if I were in Germany or Spain or England and if I knew that you others were arrested, I would come to you and be in prison with you. It is not good to flee, because none of us is guilty and our Order is good and

honest, and we are Catholics as firm in the faith as the pope, the cardinals and all the Christians in the world.[1]

Continuing, the anonymous correspondent says that the king then visited the Master and that their exchange was 'spirited', Molay reminding the king that he, the king, was not new to this, having already had Pope Boniface arrested. We probably should not give too much credence to this account, although we shouldn't reject it entirely (the letter in question contains other information that has been verified). And we can't rule out that Jacques de Molay could have taken advantage of accomplices, which might have allowed him to avoid arrest. This might be more difficult to believe since he was, of course, imprisoned.[2] As we will see, even if sequestering prisoners was not in those times a rigorously followed practice, Jacques de Molay was particularly isolated from the other detained brothers. Another letter from the commander of Miravet addressed to the master of Aragon relates important news of which the commander had been made aware; it came from a trustworthy man, Romeu de Bruguera, a Catalan Preacher brother and a master in theology at the University of Paris, who had informed the prior of the Dominicans in Barcelona.[3] According to this information, the king had imprisoned all the Templars in the Temple, 'and they were separated from each other. And so first the Master was tortured and thus he confessed publicly in the presence of many prelates and all the masters of Paris and the *bacheliers* that the Order of the Temple had been accustomed for a long time to …'. The text is incomplete, but it must have listed the accusations brought against the Order. What is important to note is that this text contains the assertion that Jacques de Molay had been tortured. We will return to this.

Jacques de Molay appeared before Guillaume de Paris and the inquisitors on 24 October.[4] At that time he was at least sixty years old, maybe sixty-five. Received into the Order in Beaune forty-two years earlier, in 1265, he had had a long and discreet career in the Orient: he is not mentioned directly in the documentation before his election to Master of the Temple in 1292 in Cyprus.[5] On 24 October he admitted that during his reception he had renounced Christ and spat on the Cross. His confession was accompanied by reservations, which would be expressed by all the Templars: he had renounced Christ with his mouth but not his heart, he had spat next to the cross, not on it. It was a minimal confession, but enough to discredit the Order. It was essential for the prosecution to obtain a confession from the Grand Master, however limited, no matter what. For that reason I think Romeu de Bruguera's information, as transmitted by the commander of Miravet, was accurate: the Grand Master was then tortured, which does not exclude the use of other means of pressure – perhaps even promises that he would be pardoned.

The king's counsellors wanted to strike while the iron was hot and, the following day, had the Master confirm his confession in front of a gathering of clerics and masters from the University of Paris. This public appearance occurred after two other similar demonstrations that had been skilfully orchestrated by the royal propaganda machine since the beginning of the affair.

The day after the arrests Guillaume de Nogaret had brought together in Notre-Dame clerics and doctors from the university to justify the Templars' arrest and set forth the prosecution's main arguments.[6] The next day, a Sunday, in the gardens of the king's palace, 'the king of France [...] had proclaimed openly and publicly, in the presence of the clergy and the people from all the parishes in Paris, all the crimes of which [the Templars] were strongly suspected'.[7] Then, on 16 October, the king wrote to his European peers (the king of Aragon, the king of England and others) to inform them of his actions and invite them to do the same in their states. In his letter to James II of Aragon, Philip briefly recalls his encounters with the pope in Lyon and Poitiers, the requests of the Inquisitor of France and the consultations he had had with advisers, clerics, masters of the university and others before making his decision.[8]

At this point the king and his advisers had no records of confessions, because the interrogations had not yet begun. This was no longer the case on 25 October. On that date, at the Temple of Paris, Guillaume de Nogaret assembled a group made up mainly of masters, doctors, *bacheliers* and students at the university: theologians, but also jurists. Guillaume de Paris, the Inquisitor, who presided over the session, had Jacques de Molay and the brothers Gérard de Causse (Gauche), Guy Dauphin, Gaucher de Liancourt and Geoffroy de Charney, all knights, all of whom had confessed in the preceding days, brought in. He asked them to confirm, in their own language, their confessions. Geoffroy de Charney had had a long career in Outremer and had performed the functions of Draper of the Order before becoming Master of Normandy in 1307; Gaucher de Liancourt had spent twenty-four years in Outremer, had been Under-Draper in 1292 and since then had exercised functions as commander of houses and bailiwicks in France. Guy Dauphin and Gérard de Causse enjoyed a certain notoriety in the order. Gérard de Causse had worked alongside Jacques de Molay in Poitiers in June

1307, as seen in an act by the Grand Master of which he was the co-signatory, and he was transferred with Jacques de Molay to Corbeil on 25 January 1308.[9] On 25 October they were, along with Jacques de Molay, the most notable of the Templars to have been interrogated – and to have confessed. They were therefore not simply associates, contrary to what has sometimes been suggested.[10]

The Grand Master confirmed his confession and recalled the origins and mission of the Order of the Temple, which had allowed him to acquire prestige and glory, until the 'enemy of the human race' turned him towards horrible crimes justly denounced by 'the bearer of light from whom nothing is hidden': that is, the king of France.[11] The next day, 26 October, before an assembly made up of even more secular and regular clerics, university masters and students, theologians and others, including most of the inquisitors working on the trial, the Templars, apart from Molay and the four who had appeared the day before, were also instructed to confirm their confessions. The same day, before that session, Jean de Tour, treasurer of the Temple of Paris, and Jean Le Moine de Coeuvres had appeared before the inquisitors.[12] By the end of these sessions thirty-seven Templars,[13] including the Grand Master, had confessed. This was a remarkable windfall for the king, who quickly spread the news, as seen in a letter addressed to James II of Aragon.[14]

On 27 October Romeu de Bruguera wrote to the king of Aragon to tell him about the two assemblies, in which he had participated as a master of the university.[15] He also recalled that six months earlier he had attended various councils where 'this matter' (perhaps discussions about the Temple?) had been discussed. Those councils would have been in May 1307, and thus at the same time as the meetings between the king and the pope, and the pope and the Grand Master, in Poitiers. This concurrence suggests that there must have been deliberations within the University of Paris about the Temple. On whose initiative? The royal advisers, as opposed to the pope? Romeu made a point of telling James II that, as a precaution, he was having a similar letter sent to him through two merchants returning to Catalonia, and through those same intermediaries he was having the same information sent to the convent of Barcelona (this was, of course, the convent of the Preacher brothers in that city). This last letter must be the one – coming from a trustworthy man, a master in theology – that the commander of Miravet cites in the letter addressed to the master of the Temple in Aragon, from which I cited a passage above.[16]

Was all this the result of torture, pure and simple, or of a more subtle bargaining – such as less harsh treatment in exchange for a favour? Either way, something must have convinced the Master to write on those same days, 25 and 26 October, a letter to all the detained Templars asking them to follow his example and acknowledge the deeds of which they were being accused.[17] 'He was made to inform all his brothers, through a letter written in his own hand, that repentance had led him to his confession, and that he exhorted them to do the same',[18] wrote two chroniclers in favour of the royal plans.

The pope's reaction

On 27 October Pope Clement reacted strongly to the king's actions. He reminded him first of the prerogatives of the Roman See and the Church: '[princes ...] nevertheless decided [...] that in matters concerning religion and especially in those in which ecclesiastical and religious persons could be harmed, they would not reserve anything for their own courts of justice, but would leave everything to the ecclesiastical courts.' And he accused Philip: 'But you, dearest son, we grieve to report, you have laid hands upon the persons and the goods of the Templars, and not just anyhow but going as far as imprisoning them.' He implicitly denounces the use of torture: '[you] have gone further and added a greater affliction to those who are already considerably afflicted by their imprisonment, an affliction which we consider it better not to mention for the moment for the sake of the Church as much as yours, if you understand our meaning.' Recalling his intentions regarding the Templar Affair and his letter of 24 August, he reproaches the king for having acted in defiance of Roman jurisdiction, which is 'an insult to and contempt of our person together with that of the Roman Church'. Not wanting to add more than necessary to the list of his grievances, Pope Clement indicates in closing that he is sending Cardinals Beranger Frédol and Étienne de Suisy (made cardinals in 1305) to Paris with the mission of informing the king of his anger and to obtain the king's promise to return the Templars, their persons and their property into the hands of the Church.[19]

The pope was not content simply to protest; he needed to take back control of the situation. His primary objective was to bring the affair under the control of the Church, as had been understood before the king's sudden and violent tactics. Putting the persons and the property of the Templars under the safeguard of ecclesiastical authority wasn't enough; it was the entire procedure that had to be taken from the hands of the king and his inquisitors, who did not have a specific mandate from the pope to act against the Order of the Temple. This was the intention of the bull *Pastoralis praeminentiae* of 22 November 1307. In it the pope asks all sovereigns and princes in Christendom to proceed with the arrest of the Templars in their states, but to place both the men and their property under the safe-keeping of the Church. He does not hide his distress at the confessions of the Templars, and that of the Grand Master in particular, but he does not pre-judge their guilt: 'But if this truth is not confirmed, after real truth has been verified, all our trouble would finish, according to the will of God, the joy will rise again. Therefore we propose to discover the truth, without delay and in any way, and, as far as God permit it us, we propose to control effectively.'[20] Before this announcement, the pope had made a point, on 17 November, of informing the king of France of his decision.[21] This follows the earlier letter of 24 August which had announced the opening of an investigation.

On 1 December, Pope Clement again wrote to Philip the Fair expressing his astonishment at learning of the insinuations being spread by the king's court suggesting that the pope had been informed and had agreed to the arrest of the Templars. While applauding the king's zeal, he 'reframed' it, as journalists today might say, and attributed all responsibility for his actions to him alone. And to drive the point home, the pope informed him that he was again sending the aforementioned cardinals to Paris. Because, as we will soon see, their first mission in November had been in vain.[22]

Two documents enable us, by cross-referencing the large amount of infor-mation they contain – and despite the distortions and factual errors that force us to study them with caution – to create a quite detailed and fairly accurate chronological account of the dealings between the pope, the king and the Grand Master in those last two months of 1307. Both from Catalan correspondents, the first document is a letter from Bernat de Banyuls, chamberlain in Corneilla (in Roussillon?), addressed to his brother, Arnau de Banyuls, commander of the Templar house of Gardeyn; the second is a letter from an unfortunately anony-mous correspondent residing in Paris and addressed to someone in Majorca. Heinrich Finke dates both letters to the beginning of February 1308.[23]

Jacques de Molay and the cardinals

Carrying out the mission the pope had announced in his letter of 27 October, the two cardinals, Beranger Frédol and Étienne de Suisy, reached Paris at the beginning of November 1307:

> The pope had sent them to discover the facts [of the Templars' confessions] with certainty. When they arrived in Paris, the king of France's council and the inquisitors simply told the cardinals that they would have to believe them because it was the *truth* [my italics], and after that statement they returned to the pope. The pope asked: did you hear it from the mouths of the Templars?
>
> No, the cardinals responded, but it came from the masters in theology and the doctors, jurists and counsellors of the king of France's court.[24]

This occurred on 7 or 8 November, when the pope was near Bordeaux.[25] According to Bernat de Banyuls, some more news reached the pope around eight days later: the king of France was announcing far and wide that the Grand Master and 250 brothers of the Temple had confessed to the crimes of which they had been accused. Bernat then provides some surprising information: ten cardinals, among them those whom the pope had recently elevated to that rank, had risen up against what was going on, making it known 'that from time immemorial [the pope] was the supreme lord of the entire world and above kings and emperors. And now they saw that the king of France was above him and they were suffering because, through the king of France's pride and arrogance, [the] right order of the world had changed.'[26] And they were threatening to resign as cardinals.[27]

The bull *Pastoralis praeminentiae* was a first response and a reminder: everything having to do with the Templars was under the authority of the Church and the pope. As for that which more specifically concerned the situation of the Templars interrogated in Paris and the authenticity of their confessions, Pope Clement sent the two cardinals back to Paris with the same objective but with stricter instructions: if the king or his counsellors (because only the latter had met with the cardinals during their first – fruitless – mission) did not comply with the pope's orders, they could be excommunicated. All of this was put in a letter dated 1 December, which the cardinals were to deliver directly into the king's hand.[28]

According to the anonymous Catalan informant, the pope furthermore declared during a consistory that if the confessions alleged by the French court were true, the Templars should be sentenced, but since he wasn't convinced of this, the two cardinals were assigned to interrogate the Templars themselves, or at least their most important representatives, meaning the Grand Master and other dignitaries of the Order.[29]

Carrying the letter from the pope, the two cardinals left the Curia some time after 1 December.[30] Our informant continues:

> And when they were in Paris, they had an audience with the king of France and gave him the letters the pope sent to him. And the king of France ordered that the Templars be delivered to the cardinals and they were given the Grand Master and many other brothers. And when they had them in their authority they asked the Master if it were true what they had heard, that he had confessed, etc.[31]

On 24 December the king wrote to the pope to tell him that he had indeed turned over the Templars to his envoys:

> Holy Father, we received with a smiling face Cardinals Béranger and Étienne, sent by you in regard to the affair of the Templars, whom we have had arrested on the request of the inquisitors delegated in our kingdom through apostolic authority. We welcomed your envoys graciously [...] For what you tell us in the name of the Church regarding the property and persons of the Templars whom you ask us to return into your hands, we agree that it be done thus, if our rights are preserved [...] We have thus put the Templars into the hands of your cardinals, in your name and in the name of the Church, as well as all the property that had been assigned for the needs of the Holy Land; we will keep them and supervise them with care, so they reach their intended destination, and without confusing them with those of our domain.[32]

In sum, if we believe what our informant says, the king and the pope seem to have engaged in a game of poker. The king's very friendly, very conciliatory tone might be explained by what he interpreted as a commitment from the pope: that he would proceed with a judgement against the Templars if it was proved that what they had admitted was true. But for that to happen the Templars had to be handed over to the cardinals. How could it be believed that the pope, who had just ordered the arrest of Templars throughout Christendom, would, a month later, determine the fate of the Order based only on the confessions (assuming they were true) obtained in Paris? And how could it be believed that the king would agree to release his catch and in good faith turn men and property over to the pope?[33]

Whatever the case, the cardinals were now in a position to interrogate the Templars detained in the Temple in Paris. Which they did, but on what date? Several facts revealed by our sources are intertwined. When the Grand Master was released to the cardinals, they asked him if it was true. He answered in the affirmative and said that he would reveal a lot more if the cardinals would allow him to speak in public. Was this before 24 December, before the king's letter? According to a document that disappeared a long time ago, but which was ana-lysed by Pierre Dupuy, the two cardinals supposedly had dinner with Hugues de Pairaud, who allegedly recanted his confession during the meal.[34] On what date was this?

Contrary to the above, Jacques de Molay is generally believed to have asked the Templars held in the Paris Temple to recant their confessions. Two testi-monies may be mentioned here: that of Jean de Châlons, whom I have already introduced, and that of Jean de Fouilloy, a renegade Templar, the first to be interrogated in Paris on 19 October 1307, who made a new deposition before the pope in Poitiers in June 1308. Jean de Fouilloy, when asked

> if he knew that some brothers had recanted their confessions, and which ones had done so, said that he didn't know, but that he had heard that. Interrogated to find out whether anyone had incited them to recant their confessions, he responded that the Master of the Order, or someone assigned by him, sent wax tablets to the brothers, going from room to room, before the king and the cardi-nals entered, to tell them they should all revoke their confessions.

Interrogated about the contents of the tablets,

> he said that in essence it was: 'know that the king and the cardinals will come to this house tomorrow; other brothers have recanted their confessions; recant yours and give these letters back to the bearer.' Interrogated to find out who had brought the tablets, he responded that it was the brother who had been received a month earlier, according to what he said, who came to the room of Dauphin [Guy Dauphin, a knight brother].[35]

This information was confirmed by Jean de Châlons when he spoke of

Templars who had fled. Also interrogated in Poitiers, he declared that a 'certain priest of the Order, Renaud, through secret letters persuaded more than sixty Templars to recant their confessions'. When asked how he knew this, he answered: 'because he wrote a letter on parchment to him and to other brothers saying that if they did not recant their confessions the Order would be destroyed; [...] and he said that brother Renaud had received the order to recant his confession from the Grand Master's brother, who was dean of Langres.'[36]

All of this seems to show above all that, in the prison that the Temple of Paris had become, the detained brothers were able to communicate among themselves quite easily, and that the Grand Master himself could have contact with the outside world, thanks to a canon brother in Langres, of whom we have no other knowledge; we know also that the cardinals were able to converse freely with the Temple dignitaries. Hugues de Pairaud was probably quite content to abandon the awful prison fare for an evening to have dinner with their eminences – if that dinner actually took place, of course.

Can we go so far as to suggest that the two cardinals willingly supported the Temple revolt of Christmas 1307? I wouldn't go quite that far, although the cryptic speech that Guillaume de Plaisians delivered in May 1308 in Poitiers could lend some weight to such a hypothesis. According to him, the recanting of confessions by the Master of the Temple and others was not the result of chance: 'And the king knows well where that came from. Because they [those who recanted their confessions] were told by a few members of the Church to remain firm, because they would find support there [in the Curia]. And the king knows well who the guilty ones are, who received money from them, and that will be brought to light.'[37]

The fact remains that the cardinals granted the Grand Master's request and offered him a public forum – it is sometimes described as a rostrum in Notre-Dame de Paris, whereas the text speaks only of a church:

And then they brought all the people together and when the church was full of people one saw the Master come in with [thirty to] forty brothers and they had the Master mount a dais as if he were going to preach. And when he was ready he said: My Lords, all that the Council of France has told you, that I and all the brothers of the Temple who are here, and many others, have confessed, is true, we have admitted everything. He then took off his mantle and his tunic, and he had already cut open his sagum along the sides and the arms, and he uncovered himself before everyone and said: you see, My Lords, that they made us say what they wanted to hear. And he showed his arms which were bruised and emaciated, so that it almost seemed they had been flayed and there remained only bones and nerves, all the skin and the flesh had been taken off his back, stomach and thighs. And he said: My Lords, such as you see me here, so are all the others without exception; let it please God and the Blessed Virgin Mary that the order of the Temple still has good discipline.[38]

From such accounts we must take the gist and not dwell too much on the 'embellishments' that their authors may have added to them. There had indeed been an interview between the cardinals and the Templars; there had indeed been instructions from the Temple dignitaries for the Templars held in the Temple in Paris to revoke their confessions. And there was that revocation by Jacques de Molay, probably public but perhaps not as theatrical as presented above. That revocation is confirmed indirectly in a text, also anonymous, but which comes from someone in the inner circle of the king's counsellors, in which the first confession of the Master and its confirmation before the masters of the university on 25 October are recalled, a confirmation that 'he still maintained for two months or more', which indeed brings us to the end of December 1307, when the Master revoked his confession.[39] Is it possible to know the exact date? Perhaps 24 December? That is the date of the letter from the king to the pope, which does not mention the event. Certainly not the 25th, Christmas Day. The 26th or 27th? The Catalan text that describes this occurrence then indicates that the cardinals, at that time convinced of the Templars' innocence, returned to meet with the pope. As for the king, according to this witness, he had already been on the road to Poitiers for two days when he was informed of the recanting; he supposedly returned in haste to Paris to write to the pope. Philip the Fair's itinerary shows no trace of such a back and forth; he was in Paris throughout that period and remained there until mid-January. It's not really clear why moreover, after two days travelling, he would have hurried back to write to the pope when he was on his way to see him.

If the royal counsellors had hoped that the pope, convinced by the confessions of the Templars, would play their game and judge the Templars quickly, they were undoubtedly disappointed. But is that what they really believed? It is doubtful.

The dispersal of the Templars of Paris (24 January–12 February 1308)

In any case, the king took the situation seriously. He needed to keep control of the Templars; there could no longer be any question of handing them over to ecclesiastical authorities. Preparations for the weddings of his third son, Charles, and of his daughter, Isabelle, were keeping him busy that January / early February. But the king had to take precautions to avoid any troublesome incidents, such as those that had marked the cardinals' visit, from happening again. The Temple in Paris was not the best place to hold the Templars and keep them from outside influences; too many people were talking. Furthermore, besides the prisoners and their guards, *frère* Guillaume Robert and his household were staying there, as were many sergeants.[40] It is not very likely that this Guillaume Robert was the Inquisitor of France, and it has been suggested that he was the Guillaume Robert who denounced the Templars, referred to by Ponsard de Gizy in 1309. The decision was made to disperse the Templars being held in Paris throughout the region. In the absence of the king, who had left for Boulogne-sur-Mer to celebrate the weddings of his children, the royal government undertook to transfer from the Paris Temple most of the Templars who were being held there. In my opinion, these measures were a direct response to the recanting of Jacques de Molay and some of the Templars held in the Paris Temple. Two royal knights who had already participated in the arrests, Guillaume de Marcilly and Hugues de la Celle, directed the transfer operation, which began on 25 January and was completed on 11 February.[41] Jacques de Molay, P. d'Acre, Gérard de Causse (du Cancer in the document) and Brother Thibaut [de Basemont], treasurer of the Temple in Paris, were the first to leave for Corbeil.[42] In total, 127 Templars were dispersed to two other places in Paris and twenty-five sites in Île-de-France, Normandy, Picardy and the Sénonais, even as far away as Orléans. Not all the Templars, as I pointed out in the preceding chapter dealing with their detention, were listed by name.

The royal government's objective was to see to it that no more than one hundred Templars at most remained in the Temple in Paris, taking into account the fact that those being held outside the Temple (in the Barbel and Preuilly residences, and in that of the bishop of Châlons) were to be taken there. The document, as presented in Table 2, proves that within Paris two other detention sites were opened: in the abbey of Sainte-Geneviève and in Saint-Martin-des-Champs.

To carry out these transfers from Paris, on 24 January the royal administration

Table 2 Dispersal of Templars from the Temple in Paris

(25 January–11 February 1308)

	Place	Number	Named
In Paris:	Sainte-Geneviève	6	0
	Saint-Martin-des-Champs	12	11
Near Paris:	Bois de Vincennes	24	10
	Saint-Denis	8	8
	Saint-Maur-des-Fossés	6	6
	Chaillot (Challuel)	6	6
In the south:	Corbeil	4	4
	Rochefort-en-Yvelines	1	1
	Montlhéry	2 + 4	2 + 1
	Villeneuve-le-Roi	2	2
	Montereau-fault-d'Yonne	1	1
	Chailly	4	–
	Bray-sur-Seine	8	8
	Pers-en-Gâtinais[43]	10	10
	Moret	1	1
	Orléans	2	2
In the north:	Dammartin-en-Goële	16	16
	Montmélian	6	6
	Thiers-sur-Thève[44]	6	0
	Nanteuil-le-Haudouin	4	4
	Crépy-en-Valois	4 + 12	4 + 12
	Creil	4 + 4	4 + 4
	Beaumont-sur-Oise	6	6
In the west:	Trappes	6	0
	Conflans[45]	6	6
	Goulet	1	1
	Vernon[46]	1	1
Totals:		177	137

mobilised 'knights, equerries, sergeants on foot and on horseback to guard the Templars en route to the castles outside Paris'.

In addition to Guillaume de Marcilly and Hugues de la Celle, the provost of Paris, the bailiff of Orléans and the bailiff of Sens were themselves charged with taking the Templars to their new prisons. They were not just any prisoners: that is, they mostly comprised the Temple dignitaries interrogated in Paris in October and November 1307. And so some special measures were taken: Guillaume de Marcilly was in charge of Jacques de Molay; the provost of Paris oversaw Hugues de Pairaud and Raimbaud de Caromb; and the bailiff of Sens accompanied Geoffroy de Charney, Gaucher de Liancourt and Guillaume d'Herblay (the young chaplain). These high-ranking royal officers were clearly not responsible for physically guarding the Templars; that job was left to the guards (six of whom are cited), who were assisted by one or two equerries or sergeants (which makes eight in all). At each of the seventeen detention sites (there were two different ones in Crépy-en-Valois), the person responsible for the Templars' transfer was also responsible for their imprisonment. They were all sergeants on horseback; there were two in Crépy-en-Valois and in Creil. In fourteen cases they were assisted by sergeants on foot.

In all, from those responsible for the operation down to the sergeants on foot responsible for guarding the Templars, twenty-eight are known by name,[47] to whom must be added twenty-five whose names are not given. A total of fifty-three men carried out the transfers.

The same document offers a rather detailed look at the cost of the operation and the cost of maintaining the Templars in their prisons. The daily wages cited were 4 *sous parisis* for a sergeant on horseback and 2 for a sergeant on foot. The most frequent occurrence was this: 'assigned to the guard of Jean Ruffaut, sergeant on horseback, who had a sergeant on foot with him, 6 Templars whom he would take to the castle of Trappes; as his wages (salary) he received 6 *livres*; those of the sergeant on foot 50 *sous* (2 *livres*, 10 *sous*); and for the expenses related to the guard of the Templars 12 *livres parisis* in hard currency.' Following the daily amount noted above, the sergeant on horseback must have received his wages for thirty days and the sergeant on foot for twenty-five days. The date of the document is not indicated, but it is probably a form of accounting done after the transfer. I can't explain the difference in days paid to the sergeant on horseback and the sergeant on foot. The total amount of wages paid for the entire operation, including the specific wages paid to some people that were different from the wages paid to the sergeants, amounted to 323 *livres* 10 *sous parisis*.

The amount spent on the maintenance of the transferred Templars in their new detention sites amounted to 322 *livres parisis*. Here again it is impossible to say what this amount corresponds to in terms of number of days' custody: twenty-five, as for the sergeants? A calculation concerning the Templars transferred on 5 February to three different places, Pers-en-Gâtinais, Saint-Maur-des-Fossés and Conflans (twenty-two Templars in all), indicates an average of 3 *livres* spent on each Templar, which, spread over twenty-five days of imprisonment, amounts to 2 *sous* 5 *deniers* per day: that is a lot if we compare it to the infinitely more precise numbers that are available for the imprisonment of the Templars in the bailiwick of Senlis in 1310–11.[48]

The document does not provide any information about the way these transfers were carried out. We can assume by looking at other cases, notably the transfer that occurred in 1310–11 in Senlis, that the prisoners of the Paris Temple were taken away in carts and in chains. Depending on how far the prison was from Paris, the transfer would have taken from one to three days, possibly even four.

These transfers marked the end of the first phase of the Templar Affair. The king had hoped to be done with it quickly; but the disruptive events at the end of 1307 and the pope's resistance did not allow that. For several months the Templars fell into semi-obscurity, but they continued to be the objects of interest in high places, in Paris and in Poitiers.

It was now time for intense manoeuvring between the pope and the king of France.

5

POWER STRUGGLE

(January–June 1308)

After Jacques de Molay's stunning reversal in Paris at the end of December 1307, Philip the Fair needed to react. The Templars – and their property – remained in the king's hands, in the king's prisons and guarded by the king's agents, as seen in the transfer of Templars from the Temple in Paris in January–February 1308. But Philip did not control the pope. During the first few months of 1308 the Templars faded from the scene. The king's foremost adversary was the pope. All eyes were on the power struggle playing out between Pope Clement and Philip the Fair.

The wedding ceremonies of the king's children, Charles, his third son, and his daughter Isabelle, were occupying the king and his court in early 1308. In the middle of January in Hesdin, Charles married Blanche, the daughter of Otto IV, count of Burgundy, and Mahaut, countess of Artois. On 25 January in Boulogne-sur-Mer, Isabelle married the king of England, Edward II. Philip stayed in Boulogne until 6 February. But he was still following the Templar Affair, as seen in the letter he wrote on 28 January to James II of Aragon to congratulate him on his action against the Templars – they had been arrested in Valencia – and his efforts against those who, in Aragon and Catalonia, had been holed up in their chateaux. He uses the occasion to bring James up to date on what had been happening in France in the Templar Affair since the time of their arrest: he had more than five hundred depositions from Templars who had admitted their crimes, copies of which he would send to James. Yet there isn't a word about the Grand Master's having revoked his confession, or a word about the mission of the cardinals in Paris in December.[1]

Four series of events will take us from Poitiers on a circular route back to Poitiers, travelling through Paris and Tours.

Poitiers: The flight of the *cubicularius* (13 February 1308)

The pope was quick to remind the king in no uncertain terms of his own point of view.

In February, probably before the 13th, Pope Clement decided to suspend the authority of the inquisitors who until then had been leading the proceedings against the Templars.

Why before 13 February? Because during the night of 12–13 one of the pope's *cubicularii* (or gentlemen of the bedchamber) in Poitiers, Giacomo da Montecucco, also commander of Lombardy, took flight.[2] Previously, on 13 October, while other Templars had been arrested, those who held curial functions in Poitiers had not been. Pope Clement, who returned to Poitiers on 15 October, immediately held a consistory during which he assured his Templar staff of his protection and advised them above all not to attempt to flee. Giacomo da Montecucco then responded to the pope on behalf of all his brothers, to thank him and to defend the Order: 'Holy Father, we are not afraid because you will defend us and preserve justice and because we are all, brothers of the Temple, good Christians.'[3] By fleeing, Giacomo da Montecucco was betraying the pope and putting his word in doubt. Clement was livid and ordered that the fugitive be found by whatever means, even offering a reward to anyone who found him and brought him back. It was in vain. Giacomo da Montecucco managed to return home to Asti. There had not yet been any attempt to arrest the Templars in Italy; he avoided all the proceedings that were later taken against the Order.[4] This happened at the worst possible time for the pope, who at that time was in the middle of a serious confrontation with the royal authorities on the subject of the Templars. The bishop of Lleida, informed of the escape by his procurator at the Curia, in turn informed the king of Aragon: the pope was furious, he said, at the idea that 'the king of France and the other princes of the world could say and allege that if he [the pope] wasn't capable of holding onto a single man, how could he guard two thousand'.[5] This affair was undermining the pope, who was still demanding that the Templars be handed over to the safe-keeping of the Church, and who – this is my hypothesis – had just made the bold decision to revoke the powers of the inquisitors. He might not have dared to do so after 13 February.

It was indeed a bold initiative because it amounted to cancelling out the royal-inquisitorial proceedings. Everything that Philip the Fair and his advisers had done in the past six months to prove the Templars' heresy and thereby justify their actions was reduced to nothing, at least formally. Later, in Poitiers, in the bull *Subit assidue* (5 July 1308) which re-established the power of the inquisitors, Pope Clement explained his decision of February: the inquisitors had acted without informing him, they had carried out proceedings in haste which had given rise to suspicions in his mind, and he had been little inclined to believe the accusations. It is conceivable that the report that the cardinals had given him on their mission in Paris had supported that position. However, by July the testimonies and the renewed confessions of the seventy-two Templars he had just heard in Poitiers caused him to change his mind and thereby justified the re-establishment of the powers of the inquisitors (without, however, excusing them for their actions).[6]

Philip the Fair reacted using various means, all of which were aimed at appealing to public opinion. This must be repeated and emphasised: historians of the Middle Ages have often had trouble grasping this appeal to 'public opinion'. But it did exist, as can be seen in the propaganda campaigns that Frederick II, in the second quarter of the thirteenth century, and Philip the Fair, at the turn of the fourteenth century, were able to orchestrate to bring that opinion over to their sides.

Arguing against the pope, the king wanted to justify his initiatives against the Templars – their arrest, interrogation and torture – and to justify his demands: the judgement, condemnation and suppression of the Order. In challenging the pope, Philip knew he was on shaky ground, and thus in a position of weakness. As Edgard Boutaric has pointed out, Philip did not want to bypass the pope, because he needed him; he just wanted to bring him over to his side.[7] It should be noted that Boutaric inverts the king's priorities: for Boutaric, the trial concerning the memory of Boniface VIII was secondary and only a means to reach his primary objective, the suppression of the Templars. In fact, the opposite is true: the primary objective was to obtain the posthumous condemnation of Boniface VIII, and that is why the king still needed the pope.

Paris: The consultation with the university (March 1308)

The king of France and his advisers had been able to orchestrate a smear campaign against Boniface VIII which went as far as physical aggression. Their campaign against Pope Clement had to be more subtle, and they had first to confront him on his terrain: prove that he was wrong to 'defend the Templars', as he was reproached for doing in scarcely veiled terms. To do this, the king submitted a series of questions to masters in theology at the University of Paris; he expected them to provide responses favourable to his views in order to shake the pope's resistance. Georges Lizerand dates this questionnaire to the beginning of February 1308.[8] Here is a summary:[9]

1. Can the king, without petitioning the Church, intervene against heretics, arrest and punish them?

2. In the 'terrible' affair of the Templars, can the temporal prince act even more completely 'or rather, because the said Templars claimed to constitute a religious Order, are the said temporal prince's hands bound so that he cannot proceed against them unless asked to do so by the Church?' For the accusation is proven by the confessions of the majority, and the Order 'was essentially a college of knights, not of clerics'.

3. Is it necessary to wait for the confessions of Templars in other kingdoms before condemning them?

4. Should a Templar from whom one has not been able to obtain a confession continue to be considered a Catholic?

5. Can the fact that ten, twenty, thirty or more Templars deny the crimes exonerate the Order, when so many others have testified against it?

6. Should the Templars' property revert to the prince, or should it be granted to the Holy Land or to the Church?

7. And if it should revert to the Holy Land, who should oversee it in the interim: the Church or the prince?

The masters in theology responded on 25 March. The responses were detailed and slightly cautious, but ultimately unambiguous. The king, regardless of the circumstances, was required to go through the Church, because the Order of the Temple was 'a religious Order [...] and exempt'. To the third question the masters responded somewhat obliquely: the confessions already obtained were enough to sanction the Order, and therefore to justify an investigation. Those who did not confess could not be considered heretics, but since it could be feared that they might 'infect' the others, measures should be taken. The Temple's property had been obtained through donations intended for the faith and the

Holy Land. That purpose remained, it should therefore be maintained with a view to that goal, and as for its safe-keeping, one must do what 'will best serve the said end'.[10] The king had lost: there could be no appeal against the clear responses to the first two questions.

Only masters in theology had been consulted, and fourteen had placed their seal at the bottom of the document relating their responses; this means that some of their colleagues did not approve the declaration, because there were twenty-two masters in theology known of at the time. They may have voiced their opinions, but probably later, on the question of a possible relapse into heresy of the Templars who, following Jacques de Molay, revoked their confessions at the end of December 1307. We will look at these questions again in Chapter 11.[11]

There are different ways of interpreting the king's questions and the responses of the Paris masters, but without question the king had received a slap in the face. In 1303, when he attacked Boniface VIII, Philip the Fair at least had the passive support of the university; he had then addressed the people of France by convoking an assembly of the estates. Despite lacking support, he did the same thing in 1308.

Pierre Dubois

In the meeting with the university masters, the king raised questions of theology and law. With his plans thwarted, he now sought out the people of France as his witnesses, and convoked an assembly of the estates in Tours. Preparations for the meeting were accompanied by a campaign of propaganda and slander, this time aimed directly at the pope. Historians have a difficult time finding all the pamphlets that comprised such propaganda. We know of two, both attributed to the same author, Pierre Dubois.[12] The two pamphlets by Dubois date from the beginning of 1308.[13] The author was from Coutances in Normandy. He studied at a university in Paris and perhaps in Orléans, where law was taught, and held the position of royal lawyer in the bailiwick of Coutances. He represented his town at the assembly of estates in 1302, and also at the one in Tours in 1308. He is known above all for his *Traité de la récupération de la Terre sainte*, which is quite interesting although its contemporary 'commercial success' is doubtful– we know of only one copy.[14] He is believed to have written the two pamphlets, because they show the same tone, aggressiveness and phraseology that he employed elsewhere against the pope and the Templars. But these texts also show many similarities to the speeches given by the royal counsellor Guillaume de Plaisians before the pope in Poitiers; because of this, some have hypothesised that Dubois was also the author of Plaisians's speech – unless it was the other way round.[15] However, the simplest solution is to assume there were two authors.

The first pamphlet, written in French, was titled *Remontrances du peuple de France* ('Admonition of the People of France'). It is presented in the form of a so-called address from the people of France to their king, imploring him to exert pressure on the pope, 'who has greatly angered the French' by his procrastination in the Templar Affair. The pope is accused of having been corrupted by the Templars' money , and of practising large-scale nepotism in granting ecclesiastical benefices. The king must therefore warn him 'to take care to follow the right path in his great seigneury'. These grievances are moderate, but they touch on a sensitive point: Pope Clement did indeed shamelessly favour his own family.

The second pamphlet is more vehement. Written in Latin, it assumes the form of a *Supplique du peuple de France au roi* ('Supplication of the French people to their king') and deals directly with the Templar Affair. The Templars are not ordinary heretics, and the Church may indeed argue its rights in the face of the demands made by the lay power. They 'must not be considered heretics; on the contrary, they are placed entirely outside the power of the Church', as seen in their confessions. It makes reference to Moses, who, without the consent of his brother Aaron, 'was made a high priest upon the order of God' and had twenty-two thousand worshippers of the golden calf massacred. Pursuing this reasoning to the end, the author declares that the king could proceed similarly 'against the entire clergy' if that clergy encouraged such transgressions. Were these texts the fruit of an elaborate strategy? Perhaps the idea was to let the king speak respectfully and in a moderate tone in his questions to the university but to let Pierre Dubois and the royal advisers spew incendiary words. The question raised in the requests to the university and in the pamphlets is the same: does the king have the right to intervene without the backing of the pope and the Church in matters of heresy?

It is hard to know exactly when these texts were written. The second one is later than the first, and was possibly written after the university's responses to the king's questions. The supplication clearly takes into account the theologians' point of view on the issue raised. It may date to the beginning of April and thus have been used during the meeting of the estates.[16] Guillaume de Plaisians, in his first speech in Poitiers on 29 May 1308, clearly knew the contents of it.

Other texts of this type probably circulated, but we have not found any trace of them in the archives.

Did the pope, or at least some ecclesiastical body, produce similar propaganda in favour of the Templars? The only known example of a *factum* defending them dates from the same period, perhaps the beginning of February, before the king sent his questions to the university.[17] The anonymous author of this *Lamentatio* in favour of the Templars is addressed to the university masters.[18] The text recalls the Gascon origins of the rumours, the arrests and the torture endured, including the fact, later repeated by the Templar Ponsard de Gizy, that thirty-six brothers were tortured to death in Paris:[19]

> In sum I say that the human language cannot express the pain, agony, misfortune, affronts and harsh torment that the aforementioned innocents have endured in the space of the three months from their arrest, because day and night they have continued to moan, to languish in prison, to cry and to shout in their torment.[20]

Then the author evokes the fate of some hundred Templars still languishing in the prisons of the sultan in Babylon (Cairo) because they refused to recant.

On the one hand, then, there were the accusatory pamphlets arguing that the king had the right to act without the pope's consent; on the other, there was a text defending the Templars, denouncing torture and the implausibility of the confessions. These themes would be developed again two years later, the former in a pamphlet wrongly dated 1308[21] and the latter in the memoranda presented by the brothers before the papal commission. This proves that those ideas circulated and that, both from the royal side and from that of the Templars, people were aware of what was going on.

Tours: The Estates General (May 1308)

The royal propaganda machine was not content simply to have slanderous pamphlets circulated. As he did in 1303 against Boniface VIII, the king appealed to 'the people of France' by summoning their representatives to gather in a *consilium generale* (which historiography would call the Estates General) on 5 May 1308 in Tours.[22] Three letters of convocation were sent out between 24 and 29 March: one addressed to the nobility, the second to the clergy and the third to towns and communities. The latter are not well defined: 'All our dear and loyal mayors, consuls, aldermen, jurats and communities in places under the insignia of our kingdom.'[23] The criterion used to select them was the existence of fairs and markets in their community. Special and individualised letters were sent to bishops and archbishops asking them to hold meetings of provincial councils to designate representatives of their dioceses (the representative would not necessarily be the bishop). The convocations for the towns were addressed to the royal bailiffs and seneschals, who were tasked with disseminating them throughout their districts as quickly as possible by making as many copies as necessary.

The designation of deputies, in response to the convocations, was done through procurations. Noblemen were convoked individually as vassals by reason of the service they owed the king; they could then designate a procurator. They didn't jump at the chance to do so, and, for the nobility, we know of only thirty-five procurators. We know of 114 for the clergy, both regular and secular. A meeting of a provincial council is documented only for the archbishoprics of Reims and Rouen. The archbishop of Narbonne, Gilles Aycelin, an important member of the royal council, claimed many obligations in order to be excused from the meeting of a provincial council. He wrote to his suffragans proposing that they designate as their representatives himself and the bishop of Toulouse. A fair number of bishops did not accept and drafted a procuration in their name, different from what Gilles Aycelin had expected.

Two hundred and sixty documents came from the towns and communities. Six towns from the bailiwick of Troyes each designated two deputies. The designation of deputies could have been the task either of municipal authorities or royal provosts when the towns were not autonomous. In Gien the royal provost convoked some forty notables, 'all bourgeois from Gien, the most qualified, and composing the best part of the town of Gien'; they chose two bourgeois 'as their procurators and special envoys' to Tours.[24]

The contents of the royal convocations sent to the nobility were brief, a bit less so for those sent to the clergy; by contrast, those that were sent to the towns were more developed. In those sent to the nobility the king simply indicated that in Tours they would be dealing with the affair of the abominable crimes of the Templars. But the towns were given a more detailed argument that provided a summary of the accusations brought against the Templars in the arrest order of 13 October 1307 and reminded them that the king and his ancestors had always been the defenders of the Catholic faith. That faith was being threatened by the crimes of the Templars – crimes they had admitted, and which were thus proven.

The king wanted to extirpate those crimes and, to that end, had to meet with the pope. Addressing the 'people of France', he said: 'We wish you to participate in this holy work, you who participate in the Christian faith.'

I won't dwell here on an analysis of the responses of the people of France to the king's convocation. This has been amply done by Malcolm Barber and Magdalena Satora from a study of the procurations assembled by Georges Picot.[25] Philip the Fair certainly did not have to worry about being snubbed the way he had been by the university masters, but the authors just mentioned have revealed much reticence among each of the three estates. Many nobles abstained from attending, claiming illness, age or pressing business. A few high-ranking prelates supported the king without reservation, but others, following the bishop of Nîmes, took precautions or voiced reservations. As for the representatives of the towns, who were the most inclined to follow the king without asking any questions, it seems that the Templar Affair was for them only an element of their political collaboration with the monarch, which was developing rapidly at the beginning of the fourteenth century.[26] The bourgeoisie of Gien, for example, were amenable, but they had hardly been persuaded by the royal propaganda, if we judge from the instructions they gave to their two deputies: they would go to Tours, or wherever it pleased the king, to hear what he had to say 'regarding the ruling, absolution, or condemnation of the Templars'.[27] So they were actually taking the pope's position: they were waiting to see.

We know nothing about the deliberations of the estates in Tours, which took place between 5 and 15 May 1308. The king arrived only on the 9th – which may have been the actual date of their opening. They closed on 15 May because on that date a certain number of deputies received the order to return home. Many, however, were to follow the king to Poitiers, where, at the head of an imposing and threatening retinue, he arrived on 26 May.[28]

Bertrand de Languissel, bishop of Nîmes, and the Templars

As I mentioned, very little was heard of the Templars during those first six months of 1308. Except in Nîmes. The bishop, Bertrand de Languissel (1280–1324), like all the bishops of the province of Narbonne, had received the archbishop Gilles Aycelin's proposal to delegate himself as their deputy to the assembly of the estates without holding a meeting of the provincial council beforehand. We have seen that some bishops of the province refused and designated their own procurators. Bertrand de Languissel did otherwise. On 22 April 1308 he summoned the eight Templars of the house of Saint-Gilles being held in Alès who came from his diocese; they had already been interrogated by Oudard de Maubuisson on 16 November 1307. Bertrand de Languissel also summoned: the bishop of Nevers, who was present at the time in the seneschalsy of Beaucaire, where he was dealing with 'difficult affairs'; Bertrand Jourdain de l'Isle, seneschal of Beaucaire; Oudard de Maubuisson; Déodat Catalan, the inquisitor; and other Preacher brothers and royal agents. They had all participated in the interrogations of November 1307. The bishop had the confession given on 16 November by one of them, Pons de Castelbon, a confession that the seven others had agreed with, read out loud. Only Pons de Castelbon was interrogated, and he confirmed his earlier confession. The seven others probably again agreed with Pons's statements.[29]

The bishop of Nîmes's initiative was directly connected to the convocation of the Estates General in Tours. He was intervening *ex officio*, convoking only the Templars of his diocese. His goal was to determine personally the truth of the confessions made by the Templars before assigning procuration to Gilles Aycelin. Bertrand de Languissel was not a fan of the king of France, or of the archbishop of Narbonne. In 1303 he had disobeyed the king and gone to Rome to the council assembled by Boniface VIII (this was before the attack in Anagni). The eight Templars didn't dare recant their confessions of 1307. Is it possible that they were unable to seize the opportunity that was being offered to them to do so? It's not clear that they had been aware of the revocation made by the Grand Master in December 1307; and then, right next to the bishop of Nîmes were all those who had forced their confessions from them in November – that must have been enough to make them nervous.[30]

As for Bertrand de Languissel, he didn't go any further and granted procuration to the archbishop of Narbonne, in completely neutral terms: only the Templar Affair would be dealt with under the procuration (*negotio templariorum*); no judgement, no speculation.[31]

From the sometimes ambiguous phrasing of some Templar depositions I have wondered whether there might not have been other appearances by Templars before the bishops in the course of 1308, and without necessarily having any connection to the meeting in Tours. Anne-Marie Chagny-Sève, looking at the interrogations before the bishop of Clermont in June 1309 (this would have been the time of the proceedings against individual Templars established by Pope Clement in August 1308[32]), cites the deposition of Bernard de Villars (June 1309), who, with thirty-three other brothers, repeated before the bishop of Clermont, Aubert Aycelin, the confession that he had made before two Preacher brothers, Étienne Bourdon and Durand Vassal. The first interrogation must have taken place in October or November 1307, so an appearance before the bishop could have taken place in 1308.[33] Some testimonies given before the papal commission seem to support the appearances before the bishops following the confessions made in 1307, and before the meeting – which was not before 1309 – of the diocesan commissions set up by the pope.

Here are a few such examples. Humbert du Puits and Jean Bertaud, both from the diocese of Poitiers, appeared in 1307 before the seneschal of Poitou, then a year later before the official of Poitiers (that is, the head of the episcopal jurisdiction or officiality) as well as Preacher and Minor brothers.[34] Gérard de Passage, from the diocese of Metz, was interrogated and tortured before the bailiff of Mâcon in October or November 1307; he was then questioned by the Preacher brothers and the bishop of Chalon-sur-Saône. He would later be questioned by the bishop of Toul (this was perhaps at the time of the proceedings before the diocesan commission ordered by the pope).[35] In these two examples the appearances before the bishop and the inquisitors are comparable to those that we saw in Aigues-Mortes and Nîmes in 1307. In contrast, Gillet de *Encreyo*, from the diocese of Reims, interrogated at the Temple in Paris by the inquisitors in 1307, later appeared twice before the bishop in the great hall of the bishop's residence. When? It could have been either in 1308 or in 1309, or both.[36]

An appearance before a local bishop in the months following the confessions made to the inquisitors and royal agents could have been a means to have proceedings that the king knew were illegal validated by the ecclesiastical authority. It remains the case that, in the absence of explicit documents, it is impossible to say anything more on the subject.

Guillaume de Plaisians in Poitiers (May–June 1308)

The king left Tours on 21 May. He stopped in Chinon on the 22nd and reached Poitiers on the 26th.[37] He was accompanied by his counsellors, his court and deputies from the Estates General in Tours. According to the ambassador of the king of Aragon, Jean Bourgogne, the reception from the pope was warm: Pope Clement, before his departure for Rome (he ended up going to Avignon), would be able to discuss with the king the matter of the Holy Land (that is, his plans for another crusade). This account can probably be attributed to Gascon humour, because clearly they were going to discuss only the Templars and Boniface VIII.

The pope held a consistory on 29 May. Jean Bourgogne's report, which we've already seen, is particularly detailed and complete, and in it he mentions and sums up everything that was said.[38]

Guillaume de Nogaret, excommunicated since the violence in Anagni, obviously could not appear before the pope. Thus it was Guillaume de Plaisians, the royal counsellor specifically in charge of the Templar Affair, who would speak first. He gave a long speech, of which we know the framework, published by Georges Lizerand.[39] Jean Bourgogne's summary enables us to state that Guillaume de Plaisians did not follow his outline to the letter. In the form of a sermon titled *Christus vincit, Christus regnat, Christus imperat* – Christ is the victor, Christ is the ruler, Christ is the commander – he repeats the great themes of the royal propaganda and demonstrates the soundness and the success of the royal undertaking against the heretical Templars, based on the hundreds of confessions obtained just about everywhere in the kingdom: 'The aforementioned facts are sound, clear, indubitable.' To place them in doubt amounted to being complicit in heresy. In relation to his plans, Guillaume de Plaisians hardened his speech against the pope and introduced some thinly veiled threats. The Order had condemned itself, and they only awaited the pope's decision, because 'the affair is in your jurisdiction alone'. And he concludes, still according to Jean Bourgogne: 'And so, Holy Father, as the king, the bishops, the barons, and all the people of this kingdom press for the rapid execution of this business, may it please you to expedite it with all immediacy! Otherwise it will be necessary for us to speak to you in another language!' This diatribe was given in the vernacular French, rather than Latin.

Then Gilles Aycelin, the archbishop of Narbonne, and Gilles Colonna, archbishop of Bourges, quickly spoke in the same vein; they were followed by a baron and two members of the bourgeoisie: one from Paris, who appeared on behalf of those who spoke the *langue d'oïl*, and the other from Toulouse, for those who spoke the *langue d'oc*. They were bringing the support of their 'estates' to the king.

The pope answered in Latin and held to his earlier positions, pointing out that the decision to arrest the Templars had never been sanctioned in writing by him. In Jean Bourgogne's report on his statement, the key phrase is this:

Since becoming pope, he knew of many Templars, and he appreciated the Order and the brothers as those he believed to be good. If, however, they are as they are said to be, he hates and will hate them in such a way that, if their errors are proved to him, as their judge he will proceed against them in a way that will do honour to the Church of God and further the faith and the whole of Christianity.

And he would act with the cardinals well and quickly, but not in haste, and with the honesty and maturity that were the hallmark of the Church.

Pope Clement took his time, but he had to grant a new meeting in the face of pressure from the king. This took place on 14 June. The new speech by Guillaume de Plaisians was much stronger and threatening.[40] He presented the king of France 'not as an accuser, denouncer or special promoter, but as the minister of God, champion of the Catholic faith, zealot of divine faith for the defence of the Church'. However, like a reed, Pope Clement bent but did not break, to the great fury of Plaisians, whose violent tone probably went beyond the king's intention.[41] No, the pope could not judge or condemn the Order until the brothers and the property of the Order were transferred to the guardianship of the Church.[42]

The king resolved to make a grand gesture. He ordered that a certain number of Templars, including the main dignitaries, be taken to Poitiers to be handed over to the pope.

The arm-wrestling had been suspended. It was now time for intense bargaining.

6

COMPROMISE: POITIERS–CHINON

(June–August 1308)

The Templars appear before the pope: Poitiers, 28 June–2 July 1308

The day after the consistory of 14 June 1308, Philip the Fair understood that continuing on the path suggested in Guillaume de Plaisians's speech could lead to violence – another Anagni, perhaps – and would be counterproductive.

On 27 June he published two letters. In the first he justified the detention of the Templars in royal prisons with his fear that they might attempt to flee, and said that their property had been seized in order to prevent it from being wrongly appropriated. Then he announced that he was going to return the men and the property to the pope and the Church through the two cardinals, Beranger Frédol and Étienne de Suisy. In the second letter he decided to relinquish royal administration of the property.[1]

Both a concrete and symbolic act, the handing of the Templars over to the pope amounted to sending seventy-two brothers to the pope, who would then be able to interrogate them. We know very little about how that operation was undertaken. It is impossible that the king would have waited until 27 June to organise the Templars' transfer, since the interrogations were to begin the following day. An English text reporting on the events in Poitiers during the month of June provides an interesting detail:

> Upon thursday after the Feast of Saint John the Baptist, the kinge of France did bringe certeyne of the templaries persons to the number of VIII or IX what were noble men [break in text] in the kingdom of France and did give and offer them to the pope and to the Churche corporall possession of theirs persons and goods. In the next week followinge the pope, with fyve cardinals, did examine those Templars.[2]

The text presents a few chronological problems. The Thursday after the feast of Saint John the Baptist, which that year fell on Sunday 24 June, was Thursday 28 June, the day of the first interrogations, which makes it difficult to believe that the Templars arrived on that day; furthermore, the pope did not wait until the following week to interrogate them. That said, the text reasonably suggests that the arrival of the Templars in Poitiers was staggered and must have begun before 26 or 27 June. An analysis of the interrogations enables us to pinpoint, to a certain extent, the places of detention the seventy-two Templars had come from. But before looking at this more closely, let's examine the documents available to us.

The figure of seventy-two Templars presented to the pope in Poitiers is the same number mentioned in the bulls *Regnans in coelis* and *Faciens misericordiam* of 12 August 1308, two texts whose importance will become clear in the following pages. The five dignitaries of the order, Jacques de Molay at the head, who were also to be presented to the pope in Poitiers did not get any further than Chinon. Should they be counted among the seventy-two? Historians have the depositions of forty of those seventy-two Templars. They can be divided into two types of documents: the *mundum*, a carefully prepared original document, on parchment, intended to be distributed by the chancellery beyond the inner circle; and the *rubrice*, a sort of rough draft on paper that remained in the chancellery.[3] These forty depositions belong in the *rubrice* category; thirty-three of them have been published by Konrad Schottmüller (numbered VII to XXXIX), and the other seven by Heinrich Finke (numbered XL to XLVI).[4]

To these forty Templars whose confessions we possess we must add seven others, who we know were interrogated in Poitiers: two are cited after the last deposition published by Heinrich Finke, with no further information: Robert de Layme (or de Yma) and Jean de Valbruan. The records of the appearances before the papal commission in Paris in 1310–11 reveal five other names. On 14 February 1310 twenty-eight Templars who came from Carcassonne appeared before the commission; six of them said they had confessed before the pope. They then confessed and denounced the Order; in 1310 they recanted their confessions and said they had lied before the pope. Two out of the six, Déodat (or Dorde) Jafet and Étienne *Trobati*, were indeed among the Templars who had made depositions before the pope in June 1308; the four others do not appear in Schottmüller's or Heinrich Finke's publications, so they should be added to the Templars present in Poitiers: they were Gaucerand de Montpezat, Jean

Costa, Gérard de *Fore Agula* and Raymond Finel.[5] On 17 February 1310 four other Templars arrived in Paris from the diocese of Auch: one of them, Adémar d'Esparre (de *Sparros*), is mentioned in the list published by Konrad Schottmül-ler; he had lied then. Another, Jean de Vaujaloux (*Valle Gelosa*), a priest from the diocese of Périgueux, does not appear on the list; he says he had made a deposi-tion before the pope and said nothing against the Order at that time. We cannot affirm whether the two other members of the group from Tarbes, Raymond de *Gladio* and Raymond Guilhem, had been interrogated in Poitiers.[6] Finally, Jean de Juvigny, who also appears on the list of Templars whose depositions we possess, appeared before the papal commission, where he recalled having been interrogated by the pope.[7] And so we must add to the forty Templars whose con-fessions before the pope are available to us these seven names: Robert de Layme (*Yma*), Jean de Valbruan, Gaucerand de Montpezat, Jean Costa, Gérard de *Fore Agula*, Raymond Finel and Jean de Vaujaloux.

In 1310 the papal commission decided not to interrogate Templars who had been heard by the pope in Poitiers. It made this decision at the moment when Jean de Juvigny came to depose before them. Immediately after announcing its decision, the commission received eight Templars; the text is not very clear, but they should not be counted among those present in Poitiers: they were in fact interrogated one after another by the commissioners in the hours and days that followed.[8]

Forty-seven out of the seventy-two Templars who appeared before the pope in Poitiers are thus identified, and we have the depositions of forty of them.[9] We must add to them the names of the five dignitaries who would be interrogated a bit later in Chinon. This gives us a total of forty-five.

We know some of the places where these Templars came from. Regard-ing the dignitaries of the Order, stuck in Chinon, and two other brothers, the information provided in the documents related to the dispersal of the Templars held at the Temple in Paris in January/February 1308 gives the precise loca-tions of their detention before they left for Poitiers: Jacques de Molay was in Corbeil, Hugues de Pairaud in Rochefort-en-Yvelines, Raimbaud de Caromb in Montlhéry, Geoffroy de Charney in Montereau, and Geoffroy de Gonneville in Vernon. They were probably brought together before setting out for Poit-iers. Mention is also made, in connection with the transfer, of Jean de Fouilloy and Gaucher de Liancout, who had been taken from the Temple of Paris to Villeneuve-le-Roi.

These seven Templars, as well as four others – Simon Chrétien, Jean de Cugy, Pierre de Montsoult and Jean de Valbruan – had been interrogated by inquisitors in Paris in October/November 1307; eight others had been interrogated in the same months in Cahors (Guillaume de Limoges, Atho de Sauvagnac, Guillaume de Trèbes), in Carcassonne (Raymond Étienne, Raymond Massol), in Toulouse (Adémar d'Esparre), in Poitiers (Géraud de Saint-Martial) and in Lusignan (Humbert de Comborn). And so nineteen out of forty-five Templars had been interrogated, which obviously does not mean that the twenty-six others had not been.

The forty Templars who deposed in Poitiers can be divided into four groups according to their geographical origins, which were indicated by the dioceses they were originally from. Eleven came from the diocese of Limoges, and one from that of Saintes, both regions near Poitiers. One of them, Aymeri Chamerlent, was ill and at his parents' home at the time of the arrests; he went to Poitiers to appear before the Curia, and that is where he was arrested.[10] A second group included the ten Templars who came from the Midi, one of whom was from Provence. Nine came from Paris and Picardy. And ten came from dioceses in Champagne and Burgundy.

The Templars in the first group were taken to Poitiers quickly; some were incarcerated there.[11] They were perhaps the seven or eight who were handed over to the pope on 27 June, as mentioned in the English document cited above.[12] As for those in the other groups who came from more distant regions, it took them several days of travel, probably in carts, to get to Poitiers. One thing is certain in any case: we must not imagine a long procession of Templars conveyed from Paris to Poitiers, stopping in Chinon to drop off the five dignitaries.[13]

Did the king and his agents hand-pick the Templars to be sent in order to avoid any surprises in Poitiers? A number of elements point to that conclusion, although they are somewhat ambiguous. Six Templars had left the Order at one time or another before being arrested or turning themselves in – I have mentioned Aymeri Chamerlent, on 'medical leave' of some sort at the time of the arrests. Pierre de Claustre, received in 1300, left the Order shortly after that to go to southern Italy, where he served the Angevins; Jacques de Bergnicourt, also received in 1300 by Hugues de Pairaud, had left the Order a year later, at night, and had gone with some family members to join the royal armies that were fighting in Flanders; he was not one of the Templars arrested on 13 October 1307.[14] Guillaume de *Resis* is described as 'once a Templar'; Étienne de Troyes, who had left the Order, went to Outremer; when he returned, he had an audience with the king of France before the arrests. Jean de Villars had left the Order seven years earlier, in 1301. To these men we may add those who claimed they would have liked to have left the Order but who had not done so because they lacked the courage: they included Jacques de Châtillon and Jean de Fouilloy.[15] Were any of these men the famous 'moles' introduced into the Order by Guillaume de Nogaret from 1305 on?

It is striking, however – and this points in the opposite direction – to note the number of Templars who said they had been tortured (eight) or threatened with torture (four),[16] such as Atho de Sauvagnac, who denounced the harsh treatment to which he had been subjected. Their attitudes are, however, ambiguous: they were tortured, but that wasn't the reason for their confessions; they maintained those confessions before the pope because they were the truth. On the one hand, the possibility of being able to talk before the pope loosened their tongues; on the other, the fear of once again, in their prisons, falling under the blows of their torturers led them, sometimes in defiance of all plausibility, to eliminate the question of torture as a direct reason for their confessions. It was only later, in 1310, during the Templars' widespread movement of revolt before the papal commission responsible for investigating the Order, that they dared take the leap and recant their confessions: Adémar d'Esparre, from the diocese of Auch, was one of them, and he stated then that he had lied before the pope in 1308 at Poitiers.[17] Similarly, on 14 February 1310 the six Templars from the diocese of Carcassonne made an identical declaration; among them was Déodat Jafet, who had been tortured.[18]

From all of these facts one has the impression that there was some indecisiveness and a bit of improvisation among the Templars: the day after 14 June the negotiations between the pope and the king were apparently arduous, but they had certainly ended before 27 June, which gave enough time to have Templars come from Champagne or Languedoc, those from the regions close to Poitiers having appeared before the papal authorities on 27 June. The pope had obtained what he wanted and could therefore not procrastinate much longer.

The interrogations took place in two phases: the first, before the cardinals, from 28 June to 1 July; the second, before the pope in person, on 2 July. The pope had assigned the task of interrogating the Templars to five cardinals: Thomas Jorz, an Englishman; Beranger Frédol and Étienne de Suisy, who from the beginning were active in the Templar Affair on behalf of the pope; Landolphe Brancacci; and Pierre Colonna. It was probably expected that each of them would interrogate a group of Templars, but in reality only four carried out their assignment. Étienne de Suisy interrogated ten; Beranger Frédol interrogated twelve; Pierre Colonna and Landolphe Brancacci together interrogated eleven Templars. According to the text published by Konrad Schottmüller, thirty-three Templars were interrogated. No information of this kind is provided for the seven Templars whose records are published by Heinrich Finke. Whatever the case, their interrogations must have taken place.

They all appeared before the pope, who assembled a consistory on 2 July; the king of France and his advisers were present. There was a reading, in Latin and the vernacular, of the confessions thus obtained, which the Templars then confirmed; they were then absolved and reconciled with the Church (i.e., they were again able to attend religious ceremonies and receive the sacraments), but without being freed because they still had to be judged; a public instrument was then drawn up by the notaries present. Templars appeared again on 10 July in the residence of the cardinal Pierre de La Chapelle, who was assisting the pope in the matter, in the presence of the cardinals who had carried out interrogations at the end of June and 1 July. According to Jean Bourgogne, who provides this information in a letter addressed to the king of Aragon dated 11 July, some fifty Templars were present, which confirms the fact that we do not have all the records of the interrogated Templars. They again confirmed their confessions; they were again granted absolution; and they were told that since the Order had not for the moment been condemned, they could retain their distinctive insignia (the mantle, cross and so on) and participate in the liturgy and sacraments, but it was out of the question for them to be freed.[19]

All of those confessions served to justify the 'vehement suspicions' of the king of France, who reiterated his strong desire for a judgement and condemnation of the Templars and their Order. The pope responded that the Church did not reject those who repented, meaning the Templars, since they had confessed their sins and renounced them; further, he had to wait for the results of the other investigations being carried out throughout Christendom before coming to a decision.[20] Another set-back for the king. The pope was working at his own pace.

Faciens misericordiam

What happened to the Templars who appeared before the pope after the session of 10 July? They were probably taken back to the detention sites they had come from. We find a few of them, ten to be exact, among those who appeared before the papal commission responsible for investigating the Order in 1310–11. Guillaume de Saint-Supplet, Jean de Valbruan and Robert de Layme appeared on 11 April 1310 but were not interrogated because they had already been questioned by the pope in 1308; in their case, the place they came from is not indicated;[21] the same is true for Jean de Juvigny, who appeared on 30 April 1310.[22]

On 14 February 1310 Déodat Jafet and Étienne *Trobati*, from Gabian, in the seneschalsy of Carcassonne, appeared to defend the Order,[23] and on 17 February it was Adémar d'Esparre's turn; he had come from the diocese of Auch. On that same day Aymeri de Chamerlent, from Poitiers, also appeared before the commission, but refused to defend the Order.[24] There is mention of Guillaume Aymeri (by Bertrand de Villars) and Guy Brughat (by Guy de La Chastaneda) for 29 March 1311: they were being held in Limoges on that date.[25] For these six Templars the information provided in the spring of 1310 shows that they had indeed returned to the places where they had been held in 1308, when they were transferred to Poitiers to appear before the pope.

After the consistory of 2 July, Pope Clement turned to something else, the 'setting to music' of the compromise reached with the king, by means of a series of bulls dealing with various aspects of the matter: turning individuals and property over to the Church; allowing the inquisitors to resume their functions; putting into place new proceedings against individuals, and the proceedings against the Order; the decision to convoke a council; and the cases of the dignitaries of the Order.

All of this concerned only the Templars. Other decisions were to be made on a project 'in passing' (a new crusade) led by the Hospitallers, and the opening – so desired by Philip the Fair – of an investigation into Boniface VIII. This wasn't a coincidence; it all hung together – everything had been laid out in the open. There had been a power struggle, then a compromise. But it did not happen without ulterior motives.

This exchange of notes between the king and the pope, most recently on the subject of the king's requests at the end of the 2 July consistory, can be dated to between 2 and 5 July. In them the concrete matters of handing over the men and property are broached. The king agrees to turn the Templars over to the Church, whose representative asks him to continue to hold them, but in the Church's name. The Temple property will be reserved for the use of the Holy Land and given over to the Church, but it will continue to be administered by people assigned by the king, at the Church's request. The Church will designate the keepers of the accounts, but the money earned from the Temple's property will be kept by the king.

But the pope imposes some conditions: the Templars will be guarded by the king's agents, but they will be presented to the pope and the bishops upon their request. It is specified that it will be the bishops who will investigate the Templars in their dioceses, the pope reserving for himself the proceedings against the dignitaries and the Order as a whole. And so the two sets of proceedings are sketched out – one against individuals, and another against the Order. They would be finalised in the following weeks. For the property, there would be two curators for each diocese: one designated by the pope, the other by the bishop. The king could secretly designate men whom he wished to have named; the same for the controllers assigned by the pope and the bishop. The Templars' money would be held by the king but earmarked for the Holy Land and for the moderate expenses related to guarding the Templars. All of this would remain effective until a final decision on the Order could be made.

Finally – and this is what enables us to date the negotiations to before 5 July – the pope responded to the king's wishes regarding the inquisitors; he 'would do everything possible with the Sacred College, although it seems contrary to his honour, so that they would be permitted, conjointly with the ordinaries [the bishops] to proceed individually against the members of the Temple'.[26] On 5 July 1308 the bull *Subit assidue* ratified this first point.[27]

In this text the pope recalls that he had previously suspended the authority of the inquisitors who had proceeded against the Templars in 1307, and he explains why. Since then, having questioned the Templars in Poitiers and having received confessions from some of them, he has decided to remove the prohibition from proceeding against them, and he assigns prelates and inquisitors to investigate them within the boundaries of their dioceses. But their activity should be directed only against individuals, and not against the state of the Order in general (*generali statu tocius ordinis*); for that latter procedure the pope would designate appropriate agents. He also recalls that he reserves for himself all investigations, proceedings and trials against the Grand Master, the Master of France (in fact, this was the Visitor, Hugues de Pairaud), the Grand Commander of Outremer and the commanders of Normandy, Poitou and Provence.

In another letter, also dated 5 July, he grants the Inquisitor of France, 'G.' (Guillaume de Paris), the right to participate in the diocesan commissions alongside the bishop, even though he had earned the pope's indignation for having acted against the Templars without his previous authorisation.[28]

Finally, on 13 July the bull *Cum per nos* established the composition of the diocesan commissions: the bishop would work with two canons, two Preacher brothers and two Minor brothers.[29]

Thus the diocesan commissions were set up. In the name of the pope and the Church they would henceforth investigate all individual Templars throughout Christendom to discover whether they were individually guilty of the errors and crimes of which they had been accused.

Between 5 and 13 July the king went back on the offensive, but aiming beyond the framework of the Templar Affair. According to an anonymous English document that I have already cited,[30] on the Saturday following the day of the Translation of Saint Thomas the Martyr (that is, 7 July),[31] the king gave his intermediary Guillaume de Plaisians several requests for the pope. Plaisians presented them to the pope on 13 July during another consistory. They were:

1. That the pope and the Curia remain in France;
2. That the pope condemn the Templars following their confessions;
3. That, if there was to be a General Council, it should take place in France;
4. That he canonise Celestine V, Boniface VIII's predecessor;
5. That he order the burning of the bones of Boniface VIII;
6. That he absolve and revoke Guillaume de Nogaret's excommunication.

The pope's responses are reported in our English document, as well as by the chronicler Ptolemy da Lucca:[32] he would not stay in France but wished instead to return to Rome, a much more practical and central place to manage the affairs of Christendom; he would deal zealously with the Templar Affair, but without departing from the rules he had set down; as far as the location of the possible council was concerned, he had no preference; to canonise someone there needed to be a miracle, which he was awaiting; Pope Boniface had shown that he was a good, Catholic man, so Pope Clement was surprised by the king's request and asked him not to repeat it, although he agreed to open an investigation; and lastly, he flatly refused to consider the request regarding Guillaume de Nogaret.

The king was thwarted once again. On 9 July he had agreed to let the

Temple's property be assigned to the Holy Land if the Order were suppressed, and in exchange the pope had authorised him to name the curators (managers) of that property.[33] And on 13 July the individual Templars were handed over to the Church via Cardinal Pierre de La Chapelle, who immediately entrusted custody of them to the king, in the name of the Church.[34]

On 21 July Philip the Fair left Poitiers, leaving a few advisers behind, including Gilles Aycelin, archbishop of Narbonne, and Guillaume de Plaisians. According to Jean Bourgogne, the envoy of the king of Aragon, they monopolised the pope's attention to such an extent that he was not able to obtain an audience to discuss the affairs of Aragon.[35] We don't know the pope's 'agenda' during the three weeks before his departure from Poitiers. If we judge from the last decisions he made, his position did not change, and he ended his stay with a true fireworks show.

On 11 August the bull *Exurgat Deus* and its related documents brought to the forefront plans for a crusade that, with the agreement of the pope, the Order of the Hospital of Saint John (whose Grand Master, Foulques de Villaret, was in the West at that time) was preparing. The archbishops and bishops were asked to implore their flocks to contribute to the enterprise. Indulgences would be granted to all those who in one way or another contributed to the success of the 'passage' to Outremer. A summary of the bull in French was to be read and published in every parish.[36] Who could not see the close connection between these decisions in favour of the Hospital's plans and the bitter battle Pope Clement was waging to make Philip the Fair agree to earmark the Temple's property entirely for the Holy Land? And who could not see that the pope was winning here too; for him there was no doubt that the Temple's property should be given to the Hospital if the Temple were suppressed, because the Hospital was the best instrument to help in the Holy Land.

The next day, 12 August, two important texts were presented during the final consistory held in Poitiers, the bulls *Regnans in coelis* and *Faciens misericordiam*.[37] These two bulls had one element in common: the history of the affair, from the moment when the pope was informed of it in Lyon up to the appearance of the seventy-two Templars in Poitiers and the interrogations of the five dignitaries being held in Chinon by the three cardinals sent by the pope. There was a problem: the interrogations carried out in Chinon took place from 17 to 20 August – that is, after the consistory of 12 August.

The object of *Regnans in coelis* was to announce the institution of proceedings against the Order, which the pope had reserved for himself: he decided that the investigation would be conducted by 'some discreet people whom he would designate to bring this to a good end'. Afterwards, judgement would be pronounced during a General Council convoked for the calends of October 1310 (it would, in fact, be pushed back another year). This council would meet in Vienne (which was not in the kingdom of France, as the king had requested, but in the Dauphiné, which fell under the control of the Empire) and would deal with the Order, its members and its property, but also with aid for the Holy Land and with Church reform. Papal time was not the same as royal time, and Philip the Fair would just have to accept that.

Faciens misericordiam, published the same day, is presented in three forms: a basic version, which was read during the consistory of 12 August but not published, and two final versions, which were published. Let's look first at these two versions. They differ by way of the audiences to whom they are addressed (that is, the names and functions of the addressees) and by the way in which they are arranged: that is, by the decisions announced (this is known as the *dispositif*). But the text of the *narratio,* which looks at the facts and events that justified the decisions, is the same in both versions.

In its initial form the bull is addressed to a specific archbishop and his suffragan bishops; the text describes the proceedings 'against specific persons' and for this borrows the provisions of the bull *Cum per nos* of 13 July, with the composition of the diocesan commissions that were to investigate in every diocese all the Templars being held in said diocese. *Faciens misericordiam* specifies the continuation of the proceedings in question: provincial councils, under the direction of the archbishop, would examine the records of the investigations and pronounce judgement and a sentence against individual Templars. In no case would the diocesan commissions or the provincial councils become involved in the proceedings against the Order in general or against the dignitaries in particular, which the pope had reserved for himself. A list of eighty-eight articles to which the Templars would have to respond accompanied the bull.[38]

In its second form, the bull *Faciens misericordiam* is addressed to the eight members whom the pope designated to make up the commission responsible for investigating the Order in the kingdom of France; the commission would be based in 'the town, the diocese and the province of Sens'. In fact, it met in Paris, which at the time was only a suffragan bishopric of the archbishopric or province of Sens. This version's mandate was obviously different from that of the first, since the goal of this commission was to investigate the Order in general and, to that end, all the Templars in the kingdom would be called to appear before it. It was noted that the commission could meet validly even in the absence of some of its members, provided there were at least three members present, two of whom were prelates.[39] The interrogations would be carried out following a list of 127 articles.[40]

There is no need to point out that the text read in Poitiers on 12 August could not have included such specifications on the organisation of the papal commission in Paris, which, as we will see, was not put into place until August 1309. It also did not include (and nor did the text of *Regnans in coelis*) the information regarding the interrogations in Chinon, which had not yet taken place. On the 12th it was an initial version of *Faciens misericordiam*, whose text, written on 8 August, is preserved in the ledgers of Pope Clement, that was read. The first part, as in the definitive texts, tells of the history of the Templar Affair, but only goes up to the interrogations in Poitiers and the absolution granted to the Templars present, which was renewed on 10 July; then the Council of Vienne is announced. Pierre de la Chapelle is assigned the task of ensuring that the dignitaries of the Order are present in order to be judged, alongside the Order. It is this text that was posted that same evening on the doors of the cathedral of Poitiers.[41]

This was not enough to satisfy the king of France's representatives, who were still in Poitiers, but at least the framework seemed fixed. Perhaps the pope was trying to get them to drop their guard. He left Poitiers the next day, 13 August, and stopped five or six leagues (roughly seven miles) farther away, in Ligugé, where he stayed for a few days. Why?

We must look to Chinon for an explanation.

Chinon (17–20 August 1308)

Five Temple dignitaries – the Grand Master, Jacques de Molay; the Visitor, Hugues de Pairaud; the Grand Commander of Outremer, Raimbaud de Caromb; the Master of Normandy, Geoffroy de Charney; and the Master of Poitou-Aquitaine, Geoffroy de Gonneville – were also meant to appear before the pope in Poitiers, but some were too ill to continue the journey on horseback, and they went no farther than Chinon, where they were held in the castle, a royal possession. The pope mentions this fact in the two bulls *Regnans in coelis* and *Faciens misericordiam*, adding: 'we absolutely wanted to know from them all the truth and know if their confessions and depositions made in front of the Inquisitor of France, in the presence of notaries and trustworthy witnesses, were truly exact (the instruments were presented to us by the Inquisitor himself).' Before closing the consistory on 12 August and leaving Poitiers the next day, Pope Clement sent three cardinals – Beranger Frédol, Étienne de Suisy and Landolphe Brancacci – on a mission. They were to go to Chinon to investigate the five dignitaries and the Order; they were to get their confessions and then prepare a public instrument that they would give to the pope in Ligugé, where he would await them.

The three cardinals left on 14 August. Jean Bourgogne, in the letter he sent to the king of Aragon on 19 August 1308, informs us of these facts and dates, although without giving the name of the castle; he talks of this castle, which was 'sixteen leagues' from Poitiers, which is almost the exact distance from there to Chinon.[42] They began their investigation on 17 August by hearing the confessions of Raimbaud de Caromb, Geoffroy de Charney and Geoffroy de Gonneville. Two days later, on 19 August, they interrogated Hugues de Pairaud, and on the 20th, Jacques de Molay, whose deposition was brief. The others returned to listen to the French translation of their depositions and confirm them. Then, having repented of and renounced their errors, they were absolved and reconciled with the Church.[43]

Historians have known of these Chinon interrogations for a long time, yet in 2007 a well-publicised initiative by the Vatican Archives, enthusiastically reported by the media (which we historians hadn't known were so excited about authentic historical documents), tried to make us believe there had been a sensational discovery. What was it?

I have already mentioned that the records of the interrogations in Poitiers existed in two forms: an official version on parchment, the *mundum*, and a draft, or *rubrice*, on paper. The forty known Poitiers depositions, published by Konrad Schottmüller and Heinrich Finke, are the *rubrice* versions. The same is true of the Chinon records that Heinrich Finke published in 1907.[44] In 2001, by chance, the historian Barbara Frale discovered in the Vatican Archives the *mundum* versions of those records. As in all archival collections throughout the world, it happens that some documents are catalogued wrongly and/or are not put in the right place, and are never discovered by researchers. There was nothing sensational in this discovery, and when Barbara Frale published the transcriptions of the documents in an appendix to her work *Il papato e il processo ai Templari* in

2003, historians interested in the Temple were clearly delighted to be able hence-forth to refer to them but found that, ultimately, they provided nothing new.[45]

And yet: 2007 was the seventh centenary celebration of the beginning of the Templar Affair. For that occasion the Vatican Archives published, in 800 copies and at a price that might rival the salary of a professional football player for Manchester United, a luxury edition, a collection in facsimile form of the documents relating to the Templar Affair preserved in the Vatican Archives. Included among them, our Chinon interrogations occupy only a few pages. A publicity campaign based solely on that 'unpublished' piece, combined with the fantasies that the name Archivio segreto del Vaticano, reworked for that purpose, might create, attracted the gullible and conspiracy theorists of all kinds.[46] One thing leading to another, newspapers throughout the world informed the public that Pope Clement had, in Chinon, absolved the Order of its errors and reinstated the Templars. That is absurd.[47]

In Chinon, Jacques de Molay and his cohort repeated the confessions they had made before the inquisitors in October and November 1307; they renounced all heresy and humbly begged for absolution. The cardinals, by order of the pope, absolved them and reintegrated them into the unity of the Church and the communion of the faithful, and allowed them to receive the sacraments. There is nothing new in this; the forty Templars interrogated in Poitiers were dealt with in the same way. But neither the dignitaries nor they were acquitted. The 'repentant' were placed, through that absolution, in the situation of penitents, liable to be sanctioned. In the end, it was through a judgement that their fate would be decided.

The interrogations of the dignitaries in Chinon can be placed on the same level as those of the forty Templars interrogated in Poitiers. In the rubrice, their interrogations are numbered from II to VI, following which there came the interrogations of Poitiers that we have, numbered from VII to XLVI. In the pope's mind, they were all part of the same, single procedure.

The Chinon manuscript thus does not add very much to what we already knew. It only confirms that the 'Chinon moment' is very enlightening as regards the pope's attitude and the way in which he intended to carry out the Templar Affair, away from any royal pressure. In July/August 1308 the Templars were still alive and their Order still extant.[48]

Three murky points still remain.

The interrogations date from 17–20 August, yet the bull *Faciens misericordiam* of 12 August mentions them as something that had already happened. For one thing, the bull was reproduced in dozens of copies which were sent throughout all Christendom, and that copying work was spread out over several days, even weeks; but, most important, it was presented at the consistory of 12 August following an initial writing dated the 8th which doesn't mention – for good reason – the interrogations in Chinon. The second version, containing the succinct account of those interrogations, could very well have been written afterwards and back-dated to correspond to the date of the consistory. Barbara Frale gives this explanation, which is all the more plausible since it is not the only occurrence of this sort.[49]

What is more difficult to understand is the fact that there is not the slightest allusion, either in Poitiers or in Chinon, to the revocation of the confessions made by the Grand Master and Hugues de Pairaud (at least) at the end of December 1307. The two cardinals who had heard that revocation, Beranger Frédol and Étienne de Suisy, were among the five cardinals who interrogated the Templars in Poitiers and the three who were sent to Chinon. One might obviously argue from that fact that there hadn't been any revocation of confessions made in Paris in December 1307, and that the source that mentioned them is not reliable. But the revocations are attested to by other sources, and are incontestable. Should we attribute this turn of events to Jacques de Molay's 'cowardice'? But he was standing before the same cardinals who had supported him in 1307. Why wouldn't he trust them again?

This brings us to the third and final point: the *mundum* or 'official' manuscript discovered by Barbara Frale indicates that the three cardinals were accompanied by public notaries and trustworthy witnesses. The notaries included Robert Condet, a cleric from the diocese of Soissons, an apostolic notary who was assigned to write down the confessions in order to prepare a public instrument; accompanying him were Umberto Vercellani (a cleric from Béziers), Nicolao Nicolas de Bénévent and Amisse d'Orléans, known as Le Ratif, all public notaries. They placed their seals and their marks of personal validation on the records. As public notary, Amisse d'Orléans was already present during the interrogations in Paris in October and November 1307. The witnesses in Chinon were: Raymond, abbot of Saint-Theoffrède in the diocese of Le Puy;[50] master Bérard de Boiano, archdeacon of Troia, in southern Italy; Raoul de Boset, canon of Paris; and Pierre de Soire, custodian of the church of Saint-Gaugery in the diocese of Cambrai.

The cardinals sent a simplified and considerably condensed report to the king of France in which they limited themselves to saying that the five dignitaries had confirmed the confessions that they had made before the inquisitors in Paris, and that the cardinals had absolved them.[51] This text, however, contains two pieces of information that do not appear in the original interrogation records. First, the Grand Master asked the cardinals to hear the confession of a sergeant brother in his entourage and to grant him absolution, which the cardinals agreed to do. Second, the cardinals appealed to the indulgence of the king so that he would act 'graciously, favourably and benignly' towards the Grand Master, Hugues de Pairaud and the Grand Commander of Outremer, who had made their confessions before them with a great deal of humility and devotion. 'Your beloved knights G. and G., as well as Jean de Janville [in charge of guarding the Templars], present with us in the above-mentioned castle and diligent in these things' could bear witness to this. 'G. and G.' are obviously the two Guillaumes, Nogaret and Plaisians.

After Christmas 1307, Jacques de Molay and his fellow Templars remained under the control of the king. As we have seen, they were transferred outside Paris and isolated from each other. From the end of June 1308 they were held captive in Chinon, a royal castle. It is reasonable to believe that during those months the king's men, under whose guard they were being held, caused them to rethink what they had said in December 1307. If the witnesses cited in the report made to the king really did attend the interrogations, it is not surprising that Jacques de Molay and his group confirmed the confessions they had made before the inquisitors in Paris the preceding autumn. Similarly, we can understand why the cardinals, who were well aware that those confessions had been revoked, didn't breathe a word of this fact, in order not to make things worse for the Temple dignitaries and put them in danger.[52] The cardinals could not absolve the dignitaries unless they confessed their errors. The interrogation of Hugues de Pairaud was short, and that of Jacques de Molay even shorter, which is perhaps not by chance: say as little as possible so as not to erase completely the revocation of the confessions of December? A precaution in case better days should come? It has been hypothesised that the royal chancellery may have doctored the text,[53] but it is difficult to see why the French royal government would have wanted to claim the two Guillaumes had appeared among the witnesses if they had not been present; it would have been better to delete any reference to them.

The king's agents were at home in Chinon, a royal fortress, and it didn't matter that the responsibility for leading the procedure had been transferred to the pope and the Church. In November 1309, on two occasions, during the depositions given by Jacques de Molay before the papal commission responsible for judging the Order which had just begun its work, the two Guillaumes invited themselves separately to the sessions although, as the records indicate, they did not need to be there. But they were there. So why were they not in Chinon in 1308?[54]

Finally, to settle (temporarily) this question of the Chinon interrogations, we must go back to the importance of the negotiations between the king and the pope in June–July 1308: there had been a compromise. There was a quid pro quo. Pope Clement, finally responding to a request that was very important to the king of France – the investigation into Boniface VIII – announced that he would look into it with the cardinals as soon as he had settled not in Rome, which was still inaccessible, but in Avignon.[55] Granted, he gave in to the king, but he kept control of the procedure, just as he regained control of the one against the Templars (and to this we should also add the reopening under the aegis of the Church of the proceedings against the bishop Guichard de Troyes).

With his compromises, did the pope abandon the Order of the Temple? It could have been the price for saving Boniface VIII's memory, as well as the Church and the papacy, but also for protecting the Hospital and keeping the crusade within the fold of the papacy. All of that was at issue in July in Poitiers. But the Templars still had to play ball: if they recognised their sins, they could be absolved and reconciled with the Church. This was perhaps the dilemma that both the dignitaries of the Temple and the cardinals sent by the pope to Chinon to interrogate them had to face.

7

CLERMONT: THE DIOCESAN COMMISSIONS

(June 1309)

The diocesan commissions are set up (August 1308–spring 1309)

Although they had been established by Pope Clement in August 1308, most of the commissions responsible for judging individual Templars in each diocese (*processus contra personas templariorum*) did not begin their work until the spring of 1309. Some were even later: the Nîmes commission did not get under way until August 1310.

There were several reasons for this delay, an obvious one being that the decisions of 12 August were of a more general nature, and it was necessary to clarify certain points in order for them to be put into practice. A modern analogy might be the drafting of a law and then its official application. More important, the power struggle between the king and the pope, although it had become less heated, still continued. Although official, the Church's control over individual Templars was not a given; the royal administration and its agents were not eager to co-operate, and the pope's administration was not really equipped to assume effective control. In addition, the pope left Poitiers in August 1308 to go to Avignon, instead of Rome, where he planned to install the Curia; travelling short distances each day, he travelled through the entire French Midi, arriving in Avignon only the following March. Dealing with the unexpected during his travels probably prevented him from keeping completely focused on the Templar Affair.

And it was the issue of the order's property that was of primary concern to him. On 5 January 1309 Pope Clement wrote to all the bishops and archbishops of the kingdom to request that they assume responsibility for administering the Temple's property. In an earlier letter the king had already authorised the transfer, which had not yet been carried out. (Can this be attributed to the king or to the bishops?) Each bishop was asked to appoint competent curators in his diocese, and the pope would assign six curators and general administrators for the entire kingdom. We are familiar with the *vidimus* (copy) of these letters that the archbishop of Tours had made on 22 February 1309.[1] In the meantime, on 15 February, the king repeated the order given to his officers to hand over the Temple property to the agents designated by the pope and the bishops. Until then, the royal chancellery had not done much to publicise the king's orders: on 27 December the pope, who was in Toulouse at the time, asked the king to send him twenty additional copies of his letter, since the papal chancellery only had six, which was far from enough to inform all the bishops.[2]

Were these new letters more effective than the earlier ones? Papal administrators were assigned, at least at the top. In the *langue d'oïl* (of northern France) two royal administrators had been assigned in 1307: Guillaume Pizdoe and Renaud Bourdon, both bourgeois from Paris; Bourdon then ceded his place to Guillaume de Flavacourt, archdeacon of Rouen. Similarly, the archbishop of Arles and the bishop of Embrun were assigned by the apostolic see to oversee the administration of the Temple's property in Provence and Burgundy.[3] This transition to co-management by the royal authorities and the Church probably led to a significant change in the way that the property was managed: it was a transition from direct involvement to a farming out of the management of the estates.[4] The king found this to his advantage: by relinquishing direct management of the property, he could sell all the goods – livestock, farm equipment and so on – because the farmer would already have his own draft animals and equipment. And so the king handed over to the Church only the land.[5]

The case of the income of Otton de Grandson shows that the Church succeeded in intervening in the control of that land. In 1296 Jacques de Molay had granted Otton de Grandson, a lord from the Franche-Comté (the county of Burgundy) originally from the region of Neuchâtel (in Switzerland), a life annuity of 2,000 *livres tournois*, to be received in two bi-annual payments at the Temple in Paris or the Temple in Lyon.[6] After the arrest of the Templars, the Temple treasury in Paris was shut down and Otton could no longer receive his income from there. He complained to the king and the pope. Both agreed with his complaint, the king, in a letter dated from Poitiers on 30 July, thus after his departure on 21 July, and the pope a bit later, on 17 August, from Ligugé, where he was spending a few days. They had probably discussed the matter together, since they both specified that the income would henceforth be collected from the proceeds earned by the Templar houses of Thors (diocese of Troyes), Coulours-en-Othe (diocese of Sens) and Épailly (diocese of Langres).[7] These houses were under royal management at the time, but since 9 July 1308 the king had turned over the Temple property to the Church. An accounting of the goods and revenue from the house of Épailly was done on 25 November 1308, and since the revenue was more than the sum of 2,000 *livres tournois*, it was not necessary to have the commanderies of Thors and Coulours make a contribution.[8] A document proves that Otton de Grandson received his pension until his death in 1328. In 1312–13 Épailly had been turned over to the Order of the Hospital.

Finally, the slow process of transferring the Temple property to the Church's jurisdiction may have been due to the afterthoughts that the king of France might have been having. On 10 March 1309 Pons, the bishop of Lleida, and Bernard de Fenouillède wrote to their sovereign, the king of Aragon: they were in Avignon, where the pope had not yet arrived, but a fair number of cardinals were present. One of them slipped 'in great secret' to these two envoys some advice intended for their master: not to give the Church the Temple property that he had sequestered (in particular, several castles) until the pope has specified what he intended to do with it. In fact, 'the king of France wanted all the Temple property, no matter in what land it may be found, to be given to his son who would be king of Jerusalem. And thus if the property were turned over to the Church it would be a great loss and a shame for all the princes in the world.'[9] The king of France agreed with the pope that the Temple property should be devoted to the needs of the Holy Land, but he had not yet agreed that, in order to achieve that purpose, it needed to be given to the Order of the Hospital. This was the as yet unannounced intention of Pope Clement.

These matters did not occupy the pope to the point of completely neglecting the investigation of individual Templars, because the king of France continued to pressure him on that subject as well. A letter from Pope Clement dated 6 May 1309 appears to be a response to several questions from the king, but also from bishops and archbishops, probably raised in earlier letters.[10] The king accused the pope of letting things drag on, thereby encouraging the Templars to recant their confessions. Furthermore – and the bishops had the same questions – he was concerned by the lack of details regarding the procedures to be followed in the episcopal commissions: would the Templars be questioned in their original diocese or in the ones they had been in in 1307? Should the Templars who had been interrogated earlier, notably by the inquisitors, be interrogated again? The pope responded: the Templars would not be transferred to their original dioceses; all would be interrogated by the diocesan commissions, even if they had already appeared before the inquisitors in 1307. He confirmed that those he had interrogated in Poitiers would not be questioned again, but he agreed that they would be judged by provincial councils. He repeated once again that he had reserved for himself the judgement of the five Temple dignitaries and of the Order as a whole (by way of papal commissions). And so the interrogations of the five dignitaries undertaken by the three cardinals sent to Chinon should probably be considered, as Barbara Frale has rightly pointed out, in the same category as those that took place in Poitiers: that is, they were interrogated as individuals.[11] They were the equivalent of those which the diocesan commissions would carry out with all the other Templars.

Did the bishops follow a template in carrying out their procedure? The bishop of Paris, Guillaume de Baufet, wrote instructions to that effect. We know of this document through a copy that has been conserved in the papers of the bishop of Angers, Guillaume Le Maire,[12] which seems to indicate that it was distributed beyond just the diocese of Paris. Moreover, its contents clearly indicate that it was intended for wide distribution.

The document first presents a template for interrogating the Templars: the place, date and manner of their reception into the Order, people present, scandalous rites and so forth. Then it lists four possible situations: Templars who continued to deny; those who recognised their sins and who continued to do so; those who first denied and then finally confessed; last, those who after having confessed later recanted their confession and now persisted in their denial. In the first and fourth cases, they would be held in harsh conditions, isolated, on bread and water (unless they were sick) and deprived of the sacraments except for confession; if, during the interrogation, they insisted that they had not erred, they would be subjected to torture. In the third case, caution was advised, as their initial denial rendered them suspect, but they would not be treated harshly. As for those who confessed and rejected the heresy, they would be absolved and treated well, but still held 'in a secure manner until there were orders to the contrary'. In fact, they all had to wait for the judgement of the provincial councils to find out the punishment they would receive.

Georges Lizerand thinks that this text came after the pope's letter of 6 May 1309.[13] However, some details provided by the Templars during their interrogations before the papal commission in 1310–11 lead us to think that it was written earlier: in the diocese of Paris and in that of Sens the commissions seem to have gathered in March or April. Either the bishop of Paris's instructions need to be assigned an earlier date or he had been asked to provide instructions after his diocese's commission had already begun to meet – instructions based on his experience, for the use of the bishops who were still hesitant, having not yet assembled their commissions. The question remains unanswered. Whatever the case, the document was certainly not distributed everywhere in France. We can see this in the only two sets of records that we have from the interrogations of the diocesan commissions in the kingdom of France: those of Clermont and those of Nîmes.[14] Neither of them, as we will see, refers to the Paris template, or to any other template for that matter.

The interrogations were to be carried out following an act of accusation made up of eighty-eight questions, which was added to the bull *Faciens misericordiam* sent to bishops and archbishops: *Articuli contra singulares personnas ordinis militiae Templi*. This questionnaire was different from the one that was used in the procedure against the Order, which contained 127 questions (see Appendix 3).

The Clermont commission (June 1309)

The records giving an account of the work of the Clermont commission are the only ones that provide concrete information about the way in which its meeting was prepared.

In carrying out the bull *Faciens misericordiam*, the bishop of Clermont appointed the members of his diocesan commission. The bishop, Aubert Aycelin, was the nephew of Gilles Aycelin, the archbishop of Narbonne and adviser to the king, who would be called upon to preside over the papal commission investigating the Order in Paris the following year. The Aycelins were a family from the Auvergne who regularly provided the Church with canons, bishops or monks. Besides Gilles Aycelin, who before becoming archbishop of Narbonne had been provost of the cathedral church of Clermont, two of Aubert's other uncles had ecclesiastical careers: Jean was bishop of Clermont from 1297 to 1301, while Hugues entered the Preaching order (Dominican) and was elevated to cardinal in 1287. Aubert had been named bishop of Clermont by the pope, who informed the cathedral chapter and the king of his choice on 11 August 1307. He swore an oath of loyalty to the king of France on 22 August and promised to respect the rights of the canons on 19 November 1307. This means that he owed his nomination neither to royal favour nor to the chapter (election by the chapter was the usual path to becoming bishop).

In the somewhat simplistic perspective adopted by many historians studying the Templar Affair – categorising the bishops and other Church dignitaries in terms of their degree of dependence (real or supposed) on the king of France – Aubert has appeared sometimes as a minion of the king who was hostile to the Templars, sometimes as independent of the king because he did not owe his nomination to him, and sometimes as a bishop obviously not compliant vis-à-vis the king but who, even so, was drawn by familial connections to support royal authority.[15] None of this means very much. I will return to this question more generally in another chapter, but for the moment suffice it to say that I am very sceptical about this way of presenting things.[16]

And so Aubert designated two canons from Clermont (Étienne Chausit and Pierre de Châlus), two Preacher brothers from the convent in the city (Guillaume Vital and Jean de Rinhac) and two Minor brothers (Arbert de Thinières and Astorg de Mareugheol [or Marvejols]). On 6 May 1309 he addressed the four curates from the parishes of Clermont, giving them these instructions: on 8 May, the Feast of the Ascension, they were publicly to summon the Templars, who were to appear before the diocesan commission the following 4 June at the hour of Prime – around six in the morning. On 8 May the four priests responded that the bishop's instructions had been carried out, and that on that same day at the hour of Mass and in the presence of a crowd of the faithful and of witnesses, the summons had been read in their respective churches. On 26 May the bishop again addressed them and asked them to repeat the summons to appear on Wednesday 28 May, which they did, and informed the bishop that same day.

Also on 28 May the bishop sent the same request to the curates or vicars of Vertaizon, Montferrand, Riom, Nonette and Auzon to summon the Templars residing in their parishes and towns to appear. Vertaizon was the seat of an episcopal castellany; the four other sites were seats of royal provostships.[17] They all had fortified castles where the Templars were being held.[18] Did all the Templars cited in the summons appear? The bishop's wording leads one to wonder. Summoned to appear were 'all those who, it has been said, have fled or gone away from the city and our diocese, or are hiding or are absent',[19] which leads one to assume that a fair number of Templars had not been arrested and were still on the run. It was probably they whom the curates of the Clermont parishes were targeting. It is doubtful that the curates had much success, since they had to repeat their appeal; if those fugitives did not appear before the commission, they would be considered to be *in absentia*. The instructions sent to the clerics of Vertaizon, Montferrand, Riom, Nonette and Auzon concerned the Templars who were being held: 'We ask you to summon peremptorily and personally each and all of the Templars who reside or are in your parish.'[20]

On Wednesday 4 June at the hour of Prime the summoned Templars appeared in a room of a building that had been recently acquired by the bishop of Clermont and was called 'the palace', probably located outside the city walls, close to the Palace Gate, north of the city.[21] There were sixty-nine of them, and a list of their names was drawn up, not in the order of their interrogations but rather, interestingly, according to their pleas: first listed were the forty Templars who confessed, then the twenty-nine who denied. And so an initial sorting had been done before this session, on the basis of earlier, but lost, interrogations, an idea supported by the fact that the twenty-nine who denied were all interrogated three days later, on the Saturday before the Feast of Saint Barnaby, which would have been 7 June. For the first forty, no specific day is given except for the last man, Pierre Aureille, who was interrogated and examined again on the Monday before the Feast of St Barnaby, 9 June; all the others – and Aureille the first time – were interrogated on 4, 5 and 6 June.

The record does not specify this, but the list of eighty-eight questions spread over fifteen articles was probably read out loud: renunciation of Christ; spitting on the cross; worshipping a cat; the absence of words consecrating the host during services; absolution by lay brothers; kissing; swearing not to leave the Order; secrecy about receptions; the practice of homosexual acts; idolatry; prohibition to reveal these practices; confession only to priests of the Order; neglecting to correct or denounce those errors; increasing through all means, even illicit ones, the wealth of the Order; and the well-known defamation of the Order.[22] Were they translated into the vernacular? This is indicated for seventeen Templars, all of whom were among the non-confessing: *in eis sibi materna lingua expositis.*[23]

A general session, at which all of them were present, took place on Tuesday 10 June. Both those who confessed and those who denied confirmed their depositions. A public instrument was drawn up, authenticated by the signatures of three notaries and by the accompanying seal of the bishop. Notwithstanding, although the record was finalised on 10 June, it is dated 4–6 June.

The results of the interrogations were probably then sent to the archbishop of Bourges, under whose jurisdiction fell the bishopric of Clermont, with a view to the future provincial council which was to pronounce judgement. While waiting, the Templars – all of them – were taken back to their prison. That is where they received the summons to appear before the papal commission responsible for examining the Order.

Other commissions throughout France

In principle, in each diocese there were commissions assigned to judge individuals. The chronicler Jean de Saint-Victor mentions this briefly: 'That year [1309], by order of the pope, the prelates of France arranged for solemn investigations into the Templars in any place of their choosing in their diocese.' [24] Lacking any records, such as those that we have for Clermont, we are informed indirectly about the meeting of other diocesan commissions through evidence provided by the Templars who deposed before the papal commission of Paris in 1310–11. These interrogations took place during the second phase of the commission's work, after the uprising by the Templars had been crushed by the iron fist of the archbishop of Sens in May 1310. The 224 Templars who appeared at that time did not defend the Order; they reiterated the confessions they had made earlier and, anxious not to contradict themselves, were careful to declare that they did not intend to recant what they had said to the bishop who had interrogated them individually. After having recognised all or some of the 'crimes' of which they were accused, the Templars were absolved by the bishop, or his official when he was absent, as was the case in Poitiers. They could then attend Mass, receive the sacraments, confess and, if they died in prison, die as Christians and be buried in consecrated ground. We can appreciate their desire not to contradict themselves.

The following table shows the dates found in the testimonies of 1310–11. [25]

Table 3 Mentions of meetings of the diocesan commissions

Diocese	Summons	Date
Amiens	14	?
Bourges	1	?
Châlons-en-Ch.	1	?
Chartres	5	?
(Clermont)	(69)	4–10 June 1309
Laon	1	?
Le Mans	1 (+5)	?
Limoges	1	?
Mâcon	2	?
(Nîmes)	1	?
Noyon	1	?
Orléans	5	?
Paris	52	March–April 1309?
Périgueux	1	December 1308?
Poitiers	11	Early 1309?
Reims	28	?
Rodez	8	?
Saintes	12	?
Sens	30	April–May 1309
Soissons	3	?
Tours	12	?

The dates that we can sometimes infer from the depositions are not precise. Of course, all mentions of the Sens province dioceses are earlier than the provincial council, held in the middle of May 1310. Guillaume d'Herblay (*de Arreblayo*), former royal chaplain, was interrogated, absolved and reconciled by the bishop of Paris thirteen months before the Council of Sens (10–12 May 1310), which would place the meeting of the diocesan commission in April 1309.[26] This dating is almost corroborated by the deposition of Baudouin de Saint-Just, who said that he had been interrogated and tortured, before the bishop of Paris in the middle of the Quadragesima, or around 9 March.[27] But Hugues de Caumont, from Rouergue, declared on 16 January 1311 that he had 'taken off his mantle when, in the past, around All Saints' Day, he was interrogated by the bishop of Paris'[28] – All Saints' Day 1309? Other cases are more problematic. Étienne de Domont was questioned in Paris, more than two years before making his deposition before the bishop.[29] He was interrogated by the inquisitors in Paris on 27 October 1307.[30] A little over two years takes us to the end of 1309 or early 1310, which does not correspond to the dates provided by Guillaume d'Herblay. One of the earliest mentions of a meeting of a diocesan commission, that of the commission of Périgueux, may be in the testimony of Consolin de Saint-Joire, which enables us to date it at the end of 1308.[31] But in these last two examples could there not be errors that could be attributed to faulty memories?

There are other, more reliable chronological references, although they are not always precise. In 1307–10 there was sometimes a vacancy in an episcopal see following the death of a bishop. The Templars allude to such a situation, mentioning the bishop 'at present' or the one who was 'formerly the bishop'. For Amiens, most of the fourteen Templars who mention their appearance before the bishop speak of 'the present bishop':[32] this was Robert de Fouilloy, who had been bishop since May 1308. However, two Templars, Thomas de Jamvalle and Martin de Marseille (in Beauvaisis), refer to Guillaume de Mâcon, formerly bishop of Amiens.[33] This situates their appearance before May 1308, thus outside the framework of the procedure against individuals established by Pope Clement in August 1308.

In Sens the bishop of Orléans had been called upon to fill in for the archbishop to pursue the investigation of the Templars of the diocese. Archbishop Étienne Bécart had died on 29 March 1309; his successor, Philippe de Marigny, bishop of Cambrai, was transferred to Sens on 6 May 1309. The bishop of Orléans intervened only for the Templar Affair, and only during the actual vacancy, in April 1309. It was a matter of investigating the Templars imprisoned only in the diocese of Sens, not throughout the archbishopric. Bécart had begun the investigation of individuals before his death, since five Templars indicate that they had been questioned by him; one of them, Étienne de Dijon, had even been reconciled through him (thus before 29 March 1309),[34] and this is perhaps also what happened with Simon de Commercy.[35] The three others – Jacques de Troyes, Gautier de Bure and Aymeri de Bure – were absolved and reconciled in Sens by the bishop of Orléans, 'the see of Sens being vacant'.[36] Aymeri de Bure, who appeared before the papal commission on 23 December 1310, also indicates that he had been questioned again by the new archbishop during the past Quadragesima: that is, between 8 March and 19 April, Easter Day. This was also the case with Jean Quentin, interrogated on 31 December 1310.[37] This means therefore that, even before being enthroned (which happened on Easter Day, 19 April 1310),[38] the new archbishop decided to review a few cases that seemed to have been settled, but nothing from the depositions of those two Templars indicates any original element that would have been likely to catch the attention of the new archbishop.

From these very fragmentary indications it is, however, possible to establish the following, relative chronology: most of the first meetings of the diocesan commissions must have occurred at the end of the first trimester of 1309; then others followed later, notably the meeting in Clermont in June. And then – this is the case with Nîmes, which we will now analyse – others were held quite a bit later, in the course of 1310.

Nîmes, August 1310 and August 1311

In general, it was true that the diocesan commissions outside France did not meet before 1310, and they were often held at the same time as the meetings of the papal commission, as was the case in Cyprus, England, Italy and even Spain. In the kingdom of France the meetings of the diocesan commission of Nîmes occurred relatively late. The archbishop of Narbonne, Gilles Aycelin, like the other archbishops of the kingdom, had received the bull *Faciens miseri-cordiam*; he had had it distributed to the bishops of his province, including the bishop of Nîmes, Bertrand de Languissel. On 5 May 1309 the archbishop wrote to him to inquire into the progress he had made: it is likely that Bertrand de Languissel proceeded in a manner identical to that of the bishop of Clermont, informing the faithful and the detained Templars. But there were many delays because the bishop fell ill, and in order to carry out the episcopal procedure he was replaced by his agent, Guillaume de Saint-Laurent, a jurist who was also curate of Durfort. He was joined by two canons, two Preacher brothers and two Minor brothers. The commission met from 22 June to 14 July 1310 in Alès, to interrogate thirty-two Templars imprisoned in that town: seven of them had been held there from the start, eight came from Nîmes, and seventeen from Aigues-Mortes. Some were missing, although it is possible that they had been transferred to Sommières.[39] The commission met sporadically: between 22 and

27 June, it met every day except the 24th; it then reconvened on 1, 2 and 3 July, and finally again on 14 July to interrogate the last four Templars. We don't know the reasons for this erratic schedule. The presentation of the testimonies in the records is also surprising, since the four depositions of 14 July precede those of 1–3 July.

The composition of the commission was in principle in conformity with the pope's instructions – two canons, two Preacher brothers and two Minor brothers – but in fact there were a few variations in the individuals present. Most notable is the absence of canons in the four sessions in July. For the rest, Guillaume de Saint-Laurent chose the simplest route: the commission was stationed in Alès, and so he recruited Preacher brothers and Minor brothers from the houses of those two orders in Alès.

The Templars interrogated at that time knew that for several months the papal commission assigned to examine the Order had been meeting in Paris. They had been informed of this, since seven of the Templars who had been interrogated in 1307 went to Paris to defend the Order. There were: Albert de Canellis, a knight from Lombardy; Guillaume de Ranc, Commander of Montpellier; and sergeants Jacques Gaillard, Pierre d'Aguzan, Jean de Tréviers, Pierre Jubin and Pons Pisani. They arrived in Paris on 10 February 1310 and were present during the general meeting called by the commission on 28 March, but we don't know whereabouts in Paris they were held.[40] Nor do we know what happened to them later – in any case, they were not called to testify before the diocesan commission of Nîmes in June and July 1310.

By contrast, when the thirty-two Templars of Alès were interrogated on those same dates, it seems they had not yet been informed of the show of strength by the archbishop of Sens on 11 May 1310, which, as we will soon see, crushed the Templars' resistance. This might explain their attitude before the diocesan com-missioners: although they had all confessed in November 1307, they recanted their confessions before Guillaume de Saint-Laurent and his team. Only three stuck to their original confession: Bertrand Arnaud, who, after having revoked his confession, returned before the commissioners to correct his deposition and admitted to having renounced Christ and having spat on the cross, and Pierre de Toulouse and Drohet de Paris.[41] These three Templars were among the first to be interrogated, in second, third and fifth positions.

The commissioners tried, however, to put those Templars who were now denying the charges in a corner by showing them their earlier depositions. This

Table 4 The diocesan commission of Nîmes in June–July 1310

	June						*July*			
	22	23	25	26	27	28	1	2	3	14
Canons:										
Pons Imbert, prior of Saint-Germain	✓	✓		✓	✓	✓				
Pons Imbert, his nephew	✓	✓	✓	✓	✓	✓				
Raimond de Rossans			✓							
Pierre Raymond, judge of the bishop in the archdeaconry of Nîmes		✓								
Preachers:										
Jean Alamandini, prior	✓		✓		✓	✓				
Raymond Girart	✓	✓	✓	✓	✓	✓				
Bernard de la Tour		✓		✓						✓
Jean *Agricola*							✓	✓		✓
Pons de Fisco, lector							✓	✓	✓	✓
Gaucelm de Barjac									✓	✓
Minors:										
Raymond Rixendes, lector	✓	✓	✓	✓	✓	✓				
Raymond de Fayheto, guard	✓	✓		✓	✓	✓	✓	✓	✓	✓
Raymond Dacuig							✓			
Raymond de Frumentières		✓						✓	✓	✓

✓ present at the session

was the case for Pons de Castelbon, the ninth to be interrogated. He denied everything. So the commissioners had the deposition he had given before the bishop of Nîmes on 22 April 1308 read out, in the vernacular. In this deposition Pons de Castelbon had renewed and confirmed the previous deposition that he had given before Oudart de Maubuisson on 16 November 1307. And so there was what we might call interpolation: the confession of 16 November was inserted in the deposition of 22 April 1308; there is even a double interpolation, since, in turn, the deposition of 22 April 1308, with the text of 1307, is interpolated in the deposition of 1310.[42] Confronted with his contradictions, Pons de Castelbon did not appear confused and answered that, 'having had on this subject sufficient deliberation, he had never made such confessions; and, if he had made them, he made them without *memoria* and through means of torture. And so he revoked them and did not wish to pursue them.'[43] Having probably heard an echo, however muted, of the 'rebellion' of the Templars in Paris, the brothers who remained in Nîmes had regained hope and found the courage to participate, in their own way, in the defence of the Order. This did not last, and the following year, in circumstances that need to be made clear (they were tortured), they were brought again before Guillaume de Saint-Laurent and the diocesan commission, and they reverted to their initial confessions of 1307. A final meeting of the diocesan commission of Nîmes was held, again in Alès, in November 1312; there had still not been a provincial council by then.[44]

We don't know whether other diocesan commissions in France met at such a late date. Let's summarise these diocesan investigations.

The procedure established by the pope in Poitiers replaced the one that had been launched by the king in 1307. By suspending the inquisitors in February 1308, the pontiff had suspended the royal-inquisitorial procedure; by reinstating those same inquisitors in July 1308, was he going in reverse and validating that procedure at the same time? No, although it was difficult for him to act as if it had never existed. It is legitimate to wonder whether, in adopting before the diocesan commissions a position that was different from the one they had taken before the royal agents and inquisitors, the Templars were placing themselves in danger. Wouldn't they have run the risk of being considered as having relapsed into heresy and thus incur the penalty of being burned at the stake? Those, however, who hadn't confessed and persisted in that position couldn't be considered as relapsed, but they were running another risk: that of not being absolved and finishing their days in prison. It was up to the council convoked by the pope in Vienne to resolve these questions.

Pressure and threats inflicted on the detained

While waiting for judgement to be pronounced, the Templars questioned by the bishops were returned to their holding cells. Those who recognised their errors and repented of them were absolved and reconciled with the Church; they could again hear Mass, confess and take communion, in short, be reintegrated into the

Christian community. Those, on the contrary, who did not confess and persisted in their denials were not reconciled (although they were allowed to receive the last rites). The sixty-nine Templars of the diocese of Clermont interrogated from 4 to 9 June 1309 appeared before the bishop on 10 June and were divided into two groups. The forty who had confessed and who confirmed their depositions were reconciled and submitted themselves completely to the mercy of the Church. Nothing is said of the twenty-nine others.

The fate of the Templars following their interrogations differed in another way: the conditions of their detention depended on whether they had acknowledged their errors or not.

The instructions given by the bishop of Paris were clear: in the course of the proceedings against individuals, torture could be used to force the Templars to tell the truth; this targeted those who insisted on denying or those who had changed their depositions. Those threats of torture, or torture itself, came after the threats that many Templars had received during the royal-inquisitorial procedure in 1307. Few of them would have been eager to endure a second round.

There are testimonies on the use of torture during the episcopal procedure: those of Templars who then appeared before the papal commission in 1310–11. Audebert de Porte did not wish at that time to recant the deposition he had given before the bishop of Poitiers (or rather, his agent) because he had been tortured beforehand.[45] This was also the case of Ponsard de Gizy and Jean du Four, or Torteville, questioned three months before appearing before the bishop and subjected to harsh treatment afterwards.[46] Consolin de Saint-Joire, a knight from the diocese of Cahors, held in Périgueux, appeared before the papal commission on 2 May 1310 with a group of brothers from the same place to defend the Order. He had been subjected to torture and to harsh treatment for a year before being interrogated by the bishop of Périgueux; then from the Friday after the Nativity to the Saturday following the Feast of Saint John the Baptist (24 June) he was held in the cold, on bread and water; this would situate his interrogation at the end of 1308. The nineteen other brothers had apparently endured the same treatment; thirteen of these nineteen had been questioned in Cahors between 8 and 27 November 1307.[47]

A very clear case of pressure, threats and torture is provided by Jean de Couchy, a Templar originally from the diocese of Langres who was imprisoned in Sens and appeared before the papal commission on 14 February 1310. He hesitated to defend the Order without the advice of his superiors. He presented a letter that the royal cleric Jean Supin supposedly gave to the Templars held in Sens at the time when the bishop of Orléans, who was filling in for the dead archbishop of Sens, came to Sens to question them. The letter was addressed to Laurent de Beaune, Commander of Épailly, and his co-detainees. And it came from Jean de Janville and Philippe de Voët (provost of the Church of Poitiers), guards of the Templars in the ecclesiastical provinces of Sens, Reims and Rouen. It let the prisoners know that the king had granted permission for the bishop of Orléans to hear their confessions and reconcile them with the Church, so that the vacancy in the see of Sens would not impact them negatively. The two royal officials asked the Templars to repeat before the bishop of Orléans the 'good confessions' they had made before. Jean Supin must have told them more: 'And know that our father the pope has ordered that all those who had confessed before the inquisitors, his delegates, and who do not want to persist in that confession, will be damned and destroyed by fire.' This was a significant lie, since the pope had never said any such thing. To increase the pressure, the two guards announced that they would go to Sens. While waiting, they asked that the detainees be lodged in decent rooms: the carrot after the stick. The papal commission summoned Jean de Janville and Philippe de Voët, who denied ever having written this letter. Summoned in turn, Jean de Couchy and Laurent de Beaune kept a low profile and declared that they had been ordered to do nothing of the sort, except to tell the truth.[48]

We need not necessarily believe them, especially when we know that Laurent de Beaune died at the stake with fifty-three other Templars condemned for having relapsed into heresy by the Council of Sens on 12 May 1310.[49] What was the 'truth' of the day? Let's also remember from this example the reference to the conditions of imprisonment and the means of pressure used by the jailers: if you co-operate, your conditions will improve, otherwise ... Essentially, the king kept control over the Templars; the comfort (no doubt quite relative) of their lodgings and the quality of their food depended on the good will of his agents and on the orders they received. Bread and water, cold, were mentioned alongside torture.

The king would have been made fearful by the sight of Templars who had gone before the ecclesiastical commissions put in place following the compromise of Poitiers rejecting their previous confessions. And it is easy to imagine that this fear incited him to continue to put pressure on the brothers before they appeared before the bishops (and then, as we will see in the next chapter, before the papal commission). It was essential that they should not be allowed to rebel. What did Jean de Couchy and Laurent de Beaune say before the bishop of Orléans after the threats of Jean de Janville and Philippe de Voët? We don't know. A year later, before the papal commission, they were still not very reassured; they declared themselves defenders of the Temple, but on the condition that they first deliberate with the Grand Master.[50]

8

THE PAPAL COMMISSION GETS OFF
TO A SLOW START
(August–November 1309)

When he wrote to the king on 6 May 1309, Pope Clement admitted that the work of the papal commission set up to judge the Order had not yet begun. He gave a few additional details on how it would function. Since many Templars were being held in the north of the kingdom, the commission would establish its base in Paris, in the archbishopric of Sens, without sending any of its members to other ecclesiastical provinces. Everything would thus happen in one place. The king of France would surely be satisfied.[1]

Paris, 8 August 1309

The members of the commission gathered for the first time on 8 August 1309 in the episcopal palace. They began by having several earlier letters from the pope establishing the commission read out loud and reproduced in the official record. The second version of the bull *Faciens misericordiam* was interpolated into the pope's letter designating the commission's eight members. In this letter the pope, arguing that it was impossible for him to carry out the investigation himself in every corner of Christendom, ordered the commissioners to post a public edict of summons in the towns, diocese and province of 'S.' (copy addressed to the archbishop of Sens) and to have appear 'those who should respond to the articles that we send you in our bull, and to others that your caution will deem necessary'.[2] The commissioners could take action against anyone who might hinder their work by using ecclesiastical censure and, if necessary, call upon the secular arm for assistance. In the event of any of them being prevented from presiding, the commission would continue to meet, provided there were at least three members in attendance, two of whom would have to be prelates.

Nine copies of this bull were produced, one for each archbishop. Michelet's book includes the copy sent to Sens. In the eight others the text is addressed differently and involves the archbishoprics of Reims, Rouen, Tours, Bourges, Lyon, Bordeaux, Auch and Narbonne.[3] The archbishops were to distribute to their suffragan bishops the commission's summons to appear. The letter from the pope was of a purely informative nature. The papal commission put it into practice on 8 August. It is worth noting that from the beginning the commission was in fact reduced to seven members. Guillaume Agarni, provost of the church of Aix, had been assigned by the pope shortly after his nomination to the commission to 'harvest' the tithes that were to be collected for two years from the clergy in the ecclesiastical provinces of Arles, Aix, Embrun, Vienne and Lyon on behalf of Prince Philip of Taranto. On 5 May 1309 Guillaume informed the commission that it would be impossible for him to do both things at the same time. He never participated in the commission's work and was never replaced.[4]

And so on 8 August 1309 the commission published, in as many copies as there were archbishoprics, an edict summoning the Templars to appear in Paris, in the great hall of the episcopal palace, the first day following the Feast of Saint Martin (12 November) at the hour of Prime (around 6 a.m.). The archbishop and the bishops were to arrange the reading, recitation and publication of that summons for the clerics and the people gathered in the cathedral church, in the great collegial churches and in the schools where there was a *Studium generale* (a university), as well as in the principal houses of the Temple Order and other places where the brothers of that Order were being held. A public instrument was to be drawn up by the notaries and sent to the papal commission. This edict of summons was co-signed by thirteen witnesses, all clerics, seven of whom, interestingly, came from the bishoprics of Clermont, Limoges, Mende and Bayeux; the bishops of these last three were members of the papal commission.[5]

The commissioners did not just send letters; they sent nuncios (or envoys) to the various ecclesiastical provinces, whose job was to put the summons directly into the hands of the archbishops and their suffragan bishops:[6]

Jean du Bois (*Johannes de Bosco*)	Sens
Jacquemard de l'Île (*Jacomardus de Insula*)	Reims
Robert Bernard (*Robertus Bernardi*)	Rouen

Colin d'Arras (*Colinus de Atrebato*)	Tours
Pierre Cochard (*Petrus Cochardi*)	Lyon
Laurent de Nanterre (*Laurencius de Nanterre*)	Bourges and bishoprics of Puy and Viviers
Jacques de *Parvocayo* (*Jacobus de Parvocayo*)	Bordeaux
Jean Pilavoine (*Johannes Pilavena*)	Narbonne
Thibaud d'Angers (*Theobaldus de Andegavis*)	Auch

This list provides an important indication of the territorial framework within which the commission exercised its power: it involved the kingdom of France strictly as it appeared at that time: that is, within the boundaries of the 'four rivers': Escaut, Meuse, Saône and Rhône. The dioceses in the Lorraine were not included, although a few Templars of the diocese of Toul, arrested in France, were examined in the place where they were being held. One detail concerning the mission of the nuncio sent to the province of Bourges is very interesting: he was also to go to the bishops of Viviers and Puy. Those two bishoprics had only recently come under the sovereignty of the king of France. The bishopric of Puy was a suffragan of Bourges, but that of Viviers was a suffragan of the archbishopric of Vienne, which was for the most part a territory of the Empire.[7]

Bazas, September/October 1309

What do we know about the way in which the nuncios carried out their mission? Almost nothing, and nothing directly, except in the bishopric of Bazas, a suffragan of the archbishopric of Auch. On 26 October 1309 the official of Bazas, Rossignol de Taleyson, informed the archbishop of Narbonne, president of the papal commission, of the way in which the commission's instructions had been applied there. Three of the four documents attached to his letter provide information about the publication of those instructions in the bishopric on 6, 7 and 8 September.[8]

It is possible to establish a chronology of the process. The commission's instructions were sent to the archbishop of Auch by Thibaud d'Angers, and perhaps also directly to the suffragan bishops, including the bishop of Bazas, in the last days of August or in early September. The bishop of Bazas, Guillaume Arnaud de la Motte, was absent at the time because he had accompanied Pope Clement, his relative, to Avignon. The pope had, in fact, been in Bazas in November 1308, and in August/September 1309 the bishop of Bazas was still in Avignon. And so it was the official of Bazas who received the summons to appear and issued it. The three attached documents reveal his activities: the summons was read on Saturday 6 September to the official court of Bazas in the presence of a dozen or so witnesses, mainly clerics but also three citizens of the town; on Sunday 7 September it was read during the dominical Masses in the three main churches of Bazas (the cathedral, Sainte-Marie and Saint Martin); and finally it was read on Monday 8 September in the church of Romestaing, the main Templar house in the bishopric.

The Templars of the commandery were being held in the prison of the officiality (or episcopal prison) in Bazas; they did not attend the readings of the summons to appear either in Bazas or in Romestaing, which is strange if the summons was meant for them. It seems that it was not until 27 October that they were informed. A fourth document dated that day states the summons to appear was read to the eight Templars held in the episcopal prison of Bazas, a reading done by the bishop's procurator, P. de *Passinhaco*, assigned by the official. The eight Templars were: Ratier de Limousin, Gaillard de *Fasenis*, Hugues de Limousin, Guillaume de la Roque (*Rocha*) and Bertrand de Trabes (all knights); P. de Lac (a sergeant); and Jacques *Caputii* and Fricon de Béarn (priests). The document raises two questions.

First, why such a late date? It is possible that the summons had been read to the Templars before 27 October and just not recorded. Equally, the late date might be explained by negotiations between the official and the Templars; the document could represent the end of those negotiations, rather than an initial declaration. In fact, we know that the Templars in Bazas did respond to the summons, saying they were prepared to go to Paris, but on the condition that they were freed and given the means to live. As for the official, he was not very keen on the Templars' departure from Bazas because he thought they might take advantage of the journey to flee – the routes weren't secure, they had friends and so on. Above all, the official wanted to be sure that they would be returned to him once their testimony had been taken in Paris, because they had not yet been judged by the provincial council (which, at that date, was generally the case). Nor did it seem that they had already been examined by the diocesan commission. (We mustn't forget that the bishop was absent and we can't be sure that he had delegated his authority to his official in order to proceed.) Perhaps, and this is only a hypothesis, there had been an exchange of correspondence between the official and his bishop, or between the official and the commissioners in Paris. On 27 October the official made a decision: he did not agree to the Templars' demands, and instead kept them in Bazas, explaining his reasons in the letter he sent to the members of the commission.

And so a second question is raised: the letter sent to the commission is dated 26 October, whereas the document is dated 27 October. This can only be explained if there had been negotiations as suggested above. There could not have been a simple misunderstanding among the Templars, the official and the commission, because if that had been the case, it would have been mentioned at some point since the papal commission, tenacious in its work, had succeeded in overcoming the obstacles that royal officers and bishops attempted to erect in order to prevent the Templars from going to Paris. And so the eight Templars of Bazas would have been on the lists of Templars who defended the Order beginning in February 1310 – at least, if they had shown their intention to do so. We can't exclude the possibility that they may have refused.

I believe that in this example it is important to note above all the lack of co-operation of the bishops, which is usually overshadowed by that of the royal agents. They defended their jurisdictions and in particular, in the Templar Affair, the prerogatives that the pope himself had given them: to investigate and judge the Templars as individuals. If, as was possible in Bazas, that investigation of individuals had not yet been carried out, we can understand the reticence of the bishop and his official, in spite of the assurances given by Pope Clement in his letter of 6 May 1309. If this explanation is correct, it might also be applied to the case of the diocese of Nîmes, which sent only a small number of Templars to Paris in 1310: in that diocese the investigation into individual Templars had not yet been undertaken at the time the papal commission began its work.

Paris, episcopal palace, November 1309

And so on 12 November 1309 the papal commission met in the great hall of the episcopal palace in Paris. Not all of the commissioners were there: two were missing, one of whom was Guillaume Agarni, who, as we have seen, never attended and was not expected. Not one Templar appeared, and the commissioners adjourned until the following day. The same thing happened the next day, and the following days, until 18 November. The commissioners passed the time by reading the letters from archbishops and bishops who reported on the implementation of the commission's orders to publish the edict of summons in their ecclesiastical dioceses and provinces.[9] Some had carried out the work correctly, others less so and a large number not at all: in fact they had not responded. The response of the official of Bazas was almost certainly included in the correspondence received, as is proved by a reference to him dated a few days later;[10] but the bishop of Paris had not responded, even though the commission was meeting in his palace.

At that point the commissioners decided to write to him and had their letter included in the record. It asked him to remember their letter of 8 August and the distribution process decided on at that time. In their great goodness they granted him eight days' extension but intimated that, by virtue of the 'holy obedience that he owes to the apostolic authority', he should see to it that all the Templars of his diocese who would like to do so appeared before them. And the commissioners added 'that against the individual brothers of said Order, and about that which concerns these same individuals, we do not intend to investigate them, but only the above-mentioned Order'. They also specified that they would see only those who wanted to come voluntarily.[11] This reminder and this specification were probably connected to the fears expressed in the letter of the official of Bazas, which were widely shared by the bishops.

On Saturday 22 November the bishop of Paris, Guillaume de Baufet, appeared before the commissioners and told them 'that he had personally been in the place where the Grand Master of the Order and brother Hugues de Pairaud, Visitor of the Order in France, and other brothers of the Order were being held' and had seen to it that they heard, first in Latin then in the vernacular, the original letters of the pope and those of the commissioners, including the edict of summons to appear. The Master and the Visitor said they wished to appear. The bishop added that he had also sent appropriate people to all the places in the city and his diocese where Templars were being held, to have the letters published and read.[12]

The commissioners immediately sent Philippe de Voët, provost of the Church of Poitiers, and Jean de Janville, royal valet, both guards of the Templars, to go and bring back the Grand Master and the Visitor, as well as any others who had informed the bishop and his envoys of their wish to appear before the commission. The bishop and the Templars' guards 'roused themselves' a bit, since before the day was out there appeared in succession a certain Jean de Melot, calling himself a Templar, a group of six Templars brought by

Jean de Janville, Hugues de Pairaud, the Visitor of the Order in France, and finally the 'so-called' Templars recently arrested by the (royal) provost of Paris.

Jean de Melot appeared in secular dress. He came from the diocese of Besançon and had worn the garb of the Temple for ten years before apostasising. He swore that he had never heard or known of any wrongdoing but didn't want to defend the Order. His speech was incoherent, and the commissioners, also taking into consideration his body language and gestures, concluded that he was *simplex* (meaning illiterate, but with an implication of what we would now call a learning disability) and sent him back to the bishop of Paris, 'who was responsible for receiving such fugitive brothers in his diocese of Paris'.[13]

The six Templars brought by Jean de Janville were certainly imprisoned in the Temple at that time. Two of them, Gérard de Causse and Thibaut de Basemont, had been transferred with Jacques de Molay from the Temple to Corbeil on 25 January 1308;[14] Rainier de Larchant had been transferred to Villeneuve-le-Roi. The three others, Regnaud de Tremblay, Raoul de Saulx and Nicolas de Troyes,[15] were not among the Templars transferred at that time, at least not among those whose names were cited. They had all been questioned in Paris in October/November 1307 and had confessed.[16] They were among the defenders of the Order before the papal commission on 18, 19 and 20 February 1310,[17] and had all come from the Temple of Paris, and the first three said that they had appeared on a previous occasion before the papal commission, namely the session of 22 November 1309.

On that day Gérard de Causse, a knight from Rouergue, spoke on their behalf and, interrogated by the commissioners about the reason for their coming, declared that he thought, after hearing the edict of summons directly from the bishop of Paris, that he would be interrogated as an individual. The commissioners told him he was mistaken and said that they were ready to hear his testimony on the Order. Was he ready to defend it? De Causse hesitated and stammered: he was but a 'simple knight, without a horse, without weapons and without land, and he could not and did not know how to defend the Order'. The five others echoed his statement.[18]

Then Hugues de Pairaud appeared. He came, he said, because the bishop of Paris had told him that the commissioners wanted to hear him talk about the Order. He begged them to implore the pope and the king to ensure that the Order's property was not embezzled and was kept to support the Holy Land. Moreover, he had been heard by the cardinals in the name of the pope (in

Chinon), and he was ready to talk before the pope. Since he did not want to say anything more in front of the commissioners, they sent him back to where he had come from.[19] Did he return to a holding cell in the Temple?

For the commissioners that Saturday 22 November was looking more and more like a waste of time. It was even worse with the last Templars who arrived. Some commissioners had learned by chance that men were being held in Paris who had supposedly come to testify about the Templars. After deliberating on this, the commissioners summoned Jean Pluvaleh, the provost of Paris (a royal agent), to provide them with an explanation. He admitted he was holding at the Châtelet, a royal prison, seven men in lay dress who were believed to be fugitive Templars. They had come to Paris with money to pay for lawyers and advisers and to find out what was happening with the Temple. The provost had had two of them tortured, but they had not revealed anything. The commissioners demanded that he bring the seven men to them immediately, which was done before the end of the day. The first, Pierre de Sornay, from the diocese of Amiens, admitted he had entered the Temple three months before the arrests, but had left it two weeks before that. He knew nothing bad about the Order. To the commissioners' question about why he had come to Paris, he answered that he had come to work and earn money because he was poor, without income and not a noble. But he didn't want to defend the Order. The six others also refused. They all came from the north of the kingdom. Two of them, Nicolas de Sarte and Hennequin Villane, who had previously served the Templars of the county of Hainaut, admitted that they had been sent to Paris by them to find out about the fate of the Templars. The commissioners returned them to the guard of the provost of Paris – all except Pierre de Sornay, the only one they considered to be truly a Templar, who would thus be returned to the guard of the bishop.[20]

Night must have finally fallen. Despite a final appeal made by the public crier, no one else appeared and the commissioners agreed to meet the following Monday at the hour of Prime.

On Monday 24 November no one appeared. There was another adjournment to the 26th. Finally, the commissioners, who were meeting in a room adjacent to the great hall, had some 'grist for the mill': the Grand Master himself, Jacques de Molay, was brought in. During this session he obtained a delay for reflection until 28 November, and so I will examine his two statements at the same time. But first let us look at the other Templars who had heard the edict of summons and appeared before the commission on the 27th. Among them was Ponsard de Gizy.

27 November: Ponsard de Gizy

I have already mentioned the deposition of Ponsard de Gizy, which denounces the 'four traitors' responsible, in his opinion, for the false accusations against the Temple.[21] Let's look at it again here. He begins by asserting that the crimes of which the Order has been accused are false and that the confessions were obtained through torture. He describes the torture and harsh treatment to which he himself had been subjected for two years; according to him, thirty-six brothers were tortured to death in Paris and others in the provinces. He is ready to defend the Order on the condition that he be given, from the Order's property, enough to live on and to defend himself. He asks for the advice of Renaud d'Orléans and Pierre de Bologne, two priests of the Order, who are mentioned for the first time here as spokesmen for the Templars. It is then that he gives the commissioners a statement in which he names the four who had defamed the Order.

On 27 November Jean de Janville and Philippe de Voët gave the commissioners a letter, which was immediately read out loud. It had been written earlier by Ponsard de Gizy, and its contents were completely different from his present statement. In it, on the contrary, he denounces crimes and abuses of the Order which are not included in the eighty-eight 'official' articles of accusation: abuses by the 'masters' against the poor brothers; sexual abuse of the sisters of the Order; admittance of unworthy brothers into the Order; simony; sending brothers they didn't like to fight on the front. Finally, he accuses the Master of France, Gérard de Villiers (who had fled at the beginning of the affair), of being responsible for the fall of the island of Ruad, off the coast of Syria, in September 1302. Ponsard de Gizy wasn't flustered: 'Because the truth doesn't seek a detour', he admitted he had written that letter in a moment of anger against the treasurer of the Temple of Paris, who had offended him. He had given the letter to his guards, so they would allow him to appear before the pope or the commissioners. Without going back on what he had just stated, Ponsard feared that his new testimony might lead to a worsening of his conditions of detention, and he asked the commissioners to protect him. They ordered the guards to change nothing in the conditions of his detention, and they obeyed.[22]

Aside from Ponsard, eleven other Templars appeared that day, including Raoul de Gizy, a relative of Ponsard, who, as well as being a commander of the houses of the Temple of Lagny-le-Sec and Beauvais, also worked in the service of the king as collector of revenue in Champagne and Brie. Four of the

Templars had been arrested, imprisoned and then interrogated in the Temple of Paris in October 1307: Raoul de Gizy, Jacques Le Verjus, Jean du Four (also known as Jean de Torteville) and Pons de Benèvre.[23] Of the others, Aymon de Barbone had been arrested in Paris but was not on the list of Templars to be interrogated. Guillaume Bouchel (*Boscelli*) was held in Pont-de-l'Arche, where he had been interrogated on 18 October 1307.[24] The five others aren't mentioned in 1307: Jean de Seraincourt, or de Celle; Jean de *Villaserva*, Gaubert de Marle, Étienne de Provins and Nicolas de Celle. The commissioners abruptly asked them: did they wish to defend the Order? Their responses, in the negative, were unanimous, and the reasons they gave were approximately the same: they didn't know the Order and couldn't defend it; they should be set free; five of them were destitute. They all intended to stick to the confessions they had made before the bishop of Paris (or of Laon, in the case of Gaubert de Marle): that is, during the diocesan procedure against individual Templars. None of those who had appeared before the inquisitors in 1307 referred to their confessions of that time; the commissioners asked them nothing on the subject. Could this indicate that the commissioners, who were thereby loyally following the pope's plans, also believed that the earlier procedure had no value?

Three months later, eight of those eleven Templars and Ponsard de Gizy would again appear before the commission as defenders of the Order, with other Templars imprisoned, as they were, in the Temple. These were: Étienne de Provins, on 18 February,[25] Ponsard de Gizy, Jean de Seraincourt, Jacques Le Verjus, Aymon de Barbone, Guillaume Bouchel, Nicolas de Celle, Jean du Four (or de Torteville) and Pons de Benèvre on 19 February.[26]

A final note. The commissioners asked Ponsard de Gizy why he had come to them. His response remains perplexing: he was there because the bishop of Paris had said that 'those who wanted to appear before the lord commissioners could go'. This says a lot about how seriously the bishop took his duty to inform the Templars. In sum, it would simply be a nice little outing in a cart between the Temple of Paris and Notre-Dame.

26 and 28 November: Jacques de Molay

This was a hearing that held a lot of promise. It took place over two days.[27] On 26 November the Grand Master appeared in the chamber behind the great hall of the episcopal palace. Did he want to defend the Order, or to say something else about it? The Grand Master responded obliquely: the Order had been established and privileged by the apostolic see, and it would therefore be strange if the see wanted to suppress it so suddenly. Although not a scholar and lacking counsel, he was ready to defend it, or he would not be worthy of the honours and advantages that he had received from the Order; but being a prisoner of the pope and the king, and not having any money, he was not in a position to do so unless he were granted help and counsel. The commissioners warned him to consider carefully, and had the deposition he had made in Chinon read aloud. He appeared very upset and shaken by it, and protested, but without explaining himself. (This reaction created problems for him, which I will discuss shortly.) At this point Guillaume de Plaisians, who the record notes had not been invited by the commissioners, entered the room. The Grand Master considered him an ally, because, he said, as knights, they respected each other. The commissioners allowed them to speak together. Guillaume de Plaisians advised Jacques de Molay not to put himself at risk unnecessarily. He probably whispered to him not to contradict what he had said in Chinon, that is – and let's cast some doubt – what he was *told* he had said. To avoid 'becoming muddled' – as he put it – the Grand Master asked for two days' extension, which was granted.[28]

And so he returned on 28 November.

The commissioners immediately got down to the matter in hand by asking him if he intended to defend the Order. Again he avoided answering directly: he was only a poor *illitteratus* (that is, he didn't know Latin) knight, but from the apostolic letters that had been read to him he understood that the pope reserved for himself the examination of him and the other Temple dignitaries. Consequently, he refused to defend the Order before the commission and asked to be transferred before the pope as quickly as possible. The commissioners replied that they were dealing not with individuals but with the Order, and this through the pope's commission. Did he intend to prevent them from carrying out that mission? No, of course not, and Jacques de Molay commended their work, but he did not stray from what would henceforth be his position: he would speak only before the pope.

In order to ease his conscience, however, he agreed to say three things about the Order:

1. He knew of no other Order in which the churches were as well maintained and the divine service better celebrated.

2. Throughout the Order, at all times, alms had been distributed.
3. He knew of no other Order where as much blood had been spilled in defending the faith.

He ended with a short, perfectly orthodox profession of faith, saying that 'when souls have been separated from bodies, then we will see who was good and who was bad; and we will then know the truth about what is currently being debated.'[29]

At that moment Guillaume de Nogaret appeared uninvited in the room, as if by chance. Supported, he said, by the text of the *Chroniques de Saint-Denis*, he reminded those in attendance that in the time of Saladin 'the Master of the Order at the time had paid homage to him and that [Saladin] explained the great misfortune experienced by the Templars [the defeat at Hattin and the loss of Jerusalem] by their practice of the vice of sodomy'.[30] Clearly upset, Jacques de Molay responded that he had never heard this, and he explained his feelings towards the former Grand Master Guillaume de Beaujeu (Molay was in the Orient for the entire duration of de Beaujeu's mastership): when Molay arrived in the Orient, he was, like many of the young knights who arrived with him, eager to fight the enemy, and he criticised the wait-and-see policy of the then Grand Master; but in time and with experience he understood that one sometimes had to compromise with the enemy to prevail.

Soon afterwards, Pierre de Safed, the Grand Master's cook, appeared. In the presence of the Grand Master and Guillaume de Nogaret he refused to defend the Order, reckoning that it had good defenders: the king and the pope.

Another adjournment

From 22 to 28 November the commission was at a standstill. The handful of Templars, all detained in Paris, who had appeared before it did not know what was expected of them. Except for one, Ponsard de Gizy. The question 'Do you intend to defend the Temple?' caught them off guard. Hugues de Pairaud and Jacques de Molay, rightly or wrongly, sensed a trap and tried to find a way out: 'I will speak only in the presence of my lawyer' (the pope, in this case). They were mistaken – or pretended to be mistaken – about the proceedings, and the commissioners were annoyed by this. Jacques de Molay still, cautiously, gave a statement in defence of his Order. It was not by chance that, during the depositions of Ponsard de Gizy and Jacques de Molay, interventions external to the commission sought to destabilise the two men: the reading of a compromising statement for the first; the presence and interventions of Guillaume de Nogaret and Guillaume de Plaisians for the second.

Thus there was a bishop (of Paris) who didn't do the commission's work, and royal agents and counsellors who sabotaged it. On 28 November the papal commissioners certainly had enough to overwhelm them. But they did not admit defeat, and took up their pens again.

On the evening of 28 November they took stock and noted that the publication of the edict of summons to appear had not been carried out correctly in most of the dioceses of the kingdom. They cited in particular Bazas, Toulouse, Clermont and Paris, where the Templars had exhibited a desire to appear in order to defend the Order but had been prevented from doing so.[31] Many bishops had still not responded to the commission to report on the execution of its orders. The commissioners thus addressed another edict of summons to the bishops. They placed their seals on it. In it they recalled their first edict, which had not been followed to the letter, and stressed once again that they would be dealing with the Order, and not with individuals. Another appearance date was fixed: 3 February 1310, after the Feast of the Purification of the Blessed Virgin. They specified that 'if the brothers [...] say that they want to respond for the Order or defend it, they should be sent before [the commission] in Paris immediately, under the watch of their guards'.[32] The letter ended by mentioning the king's missive dated 26 November, which said the same thing.

It is probable, in fact, that the head of the commission, Gilles Aycelin, a royal counsellor, had spoken to the king even before the disapproving statement of 28 November. The royal letter ordered the bailiffs and senechals of the kingdom to facilitate the appearance in Paris on 3 February of all the Templars held in their circumscriptions who wanted, of their own accord, to defend the Order. They were to be placed under strong guard during the journey, so they would not attempt to escape, and would be isolated so that there could be no collusion among them.

The commissioners had not waited until 28 November to become alarmed: between 12 and 18 November, although they were at their post each morning from the hour of Prime, no Templar appeared; they must have been very angry with Jean de Janville and Philippe de Voët, the two guards of the Templars of the (ecclesiastical) provinces of Reims, Sens and Rouen, to ask them to get to work, probably reproaching them for having acted only in Paris (but to no great effect, since no Templar had yet appeared). To defend themselves, the two men produced a letter dated 18 November, addressed to all the superintendents responsible for guarding the Templars, and to their guards, in Orléans and in the diocese of Orléans, asking them to carry out the instructions of the commissioners.[33] This letter, like that of the king of 26 November, was included in the records.

Perhaps, if I may hypothesise, we should see a connection here with the pope's decision of 13 September 1309 to summon all those who wanted to testify in favour of or against Boniface VIII to appear on 16 March 1310 in Avignon; on 18 October 1309 the pope addressed a similar summons to Guillaume de Plaisians.[34] Was it a quid pro quo or merely a coincidence? I opt for the first possibility: 'I am agreeing to the Boniface VIII affair. Your turn, Philip, to allow the Templar Affair to unfold according to the procedure I have established.' The exchanges continued between Paris and Avignon throughout 1310: the bishop of Bayeux, Guillaume Bonnet, a member of the commission, spent a good part of December 1310 in Avignon; he and Geoffroy du Plessis, a royal notary, were at the head of a royal delegation sent to meet with the pontiff. The two men gave an account of their mission to the king in a letter from Avignon dated 24 December 1310. To their great disappointment, they noted that the pope was still standing firm.[35]

9

THE PAPAL COMMISSION AT WORK

(1309–1311)

The commissioners

In 1308 in Poitiers the pope had decided to reserve judgement of the Temple dignitaries, and of the Order as a whole, for himself. The questioning of the five dignitaries in Chinon on 17–20 August 1308 by the three cardinals assigned by the pope was the equivalent of the investigations of individual Templars carried out by the bishops within their dioceses; judgement for everyone would be handed down later, at the behest of the pope. This did not happen, however, until 1314.

Since he could not carry out all the investigations into the Order throughout Christendom by himself, Pope Clement assigned responsibility for the investigation to papal commissions set up in each state. The eight members of the papal commission established for the kingdom of France – and the members of other commissions set up throughout Europe – therefore represented the pope. And so they had to be chosen carefully.

Historians of the Temple, regardless of their opinions on the guilt or innocence of the Templars, continue to put the French bishops simplistically into two camps: partisans of the pope and partisans of the king.[1] It is obviously impossible to deny that the conflict between the king and the pope (above all regarding Boniface VIII) weighed not only on the principal characters involved but also on the more mundane, but equally important, questions of control of French clergy and the king's right to have a say on the selection of bishops in his kingdom. But this was not new; such conflicts existed well before the arrival of Philip the Fair. Did the fact that the king voiced his opinion – indeed, that he sometimes imposed his choice – automatically transform a bishop into a puppet beholden to the king?[2] One must not forget that the function can sometimes change the man; the episcopal function implied responsibilities not only to the king but also to the pope and to God. To my knowledge, Philip the Fair feared God, and although he may not have feared the pope, he did need him.

Let us now take a candid look at the bishops and the other clerics, and at how they acted during the Templar Affair. They were not all deserving of admiration, but not all of them were servile cowards either. To begin with their leader, the president of the papal commission, Gilles Aycelin, archbishop of Narbonne and royal adviser: was he, as one historian put it, 'totally the creature of the king'?[3]

Gilles was an eminent adviser to the king, as important as Guillaume de Nogaret or Enguerrand de Marigny. He certainly did not have any fundamental disagreements with royal policy, and in 1302 he sided with the king by refusing to respond to Pope Boniface VIII's convocation of French bishops to Rome. The idea that he left his position at the chancellery on 22 September 1307 because he did not approve of the decision to arrest the Templars seems unfounded:[4] nine months later, in Poitiers, speaking on behalf of the clergy in the southern regions, he approved Guillaume de Plaisians's indictment of the pope and the Templars. It is clear that the king forced Gilles on Pope Clement, who, a subtle diplomat who knew the man better than historians do, perhaps did not need to be persuaded to choose him.

Who was he? A member of the Auvergnat nobility, he came from a family that had given many of its children to the Church. As we have seen, the bishop of Clermont was his nephew. He studied law and embraced an ecclesiastical career, first in Clermont, then in Narbonne, where he became archbishop in 1290. Elected archbishop of Rouen in 1311, he ended his career there and died in 1316. Throughout this period he was also one of the pillars of the royal council; he carried out many missions on behalf of the king at the Roman court and elsewhere; he deputised Guillaume de Nogaret as keeper of the seal on 27 February 1310. There is no doubt that he espoused the king's policy in the Templar Affair; however, Jean Favier believes that this was a unique occurrence, the behaviour 'of a counsellor who held his ground, and who, with absolute loyalty, often voiced his disagreement with the king', and further: 'The independent mind of Gilles Aycelin became a decisive element in political relations when the archbishop was called to preside, in the name of the pope, over the commission investigating the Order of the Temple. A faithful servant of the king, Aycelin was also fiercely consistent, which went hand in hand with his uprightness.' The king listened to, but rarely followed, the advice of Gilles Aycelin, who 'through his very independence ... was a man alone' on the council.[5]

In addition to Gilles Aycelin, three bishops were members of the commission.

Guillaume Durant the Younger, bishop of Mende from 1296, is described as 'a man of the king', a 'faithful servant of the king' or from a 'very royalist' family.[6] Did that mean that he was hostile to the pope and automatically anti-Templar? Let's take a closer look at this bishop's career. His uncle, Guillaume Durant the Elder, bishop from 1285 to 1296, died in the court of Rome. Because of this, the pope had the right to reserve the post: that is, the right to name a successor without following the usual protocol (election of the new bishop through the cathedral chapter).[7] And so Pope Boniface VIII named the deceased bishop's nephew Guillaume Durant the Younger, who at that time was canon of Mende. The bishop of Mende was also the count of Gévaudan. He fought against the jurisdictional encroachments of some local barons, as well as the pressure of the king and his local agents, who were eager to make a mark in the county. Guillaume Durant played the king against the barons, and the pope against the king. Although he was critical of the Boniface papacy's policy of concentrating power (even though he owed his see to that papacy), he nonetheless didn't submit to the king's demands in the conflict between the two powers: in 1302, defying the royal prohibition, he was among the thirty-three French bishops who attended the synod in Rome convoked by Boniface VIII.

To settle the jurisdictional conflicts between the bishop and the king, the idea of a pariage was introduced. Guillaume Durant was in favour of it, because for him it was a means of setting forth and guaranteeing his rights, which in *Mémoire relatif au paréage* he unconditionally defends against the claims asserted by the king's lawyer, who was none other than Guillaume de Plaisians. Philip the Fair did not listen to Plaisians and chose compromise, drawing up a treaty of pariage, which was definitively adopted in February 1307. The bishop and the king would each have their own administration and their jurisdiction. Common institutions, such as the common court of Gévaudan, would oversee all issues of a general nature.[8] It was probably during these harsh discussions between the king's and the bishop's lawyers that this bitter-sweet exchange happened, as reported by Julien Théry: 'Item, declared the episcopal jurist, even though the king's lawyer has alleged that the king must be adored as the earthly Lord, we will leave that to the heretics ... because we adore only the heavenly God,

Creator of heavenly and earthly things', and he referred the king's agent back to the *Decretum Gratiani*.[9]

Like Gilles Aycelin in his archbishopric of Narbonne, and most bishops in their dioceses, Guillaume Durant fiercely defended his rights – in the spiritual as well as the temporal realm – against the encroachments of the king. This did not prevent Gilles Aycelin and occasionally Guillaume Durant from advising the king, but they did so without turning into lackeys. Durant participated in the Council of Vienne, and it was possibly he who suggested to Pope Clement the solution to the trial of the Templars, of suppressing the Order without condemning it.[10] Often absent from his bishopric, the bishop had a residence in Paris, on rue de la Calandre. An active member of the papal commission for two years, this is probably where he stayed during the trial. He died in Cyprus in 1329, on his way back from a mission to prepare the next crusade envisioned by Philip VI.

Guillaume Bonnet, bishop of Bayeux, was closer to the profile of a 'man of the king', not only because he owed his election to bishop of Bayeux on 27 August 1306 to royal intervention (he was not the only one[11]) but also because he was often summoned by the king to carry out diplomatic and other missions, notably at the papal Court, as was the case in November 1310.[12]

Renaud de la Porte was bishop of Limoges from 1294 to 1316, when he was transferred to the archbishopric of Bourges; he owed his promotion to cardinal in 1320 to Pope John XXII.[13] He had fewer ties to the king, but, according to Malcolm Barber, it is unlikely that he was anti-royalist.

The other members of the commission held less important positions: Mathieu de Naples was an apostolic notary; Jean de Montlaur was archdeacon of Maguelonne. They do not seem to have been the king's men. However, Jean de Mantoue, archdeacon of Trent, and Guillaume Agarni, provost of the Church of Aix, were within the orbit of the French court, Jean being the auditor of Cardinal Pierre Colonna, the leader of the pro-French cardinals, and Guillaume a former procurator for the Angevin kings of Naples in the Roman Curia. Despite these connections, he was assigned to other tasks by the pope, and didn't take part in any of the meetings of the commission.

Thus, things were complex, and before casting judgement on the real or supposed docility of the commissioners vis-à-vis the king, we should first examine how they acted in the commission.

Where the commission met

The commission met in Paris for the first time on 8 August 1309 in the great hall (*aula*) of the episcopal palace (located south of the cathedral, along the Seine). It was in that room that the Templars who wanted to defend the Order were summoned to appear on 12 November. The interrogations of Jacques de Molay on 26 and 28 November, as well as the depositions on the 27th, probably took place in a smaller room or in an adjoining chapel.[14] After another adjournment the hearings resumed on 3 February in that same *camera*, which was nonetheless big enough to accommodate the ninety Templars who were gathered to hear the articles of accusation brought against their Order.[15] However, when the commission decided to gather all the Templars who were in Paris on 28 March, they did so outdoors, in the orchard, behind the great hall and the bishop's residence. The total number of Templars who gathered that day was 546.[16]

The following sessions, until 27 April, took place in the chapel. On 13 April, however, three members of the commission travelled to Saint-Cloud to hear Jean de Saint-Benoît, a Templar from Poitou in his eighties, who, very ill, could not travel; he was being held in a house belonging to the bishopric of Paris and died there a couple of weeks later.[17]

On 28 April 1310 the commission moved to the left bank of the Seine, to the Saint-Eloi Chapel in the abbey of Sainte-Geneviève.[18] It met there until 30 May, when it adjourned until 3 November. But on the morning of 18 May the commissioners met at the home of their president, the archbishop of Narbonne.[19] The meeting was called in order to decide on the position they should take following the actions of the archbishop of Sens on the preceding 11 and 12 May. It is possible that the president of the commission, probably very sought-after by the royal council, considered it best to carry out a rapid consultation with the other commissioners, since he himself was unable to attend the meetings; in fact, he was not at Sainte-Geneviève that afternoon or in the following days.

The commissioners were to resume their work on 3 November, but only three of them returned to the Saint-Eloi Chapel that day. Not having a 'quorum' (we will see why a bit later), the three commissioners wisely postponed the resumption of their meetings until 17 December.[20] That day, having brought in twelve Templars, the commissioners moved to another meeting space to be able to deliberate in the most favourable conditions. They chose the house of the Serpente in the parish of Saint-André-des-Arts, which belonged to the abbot of Fécamp. The commissioners held their meetings there until 23 January 1311, when they once again moved: for three days, on 26, 27 and 28 January, they met in the house of the abbot of Molesmes, located near the church of Saints Cosmas and Damian (at the corner of the current rue de l'École-de-Médecine and the boulevard Saint-Michel[21]). They did not stay there; on the 29th they moved to the convent of the Minor brothers (the Cordeliers) near by. A final move occurred on 22 March 1311: the commissioners crossed the street to stay in the house of Pierre de Savoie, archbishop of Lyon, located opposite the house of the Minor brothers.[22] It was there that they completed their work on 26 May 1311.

The reasons for their moves are not recorded, with the exception of the transfer to the house of the Serpente. They needed a big enough room because, in addition to the members of the commission, there were five or six notaries and a few other witnesses in attendance. Templars were brought there in small groups before being interrogated individually. In the second phase of the commission's work, from December 1310 to May 1311, it had probably been necessary to deal with the challenges caused by the arrival and accommmodation, for a few days, perhaps a week, of groups of Templars who had come from the provinces or the environs of the capital to be interrogated; and with them had come their guards, coachmen, horses and carts.[23] This continual coming and going must have ultimately exhausted the commission's hosts.

With the exception of the episcopal palace, all the meeting places were on the left bank of the Seine, on the hill of the abbey of Sainte-Geneviève, or at the foot of it, in an area located around the convent of the Minor brothers. The commission met only in ecclesiastical establishments: episcopal palace, convents or Parisian residences of ecclesiastics (the abbots of Molesmes and Fécamp, the archbishop of Lyon).

Table 5 Places in Paris where the commission met (1309–11)

Place	Number of daily sessions
Episcopal palace	45
Sainte-Geneviève	19
House of the Serpente	26
House of the abbot of Molesmes	3
House of the Minor brothers	40
House of Pierre de Savoie	25

Commissioners' fees

The commission met in Paris from 8 August 1309 to 26 May 1311. Altogether, there were 167 day-long meetings, interrupted by more or less lengthy periods of adjournment.

There were eight commissioners, four of whom were prelates: the archbishop of Narbonne and the bishops of Bayeux, Limoges and Mende. Of the four others, one of them, Guillaume Agarni, provost of Aix, did not participate in any of the sessions; another, Jean de Montlaur, archdeacon of Maguelonne, who fell ill, could no longer attend after 3 February 1311.

On 8 August 1308, the date of the first version of *Faciens misericordiam*, Pope Clement had granted compensation for each of the commissioners: the bishops were to receive 12 gold florins for every day they appeared, Jean de Montlaur and Jean de Mantoue 5 florins, and Guillaume Agarni 3 florins.[24]

One might think it would be rather easy to determine which commissioners attended which sessions, but the records of the members' attendance are not always clear, and the figures I give may not be completely accurate.[25]

Table 6 Work sessions and adjournments of the papal commission

Opening session	8–9 August 1309	2 days
	12–28 November 1309	13 days
First adjournment		
First phase	3 February–30 May 1310	54 days
Second adjournment		
Second phase (1)	3 November 1310	1 day
Third adjournment		
Second phase (2) (breaks for Easter and between 19 April and 7 May)	17 December 1310–26 May 1311	97 days

Four commissioners were very conscientious: especially the bishops of Mende and Limoges, who missed only two and five sessions respectively. Next were Jean de Mantoue and Mathieu de Naples who attended over 150 sessions. The bishop of Bayeux was absent on half of the days, and the archbishop of

Table 7 Commissioners' attendance at commission sessions

Names	August 1309	12–28 November 1309	3–30 May 1310	3 November 1310	17 December 1310–26 May 1311	Total
Narbonne	2	13	20+3½	–	10	45+3½
Bayeux	2	13	20	–	46	81
Mende	2	13	54	1	95	165
Limoges	2	13	52	–	95	162
M. de Naples	2	12	53	1	83	151
J. de Mantoue	2	13	48	1	90	154
J. de Montlaur	2	?	53	–	22	77

Narbonne, the president, presided rarely (at just over forty sessions). Jean de Montlaur attended regularly in the first phase of the meetings, but, as we saw above, after 3 February 1311 he was no longer able to attend due to illness.

The seven commissioners were all together only thirteen times (at a minimum), but those were critical moments: at the (aborted) start of the commission, between 12 and 28 November, and at the end of March/beginning of April 1310, when the commission was trying to establish a procedure that could accommodate the great number of Templars who had come to Paris to defend the Order. And on 27 May 1310 the seven commissioners were again together to decide on the adjournment of the commission (finalised on 30 May).

There were two types of absences: those that lasted a short time (a day or half a day), and prolonged absences. Let's now look at the reasons for them.

The reasons for short absences were probably diverse, and not always recorded, except when they concerned an illness. Jean de Mantoue was ill on 30 May 1311 and thus did not attend the session where the decision of 27 May to adjourn the commission's work was confirmed; however, a notary was sent to his home to record his agreement – he was at that time residing in the abbey of Saint-Germain-des-Prés.[26] Mathieu de Naples was also absent owing to illness on

3 and 4 February 1311; he sent his nuncio, master Roland, to present his excuses.[27] Other short absences were explained by obligations that cropped up at the last moment, but details were not always provided: Jean de Mantoue attended three interrogations on the morning of 21 May 1311, but missed two in the afternoon.[28] It happened several times that Gilles Aycelin would open a session and then leave: on 7 May 1311 he was present when eight Templars sent by the bishop of Saintes appeared, but he excused himself and left as soon as they had sworn their oaths.[29] On 16 February Mathieu de Naples slipped out during the deposition of Eudes de Châteaudun.[30] I have found seventeen partial absences during a session: five for Gilles Aycelin,[31] two for the bishop of Bayeux,[32] one for the bishop of Mende,[33] three for Jean de Mantoue,[34] two for Jean de Montlaur[35] and four for Mathieu de Naples.[36]

Prolonged absences can be explained by illness or by missions assigned by the king or the pope.

Jean de Montlaur's health was probably quite poor. On 10 November 1309 he wrote to the other members of the commission from Saint-Benoît-sur-Loire to tell them that he had fallen ill and could not continue his journey, and that he would be absent on 12 November (he must have been coming from his home in Maguelonne-Montpellier), but as soon as he felt better he would come. In fact, he appeared on 22 November.[37] A year later he took advantage of the commission's adjournment until 3 November 1310 to return home. Ill once again, he did not return on 3 November; he had alerted his colleagues in a letter dated 12 October. Informed of the new adjournment that had been decided on 3 November, and still ill, he wrote another letter on 3 December to excuse his absence. His legs and feet were affected, he could not walk and so could not without danger undertake a trip to Paris, which, moreover, his doctors advised him against. His letters were attached to the records by the commission notaries.[38] He seems to have returned on 4 January 1311, but the details are unclear. In any case, his ill health got the better of him: he no longer participated in commission meetings after 3 February 1311.[39]

Assignments from the pope and assignments from the king occasionally occupied some of the commissioners for long periods. We've already seen the case of Guillaume Agarni. Gilles Aycelin, the archbishop of Narbonne, was also one of the most eminent members of the king's council. He was sometimes summoned for a half-day or a day, as on 3 February 1311,[40] but most often his absences lasted several days: besides his presence on the king's council, on several occasions he had to fill in at the chancellery. But, like our politicians today, he knew the contents of the commission's files well and could 'breeze through' them to direct the commission's work before attending to other business. In any case, he was present when crucial matters were being discussed.

The bishop of Bayeux was also often absent, and sometimes for long periods; he made only two brief appearances between 7 and 27 February 1310.[41] On 15 April 1310, at the end of the session, he excused himself in advance for a prolonged absence of a month or more, owing both to the council of the province of Rouen, over which he was expected to preside, and to other business.[42] He did not return until 30 May, the date when the commission adjourned until 3 November. But he was not present on 3 November, because he had gone on a mission for the king to the Curia in Avignon. Since the commission then adjourned until 17 December, his dedication was not called into question.[43] He returned on 4 January 1311.[44]

Such absences were not obstacles to the commission's work, except on one occasion. The papal letters establishing the commission had fixed a quorum of three commissioners, two of whom had to be prelates, to be present for their work to be valid.[45] There were only fourteen sessions where there were only three commissioners, and in twelve of those there were two bishops. This was not the case on 3 November 1310, the day fixed for the resumption of work following the adjournment of the preceding 30 May.[46] Of the four bishops, only the bishop of Mende was present, along with Mathieu de Naples and Jean de Mantoue. The archbishop of Narbonne was not in Paris; the bishop of Bayeux, as we've just seen, was in Avignon on the king's business; and the bishop of Limoges, usually so reliable, must have turned around at the king's request when he was on his way to join the commission at the abbey of Saint-Geneviève, to oversee the opening of the next session of the *parlement*.[47] The commissioners present decided that they could not meet and postponed the session to 17 December. No Templars had appeared.

We encounter another borderline situation on 18 May 1311. On that day, however, there were four commissioners present – the bishops of Mende and Limoges, Mathieu de Naples and Jean de Montlaur – but the last two arrived late and were not able to hear the deposition of Philippe de Manin (or Manni), the first Templar to appear that morning. It was decided that he would return the next day to confirm his deposition, in the presence of the two latecomers.[48]

However tedious (and in part, unreliable) it may appear, this tallying, which as far as I know has not been of much interest to historians, is, in fact, interesting for two reasons. First (and even if by minor errors), it provides exact figures concerning the day to day unfolding of the commissioners' work – which is always better than 'impressions' – and it also provides some useful details for the debates concerning the commission's independence (or not) in relation to the king. The pillars of that institution were the bishops of Mende and Limoges, who are not considered by historiography to have been exactly the most 'servile' to the king. It is also worth noting, incidentally, that they deserted their bishoprics for months on end. The commissioners had perhaps been named by the pope on the strong recommendation of the king, but they did not work under the king's thumb, even if there was plenty of pressure to do so. Whenever the need arose, they remembered exactly what their mission involved.

Objectives and work methods

The slow start to the commission's work shows that it had to assert its independence from the king, reassure the bishops who were worried about maintaining their jurisdictional prerogatives over the Templars in their dioceses and overcome the distrust of the Templars themselves. The commissioners were compelled to define their mission clearly. To Jean du Four, who refused to defend the Order because he 'didn't want to fight with the pope and the king of France', they responded that that was not at issue, that they were the 'commissioners of the pope and not the king' and that they had a mandate from the pope to seek the truth about the objectives of the Order.[49] On 20 February 1310 they informed Gérard de Causse that they did not have the power to free the Templars, only to investigate the Order,[50] and – this was the entire gist of the polemics with Jacques de Molay – that the proceedings against the Order, for which they were responsible, were different from the proceedings against individuals. They were clearly annoyed at the Grand Master's obstinacy in refusing to recognise the nature of the proceedings they were undertaking – they reminded him of this again during his brief third appearance on 2 March 1310.[51]

On this point, however, the commission wavered a bit when it was confronted with the Templars who had been interrogated by the pope in Poitiers in 1308; first Jean de Juvigny, on 30 April 1310, then others fit into this category. The commission decided to postpone their hearings and to deliberate on the issue; it justified this position by the fact that it did not know which articles the Templars had been interrogated on in Poitiers.[52] This hesitation is curious, because the Templars interrogated by the cardinals and the pope in Poitiers and Chinon had been questioned as individuals, and they should not have been interrogated again by the bishops. However, the pope agreed that the judgement and the sentence they would receive would be handed down by the provincial councils. The papal commission, which was judging the Order, should therefore not have hesitated to interrogate them about the Order. Those Templars were in the same situation as Jacques de Molay, whom the commission reproached for confusing the two sets of proceedings, except that the situation was not of their making. We don't know the commission's final decision, but in the end it did not inter-rogate Jean de Juvigny.

The commissioners' goal, as is now clear, was to have Templars who wanted to defend the Order appear before them. For that to happen, they were ready to grant some guarantees to those who appeared. Ponsard de Gizy, the first brother who came to defend the Order and the first to recant the confession he had made under torture, was promised by the commission and the Templar prison guards that he would be protected from any reprisals.[53] Geoffroy de Gonneville, master of the province of Poitou-Aquitaine, appeared on 13 March 1310. He did not want to defend the Order, and was visibly afraid. The commissioners attempted to reassure him by saying 'that he could speak in all safety' before them, that he should not fear any threats nor any violence or torture, 'because they wouldn't allow it'.[54]

On 5 May the commission renewed its commitments in a more solemn way by receiving a group of eight Templars in the presence of four spokesmen of the Order (in the next chapter we will see how the spokesmen were assigned, and what they did). It made them swear an oath in a form that would henceforth be used throughout the proceedings. Before his interrogation each Templar had to swear on the Gospels to tell the truth either against the Order or in defence of it; his deposition would not be opened or revealed to anyone until the end of the procedure.

The commissioners thus assured the Templars of the complete autonomy of the procedure against the Order and its 'airtightness' – if I may use the term – in comparison with the proceedings against individual Templars. They were probably sincere, but eight days later this guarantee was shattered by the abrupt actions of the archbishop of Sens, who used the one (the proceedings against the Order) against the other (the proceedings against individuals).

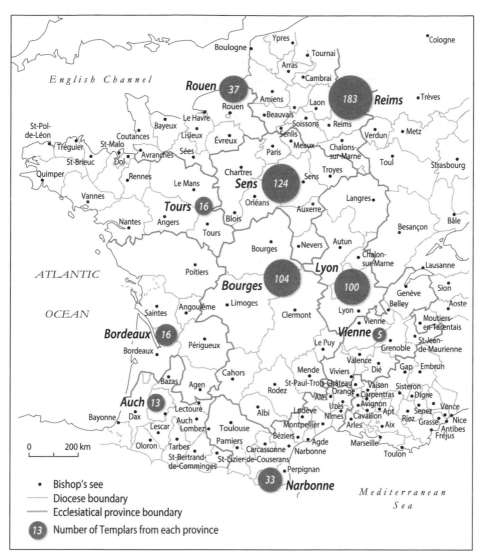

Origins of Templars who came to defend the Order in 1310

But we are not there yet. Starting on 5 February 1310 and throughout the month, Templars travelled *en masse* to Paris to defend the Order. The commission could be pleased by this, but it was also concerned: how, before that large number of men, could it proceed effectively when the date of the council was fast approaching? In February 1310 no one could have known yet that its opening would be pushed back a year. Obviously, the commissioners had not foreseen everything.

10

THE TEMPLARS' REVOLT

(February–May 1310)

Everyone arrives in Paris: February 1310

In Paris the commission was expecting only Templars who wanted to defend the Order: 'Those who wanted to defend the Order were brought to Paris [...] Those who, on the other hand, said they didn't want to defend the Order and for whom there was a public instrument, were not brought', the commissioners said on 3 April 1310.[1] On 3 February 1310 the commissioners gathered in the episcopal palace. No one came: bad weather, floods and other problems were cited; the same thing occurred the next day and the day after that. Finally, on the 6th, sixteen Templars from the diocese of Mâcon who had arrived on the 5th were brought before the commissioners. They were interrogated one by one, separately, with the others staying in the back of the room; their responses were briefly noted, then sorted into groups. Guillaume de Givresay wanted to defend the Order, in which he had never seen any evil during the thirty years he had been a member; Jean de Cissey wanted to defend the Order 'insofar as I am capable'.[2] There were fifteen men who wanted to defend the Order; the sixteenth, Gérard de Lorraine, refused because, he said, the Order was bad.

The next day, 7 February, thirty-two Templars in two groups from the diocese of Clermont appeared, all defenders of the Order; among them were the twenty-nine who had admitted nothing before the bishop of Clermont in June 1309, but also three others who had confessed and who now, however, claimed to be defenders: Gilbert Laporte, Guillaume d'Espinasse and Guillaume Brughat.[3] From then on there was a groundswell of new arrivals: up until 27 February groups of defenders arrived from throughout the kingdom. The movement slowed in March, but there were many more who came afterwards; on 2 May two more groups appeared. In total there were forty-three groups, as listed in

Table 8 below. Included in the table are the dates of arrival and the number and positions of the Templars that made up each group.

Table 8 Arrival of groups before the commission from February to May 1310

(D: defender; ND: non-defender; K: knight; S: sergeant; P: priest; ref: Michelet reference)

Date	Place of departure	No.	D	ND	K	S	P	ref.
6 February	Mâcon	16	15	1	0	15	1	vol. I, p. 57
7 February	Clermont	16	16	0	0	15	1	vol. I, pp. 58–9
7 February	Clermont	16	16	0	7	8	1	vol. I, p. 59
9 February	Sens	6	6	0	0	6	0	vol. I , p. 59
9 February	Amiens	12	12	0	0	11	1	vol. I, p. 60
9 February	Diocese of Paris	14	13	1	0	14	0	vol. I, pp. 60–61
9 February	Tours	18	18	0	0	18	0	vol. I, pp. 61–2
9 February	St-Martin-des-Ch.	15	15	0	1	11	3	vol. I, pp. 62–3
10 February	Nîmes	7	7	0	0	7	0	vol. I, p. 63
10 February	Sens	10	10	0	0	9	1	vol. I, pp. 63–4
10 February	Montlhéry	8	8	0	0	7	3	vol. I, p. 64
10 February	Temple of Paris	37	36	1	2	26	9	vol. I, pp. 64–5
10 February	L'Haÿ-les-Roses	19	19	0	0	16	3	vol. I, p. 65
12 February	Corbeil	4	4	0	0	3	1	vol. I, p. 66
12 February	Sens-Chaumont	33	33	0	1	27	5	vol. I, p. 66
13 February	Saint-Denis	7	7	0	0	6	1	vol. I, p. 67
13 February	Conflans	6	6	0	0	5	1	vol. I, p. 67
14 February	Beauvais	11	11	0	0	9	2	vol. I, p. 68
14 February	Vitry-le-François[4]	10	9	0	0	9	1	vol. I, p. 68
14 February	Tyers (Sens?)[5]	11	11	0	0	10	1	vol. I, p. 69
14 February	Carcassonne	28	28	0	1	26	1	vol. I, pp. 69–70
14 February	Sens	7	7	0	2	5	0	vol. I, pp. 70–71
14 February	Sens	27	27	0	0	26	1	vol. I, pp. 70–72
16 February	Dammartin	14	14	0	1	11	3	vol. I, p. 73
17 February	Auch	4	4	0	1	1	2	vol. I, p. 73
17 February	Toulouse	6	6	0	0	6	0	vol. I, p. 74
17 February	Crèvecoeur	18	18	0	0	17	1	vol. I, p. 74
17 February	Toulouse	7	7	0	2	4	1	vol. I , p. 74

Date	Place of departure	No.	D	ND	K	S	P	ref.
17 February	Poitiers	14	13	1	1	11	2	vol. I, p. 75
17 February	Poitiers	16	5	11	0	16	0	vol. I, p. 76
17 February	Crépy-en-Valois	8	8	0	0	6	2	vol. I, p. 77
18 February	Temple of Paris	23	11	12	0	21	2	vol. I, pp. 77–9
19 February	Temple of Paris	15	7	8	3	12	0	vol. I, pp. 79–80
23 February	Moissac (Cahors)	6	6	0	1	4	1	vol. I, p. 82
23 February	Trappes	13	12	1	0	13	0	vol. I, p. 83
25 February	Jamville (Orléans)	21	21	0	0	19	2	vol. I, p. 84
26 February	Gisors	58	58	0	5	50	3	vol. I, pp. 84–6
27 February	Vernon	13	13	0	0	12	1	vol. I, pp. 86–7
Total 1		*574*						
13 March	Bourges	15	14	1	0	15	0	vol. I, p. 89
27 March	Bourges	32	32	0	1	29	2	vol. I, pp. 98–9
27 March	Tarbes	4	4	0	1	3	0	vol. I, p. 99
Total 2		*51*						
2 May	Périgueux	19	18	1	1	17	1	vol. I, p. 230
2 May	Le Mans	8	6	2	1	7	0	vol. I, p. 230
Total 3	(3a)	*27*						
Total 1+2+3		*652*		*40*	*32*		*60*	

To this total of 652 must be added seven who were not counted upon their arrival in Paris but who were present during the meeting of 28 March and who were held in the residence of the abbot of Tiron. (Also at the residence was Pierre de Cortemple, who is listed with a group from Sens who arrived on 14 February.)[6] So there were 659 Templars who came to Paris.

The province of France (including Normandy) sent 58.5 per cent of the groups; the other provinces (Poitou-Aquitaine, Auvergne, Provence) sent 41.5 per cent. The absence of Brittany (which was part of the Poitou-Aquitaine province) should be noted. The names of the Templars were recorded as they arrived, as were the dioceses from which they came, and their positions and, for some, their functions in the Order. Sergeant brothers were in the great majority (565); there were only 32 knights and 60 priests. Appendix 4 provides a more detailed table listing the number of Templars per diocese of origin.

Table 9 Geographical breakdown by Temple province

France	Paris and diocese	11 groups
	Picardy	4 groups
	Champagne-Brie	4 groups
	Sens-Orléans	5 groups
	Normandy	2 groups
	Burgundy	1 group
Poitou-Aquitaine		5 groups
Auvergne		4 groups
Provence		7 groups

The lists of Templars

Upon their arrival in Paris the Templars were held in prisons under ecclesiastical control and were visited between 31 March and 7 April 1310 by notaries who recorded their presence. A group may have been split up or combined with another group, depending on the size of the detention space. And it was from these prisons that the brothers defending the Order were brought, on 28 March 1310, to the episcopal palace for a gathering that would prove to be decisive in the Templar Affair. For the time being what is important is that, for that occasion, a list was drawn up of almost all the Templars present in Paris, including those who had arrived the day before, on 27 March. There should have been 625, but there were only 546 on the list.

Thus we have three principal lists of Templars who came to Paris to defend the Order: the one drawn up while the groups were arriving in Paris; the one created during the general meeting of 28 March; and the one listing the Templars in the places where they were being held.[7] To those lists we must add the secondary lists, such as the one showing ninety brothers who had been assembled by the commissioners on 14 March 1310.[8] The same Templars, though not all of them, appeared on each of the lists. I will now briefly point out the main differences between the lists.

Not all of the Templars who had come to Paris were included in the list of detention sites; many have been omitted, since only 453 brothers are counted on this third list. This disparity might be attributable to oversight: it is not known where the sixteen Templars from the diocese of Mâcon who arrived on 6 February were being held, or those from Nîmes and Montlhéry who arrived on 9 February. Above all, it may be due to the fact that lists were not drawn up for all the holding places visited, and that not all were visited by notaries: this is the case for the seven Templars who arrived on 13 February from Saint-Denis, near Paris, where they had been imprisoned.[9]

Not all of the Templars who came to Paris before 28 March 1310 were present at the meeting that day: at least seventy-nine names are missing from the record for that date. We mustn't rule out errors committed by the scribes responsible for drawing up the lists: omissions, graphical errors, confusion among homonyms. Nor must we exclude cases of illness, not always mentioned by the scribes, or death. What is more curious is the absence of entire groups: the six Templars from the diocese of Sens who arrived on 9 February, whom the notaries visited on 6 April in the residence of Gossoyn de Brabant, were absent on 28 March, when all six of them had declared themselves to be defenders of the Temple. Another two groups who had also come from Sens, numbering thirty-four men, had arrived on 14 February but were not on the list of 28 March. When the notaries visited them on 2 April in the residence of the abbot of Preuilly, where they were being held, there were only twenty-seven of them, and the notaries were told that they had gone to the meeting in the bishopric's gardens on 28 March. There is an even more troubling case that I've already mentioned: eight Templars probably from the diocese of Sens, held in the residence of the abbot of Tiron and present on 28 March, had not been registered on their arrival in Paris, except for one, Pierre de Cortemple.[10]

Finally, it is probable – and this is logical – that the commissioners did not summon to the meeting of 28 March those Templars who refused to defend the Order: Gérard de Lorraine, the only one of the sixteen Templars from Mâcon to refuse, did not come,[11] nor did the seven non-defenders in the group from Gisors[12] or the five from the group being held at the Temple.[13] But this did not happen systematically: in this same Temple group those who hesitated and did not say frankly that they refused to defend the Order – there were twelve of them – participated in the meeting of the 28th.[14] Two groups had arrived from Poitiers on 17 February; in the first, Humbert de Reffiet refused to defend the Order, and he did not attend the meeting on 28 March; however, in the second group, eleven out of the sixteen brothers refused to defend the Order, but four still attended the meeting.[15]

The groups of Templars who arrived in Paris in February and March 1310 remained together; some groups had been split into two, others grouped together, but at no time were these men isolated or kept in secret. Before as well as after their stay in Paris the ten Templars who had been transferred from the Temple of Paris to Pers-en-Gâtinais (?) in the diocese of Sens on 5 February 1308 stayed there for two years before being taken back to the capital on 10 February 1310 to defend the Order before the papal commission; still together, they were held in the Penne Vayrié residence on the rue de Lucumdella (Lieudelle),[16] and the twelve 'Flemish' Templars from Amiens who arrived on 9 February were held as a group in Beauvais from September 1310 to April 1312.[17] Thus there was ample opportunity for the Templars to communicate with each other. It is worth saying that, unlike the royal counsellors and agents, the papal commissioners did not ask for anything more.

The prisons of Paris

Let's now go into the places that served as prisons for the Templars held in Paris. In 1307 the majority of Templars had been imprisoned in the Paris Temple, but also in the Barbel and Preuilly abbatial residences, and in the bishops' residence in Châlons-en-Champagne. During the dispersal that occurred in January–February 1308 those being held in these establishments were taken to the Temple, although twelve of them were sent to Saint-Martin-des-Champs, and six others to Sainte-Geneviève. Among the forty-three groups of Templars who came to Paris in February 1310, four were taken to prisons in Paris: three to the Temple and one to Saint-Martin-des-Champs, whose Parisian territory bordered the Villeneuve of the Temple. The Temple and Saint-Martin were therefore the two permanent places where the Templars were held in Paris.

The influx of Templars in February 1310 forced the opening of new prisons, and, as we have noted, the papal commission saw to it that they were under ecclesiastical jurisdiction.[18] Thanks to the visits of the commission notaries between 31 March and 7 April 1310, we know of twenty-eight of these centres, including the Temple and Saint-Martin-des-Champs, the abbey of Sainte-Geneviève and the residence of the abbot of Preuilly, already commissioned in 1307. Let's set aside the Temple for the time being: out of the remaining twenty-seven places, ten were religious establishments (abbeys, residences of bishops or abbots) and seventeen were the houses of individuals. The following table lists them in the

Table 10 Detention sites of Templars in Paris, 1310

No.	Prison	Location	Templars	Michelet reference
1	Guillaume de la Huce residence	rue du Marché Palu (rue de la Cité today)	18	vol. I, p. 113
2	Temple	Temple grounds	75	vol. I, pp. 114–15
3	St-Martin-des-Champs	Conservatoire des Arts et Métiers	13	vol. I, p. 116
4	Late bishop of Amiens' residence	Porte Saint-Marcel	14	vol. I, p. 117
5	Count of Savoie's residence	Porte Saint-Marcel	18	vol. I, p. 18
6	Bishop of Beauvais's residence	between Sainte-Geneviève and the Preaching brothers	21	vol. I, pp. 118–19
7	Sainte-Geneviève	place du Panthéon	27	vol. I, p. 119
8	Prior of Cornay's residence	not identified	21	vol. I, p. 125
9	Serene residence	rue Cithare	12	vol. I, pp. 125–6[19]
10	Abbot of Lagny's residence	Porte du Temple	11	vol. I, p. 129
11	Leuragie residence	rue de Chaume	11	vol. I, p. 130[20]
12	Richard des Poulies residence	rue du Temple	47 (-4)	vol. I, pp. 130–31, 159[21]
13	Abbey Saint-Magliore	rue Saint-Martin	12	vol. I, pp. 131 162
14	Nicolas Hondrée residence	rue des Prêcheurs	10	vol. I, p. 132
15	Jean Legrant residence	pointe Saint-Eustache	30+7	vol. I, p. 133
16	L'Ocrea residence	Croix du Tirol, rue Saint-Christophe	13	vol. I, pp. 133–4
17	Robert Anudei residence	place aux Porcs	7	vol. I, p. 134
18	Blavot residence	Porte Saint-Antoine	13	vol. I, p. 135
19	Guillaume de Marcilhiaco	Porte Saint-Antoine	9	vol. I, p. 135
20	Jean de Chaminis residence	Porte Baudoyer	7	vol. I, p. 136
21	Abbot of Tiron's residence	Porte Baudoyer	8	vol. I, p. 136
22	Abbot of Preuilly's residence[22]	rue de la Mortellerie	27 (-1)	vol. I, p. 137
23	Jean Rossel residence	Church of Saint-Jean-en-Grêve	28	vol. I, pp. 138–9
24	Penne Vayrie residence	rue de Lucumdella	23 (-1)	vol. I, p. 153[23]
25	Guillaume de Domont residence	rue Neuve-Notre-Dame	4	vol. I, p. 153
26	Gossoyn de Brabant residence	grande rue Saint-Jacques	6	vol. I, p. 158
27	Clairvaux residence	rue Saint-Martin	11	vol. I, p. 160
28	Guillaume de Latingi residence	Carrefour Guilhoré	4	vol. I, p. 164[24]

order in which they are mentioned in the records of visits made by the notaries. I've noted them on the map that follows. Identifications are proposed from indications provided by the dictionary of Jacques Hillairet and the city map of Paris under Philip the Fair drawn by Albert Lenoir and included in the book by Hercule Géraud and the *Atlas de Paris au Moyen Age*.[25]

The list of prisons and the map provided here refer only to the first phase of the commission's work, during which more than 650 Templars converged on Paris. In the second phase of its work, after December 1310, the brothers who were interrogated had been brought gradually from the provinces in small groups, and they left once their depositions had been taken. The records provide no information about their stay or the places where they were lodged. Documents concerning the detention of Templars in various places in the bailiwick of Senlis do provide very useful information, as we will see, but unfortunately do not fill this gap for Paris.

As far as we can determine, the Templars were guarded by royal sergeants who were assigned by the ecclesiastical authorities. Two are cited: Colard d'Évreux, who guarded the Templars at the Leuragié residence,[26] and Guillaume de Latingi (or perhaps Latigny), who guarded those in the abbey of Saint-Martin-des-Champs.[27]

The Templars received a daily allowance to cover the costs of their detention, the funds for which were taken from the revenue earned by Temple property under sequestration. On 28 March, during the general meeting that brought all the Templars together in the bishopric orchard, one of their spokesmen, Pierre de Bologne, complained of his situation. The complaint was picked up over the following days by the Templars being held in Saint-Martin-des-Champs, who demanded 'that our income be increased because it is too small',[28] and by those being held in the residence of the abbot of Tiron; they wrote a memorandum to the commission on the issue. According to them, the allowance of 12 *deniers* (or 1 *sou*) per day that they received did not cover their costs: they had to pay for their bed (1 *sou* 9 *deniers* per week), food (2 *sous* 6 *deniers* per week), washing of linen and clothing every two weeks (1 *sou* 6 *deniers* every two weeks) and the purchase of logs and candles (2 *sous* 4 *deniers* per week). Weekly expenses amounted to 7 *sous* 4 *deniers*, to which were added, though less regularly, expenses associated with the trial: the putting on and taking off of shackles during their transport under guard (2 *sous*), and crossing the Seine by boat when they were transferred from the right bank (location of their prison) to the Cité to appear before the

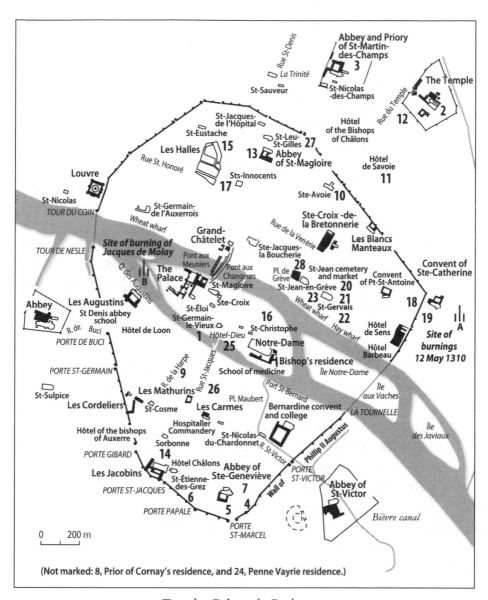

Templar Prisons in Paris, 1310

commission, which at that time was headquartered in the episcopal palace (16 *deniers*). The allowance of 7 *sous* per week was clearly not enough.[29]

28 March, in the bishopric orchard

A lot of Templars came to Paris, and the commission must have been pleased with the turnout, but there were so many of them that the commissioners had to find a way to proceed efficiently with their work. This was the goal of the meeting of 28 March, which would take on extreme importance, given what happened afterwards.

The first way in which this goal was enacted was in the reading of the 127 articles to all the brothers, first in Latin, then in the vernacular. However, as soon as the reading in Latin was done, the Templars protested and refused to listen again – in French – to the turpitude and lies that their Order was being accused of. The commissioners did not insist, and went on to the second task of the meeting: to have the Templars in attendance designate official proxies to represent them, since there were too many of them to be heard individually – there could be six, eight, ten proxies or more. The commissioners assured them that they would be free to talk and deliberate among themselves and with all the Templars regarding what they might propose for the defence of the Order. The commissioners then left to allow the brothers to deliberate.

When the commissioners returned, two brothers spoke on behalf of all those in attendance: Renaud de Provins, a priest, ex-commander of the Temple house in Orléans, and Pierre de Bologne, also a priest, who was the Order's head procurator at the Roman court. They were both 'lettered', or literate. They quickly presented a list of grievances from their fellow Templars concerning the conditions of their detention: some were in chains; their religious habits had been removed; they were deprived of the sacraments; and those who died were denied burial in consecrated ground. They were unable to designate proxies without the approval of the Master, to whom they had sworn obedience. Thus they requested a meeting with him and with other 'superiors' of the Order. If the Master did not want to or could not meet with them, they would decide how to proceed. They concluded with an argument that had been presented on many occasions: the great majority of the brothers were 'simple and illiterate' and needed counsel. Finally, they complained that many of the brothers who wanted to defend the Order were not there because they had been prevented from coming, and they cited as examples Raymond de Vassignac, knight of the diocese of Limoges, and Mathieu de Clichy, from the diocese of Paris.[30] All this 'was written by us, notaries, and proposed and dictated by them, before the said commissioners and read in Latin and repeated in the vernacular'.

The commissioners answered that they were ready to receive the proxies, that it was beyond their control if the Master didn't want to defend the Order and that all the brothers who wanted to defend the Order had been summoned. They sent someone to get the two Templars cited by the two spokesmen. Then the archbishop of Narbonne spoke:

> Brothers, you have heard what we had to say to you and inform you of. Decide today, while you are here, because the affair will begin to move fast, the date of the general council is approaching. We must hasten things. It is up to you, as has been said, who have appeared before us to defend the Order, to hasten things along. And thus we will do what must be done according to the law. Know that we do not intend to bring you all together again, but we want to proceed within the form that has been assigned to us.[31]

The bishop of Bayeux had the final word: 'Tomorrow, Sunday, we will not meet; nor on Monday. But on Tuesday the commission's notaries and scribes will circulate among you to hear what you have decided on the aforementioned things' – that is, the designation of proxies. The threat was scarcely veiled. Afterwards they would proceed formally: that is, following the questionnaire of the 127 articles.

The session was then adjourned, and the records note the names of the 546 Templars present. The meeting essentially revealed this:

1. Clearly, the commissioners were floundering; on 28 March the general council was still set for October 1310; they needed to hurry to proceed, to proceed according to the law. What did that mean? Interrogate the Templars one by one? That was impossible. And so they had at all costs to ensure that the Templars assign proxies.
2. As for the Templars, they were at an impasse. They were technically right about the proxies: they could not assign any without the Master's approval. This was the proof that the Order still existed legally in spite of the ill treatment the brothers had endured for three

years. But what could they do if the Grand Master himself was out
of the picture by refusing to defend the Order? They had two days
to decide.

Were the Templars, having returned to their prisons, able to confer? Were
Renaud de Provins and Pierre de Bologne, who acted not as proxies but as
simple spokesmen, able to meet with them? That is very unlikely.

And so the commissioners met at the episcopal palace on the morning of
Tuesday 31 March. Two Templars appeared before them. The first was Raymond
de Vassignac, whom they had had brought to them, and who appeared in a
secular habit. He was no longer a Templar and refused to defend the Order: 'He
wouldn't have removed his habit of the Order if he had wanted to defend it.'[32]
The other Templar had not been cited by Pierre de Bologne on 28 March: this
was Mathieu de l'Étang, from the diocese of Tours; he stated that he had only
seen good in the Order, but added 'that he neither would nor could say anything
more to defend it'. He belonged to the group from Poitiers that had arrived on 17
February, and he had then declared himself, as did all bar one of the brothers in
the group, a defender of the Temple.[33] He was being held in Sainte-Geneviève,
and the following day he went to see the notaries who were visiting the Templars
in their prison to tell them that he entrusted to the Master the care of defending
the Order, contrary to what he had said to the commissioners (the day before, or
17 February?); he also told them that he had not participated in the meeting of
28 March and had not co-signed the memorandum in favour of the Order that
his co-detainees had given them (see below).[34]

This certainly appears to be an echo of the threat merely mentioned by the
bishop of Bayeux on 28 March. Would the commission receive the depositions
of Templars accusing the Order, or defending it weakly, even recanting their
past attitudes in a way that destabilised the Templars? We will later see that this
way of proceeding would become prevalent throughout the month of April.

Mathieu de Clichy, whom Pierre de Bologne had indeed cited (unlike Mathieu
d'Etang), appeared the next day before the commissioners and reiterated his
desire to defend the Order. He was being held in the Temple, as was Pierre de
Bologne; it is quite strange that Pierre de Bologne cited him among the brothers
being prevented from coming to defend the Order.[35]

Immediately after they heard these two Templars, the commissioners sent
notaries to visit the other detainees in their prisons to find out if they wanted

to name proxies and if they wanted to say or write something in favour of the Order. They also ordered Philippe de Voët and Jean de Janville to bring Renaud de Provins and Pierre de Bologne, as well as two knights from Auvergne who had not been mentioned on 28 March, Guillaume de Chambonnet (or Chamborand) and Bertrand de Sartiges, to appear before them the next day, 1 April. These four men would henceforth form the quartet of spokesmen who incarnated the Templar resistance and ensured its representation before the commission.

Before following the notaries on their rounds, it might be useful to include here a brief digression on the linguistic problems, the problems of communication among those 'illiterate' Templars and the educated commissioners. To be 'illiterate' meant one did not know Latin, or knew it badly, and therefore could not express oneself orally in that idiom. The language of the trial was the vernacular, the French *langue d'oïl*. That already posed a problem for the Templars from the Midi, who spoke the *langue d'oc* and who complained about not being able to use it, as they had expected. Raymond Guillaume de Bencha protested before the notaries that he was not able to deliberate during the meeting of March 28 because he was kept apart from the other Templars wanting to defend the Order, 'adding that, if he and the others particularly of the *langue occitane* were gathered in the same place, they would deliberate on the question [of proxies] and they would respond fully to all the questions of the commissioners'.[36] And he repeated his request to be placed with others who spoke the *langue occitane*.

The depositions were thus given in the vernacular. The notaries translated them into Latin when they redacted the records of the sessions. Similarly, all the texts of the proceedings, and in particular the 127 articles, were written in Latin and had to be translated into the vernacular. This is what was done on 13 March for the ninety Templars summoned by the commissioners; and that is what the commissioners planned to do during the meeting of 28 March, but they had to abandon the idea in the face of protests by the Templars who knew by heart the nonsense the Order was being accused of, and did not want to hear it again.

For communications in writing, the commissioners told the notaries who were to visit the brothers to facilitate things for them by providing writing materials, paper or parchment, quills and ink; they could also take down through dictation what the Templars wanted the commission to know. All the memoranda written by the Templars on behalf of a group are in French – one of them in the *langue d'oc* – except one, the famous document known as 'The Knights

Templar's Prayer', which was written in Latin on parchment and was sent by Hélie Aymeri on behalf of the detainees in the abbey of Sainte-Geneviève. Hélie apologised for any errors in his Latin and asked the notaries to correct them.[37]

The prison visits

Five notaries – Florimond Dondedieu, Bernard Filliol, Bernard Humbaud, Jean Louet and Jean de Fellines – left the same day to visit the Templars. On the way, two others joined them: Hugues Nicolas and Guillaume Raoul. They would work on the afternoon of 31 March, and the mornings of 1 and 2 April; they interrupted their visits at midday on Wednesday 1 April to return to the commissioners who were hearing the four Templars' spokesmen at the episcopal palace: a fifth brother, Robert Vigier, also from the diocese of Clermont, joined them.[38]

The notaries visited twenty-three prisons. During each visit they asked the detainees if they wanted to designate proxies and present orally or in writing a document in defence of the Temple. The notaries would make note of their decision and would inform the commissioners.

The prisoners unanimously wanted to defend the Order and to reject the lies of the prosecution: the Order was good and holy. Some – the Templars from the abbey of Sainte-Geneviève just mentioned, for example – had already written a memorandum that they gave to the notaries. As regarded the defence of the Order, then, the Templars' attitude was firm and proactive; they defended the Temple orally and through writing. Only one, Aymon de Pratemi, out of the twenty-eight held in the residence of Jean Rossel, did not join his companions: he was '*simplex*', uneducated, and he did not want to defend the Order, and especially not against the pope and the king. He was not a heretic, and he asked to leave the Order to live in the outside world or in another religious house. He asked to be taken before the commissioners, at least before the bishop of Limoges (whose diocese he came from[39]).

In contrast, the attitude of the brothers on the question of the designation of proxies was less clear (beneath an apparent unanimity in refusal). We should note that Pierre de Bologne and his three companions 'who had spoken for all the other Templars on the preceding Saturday [28 March]'[40] were naturally considered to be their spokesmen.

Did the commissioners grant permission, on 28 March, for these four spokesmen to accompany the notaries on their prison visits? Although this does not appear in the records, the Templars had in any event understood this to be the case: 'They were told on the preceding Saturday that Jean de Janville would bring to each of their groups Pierre de Bologne, Renaud de Provins, priests, Guillaume de Chambonnet, knight, and others, so that they might deliberate among them', said the Templars held in the residence of Guillaume de la Huce, the first place visited on 31 March; without them, they could not designate proxies.[41] The detainees in the residence of the abbot of Preuilly also insisted that the presence of these brothers had been announced on 28 March.[42] This expectation was repeated by other groups: they wanted to be able to deliberate with the spokesmen, or at least with one of them; the name of Renaud de Provins is cited by the Templars in the residence of the bishop of Amiens, those in the residence of Robert Anudei and those in the Blavot residence.[43] The commission granted the Templars' request: the four spokesmen accompanied the notaries during the second round of prison visits the following 6–7 April.

The great majority of brothers refused to designate proxies without the approval of the Master and the 'superiors of the Order' and while they were in captivity. But behind this façade of refusal the reality was more complicated. The eleven detainees in the residence of the abbot of Lagny said no 'because they had a leader and superiors'. However, they were ready to have proxies 'who would speak for them' and, 'after that, those eleven Templars said that they made brothers Jean Lozon (or Lochon), Pierre de Landres, and Laurent de Provins and Bernard (or Bertrand) de Saint-Paul proxies [...] to defend the Order before the commissioners'.[44] Weren't they playing with words? The men they had designated as proxies were the spokesmen of their group. Who used the word 'proxy'? The Templars or the commission's scribes? The detainees of the abbey of Sainte-Geneviève were unable to deliberate on the question in the absence of counsel, but nonetheless named Geoffroy de Gonneville, Guillaume de Chambonnet, Guillaume de Bléré de Chatallone, Pierre Malian, Hélie Aymeri and Pierre de Lugni: that is, six 'defenders of the Order to tell the commissioners the reasons and good and legitimate defences in favour of the Order'.[45] Only the last two were being held in the abbey, and it is curious to see the Templars choose Guillaume de Gonneville, the commander of Poitou-Aquitaine, who had refused, like the other dignitaries, to defend the Order; but, coming from the diocese of Poitiers, they must have known him.[46] Here too we must ask the question: did the term 'proxy' used in the records come from the Templars or from the scribes? I think there was some manipulation on the part of those who redacted the records. In general, the Templars' attitude was this: no to proxies, yes to spokesmen. The memorandum presented on 3 April on behalf of the eight groups of Templars who were able to meet includes at the bottom the names of the spokesmen (one or two) from each group.[47]

The notaries visited only twenty-three of the prisons. They probably would have finished their work on Friday 3 April, but the commission had planned to meet on that day and the notaries had to attend the meeting. The commissioners would give them additional work to do.

Jean de Montréal read a memorandum on behalf of the Templars (one hundred in all) from eight prisons: the residences of Blavot, l'Ocrea, Robert Anudei, Guillaume de Marcilly, Nicolas Hondrée, Jean de Chaminis (or Chaume), Richard des Poulies and the abbey of Saint Magloire. Each group was represented before the commission by one or two brothers (four for those in the residence of Richard des Poulies[48]). Immediately afterwards, a memorandum from the Templars in the Leuragié residence was presented by Colard d'Évreux, guard of those Templars.[49] The commissioners sent the notaries to verify that those memoranda indeed represented the opinions of all the brothers in those prisons. And so on the afternoons of 3 and 4 April the notaries, with only that goal, visited the residences of Leuragié, Richard des Poulies and Guillaume de Marcilly,[50] Jean de Chaminis (or Chaume) and Blavot.[51] Each time the Templars confirmed what their spokesmen had said. Only the residences of Saint Magloire, Nicolas Hondrée, l'Ocrea and Robert Anudei remained to be visited for confirmation. This was done on Monday 7 April by another team of notaries: Bernard Humbaud, Hugues Nicolas, Guillaume Raoul and Jean Louet.[52]

On that date the first team of notaries revisited the prisons they had already been to on 31 March or 1 or 2 April: the residences of Leuragié, Richard des Poulies, Guillaume de Marcilly, Jean de Chaminis and Blavot. In the first one, the notaries took the opportunity to again ask the Templars if they wanted to designate proxies; they met with the same refusal as two days earlier.[53] On 4 April they resumed the visits that had been interrupted because of the interlude to verify the memorandum of Jean de Montréal: the residences of the abbot of Tiron, the abbot of Preuilly and Jean Rossel. The residences of Penne Vayrié and of Guillaume de Domont were visited for the first time[54] on Sunday morning, 5 April. The four Templars in that last prison made an easy-going group: if the other brothers wanted to assign proxies, they agreed with them, but if they didn't want to, they also agreed; in the meantime, Pierre de Bologne and Renaud de Provins seemed like very good spokesmen to them.[55]

A bit discouraged, the notaries returned to the commissioners at the end of the morning. They found the bishop of Bayeux, and told him that 'many of the brothers, almost all of them asked to seek counsel with the brothers Renaud de Provins and Pierre de Bologne and a few others'.[56] The bishop informed them that the commissioners intended to begin the proceedings the following Tuesday; he asked them to pick up again their pilgrim's staffs and pay some quick visits to the prisons, but this time accompanied by the four Templar spokesmen, along with this threat: they had two days to come to a decision.

On Sunday afternoon the lawyer Amisse (d'Orléans), Bernard Filliol and Florimond Dondedieu (aided by Jean de Fellines), accompanied by the four spokesmen brothers, again wound through the streets of Paris, following an itinerary that did not always take the fastest route (see map): three prisons were visited that Sunday afternoon; twenty-one on Monday and three on the morning of Tuesday the 7th, before the meeting of the commission.

The records of this second round of visits are different from the earlier ones. During the first visit on each of the four half-days the notaries wrote down the declarations of the Templars on site; for the following visits they were content to write: 'They said the same thing as …'. On the morning of the 6th the notaries began with the bishop of Amiens's residence, where the Templars again said that without the approval of the Master they could not designate proxies, but that they agreed personally to defend the Order, 'begging that, at the general council, or in any place where the religious status of the Temple would be dealt with, they could be present, or at least through proxies'. They were happy for the four to defend the Order before the commissioners.[57] Following this, the record notes, all the other groups visited: 'Responded as they had before.' The presence of the four spokesmen had a magical effect: all the Templars started speaking as one man. And so they were as good as the king's agents or the inquisitors of Guillaume de Paris at obtaining answers to the questions asked, whether they were the right ones or not.

The 'memoranda' in defence of the Order

Instead of designating proxies, the Templars chose spokesmen who were also their advisers. They also, at least some of them, wrote texts in defence of the

Temple. These texts are important because, given the time when they were produced, they show us the true positions of the Templars in this affair. If it is
difficult to accept fully the depositions made during the interrogations, knowing
the way in which the 'confessions' were obtained, we can, in contrast, have faith
in what the brothers said during the few weeks when, overcoming their fear,
they expressed themselves in confidence before the commissioners, who they
believed would listen to them without preconceived judgements.

On 28 March, let's recall, the Templars were able to deliberate among themselves in the bishopric orchard and already present some complaints and demands
through the intermediary of Renaud de Provins and Pierre de Bologne which
involved above all the conditions of their detention. As we've seen, during their
visits to the prisons the notaries encouraged the detainees to put into writing
what they had to say to defend the Order. There were ten memoranda given to
the notaries and the commissioners. They came from:

- a group of detainees in a single place of detention: the Temple of
  Paris, Sainte-Geneviève (the famous 'Knights Templar's Prayer'),
  Saint-Martin-des-Champs, the residences of Leuragié, the abbot of
  Tiron, Jean Rossel and Richard des Poulies;[58]
- several groups (eight in this case), presenting a common
  memorandum: the one read by Jean de Montréal on 3 April;[59]
- four spokesmen of the Order, sometimes associated with others;
  there were two texts during this short period, 1 and 7 April,[60] and two
  others a bit later, but they were presented in a very different context,
  which we will look at in the following chapter.

The memoranda of the four spokesmen were written in Latin, as was the one
submitted by the Templars of Sainte-Geneviève; the others were in French, the
one from the brothers in the Richard des Poulies residence being in the *langue
d'oc*. As mentioned, it was the notaries, not the Templars themselves, who gave
the texts to the commissioners. The Templars detained in the abbey of Tiron
did, however, try to do so. When the notaries appeared there on 4 April, they
met two Templars who had apparently just returned from the episcopal palace,
where they thought they would find the commissioners: the notaries asked them
what they were planning to do there, to which they replied that they had gone
to deliver a memorandum; they then gave it to the notaries, who conveyed it. As

an aside, let's note that the Templars enjoyed a certain freedom of movement, even if, as one might imagine, our two brothers did not make the trip alone.[61]

Other groups indicated that they intended to write a memorandum, but did not do so. This was the case of the detainees in the residence of the abbot of Lagny, who asked for parchment and encaustic,[62] and those in the residence of the abbot of Preuilly as well. Such was also the intention of the groups in the residences of Jean Le Grant, Robert Anudei, Penne Vayrié and Guillaume de Domont.[63] In the end, the only group whose intent and subsequent action we know of is that in the residence of Richard des Poulies; the Templars there announced their intention on 1 April and were ready, as we have seen, to send two of their group to deliver their memorandum to the commissioners, although they ended up giving it to the notaries on 3 April.

The memorandum read by Jean de Montréal on behalf of the Templars in eight detention sites is of particular interest, if only because it is proof of the contacts that were formed among groups of detainees; unfortunately, nothing is said about the way in which this collusion might have been carried out. One hundred Templars were involved; they were being held in five sites on the right bank, two on the Île de la Cité and one on the left bank. None of these places appears to have been very close to any of the others. Perhaps it was during the meeting of 28 March that contacts were made.

We've already had a look at the memoranda denouncing the conditions of detention, notably the text presented by the brothers at Saint-Martin-des-Champs. In the other texts the Templars defend a good and holy Order, subject to the Holy Church; they recall the Order's mission in the Holy Land; they invoke the patronage of the Virgin, of Saint Bernard, of Saint Louis; they denounce the false confessions and lies obtained through torture and ill treatment, threats and corruption: 'The suffering of one brought on the terror of many.' Some readily blamed the Master, who, in confessing, had lied;[64] they ask for the pure and simple annulment of the procedures of 1307 because at that time the privileges of the Order were taken away. Others say that, if the Order had been evil, sons would not have followed their fathers, nephews their uncles, into the Order; they would not be there, on bread and water, in irons, to defend it. They all asked to be set free to be able to defend the Order and choose proxies. They wanted to be allowed the sacraments. Finally, they asked to be able to attend the upcoming General Council.

Among these memoranda, two stand out.

The so-called 'Knights Templar's Prayer', presented on 1 April by Hélie Aymeri from the diocese of Limoges, on behalf of the Templars in Sainte-Geneviève, is certainly the most moving: 'May the grace of the Holy Spirit assist us. May Mary, Star of the Sea, lead us to salvation. Amen.' There followed an invocation to God and Christ to deliver the brothers of the Temple from their anguish and enable them to escape the howling devil, and, beyond that, to enlighten and save the Christian people. The Order of the 'Temple of Christ' founded in honor of the Virgin 'in the General Council by the blessed Bernard',[65] is now held captive by the king of France, a victim of lies and calumny. The Lord is invoked so he will open the eyes of King Philip so he will 'reconquer the Holy Land with us'. Then come the prayers. To Mary: 'May our adversaries return to the truth and to charity.' To Christ: 'Just as you know we are innocent of the crimes of which we are accused, so too allow us to observe our vows.'[66]

Let's compare this text with the one presented on 3 April by Jean de Montréal on behalf of the eight groups of Templars.[67] He begins by defending the Templars' faith, which is the 'Catholic faith of Rome', and their religious practices: recitation of the hours, fasting, communion three times a year, celebration of the cult of the dead, practice of charity and hospitality, celebration of religious feast days and attending processions and so on. Their churches were dedicated to Our Lady; they wear the red cross in honour of Christ's Passion.

Their Order continuously attracted laymen, which could not have happened if it had been evil. Some brothers became bishops or archbishops;[68] others served the pope as *cubicularius*, or the king as chaplain and treasurer, without being suspected of wrongdoing. If the Order had been evil, the prelates, the nobles and the commoners would not have sought to associate themselves with the devotions of the brothers and their houses; they would not have assumed the mantle of the Order when they were at death's door.[69]

Finally, the Order's actions 'in places bordering the lands of the Saracen, in the time of King Louis, the king of England [Richard Lionheart?], where sometimes the entire convent was lost [here, in the sense of all the fighting members]'. And he evokes the death of Guillaume de Beaujeu in Acre with more than 300 brothers, the battles in Spain and the long periods of captivity in the jails of the sultan of Cairo for the Templars who refused to renounce their faith. Would the brothers have kept the holy cross if they had been 'bad men'? Would the crown of thorns of Our Lord have blossomed in the hands of chaplains on Good Friday if they were heretics? Would the holy bodies they guarded (the relics of

Saint Euphemia, for example) continue to perform miracles? And in conclusion, 'more than [20,000] brothers have died in Outremer for the faith of God'. The Templars were ready to defend the Order against anyone who defamed them, except 'against our lord the King and our lord the Pope'. And, to conclude, the speaker rejected the 'erroneous articles' with which the Order had been charged.

This text puts forward the chivalrous side of the Order: the simple and profound faith of the brothers, the Order's orientation toward the lay world, its engagement, its deeds in battle and its sacrifices in favour of the faith and the Holy Land. Jean de Montréal says this to the commissioners: he and the brothers who accompanied him were 'lay and simple (*simplex*)'. As for the 'Prayer', it evoked the religious and spiritual side of the Order. The Temple was a religious and military Order, an Order that the king and the inquisitors did not have the right to judge. The commissioners, all men of the Church, knew this well. Which explains the discomfort and unease they show in their responses to the words of the 'simple' Jean de Montréal, as well as to those of the more expert Pierre de Bologne or Renaud de Provins, who presented them with texts based more on reason and law than on emotion.

On 1 April, Renaud de Provins appeared before the commission on behalf of the spokesmen. Besides a renewed request to be freed, he requested a confrontation with the Templars who had accused the Order in order to verify their testimonies and the conditions under which they had been led to testify. He declared that the commission could not proceed against the Order except under three conditions: through the path of accusation, but then the accusers would have to be produced; through the path of denunciation, but then the denouncer or denouncers would have had to have acted beforehand to attempt to have what they were denouncing corrected; through official channels, but in that case the Templars should be able to defend their cause without restriction, therefore, while being free.[70]

On 7 April, on behalf of all the Templars, the four spokesmen and six other Templars presented a memorandum that Pierre de Bologne read out loud.[71] He again explains why they cannot act as proxies, but that they wish to be present at the council if they are freed. Everything that is said against the Order by detained brothers is inadmissible. Pierre denounces the pressures of all sorts, the presence of laymen at the interrogations, the promises, the threats and the violence: 'One cannot be at all surprised that there are some who lie; rather it is suprising that there are some who support the truth.' Outside the kingdom of

France no Temple brother had proffered such lies. Pierre de Bologne then recalls the founding of the Order, its mission, its Rule and its profession of faith. All that has been said against the Order is false and was proclaimed by false Christians, apostates, heretics who, by inventing these crimes, tricked the pope and the king. He rejects the official procedure, because according to him the Templars were not defamed before their arrest. As long as they are in the hands or subject to the threats of those who uttered such lies, the Templars could have no guarantees. And even now the threats are common and fear still keeps many brothers from testifying in favour of the Order.[72]

After this intervention by the four spokesmen, Jean de Montréal read the memorandum that he presented in the *langue d'oc* on behalf of the detainees in the residence of Richard des Poulies.[73] The commissioners' response was a general one. They indeed heard Pierre de Bologne and the other spokesmen, but they were there only to listen, not to decide anything at all (and, in particular, not the release of the brothers). They recalled the papal bulls that founded their mission: in them the Templars are accused of heresy; they are indeed defamed and thus fall under ordinary and inquisitorial jurisdictions; their privileges of exemption do not apply on this point.

However, concerned with the brothers' well-being, the commissioners would now proceed with the (127) articles that the pope had sent them, but they would still receive anyone who would like to say anything more in defence of the Temple. On the following 11 April, the Saturday before Palm Sunday, the commissioners decided that Pierre de Bologne and his three colleagues whom the Templars had proposed to represent them would be admitted to the sessions, where they could interrogate the Templars as to the articles and could present their observations at any time.[74] In fact, although until this point they had been spokesmen of the Templars gathered in Paris to defend the Order, they now became official procurators of the Order in the proceedings that were then beginning with other Templars who were there to testify for the prosecution.

We cannot conclude this very important phase of the Templar Affair without bringing up the contradictions that existed within the papal commission. It wanted to bring together in Paris only the Templars who wished to defend the Order; more than six hundred came. It wanted them to choose proxies; it accepted their spokesmen. It ordered them to present, orally or in writing, their arguments in defence of the Order; they did so while almost unanimously rejecting the errors and lies and horrors of which the Order was accused. What was the outcome of all this? Nothing. The commissioners were there to listen and only to listen.[75] Nothing prevented them from interrogating individually, in accordance with the 127 articles, those spokesmen whom the Templars, defenders of the Order (who were indeed too numerous for all to be interrogated), had chosen. Instead of doing that, already changing course by agreeing to see the spokesmen, the commissioners began their interrogations by having other Templars who were going to testify for the prosecution appear before them.

All the commissioners, with Gilles Aycelin, archbishop of Narbonne in the lead, were present during the meetings of the commission during those two weeks: 28 and 31 March, 1, 3, 7 and 11 April. This indicates just how important these days really were. The commissioners were not, however, occupied all day long, since they sent notaries, twice, to visit the prisons, and they had to wait for the notaries' reports. They could thus see to other business. This was true of Gilles Aycelin, who was able to sit on the royal council while closely following the commission's work. Were there orders from within the royal court that he took it upon himself to have applied? We don't know, but one can't avoid noting that there was a slight change in the commission's work, and that he was perhaps the one chiefly responsible for it: the trial was to proceed following the rules, but that still didn't mean it should be allowed to escape from the framework in which the king and perhaps henceforth the pope wanted to maintain it. The Templars who came to Paris in February defended the Order completely. The commissioners responded that they were accused of heresy, which was no small thing; they asked the Templars to prove, not that they were innocent, but that they weren't heretics. This was a shifting that would become manifest during the month of April before, in May, a show of strength would definitively settle the question.

It remained true that during those three months the Templars, all of them, took some risks; this would be brought home to them on 12 May. All of which gives even more weight to their protestations of innocence and further discredits the 'confessions' obtained through torture.

The spokesmen for the Temple

The four spokesmen whom the Templars chose included two priests of the Order and two knights from Auvergne.

Pierre de Bologne

Pierre de Bologne de Rotis was born in 1263 into a family of that name which a lively tradition, but one without true foundations, claimed to be originally from Bergamo. He probably studied law at the University of Bologna and entered the Temple in that city in 1282, received by Guillaume de Noves, who was commander of Lombardy at that time. He was present in Venice in 1288, when he attended an Order reception. His intellectual training led him to be chosen as general procurator of the Order at the Roman Curia, probably beginning in 1298. He followed the Curia to France, and in particular to Poitiers, when Pope Clement was elected. He was in Paris when he was arrested and imprisoned in the Temple and interrogated on 7 November 1307 (he confessed); he was transferred from the Temple to the Bois de Vincennes on 30 January 1308 with twenty-three other Templars, including Renaud de Provins. He was taken back to the Temple when he proved to be a defender of the Order in February 1310. He very quickly assumed the task of spokesman for the Templars. Undoubtedly brought before the Council of Sens on 11 and 12 May 1310, he probably saved his skin by returning to his initial confession, but his escape in the following days and his return to Italy are noted in the records of the papal commission.[76] In Bologna he escaped the pursuits undertaken against the Templars, as the archbishop of Ravenna, Rinaldo da Concorrezzo, who presided over the papal commission in north-east Italy (including Emilia-Romagna), did not recognise as valid the confessions obtained under torture, and the Templars who appeared before him were exonerated. Pierre's death in Bologna is noted with a very laudatory epitaph dated 6 May 1329:

> Brother Pierre Rota, general procurator of the Order of the Knights Templar, who, after the year 1315, went to that of the Hierosolymitans [the Order of the Hospital,] a very strong champion of the Faith who, in a thousand trials, confirmed with his own blood the truth of the Christian religion, finding himself in Bologna, where he had his house following the installation in the same area of the Rota de Bergame family, finished his life and was interred in the church of Sainte-Marie du Temple, called the 'Maggione'.[77]

Renaud de Provins

A native of Provins, he was also known by the name of Renaud d'Orléans, because he was commander of the Temple house in that city at the time of his arrest in 1307. He was born around 1271, learned Latin and entered the Order as a priest in 1292 in Provins. We know nothing about his career up to his arrest and interrogation before the inquisitors in Paris on 7 November 1307; at that time he recognised the errors of the Temple. He was transferred to the Bois de Vincennes on 30 January 1308 (with Pierre de Bologne), then returned to Paris to defend the Order in February 1310; he became one of the four spokesmen. Taken before the Council of Sens, he was condemned to life in prison, defrocked and banned from the Minor and Major orders, a sentence communicated to the papal commission, before which he appeared for the last time on 5 March 1311. All trace of him was then lost.

Bertrand de Sartiges

He was from a noble family, a native of the diocese of Clermont (Sartiges, commune of Sourniac, canton of Mauriac, Puy-de-Dôme). A knight, he was received into the Order in Tartus, Syria, in 1279 by Adémar de Peyrusse. He returned to the West before 1299/1301, the date when he attended a reception in Auvergne. Arrested in the diocese of Clermont, he appeared before the episcopal commission in June 1309, where he denied the accusations made against the Order. He went to Paris in February 1310 as defender of the Order and became one of the spokesmen of the Templars until 17 December. On that date, like Guillaume de Chambonnet, he renounced the post, because of the absence of his two priest companions. Nothing more is known of him.

Guillaume de Chambonnet (Chamborand)

A knight from the diocese of Limoges (Chamborand, canton of Grand-Bourg, Creuse), he was received into the Order in the Limousine commandery of Paulhac in 1276. He probably spent most of his Temple career in the East – he was still recorded in Limassol in the first half of 1304. Having returned to the West, he became commander of the Limousine house of Blaudeix. Appearing before the bishop of Clermont in June 1309, he admitted nothing. He was a defender of the Order in Paris in 1310 and became one of the four spokesmen for the brothers. Like Bertrand de Sartiges, he stepped down on 17 December, and there is no trace of him after that.

THE COUNCIL OF SENS: THE REVOLT IS QUELLED

(11–12 May 1310)

The tide turns

On 11 April, the day before Palm Sunday, with almost all the commissioners (except Jean de Mantoue) in attendance, the commission summoned the four Templar spokesmen to appear. When they had arrived, the commissioners had eight men brought in: Jean de *Scivriaco* and master Jean de *Fallegio*, alleged brothers of the Order, were in secular habits; Jean de Juvigny and Jean de Crèvecoeur were wearing the habit; Jean Thaiafer, Huguet de Bure, Geoffroy de Thatan and Jean l'Anglais (from the diocese of London),[1] brothers of the Order, wearing the Templar-style beard and carrying their habits, threw them on the ground before the commissioners, saying they no longer wished to wear them. The commissioners ordered them to pick them up and to throw them down somewhere else. Then eleven bearded Templars (plus a twelfth, Gérard de Passage, who was clean-shaven) entered, but without habits, and finally four others who were not Templars: Raoul de Presles, a jurist, Guichard de Marciac, knight, Jean de *Vassegio*, knight, and Nicolas Simon, valet or equerry.[2]

The commissioners first interrogated Raoul de Presles and Nicolas Simon, who were witnesses for the prosecution, but the interrogation was interrupted owing to news of Jean de Saint-Benoît, one of the deans of the imprisoned Templars, commander of the house of Île-Bouchard, who was being held in Saint-Cloud in a dependency of the bishopric of Paris; he was very ill, at death's door, and could not be transported. On the morning of the 13th the bishops of Bayeux and Limoges, Jean de Montlaur and two or three notaries went to Saint-Cloud to take his deposition.[3] They returned to Paris early enough to hear

Guichard de Marciac, whose deposition would be continued the following day.[4] Then the Templars Jean Thaiafer and Jean l'Anglais were interrogated. The hearing of Jean l'Anglais was interrupted by nightfall and was continued on 23 April, after Easter services.[5]

These interrogations were carried out following the list of 127 articles of accusation, and the witnesses interrogated were all witnesses for the prosecution.

Then the other Templars who had appeared before the commission on 11 April were heard: Huguet de Bure on 24 April; Gérard de Passage on 27 and 28 April; and Geoffroy de Thatan on 29 April.[6] On 2 May the last two groups of Templars who had come to defend the Order arrived: those from Périgueux and Le Mans. On 4 May, Jean de Juvigny appeared, and in relation to his case the commissioners discussed that of the brothers who had already been examined by the pope in Poitiers. Eight other Templars then appeared, whom the commissioners interrogated over the following days, keeping to a sustained rhythm of one per day: Raymond de Vassignac on 6 May, Baudouin de Saint-Just on the 7th, Gillet de *Encreyo* on the 8th and Jacques de Troyes on the 9th.[7]

On Sunday 10 May the commissioners did not meet, but on that day the four Templar spokesmen asked to see them urgently, horrified by the news they had just heard: the archbishop of Sens had decided to assemble in Paris the next day, Monday, the council of the ecclesiastical province of Sens to judge the Templars from that province, who had been examined as individuals the previous year by the diocesan commissions. The Templar spokesmen were received and explained their fears.[8] I will discuss in a moment in detail these three days – 10, 11 and 12 May – which were of crucial importance for the Temple.

From the series of interrogations above it is noteworthy, first, that the commission took its time. The lengthy records reveal all the minutiae upon which the commissioners focused: each article, or each group of articles, was the object of questions and responses. All the testimony was for the prosecution, both that of the eleven Templars interrogated and that of the three non-Templars. Four of the Templars had already proven to be non-defenders of the Order: Jean Bertaud or *Bochandi*, Thomas de Chamino,[9] Baudouin de Saint-Just[10] and Raymond de Vassignac.[11] The Templar spokesmen attended these depositions; they intervened twice, offering memoranda that were added to the record.

On 23 April, Pierre de Bologne repeated the general complaints that the Templars had already expressed against the lies, falsities and conditions of their captivity. Realising that most of the brothers who were now going to appear before the commissioners would testify against the Order, Pierre asked that they be kept apart so as not to influence each other, and that their depositions be kept secret until the end of the investigation. He ended by citing the exemplary case – at least he considered it as such – of Adam de Vallencourt, a noble knight who was granted permission to change Orders and enter that of the Carthusians, but who soon afterwards begged to return to the Temple. In the presence of his friends and relatives he waited naked at the door of the chapter so he would be taken back; in exchange for his return he endured the penance stated in the Rule: he ate on the ground, on his mantle, for a year and a day. Since he was from Paris and had not appeared to defend the Order, Pierre de Bologne asked the commissioners to have him brought in, 'because it is not believable that such a man [...] would accept such a penance if the Order were so evil'.[12] The commission only recorded Pierre de Bologne's remarks. Adam de Vallencourt was interrogated later, on 18 January 1311, and denounced the turpitude of the Order.[13]

On 5 May the Templar spokesmen intervened before the eight Templars who were to appear that day could swear an oath, to denounce the fact that some of them were not Templars. One of them, Thomas de Chamino, responded that he had been at the meeting in the bishopric orchard with those who wanted to defend the Temple, but that now he no longer wanted to defend it.[14] Pierre de Bologne and his companions were now on the defensive. Obviously the role the commissioners expected them to play was very badly defined. What was their role, in fact? They were bit players, and the dramatic events of 11 and 12 May would reveal this clearly.

The Council of Sens, 11 and 12 May

Let's return to Sunday, 10 May, and to the horrified intervention of Pierre de Bologne at the news of the convocation of the council of the province of Sens. In his opinion the council was going to be called 'to judge many of our brothers who had appeared to defend the Order and to force them to renounce it'. And so he appealed against the decision of the archbishop of Sens and proposed to have this appeal read. The president of the commission replied that it was not the commissioners' role to present appeals, but if the Templars had something to say in favour of the Temple, they would happily listen to it. Pierre de Bologne then submitted a memorandum in which he called upon the pope, the apostolic see and the apostles, and asked that he and his companions be brought before the pope as soon as possible; furthermore, he asked the commission to put one or two notaries at their disposal to help them write their appeal in the appropriate form. While waiting, Pierre de Bologne asked for the archbishop of Sens to defer any decision and for the commissioners to ask all the archbishops not to undertake similar measures. He submitted another memorandum, this time addressed to the archbishop of Sens: in it he reiterated the protest of the spokesmen against the archbishop's harsh initiative and informed him of the appeal in process at the court of Rome.

The first memorandum was read without Pierre de Bologne and his companions in attendance. Having heard it, the archbishop of Narbonne left the room claiming he had a Mass to celebrate or to attend.[15] Very annoyed, the other commissioners postponed their response until after vespers.

The commissioners' response is worth reproducing:

> The affair with which the archbishop of Sens and his suffragans were concerned related to their council and was completely different and separate from [the commission's]; they, themselves, didn't know what the council would be discussing. Just as we are assigned by the apostolic see to deal with our affair, so too the archbishop of Sens and his suffragans are assigned to deal with theirs in the council; the said commissioners had no power over them. Because of this it does not seem to us on the face of it that we have anything to say in opposition to the said archbishop of Sens or to the other prelates regarding the pursuits undertaken by them against the individuals of the Order; however, we will deliberate further on this and will do what should be done.[16]

What hypocrisy! However, this response had the merit of highlighting the breach into which the archbishop of Sens would step in blocking the Templars' revolt. For the commissioners there were two strictly distinct sets of proceedings – the one against individuals and the one against the Order – and a Templar could say one thing in the first and its opposite in the second without there being any consequences. But was this true? No, said the archbishop of Sens. This was the weak link in the dual proceedings set in motion by the pope in Poitiers: the connection between the two sets of proceedings had not been specified, and anyone could interpret the connection as they wished. The commissioners had acted correctly: they did not confront the Templars who arrived to defend the Temple with the confessions they had made before the inquisitors or the bishops.

As for the archbishop of Sens, he considered that the confessions, regardless of the proceedings, remained in place, and that to revoke them was heretical and therefore indicated relapse. Guillaume de Plaisians had probably intimated this to Jacques de Molay in November 1309. There was consistency in the king's and his agents' way of proceeding.

Philippe de Marigny was the younger brother of one Enguerrand de Marigny, who held high-level roles in the royal council. Young Philippe had begun a career in service to the king as a secretary and a tax collector first in Paris, then in the region of Caux, before turning to an ecclesiastical career. He did not attend university but instead accumulated canonries (Cambrai, Meaux, Issoudun and others) before being promoted to bishop of Cambrai by Pope Clement on 22 January 1306. The old archbishop of Sens, Étienne Bécart, died on 29 March 1309. Pope Clement blocked the election of a new archbishop by the chapter (which was the normal procedure) by reserving the see on 23 April, probably at the request of the king. The pope transferred Philippe de Marigny from Cambrai to Sens on 6 May, but the newly promoted man did not receive the pallium (the symbol of his new role) until 22 December 1309, and was only enthroned at Easter, 19 April 1310. This does not mean that he waited until that date to intervene in the archbishopric's affairs.[17] The gathering of the provincial council in Paris had not been improvised in a few days' time. In fact, it was an initiative decided on from on high. The bishop of Bayeux, at the end of the 15 April session, had announced that he was going to be absent for several weeks to prepare for the council of the province of Rouen;[18] this was a council similar to those of the provinces of Sens and Reims.

On 10 May the commissioners did not do anything. The next day they acted as if nothing was wrong and interrogated Humbert du Puits, a brother from the diocese of Poitiers, who was wearing the habit and beard of the brothers of the Temple. Already interrogated, first by Jean de Janville and the seneschal of Poitou, questioned three times 'because he didn't confess what they wanted', held in chains and placed on bread and water for thirty-six weeks, interrogated by the official of Poitiers (within the framework of the proceedings against individuals?), he denied having been received into the Order while renouncing Christ.[19] The same scenario was repeated the next day when another brother from Poitiers, Jean Bertaud, who had confessed under threats, was interrogated.[20] It was during his interrogation, before the hour of Prime (our commissioners were early risers), that the news arrived that fifty-four Templars defending the Order before the papal commission had been sentenced by the Council of Sens to be burned at the stake.

This time the commissioners were forced to react, and they sent Philippe de Voët and the notary Amisse d'Orléans to the archbishop of Sens to implore him to act with circumspection and to postpone carrying out the sentence. Many Templars, as the provost of the Church of Poitiers could testify, had, when at death's door and at the peril of their souls, denied the crimes of which the Order was accused. In addition, carrying out the sentence would halt the proceedings against the Order, as no one else would want to testify, and would thus render pointless the commission's work. They also pointed out that the four spokesmen for the Order's defenders had placed an appeal before the pope the preceding Sunday.[21]

There is nothing else in the record. It was only the next day, 13 May, when the commissioners had resumed their daily work, that it was learned by way of Aimeri de Villiers-le-Duc, a Templar from the diocese of Langres, whom the commissioners were getting ready to interrogate, that the fifty-four condemned Templars had been burned at the stake the day before. He was pale and agitated; he spoke incoherently and gesticulated wildly. Everything the Templars were accused of was false, but he had seen the day before his fifty-four companions led to the stake and he knew that they had been burned. And so he no longer wanted to say anything for fear of incurring the same fate, because he knew he couldn't endure the flames; he would admit everything, he was even ready to say he had killed the Lord if he were threatened with the stake.[22] The commissioners cut his torment short and stopped his hearing. Sensing that they would obtain nothing else from him or other Templars that day, they adjourned until 18 May.

The Templars at the Council of Sens

No documents from the meeting of the Council of Sens (or that of Reims) have been preserved. It involved all the Templars arrested and detained in the suffragan dioceses of the province who had been questioned by the diocesan commissions – that is, the dioceses of Sens, Auxerre, Nevers, Troyes, Meaux, Paris, Chartres and Orléans. And it included the Templars who had been defending the Order as well as those who had refused to do so; the former were among the Templars registered in Paris in February and March 1310; the latter, having remained in their prisons in Sens, were not registered. The council for the province of Sens had gathered in Paris on 11 May; there is sadly no list of Templars from this meeting.[23] Remember that the papal commissioners had left the palace of the bishop of Paris on 28 April to hold their audiences in the abbey of Sainte-Geneviève. Should this be seen as a link of cause and effect? If that were the case – but this is only a hypothesis – it would support the idea that the convening of the Council of Sens was not a last-minute decision.

Thus it is impossible to know the names of all the Templars directly affected by the meeting of the Council of Sens. We can, of course, assume that all the brothers who came to Paris in February and March, brought from places of detention located in the diocese of Paris and other suffragan dioceses of Sens, were potentially answerable to the Sens council.

From the diocese of Sens there were four groups and 50 Templars, from the diocese of Paris nine detention sites and 160 Templars, from the diocese of Meaux two sites and 32 Templars, and from the diocese of Orléans one site and 21 Templars. This amounts to 263 Templars, almost all defending the Order, from four dioceses out of eight.

The same calculation can be done for the province of Reims, which included eleven dioceses: Reims, Châlons-en-Champagne, Laon, Senlis, Beauvais, Soissons, Noyon, Amiens, Thérouanne, Arras and Cambrai: fifty-two Templars came from four dioceses (Amiens, Beauvais, Châlons, and Senlis).

All of this is only of expository value.

The numbers gleaned from the depositions given by the Templars interrogated in the second phase of the papal commission's work between 17 December 1310 and 26 May 1311 are more reliable, but necessarily incomplete. There were fifty-eight Templars who said that they had been present at the Council of Sens in Paris, and twenty-seven at the Council of Reims in Senlis (see Appendix 5). Out of the fifty-eight Templars present at Sens, forty-five appeared before the papal commission in February/March 1310, thirty-one as defenders and twelve as non-defenders, two being somewhere in between. Thirteen had not appeared before the commission on those dates and thus should be considered non-defenders.

In Senlis, out of the twenty-seven, nineteen had been present before the papal commission, seventeen as defenders, one as non-defender, and one having a more ambiguous position: Wirmond de Sanconi, from the diocese of Soissons, 'knew of nothing other than good in the Order and said he didn't understand what "to defend" meant'.[24] The eight who did not appear then must have been non-defenders.

According to the chroniclers Jean de Saint-Victor and Guillaume de Nangis, three categories of accused were established by the members of the Sens council: those who had acknowledged the Templars' crimes and had never swayed, or who after having denied the crimes henceforth acknowledged them; those who had always denied those same crimes despite the evidence and despite torture; and those who after having acknowledged the crimes had recanted their confessions and henceforth remained in error. The first group would be reconciled with the Church and freed after a penance that remained to be determined; the second group would be sentenced to a perpetual 'wall', meaning life in prison; the third would be considered as relapsed heretics and handed over to the secular arm to be burned at the stake.[25] This was the case of the fifty-four Templars burned on 12 May.

Burning at the stake: 12 May

And so on 12 May fifty-four brothers were taken in wagons to a location near the Porte Saint-Antoine; a large pyre had been prepared in a field facing the priory of Val-des-Écoliers.[26] Let's look at an account of what happened, as told by Guillaume de Nangis:

> The council of the province of Sens was held in Paris from the 11th to the 26th for the Templar Affair, with the permission of its president Philippe, then archbishop of Paris [sic]. After they had carefully examined the actions of each Templar and everything related to them, and looked truthfully at the nature and the circumstances of their crimes, so that the degree of punishment would be proportional to the crimes, according to the advice of doctors of divine and canon law, and upon the approval of the holy council, it was definitively ordered that some of the Templars would be simply stripped of their vows to the Order, others made free, safe and sound following the completion of a penance that would be ordered for them, others locked up, a great number imprisoned for life, and finally some, as relapsed, delivered to the secular arm as ordered by canon laws on the subject of similar relapses, whether they were part of a religious military order or had been admitted into the holy orders; this was done, following the decrees of the bishops, after they had been stripped of their status by the bishop. This is why fifty-nine Templars were burned outside Paris, in a field not far from an abbey of nuns called Saint-Antoine.[27]

However, all, without exception, refused to admit the crimes of which they were accused, and continued with constancy and firmness in overall denial, always declaring that it was without motive and unjustly that they had been delivered to death, which a lot of people couldn't see without great astonishment and excessive stupor. Around the same time there was convoked in Senlis, in the province of Reims, a council and, on that occasion, as at the council of the province of Sens held in Paris for the Templar Affair, there was a trial of nine among them who were then burned.[28]

The sessions of the Sens council continued until 26 May, the chronicler tells us; five more Templars were sentenced to the stake. Let's cite here a little-known text by a royal cleric who had been the king's tutor, Guillaume d'Ercuis, who, in a few lines, sums up all the information available on these executions:

This year, on Tuesday during the feast day of Saints Nereus, Achilleus and Pancrace, the 12th day of May, between terce and noon, between Saint-Antoine of Paris and the windmill, were burned fifty-four Templars for the bad faith they proved. The same soon afterwards in Senlis, nine; the same not long after in Paris, five, including brother Jean de Taverny, who was chaplain to the king Philip of France.[29]

This second Paris burning was on 27 May, the day after the final session of the Council of Sens.[30] The burning in Senlis, where nine Templars were executed, came 'around the same time', according to Guillaume de Nangis; afterwards, according to Guillaume d'Ercuis; in the following month, according to Bernard Gui; on 2 July, according to Gilles Le Muisit.[31]

It is almost impossible to create a list of those who were executed, although François J. M. Raynouard has attempted to do so.[32] Eight Templars are mentioned by name as having been burned by those interrogated after May/June 1310: seven in Paris and one in Senlis.

We must add Jean de Taverny, former royal chaplain, who was among the five burned in Paris on 27 May.[33]

All, except for Martin de Nicey, appeared before the papal commission in February/March; five defended the Order without hesitation. Henri d'Aulisi and Laurent de Beaune were less assertive: like their five companions who arrived from the diocese of Sens on 14 February 1310, they responded to the

Table 11 Templars burned on 12 May 1310

Name	Cited by	Michelet references
Raoul de Frénoy	Mathieu de Tillay	Michelet, vol. I, p. 363
Gautier de Bullens	Mathieu de Cressonessart	Michelet, vol. I, p. 535
Guy de Nicey	Gautier de Bure	Michelet, vol. I, pp. 538–40
Martin de Nicey	Gautier de Bure	Michelet, vol. I, pp. 538–40
Jacques de Saci	Pierre de Sarcelles	Michelet, vol. I, p. 575
Laurent de Beaune	Henri de Faverolles	Michelet, vol. I, p. 591
Henri d'Aulisi or de Anglesi	Jean de Buffavent	Michelet, vol. I, p. 509
Lucas de Sernay (Sornavo)	Jean Bochier	Michelet, vol. II, p. 77

commissioners' question, 'Do you wish to defend the Order?' by saying they wanted to discuss things with the Master.[34] Their position subsequently became firmer, and in Sens they must have recanted the confessions made in the past, which led to their being burned at the stake.

The repression did not just involve the living. At approximately the same time 'the bones of a Templar who had been dead for a long time, known as Jean de Tour, once treasurer of the Temple of Paris, were exhumed and burned like those of a heretic because it had been discovered that he was implicated in the trial already brought against the Templar Order.'[35]

Relapsed or not?

As I've mentioned, the connection between the proceedings against individuals and those against the Order was the weak link in the dual proceedings put in place by the pope in Poitiers in August 1308.

When they appeared before the papal commission in February 1310, many Templars had already appeared before the diocesan commissions, where they were questioned as individuals. Not all, however, since some commissions met only later: that of Nîmes, for example. Following logic, it seems to have been tacitly accepted that the second phase of the proceedings – judgement – was to take place after the Council of Vienne, responsible for judging the Order, had met: it was in that council that, once a decision had been made regarding the Order's future, decisions would be made involving individuals. However, nothing prevented provincial councils from meeting beforehand; thus the archbishops of Sens, Reims and Rouen were certainly within their rights in convening their councils.

The two proceedings could not interfere with each other's work, as I've said. Many Templars (but not all: see what happened in Clermont in 1309) who went to Paris to defend the Order acknowledged all or some of the 'crimes' with which the Templars had been charged before the diocesan commissions. Did they recant those confessions before the papal commission? At the date of the Council of Sens, no. Arriving in groups, they affirmed their intention to defend the Order, but they had not been interrogated by the commissioners and thus did not find themselves faced with the dilemma of whether or not to recant their previous confessions. It was collectively, and not as individuals, that they rejected the accusations as vile lies and falsehoods.

On 11 May the Council of Sens (and shortly afterwards the Council of Reims) determined that the fact that they presented themselves as defenders of the Order before the papal commission was the equivalent of revoking a confession made before the diocesan commissions. Later, duly warned, the Templars interrogated by the papal commission would be careful to confirm that they in no way intended to recant what they might have said earlier in front of the bishops. Given the potentially large number of Templars present at the Council of Sens, the fifty-four who were sentenced and burned were probably in the minority. In front of the Council, we must imagine that the brothers had been instructed to resolve any contradiction between their earlier confessions and their position in favour of the Order. Some chose to hide their position as defender of the Order; others maintained their position and thus created the contradiction in which the members of the Council of Sens wanted to entrap them. Exploiting this weakness, the archbishop of Sens determined that they were returning to their earlier errors, to heresy (since for the king's henchmen it was heresy); they had relapsed into heresy and would therefore be burned at the stake. According to the chronicles, that is exactly how events unfolded: the fifty-four taken to the pyre, fully aware of the situation, chose martyrdom. This is what Bernard Gui writes in his chronicle *Des gestes glorieux des Français*:

> What is surprising is that they all absolutely recanted the confessions they had made separately during their trial, during which they had sworn to declare the truth, and they said that they had earlier told lies and given false depositions, giving no other reasons for their initial confessions than the violence and cruelty of torture.[36]

The continuation of Guillaume de Nangis's chronicle is even more specific:

> However all, without exception, refused to admit the crimes of which they were accused and persisted with constancy and firmness in a general denial, not ceasing to declare that it was without motive and unjustly that they had been sentenced to death; which a large number of people couldn't witness without great astonishment and excessive stupor.[37]

The writer of the *Grandes chroniques de France* (this was the official chronicle, translated from the *Chroniques de Saint-Denis*) was more disconcerted: 'Despite the very cruel suffering that they endured, they refused to recant, for which, according to what we believed, they could incur perpetual damnation, because they put the small people in very great error.' [38] By their refusal to recant the Templars might undermine the accusations of the king and the Church in the eyes of ordinary people. It clearly did not occur to these historians close to the royal court that the Templars could have been telling the truth. They were necessarily guilty because the king said so.

This brings us to the question: was there really relapse into heresy? We possess several documents whose dating is problematic. First, there is an anonymous document published by Georges Lizerand, who dates it from 1308 and attributes it to Guillaume de Plaisians, but which was almost certainly written later. Indeed the anonymous author, responding to an initial question on the fate to be reserved for the Grand Master Jacques de Molay, actually includes Molay's responses to the cardinals in Chinon in August 1308. It has thus been proposed that the text should be dated to 1310. The contents of this tract may confirm that date. Let's skip the first question, involving Jacques de Molay, and go to the second, which deals with the statutes and secrets of the Order which, according to our author, constitute the very essence of the Templars' profession of faith. Given that that essence was corrupt, by committing himself – even unwittingly – to the Order, a new brother only aggravated that corruption. The third question relates very closely to the context of the first part of the year 1310. Should there be a – or more than one – defender of the Order in this affair? No, responds the author, who distinguishes between the two sets of proceedings while artfully intertwining them. In the trial against individuals there were no defenders. If one proceeded against the entire Order through the path of direct accusation, it would be potentially possible to envision a defender, but there was not an accusation; there was no need for one since 'it is from the accusations brought by countless Templars that the corruption of the Order clearly stands out for the Church'. One need not accuse, only eradicate: 'The king isn't speaking as an accuser, or as a party to the trial, but as minister of God, defender and champion of the faith.' He calls upon the Church, which was sleeping, to wake up and act: 'The Church need not proceed against the entire Order through the path of judgement, but through the path of temporary allowance.' It is impossible that this Order could still be useful; to keep it would be a scandal, and the Church owed it to itself to eliminate the scandal. This opinion sparks our interest when we realise that it is the one Pope Clement adopted in Vienne: the suppression of the Order not through the path of judgement but through the path of temporary allowance: that is, a pure and simple administrative suppression. Finally, responding to the fourth question, the author rejects the idea that the existence of innocents in the Order could be an argument in favour of keeping it; in any case, there could not be innocents in such an Order, all of whose members have been, to various degrees, corrupted.[39]

For the purposes of this chapter it is obviously the third question that is of interest: on the one hand because blending the two proceedings was considered normal, and on the other, because any notion of defending the Temple was rejected. In sum, the papal commission, in asking completely corrupted Templars to name proxies to represent them in the defence of the Order, was wasting its time and contributing to prolonging a great scandal, to the great peril of the Church of God. One need not have been a great cleric to understand that behind this criticism of the papal commission it was the pope who was being targeted.

Rather than Guillaume de Plaisians, today we attribute this text to the theologian Jean de Pouilly, who became master of the University of Paris at the beginning of 1307, because at the Council of Vienne he expressed part of the argument developed in this anonymous text in his interventions in support of the theory of relapse. But let's remain cautious: the idea that Jean de Pouilly was the author of the text, like the date of its writing, remains hypothetical. The only solid point likely to support the date of 1310 is the connection between the third question above and the work of the papal commission in the first half of 1310, but we must point out that there is no question of relapse in the text.

It is at issue, however, in another text, which is unfortunately just as problematic. According to Noël Valois, in his study of Jean de Pouilly, prelates from various places who then gathered in Paris would have raised the question of relapse with academics.[40] In question 15 of the *Quodlibet V* that he wrote after the end of the Council in May 1312, Jean de Pouilly indicates that 'the year the Templars were arrested, many questions and articles on the Templars were raised with the doctors by prelates from various provinces gathered in Paris'. From these indications it has been proposed that those questions – posed by the bishops, it should be stressed, and not by the king (and thus different from those raised by him to which the university responded on 25 March 1308) – should be dated to the beginning of 1308.[41]

At the Council of Vienne, Jean de Pouilly defended a position that he had held for a long time: that is, that the Templars who had made confessions and later recanted them were relapsed. He developed his argument against those who defended the opposite position in that *Quodlibet*.[42] He does not seem to have been followed by other theologians, since there is mention of a vote by masters of the university in which only two supported his point of view, as opposed to nineteen who rejected it.[43] But when did that vote take place? We must remember that in March 1308 the masters in theology had responded – unfavourably – to the questions asked by the king; still there were only fourteen of them who had placed their seal at the bottom of the document. This means that some had not approved that declaration. We must compare that number of fourteen and those names with the twenty-two masters in theology known of at the time.[44] Did this vote take place at the beginning of 1308, in response to the questions raised by the bishops gathered in Paris, as suggested by the chronological information provided by Jean de Pouilly? This is the opinion of Karl Ubl.[45]

This proposed date – 1308 – leaves me doubtful, because I don't see which meeting of bishops might have been held in Paris at that time. No source mentions it. It would have taken place before the papal proceedings had been decided on and, more important, implemented. Wouldn't such a request of the bishops

be more in line with the agenda of the council of the province of Sens in May
1310? The question must be asked.

In May 1310 the bishops who gathered in the council of the province of Sens
in Paris, like the members of the papal commission, were perhaps aware of the
point of view of Jean de Pouilly (or the anonymous author of the tract) on
the two sets of proceedings and of the possible response of the masters of the
university to the bishops on the question of relapse. Perhaps armed with these
two opinions, the prelates of the Council of Sens, then completely espousing
the point of view of the royal council, thought that the papal commission was
veering off course. The king, his counsellors and the archbishop of Sens did
not bother with juridical quibbles, and they would not have taken into account
the opinions of the Parisian masters on relapse, preferring to follow the extreme
minority opinion of Jean de Pouilly: defence or not, relapse or not, it was necessary to finish with this affair, which had gone on for too long. On 11 and 12 May
they made a show of strength, which, in the short term, paid off.

After 12 May

The meetings of the Council of Sens continued until 26 May.[46] As well as sen-
tencing five more Templars to the stake, they examined the case of Renaud de
Provins, one of the four Templar spokesmen. On the morning of 18 May the
papal commissioners gathered at the residence of Gilles Aycelin and decided to
send Philippe de Voët, guard of the Templars, and the lawyer Amisse d'Orléans,
royal cleric, to the archbishop of Sens and his council in order to inform them
of the missions assigned to the papal commission by Pope Clement. Among the
many Templars who had offered to defend the Order they identified Renaud
de Provins; he had worked hard to defend the Order and the commissioners
had allowed him, with his three colleagues, to 'come before said commissioners
under full and sure guard as often and at any time they would like to defend the
Order'.[47] The commissioners asked the archbishop of Sens to take this situation into account because 'it was said that brother Renaud had been summoned
before him to respond in the investigation made against him as well as against
the other persons of said Order about which it was said that it was ongoing'. By
attracting the archbishop and his council's attention to this case, the commissioners specified, however, that they did not intend to infringe on the council's work.

In the afternoon the commissioners – the archbishop of Narbonne being absent – received the envoys of the archbishop of Sens and of the council: Pierre de Mossa, Michel Mauconduit and Jean Coccard, all canons of Orléans. They emphasised that the investigation into brother Renaud (and others) had begun two years earlier and that the council had met to conclude it by pronouncing judgement. They thus insolently asked the commissioners to tell them what they meant by the announcement that they had sent that very morning. The commissioners responded that what they had said was perfectly clear, but that, in the absence of the archbishop of Narbonne, they had nothing to add. They also reminded them that, according to their information, the appeal made on 10 May by the four spokesmen had not been brought to the attention of the council.[48]

The envoys of the council had scarcely left when the Temple spokesmen arrived: Guillaume de Chambonnet, Bertrand de Sartiges and … Renaud de Provins. Renaud was safe for the moment. Probably Philippe de Marigny and the bishops of the council had reflected: they really could not block the papal proceedings by preventing one of the Templar spokesmen from carrying out his role before the commission, even if that role appeared increasingly to be in vain. But although Renaud de Provins was there, Pierre de Bologne had disappeared, 'separated from their society', said his colleagues, who 'didn't know why'.[49] They could not continue their task without him. At this news the commissions once again sent Jean de Janville and Philippe de Voët away with an order to bring back Pierre de Bologne the next morning. He did not appear. It was said that he had been sequestered, assassinated or had met another fate. In fact, he had fled. Pierre de Bologne, an Italian Templar, had been arrested in the diocese of Paris and was thus subject to the jurisdiction of the bishop of Paris and answerable to the Council of Sens; like Renaud de Provins, he risked being burned at the stake unless he confessed. Like him, he probably would have received a reprieve, but the risk remained. Pierre did not want to take that risk and instead took flight; his functions as general procurator of the Order at the Roman Curia had probably enabled him to make good connections there. He may have had accomplices in his escape, as the *cubicularius* Giacomo da Montecucco did in 1308. He returned to Italy and Bologna and was never troubled again, and died around 1329.[50]

The next day, 19 May, forty-four Templars appeared: up to then they had wanted to defend the Order; they now withdrew their defence.[51] The notaries recorded their names (see Appendix 6). Out of those forty-four, thirty-eight were held in the Temple of Paris (as Pierre de Bologne had been), four in the residence of the abbot of Preuilly, one in the residence of Jean Le Grant, and a last one, Jean de Saint-Leu, in an unknown location, since he does not appear on the lists drawn up in February/March 1310. Out of the thirty-eight Templars in the Temple of Paris, twenty-seven were unreservedly defenders of the Order, nine had expressed some reservations (on the condition that they be freed, with the advice of the Master), and two, who had at first said they were non-defenders, must have changed their minds later, since they were now withdrawing their testimony.[52] The Temple of Paris, despite the presence of Pierre de Bologne, was thus not the most steadfast centre for the defence of the Temple. Quite the opposite. It was there that royal pressure could continue to be exerted most effectively.

Learning that the meeting of the Council of Vienne had been postponed for a year, on 31 May the commission decided to adjourn until 3 November. We know that this was a useless session and that the commission did not truly resume work until 17 December 1310. On that day Guillaume de Chambonnet and Bertrand de Sartiges were present, and they declared that they continued to make their appeal (against the decisions of the Council of Sens?), but since 'they were illiterate laymen, they asked that brother Renaud de Provins and brother Pierre de Bologne join them'; they again asked to be freed and to receive counsel. The commissioners replied that the brothers Renaud and Pierre had voluntarily renounced their defence of the Order and had returned to their initial confessions; that, following his retraction, brother Pierre had escaped prison and had fled; and that brother Renaud could no longer be admitted to defend the Order because he was under the threat of punishment by the Council of Sens. The two knights then renounced their defence and left.[53]

Renaud de Provins appeared once more before the papal commission, no longer as a defender of the Temple but as a Templar sentenced by the Council of Sens. In fact, the council held other sessions in addition to that of the month of May 1310. It met in March 1311 and again after 15 August 1311, always with the Templar Affair on its agenda.[54] On 5 March 1311 three priests of the Temple who had just been sentenced by the Council of Sens were brought before the commission, among them Renaud de Provins. They had been excluded from all the Major and Minor orders, deprived of all ecclesiastical privileges, stripped of the habit of the Temple and sentenced to life imprisonment in various forms. It is because they had returned to their initial confessions that Renaud and his two companions escaped the stake. Three other brothers, a knight and two sergeants, were given the same sentences.[55] The commission took note and immediately afterwards proceeded to interrogate Lambert de Cormelles.

12

INTERLUDE: IN THE PRISONS OF SENLIS

(June 1310–1312)

When the papal commission adjourned on 30 May 1310, there were more than six hundred Templars in Paris. What did they do with all those 'criminals' for the five months (in reality, seven) while the procedure was interrupted? They couldn't all stay in Paris. Did they go back to the detention sites where they had been imprisoned before they came to the capital? That is most likely. But, as a document concerning the Templars from Gisors indicates, there were a few transfers elsewhere.

From prisons in Paris to prisons in Senlis[1]

On 26 February 1310 an impressive group of fifty-eight Templars who had previously been held in Gisors arrived in Paris to defend the Order.[2] Thirty-seven were imprisoned in the residence of Jean Le Grant;[3] we don't know where the others went. A large number of them, but not all, were present at the meeting of 28 March. What became of them after the archbishop of Sens's show of strength and the adjournment of the papal commission? Through an act dated 16 June 1310, Philippe de Voët and Jean de Janville conferred on Pierre Proventel (or Provenchère) the job of guarding nine Templars who had been under the guard of Robert de Vernon in Gisors.[4] They asked the keepers of the Temple property to pay Proventel the usual sum of 12 *deniers parisis* per day and per person for the maintenance and food of the Templars. Their letter is included in a missive from Guillaume de Gisors, archdeacon of Auge in the church of Lisieux, who adds that he gave the money to Pierre Proventel to 'take the Templars from

Paris to Compiègne', where they would henceforth be held prisoner. In a later act, dated February 1312, Pierre Proventel swore an oath that on 3 July 1310 he had received from the farmer of the Temple house of Compiègne[5] the sum of 79 *livres parisis* as his fee for the maintenance of the nine Templars for the period of 3 July to All Saints Day 1310.[6] Seven of these nine Templars are also on the list of brothers who came from Gisors on 26 February 1310: Henri Zappellans or Chapelain, Anceau de *Rocheria*, Énard de Valdencia, Guillaume de Roy, Geoffroy de Cera or de La Fère-en-Champagne, Robert Harlé or de Hermenonville, and Dreux de Chevru;[7] the two others, Robert de Mortefontaine and Robert de Monts-de-Soissons, perhaps appear under different names.

We don't know the reasons why those nine Templars were not taken back to Gisors. They are catalogued as 'non-reconciled': that is, they had not been absolved and reconciled with the Church by a diocesan commission. They attended neither the Council of Sens nor that of Reims in May 1310. They were from different dioceses: Toul, Sens, Châlons-en-Champagne, Trêves but also Soissons (Guillaume de Roy), Laon (Geoffroy de La Fère) and Senlis (Robert Harlé). Was there a link – a tenuous one – between those origins and their imprisonment in Compiègne? It seems unlikely.

In any case this example enables us to follow continuously a group of Templars between February and July 1310: first held in Gisors, then in Paris, and later transferred to Compiègne at the beginning of June 1310. They were still there in 1311. This reveals what must have been the general rule in the bailiwick of Senlis and elsewhere. The date noted in our document of 16 June is important: 1 June, or the exact moment when the commission adjourned its work for several months. On that date and in the following few days or weeks there must have been a vast movement to disperse the Templars: those in command did not want them to remain concentrated in Paris.

The bailiwick of Senlis, from which the example examined above was taken, is of special interest because we have found no fewer than 123 acts from there regarding the detention of Templars beginning in June/July 1310.[8] This is a unique case. The acts are essentially receipts through which the person responsible for guarding a group of Templars acknowledges receiving the sums necessary to guard and keep them from Renier de Creil, the commissioner in charge of the Templar goods in the bailiwick of Senlis. In addition to these receipts, eight other acts provide different, but just as interesting, information. There is a receipt for work carried out in the Senlis house where twelve Templars

Table 12 Detention sites in the bailiwick of Senlis (1310–12)

Site	Guards	Number	Reconciled (R) or not reconciled (NR)
Abbey of Auchy (Villers-Saint-Paul)	Guillaume de Glatigny	12	(R)
Asnières-sur-Oise	Guiard d'Asnières	8	(R)
Beauvais	Daniel Grant	12	(NR)
Crépy	Pierre de la Cloche	10	(R)
Luzarches	Nicolas d'Évreux	10	(R)
Montmélian	Guillot de Senlis Simon de St-Pierreavy	11	(NR)
Plailly	Pierre de Plailly	16 (11)	(NR)
Pont (Compiègne)	Pierre Proventel	9	(NR)
In Senlis: residence of Jean Le Gagneur	Michel Gosselin Colin Alart	12	(R)
residence of Pierre de la Cloche	Pierre de la Cloche	10	(NR)
Thiers-sur-Thève	Jean Le Sarnoizier	12	(NR)

were being held,[9] three acts concerning the costs of transporting Templars going to Paris (and the return trip) to depose before the papal commission,[10] three acts involving the escape of six Templars from the Plailly residence, and the capture of one of them.[11] And an eighth act concerns the nomination, in December 1310, of Guillaume de Gisors, provost of Auge in the church of Lisieux, as curator of Temple goods in the kingdom of France alongside Guillaume Pizdoe, provost of the Paris merchants.[12]

There were eleven groups of Templars (ranging from eight to sixteen men per group) who were detained in eleven sites in ten localities in the bailiwick of Senlis (there were two in Senlis). The group of Templars originally held in Beauvais was later transferred to Senlis (to a third detention site in that city about which the documentation provides no specifics), then to Asnières, where it

joined a group that was already imprisoned there. I refer the reader to Appendix
8 for a complete table of the detention sites and the Templars being held in them.
But for the purposes of what follows, the data are summed up here in Table 12.

Of 122 Templars held in the bailiwick of Senlis, 117 are identified; the Plailly
group, with 16 men in July 1310, was reduced to 11 in the following month owing
to the escape of 5 of them. We have only some of the monthly receipts between
July and the end of 1311, even 1312, but this does not suggest that the Templars'
presence was discontinuous; documents are missing, and we may safely assume
that there was a continuity in detention from July 1310, interrupted only by the
transporting to Paris, during a period of around two weeks, of the reconciled
Templars who were to depose before the papal commission. Here, too, documents enable us to see how that unfolded.

The imprisoned Templars were either reconciled (52 of them) or non-reconciled (70, including the 5 escapees). The former had recognised the errors and
crimes attributed to the Templars at one point or another during the proceedings, before a diocesan commission or during the judgement by the Councils of
Sens or Reims: this is the case of the Templars imprisoned in Crépy, all of whom
were reconciled at the Council of Reims.[13] The more numerous Templars who
were not reconciled either denied the accusations made against the Order before
the diocesan commissions (unless they had not yet appeared before them, which
is possible) or later recanted their confessions. Reconciled or not reconciled,
all but one[14] of the identified brothers (117) were present in February/March
before the papal commission, 108 as defenders of the Order, 8 as non-defenders.
None appears among the 44 Templars who on 19 May publicly refused to defend
the Temple. None of the 65 non-reconciled Templars who have been identified
was subsequently interrogated during the second phase of the papal commission's work. As for those who were reconciled, 38 out of 52 made depositions
before the commission beginning on 17 December 1310; their depositions show
they were being careful not to risk contradicting what they had stated before the
bishops.

These facts and figures clearly show the magnitude and persistence of the
Templars' resistance well after the actions taken by the archbishop of Sens and
his colleague in Reims. Those resisters, we must repeat, knew perfectly well that
they would be sentenced to a lifelong 'wall', meaning life in prison. This sheds
new light on the conclusions usually drawn by historians who look only at the
'confessions' of the interrogated Templars.

The conditions of detention

The costs associated with the detention of the Templars were given in detail on the receipts. Each month Renier de Creil paid a sum to those who were assigned to guard a group. It was divided into three types of expenses:

- the administration and maintenance/food of the detained Templars. There were also extra sums, paid in three instalments – on All Saints' Day, Brandons (February) and 1 August – which were for clothing, linen and necessary household objects, which were usually accounted for on separate receipts;
- the salaries of the guards and their valets;
- fees for the priest responsible for the spiritual health of only the reconciled Templars.

The money to be paid was taken from the revenue earned off the Temple property, which in the bailiwick of Senlis was managed by Renier de Creil.

The sum allocated for the daily needs of the Templars was 12 or 16 *deniers parisis* per day per Templar. Let's recall the memorandum presented on Saturday 4 April 1310 by the brothers imprisoned in Paris in the residence of the abbot of Tiron: they complained of the insufficiency of the 'wages' of 12 *deniers* per day that they received to pay their living expenses.[15] The Templars held in Villers-Saint-Paul, Asnières, Crépy, Luzarches and the residence of Jean Le Gagneur in Senlis received 16 *deniers* per day, the others 12, although we are unable to explain that difference. Clothing and household items were provided on three occasions. The receipt of 16 February 1311 involving the Templars of Senlis provides a few bits of information: the two guards, Michel Gosselin and Colin Alart, were to receive annually in three instalments a sum of 60 *sous tournois* (or 48 *sous parisis*) for a knight or priest brother, and 40 *sous tournois* (or 32 *sous parisis*) for a sergeant brother.[16] It was from these sums that clothing was provided, but the practical details varied. In March 1311, for the period of Brandons, the Templars of Villers-Saint-Paul received 6 *livres*, 18 *sous*, 8 *deniers parisis*, which broke down to 10 *sous* 8 *deniers* for each of the ten sergeants and 16 *sous* for the two priests; for all three periods the sum amounted to 20 *livres* 16 *sous*, which indeed corresponds to 32 *sous* per year for each sergeant and 48 *sous* for a priest.[17] But often the amount of money involved is not indicated, despite the inclusion of details of the goods supplied; I will give an example below.

In all, seventeen receipts concern such supplies, and there is at least one for each of the eleven groups of Templars. Sometimes we find an additional detail: in Beauvais, 32 *sous parisis* were allotted for the 'making of twelve sets of robes';[18] in Luzarches the prisoners' guard received 4 *sous* for 'carrying' the robes and stockings from Senlis to Luzarches.[19]

A receipt dated March 1311 from Pierre de Plailly, who guarded eleven Templars, describes in minute detail the clothing provided to the Templars in each of the three above-mentioned periods: eleven sets of robes, overcoats and hoods lined with white lambskin, except one overcoat, one hood and two sets of sleeves that were lined in black; twenty headpieces, one hat; eleven buckskin breeches, twenty-two sets of long robes; eleven pairs of hose; and eleven pairs of cordovan boots that all went up to the knee, except for two pairs.[20] We find some or all of these same articles in other receipts. What is noteworthy is that there is no mention, among this clothing, of mantles, the habit that was such an important element of the Templar identity. Clearly the Templars' jailers, in their manual of duties, were not obliged to provide or maintain the Templars' habits.

The budget allotted for the hiring of priests is small. A priest came to the prisons three times a week to celebrate services for the reconciled Templars. His salary was 6 *sous* per month, except in Villers-Saint-Paul, where it was 8 *sous*. In Crépy a lump sum of 32 *sous* was paid in December for a period that perhaps corresponded to the five preceding months.[21] The non-reconciled Templars were denied spiritual guidance except when they were dying. This was an additional pressure on them, which highlights the courage and commitment they showed in defending their Order.

The third category of costs involved those associated with the guarding of the prisoners. The number of detainees varied from eight to twelve; in Plailly there must originally have been sixteen, but, given the five escapees, there would only have been eleven. In eight sites out of eleven there was one guard assisted by a valet; there were two valets in Montmélian and three in Plailly; in Senlis two guards, each assisted by a valet, guarded twelve Templars. The detention sites were castles, both royal and private: the (bishop's) tower of Beauvais; the castles of Saint-Aubin de Crépy, la Mote de Luzarches, Montmélian, Pont in Compiègne and Thiers sur Thève (belonging to the bishop of Beauvais); an abbey (Auchy in Villers-Saint-Paul); private residences, those of Guiard d'Asnières, Pierre de Plailly, the late Jean Le Gagneur and Pierre de la Cloche. The latter was responsible for two detention sites: his residence in Senlis and the Saint-Aubin castle in

Crépy. Almost all these guards served the king: four valets (Guiard d'Asnières, Daniel Grant, Pierre de la Cloche and Pierre Proventel); three cavalry sergeants from Châtelet in Paris (Nicolas d'Évreux, Guillot de Senlis and Jean Le Sarnoizier); and a royal knight, Pierre de Plailly. We don't know the titles – if they had any – of Guillaume de Glatigny in Villers-Saint-Paul or Michel Gosselin and Colin Alart (or de Gisors) in Senlis.

Perhaps it was because he was responsible for guarding two prisons that Pierre de la Cloche was assisted by three valets. For Pierre de Plailly, who was in the same situation, the reason was perhaps different: service to the king probably took up more time for a royal knight than for a valet, and it is quite possible that he was forced to be absent more often. It is probably for the same reason that Jeannot de Bertranfosse represented him before the tax collector and the royal authorities in Senlis to receive his income in October 1311.[22]

The group of twelve Templars held in Beauvais from at least September 1310 was reduced to eleven after April 1311, and was then transferred to an unspecified location in Senlis between June and October 1311, under the guard of Daniel Grant. Another transfer occurred before April 1312: the eleven Templars then found themselves in Asnières, under the guard of Guiard d'Asnières.[23]

Two figures – 122 and 117 – are given for the number of Templars in Senlis at the beginning of their detention in the second half of 1310. Their numbers then begin to decrease: by one for the group of Beauvais (and then Senlis and Asnières: Henri de Brabant),[24] by one in Senlis (not identified)[25] and by two in Luzarches (Pierre de Saint-Just and Jean Gambier).[26] The Plailly group, initially reduced by the escape of five Templars, lost two more before March 1312 (Gossuin de Bruges and Thomas de Ville Savoir).[27] The group from Asnières, with eight men at the beginning, lost one in February 1311 (Hugues d'Ailly) and three in October (Gilles d'Oisemont, Pierre de Saint-Leu and Nicolas Le Monnier);[28] it would then increase with the Templars who were transferred from Beauvais. However, in Thiers a twelfth prisoner, Renier de Ploisy, from Soissons, joined the initial eleven in October 1311.[29] Do we know what happened to those Templars who disappeared from the lists? There is no further trace of Henri de Brabant or Pierre de Saint-Leu. Hugues d'Ailly, mentioned for the last time in Senlis in February 1311, was said to be dead by Pierre de Sainte-Maxence, interrogated on 1 March 1311.[30] Gilles d'Oisemont, curate from Oisemont, was none other than Gilles de Rotangi, a priest brother from the diocese of Amiens mentioned many times during the interrogations; he appeared before the papal

commission on 26 and 27 January 1311 and was summoned before it again on
30 March.[31] He is thus mentioned for the last time in June 1311, just like Pierre
de Saint-Leu, who did not appear before the commission. Nicolas Le Monnier
could be the same man as Nicolas de Méanvoy, from the diocese of Amiens,
who was also in Paris on 26 January and interrogated by the commissioners on
1 February.[32] Jean Gambier and Pierre de Saint-Just swore an oath before the
commission on 26 January 1311 and were respectively interrogated on the 29th
and 30th.[33] None of this tells us anything about their fate after the final mention
given in the documents from Senlis.

Escape from Plailly

We don't know exactly what measures and precautions were taken in guarding
the Templars being held in the prisons of the bailiwick of Senlis. They don't
seem to have been chained up, a precaution that was taken during their movements and transfers. Guarding them was probably easier and stricter in the
castles than in the residences of individuals such as Pierre de la Cloche in Senlis
or Crépy, or that of Pierre de Plailly. In any event, the only escape mentioned in
the documentation is from Plailly.

Pierre de Plailly was assigned the guard of sixteen Templars in July 1310 – he
was paid to guard them and for their maintenance in July and August[34] – but later
there were only eleven. An escape occurred during that period of July / August,
and we know that one of the escapees was Philippe de Tréfons (or Treffon).
The abbot of the monastery of Saint-Éloi of Noyon, in a letter dated 22 December 1310, informs us that at the request of an equerry, whose name he does not
recall, Philippe de Tréfons had been arrested in the grounds of the abbey by its
sergeants on 1 September; he had been held in the abbey prison from that date
until 6 December. The abbot adds in his letter that this Templar had escaped
with several of his companions from the prison of 'the noble man lord Pierre
de Plailly, knight'.[35] Plailly thus resumed guarding only one of the escapees,
and only after 6 December. But in the invoices for September 1310 submitted by
Pierre de Plailly, there is mention of eleven Templars, among whom appears,
when the names are given, Philippe de Tréfons.[36] So there must have been six
escapees, only one of whom was captured.

But Pierre de Plailly wanted to receive the sums anticipated for the maintenance and administration of the eleven Templars, including Philippe de Tréfons,

from September 1310 to October 1311: knowing the fugitive had been recaptured and imprisoned among the monks of Noyon, he anticipated his return to Plailly. The tax collector of Senlis did not see it that way and refused to pay him what he requested. Pierre complained to Philippe de Voët and Jean de Janville, who are described in these documents as royal sergeants at arms, and who, as we know because we've encountered them in that function many times, were responsible for the guard of all the Templars in the north of the kingdom. They decided in favour of Pierre de Plailly and, on 7 November 1310, ordered Renier de Creil to pay him in the usual way both for the Templars that he was holding and for 'those that you know he will recover'.[37] The order must have been carried out since, on 23 November 1310, Pierre received the sum of 4 *livres* 12 *sous parisis* 'for the costs of a Templar who escaped from the prison of Plailly and was captured the first day of September'. This sum was for the period of 1 September to 1 December, or ninety-two days, which corresponded to the daily maintenance of 12 *deniers* per day (1 *sou*) of a Templar held in Plailly.[38]

From what we have learned, the other Templars who escaped were never caught. The group was reduced to nine in March 1312, the date of the last receipt known to involve the group:[39] Gossuin de Bruges and Thomas de Ville Savoir are not on it, and while nothing suggests that they escaped or died, the latter seems the likeliest explanation.

The overall cost of the Templars' imprisonment

To conclude with the detention of the Templars in the bailiwick of Senlis, I would like to look briefly at the overall costs of that incarceration. Table 13 provides a summary of data from the three categories of monthly receipts: the administration and maintenance of the detainees; the wages of the guards; and the salary of a priest when his services were required – that is, for the reconciled Templars.

Although we don't possess all the receipts for the eighteen-month period from July 1310 to December 1311, we do know that the detention was continuous. Therefore, it is worth presenting a calculation of costs that spans twelve months. The daily cost of maintaining the detainees was either 12 *deniers parisis* per day (1 *sou*) (A) or 16 *deniers* (B); the daily wages for the Templars' guards were 3 *sous* per day for the main guard and 1 *sou* per day for a valet. This opens up into four categories: (C) – 4 *sous* per day (one valet); (D) – 5 *sous* per day

Table 13 The costs of detaining the Templars in the bailiwick of Senlis

Site	Maintenance	Guard	Priest
Auchy (Villers-Saint-Paul)	B 292 *l*.	D 89 *l*. 15 *s*.	H 4 *l*. 16 *s*.
Asnières	A 146 *l*.	C 73 *l*. 16 *s*.	G 3 *l*. 12 *s*.
Beauvais	A 219 *l*.	C 73 *l*. 16 *s*.	–
Crépy	B 243 *l*. 6 *s*. 8 *d*.	C 73 *l*. 16 *s*.	G 3 *l*. 12 *s*.
Luzarches	B 243 *l*. 6 *s*. 8 *d*.	C 73 *l*. 16 *s*.	G 3 *l*. 12 *s*.
Montmélian	A 200 *l*. 15 *s*.	C 73 *l*. 16 *s*. D 89 *l*. 15 *s*.	–
Plailly	A 200 *l*. 15 *s*.	E 109 *l*. 10 *s*.	–
Pont (Compiègne)	A 164 *l*. 15 *s*.	C 73 *l*. 16 *s*.	–
Senlis 1	B 292 *l*.	F 146 *l*. 8 *s*.	G 3 *l*. 12 *s*.
Senlis 2	A 146 *l*.	C 73 *l*. 16 *s*.	–
Thiers-sur-Thève	A 200 *l*. 15 *s*.	C 73 *l*. 16 *s*.	–
Total	*2348 l. 2 s. 8 d.*	*936 l. 1 s.* *or 952 l.*	*191 l. 4 s.*

(two valets); (E) – 6 *sous* per day (three valets); (F) – 8 *sous* per day (two guards and two valets). Finally, for the salaries of the priest we have either 6 *sous* per month (G) or 8 *sous* (H).

For each prison I have noted the number of Templars being guarded at the beginning, without taking into account the few disappearances noted during the period, except for Plailly, where I have retained the number of eleven Templars (after the escape). The only uncertainty comes from the calculation of the wages in Montmélian, where the receipts of July and September 1310 suggest only one valet, while those of November 1310 to March 1311 suggest two. I didn't attempt to give an average and decided to present two accounts for this house, one calculated on a single valet (C numbers) and the other calculated on two (D numbers).

And so for one year we arrive at a total of 3,303 *livres 6 sous 8 deniers parisis* (or 3,319 *livres* 6 *sous* 8 *deniers*), 30.6 per cent of which was for the wages of the royal agents and their valets. This sum was for 117 Templars and was paid with no particular difficulty out of the sequestered Templar property in the bailiwick. It was spent on the maintenance and daily expenses of each Templar for one year: 18 *livres* 5 *sous parisis* (at 12 *deniers*/day) or 24 *livres* 6 *sous* 8 *deniers* (at 16 *deniers*/day); to these sums had to be added the costs of clothing and household items, as well as the cost of their guard, which cannot be calculated for each Templar because it was not proportional to their numbers (the 30 per cent I indicated above is only for purposes of an overview of the whole). The annual cost of guarding a thousand Templars might thus be calculated at a number somewhere between a minimum of 18,250 *livres parisis* and a maximum of 24,333 *livres* 6 *sous* 8 *deniers*. We can double this figure (to two thousand imprisoned Templars) and increase it by around 35 per cent (clothing, priests, guards' wages). This can't have been too much of a burden on royal finances; at most it would have been a sum to recoup from the revenue earned from the sequestered Temple property.

13

THE SECOND PHASE OF INTERROGATIONS

(Paris, 1311)

Work resumes: 17 December 1310

On 30 May 1310 the papal commission had adjourned until 3 November. On that day the 'quorum' necessary for the commission to meet legitimately had not been reached: there were indeed three commissioners, but there was only one bishop. The meeting was postponed until 17 December. On that date the requisite number of members were present; also in attendance were two Templar spokesmen, Guillaume de Chambonnet and Bertrand de Sartiges, who, in the definitive absence of Pierre de Bologne and Renaud de Provins, abandoned their mission and left. A group of twelve Templars then arrived, and each of them swore an oath. That is when the commissioners decided to change their meeting venue and leave the abbey of Sainte-Geneviève, moving to the house of the Serpente, owned by the abbey of Fécamp in the parish of Saint-André-des-Arts. Once settled in their new location, they read two letters from Jean de Montlaur, the archdeacon of Maguelonne, who sent his excuses for his absence, as illness had kept him in Montpellier; they then opened the session.[1] It was only the following day, 18 December, that they interrogated the first witness, Jean de Thara, a native of the diocese of Beauvais, following the 127 articles of accusation in the questionnaire established in Poitiers in 1308.

From that day on the commission met continuously until 26 May 1311. During those five months 210 Templars appeared and swore an oath; one of them, Jean Picard, was not interrogated,[2] but two Templars who were not part of a group were: Lambert de Cormeilles, from the diocese of Paris, on 23 January, and Humbaud de la Boyssade, on 20 March.[3] And so from that period we have the depositions of 211 brothers, as well as three non-Templars.[4] All the arguments that follow are based on this homogeneous corpus of depositions.[5] Of particular interest are:

- those who had already appeared in 1307: there were thirty-five who had appeared before the inquisitors in Paris in October and November 1307 (see Appendix 7);
- those who had been present, most often as defenders of the Order, in February/March 1310: there were eighty-seven of these, seventy of whom were defenders of the Order, nine who said 'yes, but …,' seven non-defenders and one, Barthélemy de Troyes, who was uncertain;[6]
- those who, among those latter, withdrew their defence of the Order on 19 May: there were thirty-one of these.

Thus most of those who were interrogated in 1311 did not wish (or, let's be cautious, were unable) to defend the Order. It is important to note, however, that a large number of Templars who had appeared to defend the Order decided not to, though without announcing their decision publicly on 19 May; Pierre de Bologne and Renaud de Provins were perhaps among these men; Rainard de Bort from Auvergne too, as we will see.

The diocesan procedure in the bishopric of Clermont in June 1309 provides additional details.[7] Let's recall that, out of the sixty-nine Templars interrogated by the bishop, forty had confessed and twenty-nine had denied the charges; these twenty-nine, as well as three 'confessors', had come to Paris on 7 February to defend the Order.[8] None of these thirty-two brothers appeared in 1311, except Rainard de Bort, who was interrogated on 2 April.[9] However, twenty of the forty Templars from Clermont who had confessed (and the thirty-seven who had not come in February 1310 to defend the Order) came in two groups of ten. They were held in Riom. The first group appeared before the commission to swear an oath on 29 March, the second on 19 May.[10] Rainard de Bort appeared on 1 April with eight other Templars who had come from various other dioceses, and he was interrogated the following day. These Templars were absolved and reconciled with the Church as individuals; they had not yet been judged and sanctioned; except for potential questioning of the confessions they had made in Clermont, they risked nothing. Why did only twenty come? On what basis was the choice of whether or not to go to Paris to testify made? Was it voluntary? A sorting by the royal or episcopal authorities? There is no way to know. The papal commission had perhaps intervened, as is suggested by the example of the Templars who came from the diocese of Saintes, which we will examine shortly. After having been overwhelmed by the number of defenders of the Order in 1310, did the commission not want to deal with the same situation in 1311, and perhaps fix a quota on its own? We can't answer this question.

But was a choice actually made? The 211 Templars interrogated indicated that they had been absolved and reconciled with the Church by a bishop: eighty-five had been reconciled by the bishops of the province of Sens, forty-seven by those of the province of Reims, and forty-four by bishops of the province of Bourges; then came Bordeaux, with twenty-one, Lyon with two and Narbonne with one. The two provinces where there had been councils and burnings at the stake – Sens and Reims – provided close to two-thirds of the witnesses in 1311. This was not by chance, since the commissioners summoned first of all Templars who were located closest to them, and who were the most submissive or resigned. This is a hypothesis supported, it seems, by the following examination of the conditions in which the Templars were brought to Paris in order to respond to the commissioners' questions.

In carts on the roads of France

The records indicate the arrival of groups of Templars at almost regular intervals; they appeared collectively before the commission to swear an oath before being interrogated individually in the days that followed. All of this can be found in Appendix 9. There were thirty-one groups, of between one and twenty Templars, that arrived during the five months of 1311. No information is given about where the Templars in these groups set off from, except in the case of the brothers who came from the diocese of Saintes: on 7 May 1311 there were seven of them, who were 'sent upon the request of the said lord commissioners by Guy [de Neuville], bishop of Saintes'. The bishop had sent a letter, the contents of which are included in the record.[11]

The letter is dated the Sunday after the Octave of Easter, or 25 April, and it is a response to the request of the commissioners, whose letter reached the bishop on the Friday. The bishop says he sent seven Templars out of the nine 'who, by special mandate of our Holy Father, we are holding'. Brother Hugues, commander of Civrac (this was Hugues Raynaud[12]), and brother Pierre Auriol would in fact not be travelling because they were too ill and incapacitated, as was confirmed by two royal sergeants who had seen them in prison. The seven left in the days that followed 25 April and appeared before the commission on 7 May; that same day the first of them, Guillaume de Soromina (or Sorolme), was interrogated; two others, Guillaume Audebon and Hugues de Narsac, were questioned the following day; on Monday 10 May it was the turn of Hélie *Costati*, Géraud de Mursac and Pierre de Nobiliac; finally, Pierre Lavergne gave his deposition on Tuesday the 11th.[13] And then six more Templars arrived to swear an oath. It is a safe assumption that the seven Templars were taken back to Saintes shortly after 11 May. Their return journey and stay lasted about four weeks.

Other depositions give some information of the same kind but are less specific. Six brothers came from La Rochelle, also in the diocese of Saintes: at the end of his deposition the commissioners asked Hélie Raynaud if he 'agreed with the five preceding witnesses, who were brought from La Rochelle together'.[14] Those six Templars arrived on 8 March and were interrogated that day and on 9 March; Guillaume de Légé (du Liège), in his eighties, acknowledged the errors, but the five others denied them; they were nonetheless absolved and reconciled by the bishop of Saintes and refused to defend the Order.

It is through documentation outside the official trial records that we obtain the most concrete information about the comings and goings of the Templars between their prisons and Paris.[15] Let's now look again at the bailiwick of Senlis: two accounting documents detail the costs associated with the transporting of three Templars taken from Senlis to Paris to appear before the commission.[16]

Pierre de Sainte-Maxence, Gérard de Monacheville (Moineville) and Guillaume de Lafons (or Fonte, or Clefons), three reconciled Templars, had been held in Senlis in the residence of Jean Le Gagneur since at least the month of September 1310 (see Appendix 8). On Wednesday 17 February 1311, the Wednesday before Shrovetide (from Sunday 21 to Shrove Tuesday 23 February), their two guards, Colin de Gisors (this was Colin Alart) and Michelet (Michel Gosselin), were ordered by Jean de Janville, royal sergeant in arms, and one of the two men (the other was Philippe de Voët) responsible for guarding the Templars in the north of the kingdom, to bring these three Templars to Paris under secure escort so they could testify before the papal commission. They were to arrive in Paris at the latest by the Friday after Shrovetide, or 26 February. A second act containing the expenses incurred for this return journey indicates that Colin

Alart, Michel Gosselin and their prisoners left on the Thursday after the Feast Day of Saint Mark the apostle (which is scarcely plausible since the Feast of Saint Mark is 25 April). According to the expense report for this trip, to which I will return, the journey occurred on Thursday and our Templars were thus in Paris on Friday the 26th. They were held in the residence of the bishop of Laon, located next to the church of the Cordeliers (Franciscans or Minor brothers). On Saturday 27 February they swore an oath before the commissioners, who since 29 January had been meeting at the house of the Minor brothers:[17] they 'swore on the holy Gospels to tell the whole and complete truth following the form of the oath practised earlier by the other brothers after they had been told of it in the vernacular'.[18]

The commission did not meet on Sunday. On Monday 1 March, Guillaume de Lafons (Fonte) and Pierre de Saint-Maxence were interrogated; Gérard de Monacheville gave his deposition the following day.[19] They were very careful to say that they did not intend to recant the depositions they had given before the bishop of Soissons (Guillaume and Gérard) or the archbishop of Reims (Pierre).[20] None of them was wearing the mantle of the Order, and they had shaved their beards. They had not participated in the defence of the Order in 1310. The documents provide some concrete information about their trip. They were in chains and transported in a cart; there was a blacksmith with them. Two sergeants on horseback joined Colin Alart and Michel Gosselin, as did valets to take care of the horses. The costs and wages were divided into two categories: those associated with the return journey and those for the stay in Paris. For the journey the renting of chains and a cart, and the wages of the sergeants on horseback and the valets, as well as the maintenance of the horses were accounted for. The stay in Paris was calculated over eight days (eight days' lodging), and it included the wages of a valet assigned specifically to take the Templars to the commissioners and to bring them back. For this 94 *sous* 10 *deniers parisis* were spent; a sum of 105 *sous parisis* in addition was allocated to Colin Alart and Michel Gosselin 'for the expenses that they had in addition to their wages, going and coming, and all that they spent'. In all, the trip cost 199 *sous* 10 *deniers*, or 9 *livres* 19 *sous* 10 *deniers*.

Among the expenses incurred during this trip, there was an additional sum of 4 *sous parisis* noted for the renting of a horse used to transfer another Templar, Guy de Belleville, from Senlis to Villers-Saint-Paul, to the residence of the abbot of Auchy, and to bring back two other brothers, Jean de Bollencourt and

Hugues d'Ailly, respectively held in Villers-Saint-Paul and Asnières-sur-Oise. The transfer of the first must have been done on the outward journey, that of the two others on the return: perhaps from Paris, since Jean de Bollencourt had been interrogated there on 28 January.[21]

At the beginning of March, Michel Gosselin submitted an invoice for a sum of 109 *sous parisis* 'for taking and bringing back three Templars from Senlis to Paris, and from Paris to Senlis, and for the time that they spent [in Paris] to be examined [by the papal commission] ... by command of Jean de Janville'. This invoice was attached to Janville's letter of command.[22] The sum of 109 *sous* indeed corresponds to the 105 for additional wages, increased by the 4 allocated for the renting of an additional horse.

We have two other documents relating to the Templars who were guarded by Colin Alart and Michel Gosselin in Senlis and to their transporting to Paris.

The first dates from April 1311: Colin Alart and Michel Gosselin submitted an invoice for the sum of 37 *livres* and 10 *sous parisis* for the food and guarding, in March (thirty-one days), of twelve Templars, 'of which there were seven in Paris at the home of Hue d'Oisemont to whom were sent wages each month'.[23] Among the Templars that Colin and Michel guarded in Senlis we find, in addition to the three brothers just mentioned, six other brothers who were indeed in Paris, but on 26 January, and who were interrogated over the following days: Foulques de Neuilly on 31 January, Adelin de Lignières and Nicolas de Méannay on 1 February, Thomas de Boncourt and Jean de Grèz on 2 February, and Hugues d'Oisemont on 4 February.[24] These six Templars who came from Senlis on 26 January were accompanied by two others who were being held in Luzarche: Jean Le Gambier, interrogated on 29 January, and Pierre de Saint-Just, interrogated on 30 January.[25] The invoice of April was indeed for the thirty-one days of the month of March; did that mean they were still in Paris in March? This is difficult to say, especially since another act refers to January 1311, but the beginning of it is partially destroyed, and there is a figure indicating four Templars that does not correspond to the contents of the act that refers to seven Templars.[26]

Let's look at the second document.

Colin Alart and Michel Gosselin took four Templars back and forth from Senlis to Paris. They were paid for three days of return travel at the rate of 8 *sous* per day, or 24 *sous*; we must then account for the cost of renting two horses that two Templars rode on both journeys, two valets, and the expenses related to the horses, and two men on horseback leading the two Templars, again for three days. The Templars stayed in Paris twelve days, and a valet had to be hired to assist their guards, and sums paid for 'the board and three beds for the twelve days they were examined by the prelates'.

And that was not all; the act continues, mentioning 'the return of V [five] Templars from Paris to Senlis' in a cart over two days 'return'; and added to other rental costs were the wages of a 'blacksmith' hired for the two carts, and two men on horseback to lead them. This accounting indeed corresponds to the 'transporting' of seven Templars at the end of January: two Templars made the trip on horseback, five in a cart. Their stay in Paris lasted twelve days; they appeared before the commission on 26 January and the first of them was interrogated on 30 January, the last on 4 February. Except that seven isn't four and, out of the seven, only six were interrogated. These are small, irritating problems that prevent us from making full use of these documents.

However, let's not lose sight of what is important: these texts open a window onto the conditions of the Templars' movements from their places of detention to Paris, and onto the entirety of their stay in the kingdom's capital. There is every reason to believe that what was true for the Templars of Senlis was true in the rest of the kingdom. It is still a shame that we don't have similar documents for the transfer of brothers from Saintes or from a detention site that was even further from Paris.

The interrogations: against a backdrop of relapse

I will not undertake a case-by-case analysis of the interrogations of this period. The Templars arrived in small groups, swore an oath and in the days that followed were interrogated individually, following the 127 articles of accusation. I refer the reader to the comprehensive table in Appendix 9. Nor will I compare the depositions of the Templars given before the papal commission with those they may have given earlier. An excellent analysis has already been done by Anne-Marie Chagny-Sève for the twenty-one Templars from the diocese of Clermont interrogated in 1309 and 1311.[27] She has revealed differences in chronology, omissions and new details that have come to light. However, we should not attribute too much importance to these variations among the testimony, which was oriented in large part by the questions and the curiosity of the judges: what those of 1307 or 1309 wanted was not the same as what the papal commissioners hoped to obtain in 1311.

The commission proceeded meticulously, asking more and more questions in order to get the witnesses to describe the exact conditions in which their reception into the Order took place, the ritual that was followed and any possible errors; in every case, it was a matter of determining the nature, heretical or not, of the reception ceremony. The records are long, especially at the beginning, the apogee being the deposition of Gérard de Causse, which runs to fifteen pages, whereas his interrogation of 1307 took only one page.[28] Of the fifteen pages ten are devoted to the first four of the 127 articles, which primarily involved the renunciation of Christ, which, let's recall, had been considered the manifest proof of the Templars' heresy by the king and his collaborators since 1307. The commissioners' insistence on this point was not meant to 'entrap' the Templars; rather, without questioning individual errors, they hoped to absolve the Order of the accusation of heresy.

The Templars who arrived at this time knew what had happened to some of their brothers at the councils of Sens and Reims. The panicky fear expressed by Aimeri de Villiers-le-Duc on 13 May 1310, the day after the burning of the fifty-four brothers, became a perhaps less out-of-control fear, but it was still just as manifest in those who testified starting in December. The Templars had understood well what it meant to be relapsed: they should above all not recant previous confessions, and above all not alter their testimony. The seven Templars who swore an oath on 11 January specified 'that in no way did they intend to recant the confessions they had made before their ordinaries [the bishops] but that they intended to persevere in their confessions'.[29] Seven others, who swore an oath on 27 January, promised to tell the full and complete truth, but they protested, before swearing, that if 'because of their simplicity, they said something that contradicted the depositions made by them earlier, that shouldn't be held against them because they said they wanted to stay with the depositions they had given and not go back on them'.[30] This was duly noted by the commissioners; moreover, they assured the Templars that the contents of their depositions would not be divulged for the duration of the procedure, and that they could speak in complete confidence and security.

The great majority of Templars thus sought guarantees, and they repeated, often *a minima*, their earlier confessions made before the diocesan commission before which they had appeared (it is through their testimony, as I said, that the meetings of a large number of these commissions are known). The deposition of Mathieu de Cressonessart, who appeared for a time as one of the Templar spokesmen alongside Pierre de Bologne and other defenders of the Order, provides a significant example of this. He is the object of a thorough study by Sean L. Field, the essential part of which I will now look at, while adding some details to it.[31]

Originally from Cressonsacq in the diocese of Beauvais,[32] Mathieu was born around 1275 and was received into the Temple of Paris, as a sergeant, in 1294. At the time of his arrest in 1307 he was commander of the house of Bellinval in Ponthieu.[33] He was perhaps related to the family of the minor nobility of Cressonessart, holders of the seigneury of the same name, and also to Guiard de Cressonessart, sentenced to life imprisonment on 31 May 1310 for having supported Marguerite Porète, who was condemned for heresy and burned on 31 May.[34] Mathieu was imprisoned in the diocese of Amiens, in any case in a suffragan diocese of the province of Reims. It was there that he was questioned by a diocesan commission, during which he seems to have acknowledged all or some of the accusations brought against the Temple. He was transferred to Crèvecoeur-en-Brie, in the diocese of Meaux, some time before February 1310: he was taken from there to Paris on 17 February with seventeen other brothers to appear before the papal commission as defenders of the Order. He was held with ten other members of this group in the residence of Leuragié, or of la Rabiose, located on rue de Chaume, a street located within the boundaries of the Villeneuve of the Temple and parallel to the rue du Temple, outside the Wall of Philip Augustus.[35] In this new quarter there was also the residence of Richard des Poulies, in the street of the same name, which housed another group of Templars. Mathieu participated actively in the defence of the Temple since he was one of the three representatives of the detainees in the residence of Leuragié who read a memorandum to defend the Order on 3 April 1310,[36] and on 7 April he was one of the five other spokesmen cited who, along with the four 'permanents', if I may call them that – Pierre de Bologne, Renaud de Provins, Guillaume de Chambonnet and Bertrand de Sartiges – presented a memorandum on behalf of all the Templars present in Paris.[37]

However, Mathieu ultimately decided not to defend the Order: present at the council of the province of Reims in Senlis in May 1310, he was absolved there and reconciled with the Church, a sign that he had returned to his previous declarations. From Senlis (the papal commission having suspended its work at the end of May 1310), he was taken to Crépy-en-Valois: he was imprisoned with seven other reconciled Templars in the castle of Saint-Aubin under the guard of Pierre de la Cloche, royal valet. Several invoices attest to his presence from August 1310 until at least April 1311 (see Appendix 8). He was taken from Crépy to Paris on 8 February 1311 to be interrogated there by the papal commissioners on the 12th; it is the deposition from this interrogation that Sean L. Field analyses in detail.[38] He then returned to Crépy, where his presence was recorded for the last time in April 1311. He was probably liberated after the end of the Council of Vienne, as were most of the reconciled Templars, but we don't know what became of him.

All the same, the commissioners, even if their convictions were now well established, were perhaps not completely satisfied with those stereotypical confessions, as they knew perfectly well how they were obtained. This is seen in the way in which they conducted themselves with Jean de Boilhencourt (or de Pollencourt, or de Polhencourt), of the diocese of Noyon, interrogated on 9 January.[39] He was born around 1281 and was received into the Order in 1301 in the house of La Ronzière.[40] He confessed and was reconciled by the bishop of Amiens; 'he said and insisted several times that he wanted to retain the confession he had first made before the bishop of Amiens and his predecessor and that he had then confessed to having denied Christ during his reception.' As noted in the record, he was very upset and pale; the commissioners urged him to stick to the truth to save his soul, and not to the earlier confession, unless 'that was the truth', and they assured him that he risked nothing and that his testimony would not be revealed. And so Jean de Boilhencourt buckled and recanted his declarations: he had not renounced Christ, hadn't spat on the cross and so on. He had confessed before the inquisitors out of fear of death and because Gilles de Rotangi, the priest brother with whom he was imprisoned in Montreuil-sur-Mer, had said that they would die if they did not acknowledge the errors of which the Templars were accused. He later confessed his false confession before a Minor brother since he was unable to do so before the bishop of Amiens. The brother had absolved him and had advised him not to make any more false confessions.

There was quite a scene on 12 January: brother Jean de Boilhencourt appeared again before the commissioners and recanted his denials. He had lied; he had indeed denied Christ, had indeed spat on the cross. The commissioners were perplexed: had he spoken of his earlier deposition to anyone? Had he been bribed? No, and he repeated his confession, even adding that he had heard, after his arrest, that the Templars worshipped a cat.[41] The commissioners had done nothing to prompt this, and probably did not believe this last deposition, especially as some other Templars continued to deny, claiming torture and pressure as reasons for their previous confessions.

This was the case of Thomas de Pampelune and Pierre Thibaud, among others, who were interrogated on 9 March.[42] On 22 March, Martin de Montrichard, Jean Durand, Jean de Ruivans, just like the earlier witnesses from the province of Poitou, also rejected the accusations, but on the 24th they returned before the commission to acknowledge the renunciation of Christ and the spitting. Interrogated by the commissioners on the reasons for that reversal, they invoked their stupidity.[43] There was a face-off between the Templars who were afraid and a commission certainly concerned with maintaining a balance between the way in which it dealt with the brothers and an attempt not to appear to be prejudging the truth, while being incapable of offering sufficient reassurances to convince the Templars to speak completely freely. What did the commission attempt, what did it do to protect Renaud de Provins, Jean de Mortefontaine and Guillaume de Hoymont, three defrocked priests sentenced to life in prison by the Council of Sens, as were Renaud de Cugnières, Pierre de Clermont-en-Beauvaisis and Bernard de Sornay?[44] The commission recorded their appearance and continued with its work.

The dozen Templars who still took the risk of hesitating should not be the trees hiding the wood: the burnings of May 1310 did not just break the will of the Templars; it also weakened the commissioners' ability to carry out an investigation that had an appearance of impartiality.

The beard and the mantle

On 11 April 1310 – that is, before the meeting of the Council of Sens – twenty Templars appeared before the commission, in no particular order.[45] Jean de *Scivriaco* and Jean de *Fallegio* were wearing secular habits but said they were brothers of the Order. Jean de Juvigny and Jean de Crèvecoeur wore the mantle, or habit, of the Order.[46] Jean Thaiafer, Huguet de Bure, Geoffroy de Thatan and Jean l'Anglais de Hinquemate said they were brothers of the Order and had the Templar-style beard.[47] They were holding their mantles in their hands, and suddenly threw them violently on the ground in front of the commissioners, saying they no longer wanted to wear the habit of the Order. To this the commissioners angrily responded that they should go elsewhere if they wanted to do that, not do it in front of the commission. Finally, a group of twelve Templars arrived:

none was wearing the habit, but eleven out of the twelve had the beard – only Gérard de Passage was clean-shaven.

On the following 14 April Jean Thaiafer was interrogated: he 'was wearing clothing of grey homespun without the mantle and habit of the Order of the Temple', and he had just shaved his beard.[48] Henceforth the records of the successive interrogations carefully noted the responses to these questions: were the brothers wearing the habit or not? Had they shaved their beards or not?[49] A look at the 211 Templars interrogated from 17 December 1310 to 26 May 1311 reveals that sixty-three appeared wearing the mantle, and 144 weren't wearing it; four weren't wearing theirs because they were so worn out that they weren't wearable; however, they were sporting beards, so they should be added to the sixty-three wearing the mantle. Beards weren't always mentioned, but in general they were associated with the wearing of the habit. Only one of the sixty-three didn't have a beard: Baudouin de Gizy had to shave owing to an illness. In the case of the 144 not wearing the mantle, the absence of a beard was signalled for only sixty-five of them, but we shouldn't place too much importance on this.

The brothers gave several explanations for not wearing the habit. For twenty-four of them their habit was in tatters, and they hadn't been given another one.[50] Barthélemy de Glans sold his mantle,[51] and Henri de Faverolles, even more charitable than Saint Martin, gave his to a brother who did not have one.[52] Hugues de Faur no longer wore a mantle because it was too worn out, but he refused to shave, which meant that he still considered himself a supporter of the Order.[53]

Twenty-four brothers also mentioned the pressures (including being forced) they had had to endure to renounce the mantle: Étienne de Dijon had been stripped of his two weeks after his arrest by the sergeants of the duke of Burgundy.[54] Three took it off at the moment of their arrest under pressure from the royal provost of Château-Landon;[55] others were stripped of it by the sergeants at the prison of Sens;[56] and it was the knight who arrested Pierre de Saint-Mamert who took off his mantle.[57]

Many (fifty-two) removed their mantle – and some specified 'voluntarily' – at the Council of Sens or at the Council of Reims (twenty-eight); a few did so before a diocesan commission: Jean de Boilhencourt before the commission of Amiens (he was originally from that diocese), Othon de Châteaudun before the one in Orléans, and Hugues de Caumont, Albert de Canellis and Renaud Bergeron in Paris.[58]

The geographical locations where these acts of removal or non-removal of the mantle occurred are telling. The majority of Templars who no longer wore the habit and had shaved their beards came from the north of the kingdom. It seems clear, notably at the Councils of Sens and Reims, that they were pressured into doing so, and so too in the prisons of Sens, by, for example, royal officers. The Templars who, in contrast, were still wearing the mantle and had beards had been reconciled by the bishops in the central and southern parts of the kingdom: five in Poitiers, twelve in Saintes, nine in Tours, thirteen in Limoges, eleven in Clermont (but the second group of ten, also from Clermont, although they arrived later, had abandoned the mantle and the beard) and eight in Rodez.

Six others were reconciled by the bishop of Paris. This represents only a minority of Templars reconciled by that bishop, but it indicates the resistance of the Templars even before a bishop – Guillaume de Baufet – who, as we have seen, was not on their side.

The undeniable resistance of the Templars is not enough in itself to explain that 'geography of the beard and the habit'. The bishops' attitudes also played a role here: they demonstrated a strong character in the face of royal injunctions, because there were royal agents everywhere who put pressure on the brothers, regardless of whether they had been guards of the Templars on behalf of the Church. Jean de Janville was naturally one of them; he persuaded Renaud de Villemoison to shave after he had taken off his habit at the Council of Sens.[59]

To renounce the habit meant breaking with the Order, rejecting it. Étienne de Caumont, a Templar from Rouergue who had taken off the mantle when he appeared before the bishop of Paris, asked him if he should also shave his beard. The bishop did not say yes or no, merely replied that he should do what he wanted. Étienne explained to the commission that he had continued to wear the mantle up to then to show he was of a religion (a religious Order), but not as a sign of approval or disapproval of the Temple.[60] Albert de Canellis, interrogated on 20 January 1311, said 'that he wasn't wearing the mantle of the Order because he had taken it off voluntarily before the bishop of Paris with the intention, since he had and was holding this mantle from the Church, of giving it back to the Church'.[61] And Raymond de Vassignac, who appeared in a secular, 'non-Templar', habit, refused to defend the Order, adding 'that he wouldn't have taken off the habit of the Order if he had wanted to defend it'.[62]

The Templars were thus well aware of what the gesture meant: it signified a rupture with the Order. By contrast, wearing the habit was an act of resistance. The Templars who had come from Corbeil and from the bailiwick of Chaumont on 12 February 1310 to defend the Order repeatedly asked for their habits to be given back to them.[63] Similarly, a bit later, the Templars held in the residence of the abbot of Preuilly complained of having been stripped of their habits and asked for them to be given back to them.[64] Pierre de Bologne, on behalf of all of them, made the same request on 28 March.

They were reassured by what had been said to the Templars in Poitiers on 10 July 1308 during a meeting in the residence of Cardinal Pierre de La Chapelle after they had been absolved: the Order for the moment not being condemned, they could preserve its distinctive insignia, the mantle and the cross.[65]

Without waiting for the decision of the forthcoming council, the bishops of the province of Sens, under the direction of Philippe de Marigny, had the habits removed from the Templars whom they judged as individuals. On 5 March 1311, in condemning Renaud de Provins and two other priests of the Order, they also stripped them of the habit of the Temple.[66] In Vienne the pope suppressed 'said Order of the Temple, its rule, habit and name'.[67]

14

THE COUNCIL OF VIENNE AND THE
BURNING OF JACQUES DE MOLAY
(1311–1314)

The end of the papal investigations

On 26 May 1311 the Paris commission interrogated three more Templars: Jean de Chali, who was arrested while he was trying to escape, had been reconciled by the bishop of Mâcon; Pierre de Modies, who was also on the run when he was arrested, had also been reconciled by the bishop of Mâcon; Renaud Beaupoil, who was in Lorraine at the time of the arrests, escaped for a while and was never interrogated by a prelate. None of these three was a defender of the Temple.[1] Following their depositions, the four commissioners present, wanting to put an end to their investigation, wrote to the bishop of Bayeux, 'G.' (this was Guillaume Bonnet), who was in Avignon with the pope at the time. In fact, he was on the road to Paris to join Gilles Aycelin in Pontoise, where the parliament was to meet. Being unable to leave the sessions of the royal council, Gilles Aycelin and Guillaume Bonnet asked the four commissioners – the bishops of Mende and Limoges, Mathieu de Naples and Jean de Mantoue – to come to where they and the king were meeting in Maubuisson, near Pontoise, on 5 June to discuss the termination of the investigation.[2]

By that date the commissioners felt they had gathered sufficient 'material' from the Templars who had testified before them and the seventy-two others who had been examined by the pope in Poitiers in 1308 – sufficient and representative, because Templars who had been received in various parts of the kingdom and Outremer had appeared. Let's note, all the same, that they were representative only of the Templars who had confessed.

And so, the end of the investigations by the papal commission was decided upon on 5 June in the presence of the king, the members of the commission, Guy, Count of Saint-Pol, Guillaume de Plaisians, Geoffroy du Plessis, a papal notary, the lawyer Amisse d'Orléans and the five notaries who had assisted the commissioners throughout the proceedings. A record in two copies, constituting two original documents, was prepared; one, prepared by two notaries on parchment, was sent to the pope; the other, written out by Florimond Dondedieu (he himself specified this) over 291½ folios, and co-signed by the four other notaries, was deposited in the Treasury (the Archives, among other places) of Notre-Dame in Paris.[3]

The last Templars who were interrogated were taken back to their prisons. The many invoices available from the bailiwick of Senlis confirm the detention of the brothers until the end of 1311 – and even later, into the first months of 1312. They had only to wait for the final decisions of the Council of Vienne.

However, some Templars in the kingdom were still involved in the proceedings, notably the proceedings against individuals.[4] Let's return to Alès, in the diocese of Nîmes. We may recall that the diocesan commission there had not met until 1310, from 19 June to 14 July, and that the Templars present at the time had almost unanimously rejected the accusations brought against the Order, thereby recanting the confessions they had made in the autumn of 1307.[5] More than a year later, on 29 August 1311, Guillaume de Saint-Laurent, who was authorised by the bishop of Nîmes, Bertrand de Languissel, again summoned the Templars of the diocese to Alès; he was assisted by six other clerics: two canons, two Preaching brothers and two Minor brothers. The object of this session was to have the Templars from Nîmes return to the 'truth': that is, to the truth of the royal agents and inquisitors of 1307. To obtain this 'truth' from them, they had been tortured: 'And one must know that these brothers were put to the question moderately, three weeks and more earlier; and since then they have not been put to the question.'[6] Naturally, all the twenty-nine Templars present (there had been thirty-three the year before) this time recognised their sins.

Why this second session a year after the first? The pope was responsible for this turn of events. With the date of the Council approaching, Pope Clement was receiving information that greatly alarmed him: in Italy, Spain, Germany and England, where proceedings had been delayed, the Templars continued to refuse to confess. In that year, 1311, the pope had made a decision: he had succeeded in saving the memory of Boniface VIII by retaining control over the investigation that he had conceded to Philip the Fair;[7] but it was a quid pro quo: he had to let go of the Temple and the Templars. It did not matter at this point if he wanted to save the Order or not. By 1311 he could no longer save it, but he could still save individual Templars … provided they confessed, that they recognised the truth: that is, the errors for which they would be pardoned. If, on the contrary, they maintained *their* truth, they risked the worst. And so, wherever interrogations of individuals were dragging on, wherever a diocesan commission could not obtain confessions, it had to double down, using the main threat – torture – if necessary. Pope Clement probably did not like that, but it was essential. On 18 March 1311 he addressed the Spanish bishops; on 27 June he again addressed them, as well as the Italian bishops; and on 13 August he addressed the bishops of Cyprus: they must use torture – moderately – to obtain confessions.[8] We don't have such a document addressed to the bishop of Nîmes, but the facts are there.

All the documents concerning the proceedings undertaken against the Order and individuals had to be delivered to the pope. He convened a special commission in the priory of Groseau, in the town of Malaucène, which for days throughout the summer examined the records of the investigations in order to synthesise them. The records of the papal commission in Paris were brought to the pope by messengers who left Pontoise on 6 June. On the 18th, Pope Clement wrote to the archbishops of the kingdom of France asking them to send him 'the investigation against the Templars undertaken in their province': Sens, Reims, Tours, Bourges, Bordeaux, Auch and Narbonne.[9] Regarding the province of Narbonne, there was a problem because its archbishop, Gilles Aycelin, the president of the papal commission in Paris, had just been transferred to the see of Rouen. Addressing him directly, the pope wrote: 'Furthermore, because you, as we discovered before your transfer from Narbonne to Rouen, had ordered the convening of the council of the province of Narbonne regarding the Templar Affair, we wish you not to defer the meeting on the date fixed in the convocation.'[10] And he specified, still addressing Aycelin, that if he could not do so, he should take care to inform the pope.

This explains why the province of Rouen is not included in the letters Pope Clement sent on 18 June, but it also suggests that the council of the province of Narbonne had not yet met in the summer of 1311, when Guillaume de Saint-Laurent summoned the diocesan commission of Nîmes, on 29 August. What about other places, in Bordeaux, Auch, Tours and elsewhere? Only meetings of the provincial councils of Sens and Reims are noted in the documentation. This does not mean that there had not been others. In any event, the pope, in his letters of 18 June addressed to the archbishops, was interested in the records of the diocesan commissions just as much as those of the provincial councils; the archbishops, even if they had not yet convened a provincial council, must have had documents issuing from the diocesan commissions.

The Council of Vienne and the defence of the Templars

The bull *Regnans in coelis* of August 1308 contains the list of archbishops, bishops, abbots and other clerics who were summoned by name to the Council; others could be represented by proxies. Finally, those who were not summoned or who could not attend could express their views on the subjects dealt with in the Council by sending written memoranda.[11]

According to the study undertaken by Ewald Müller, about 170 clerics ('fathers' of the council) took part in the Council, 108 of whom were archbishops and bishops. A third of these came from the kingdom of France; this figure should be compared with the number of convocations: 230 bishops and archbishops had been summoned, which means that not all of them attended.

The Council held only three plenary sessions: the opening session, on 16 October, when the pope reminded the attendees of the Council's three objectives (the fate of the Temple, the Crusades and Church reform), and on 3 April and 6 May, the day the Council adjourned, these last two sessions being devoted to issues involving the Templars.

Much of the Council's work was done in commissions. The calendar followed the evolution of the Templar Affair, which the commissions began by examining; the other items on the agenda were dealt with during gaps in the calendar. In fact, the examination of the Templar Affair depended greatly on things beyond the Council's control, the main one being the arrival of the king of France, for whom they had to wait: 'We dare decide nothing without the knowledge of the king of France, and thus ultimately, in everything, we do only what he wants', noted the envoy of the king of Aragon on 12 December 1311 – and when they did not know what he wanted, they did nothing and went on to something else. The entire Council worked under this threat, this fear, this anxiety: what would the king of France do, say, think?

However, on 16 October they were not yet at this point.

And so a large commission was put in place to deal with the Temple. It was made up of fifty members, chosen from every sector of Christendom (French bishops were not in the majority). This clearly indicated the pope's wishes (the fact that those wishes were often blocked or thwarted by pressure from the king of France did not prevent them from existing): every opinion and option should be expressed; no decisions would be made without prior discussion and without seeking the opinions of all of Christendom as represented at the Council. Within this large commission, a smaller commission presided over by the Patriarch of Aquileia prepared its work. Its members had in hand the records of all the investigations carried out by the papal commissions (and not just the biased synthesis that had been done in Groseau), and the memoranda from the bishops who were not in attendance, only one of which still exists: that of Guillaume Le Maire, bishop of Angers, who was very hostile to the Templars. The commission came out of the Council, and so the Council was not neglected even outside its plenary sessions. However, in spite of the pope's intentions, the Council and the large commission were ultimately completely marginalised when the king and his agents arrived. Everything was then dealt with between the royal envoys and the pope, outside the control of the Council. In the end, the Council could do nothing more than accept the decisions imposed authoritatively by the pope.

A defence of the Temple before the Council had been proposed by the pope himself, in Poitiers in 1308. Cardinal Pierre de la Chapelle, during a final meeting held on 10 July 1308 with Templars who had been previously interrogated, had made two specific rulings: that the Order could have defenders, and that its dignitaries could be present at the Council to be judged there, along with the Order. The text of these rulings was posted the same evening on the doors of the cathedral of Poitiers and was included in the bull *Faciens misericordiam* of 12 August 1312: it authorised the presence of 'representatives or appropriate defenders', as well as of dignitaries and commanders.[12] In 1310 the Templars who had gone to Paris to defend the Order remembered those promises very well. The day after the gathering of the Templars in the bishopric orchard on 28 March 1310, Pierre de Bologne, speaking on behalf of the brothers held in the Temple of Paris, asked 'that they be present at the general Council in person or through the representation of other brothers'.[13] The request was repeated by most Templars when the notaries of the papal commission visited them in their Paris prisons. Thus the detainees in the residence of the bishop of Amiens implored 'that, at the general council or anywhere else where the status of the religious order of the Temple is being dealt with, they could be present'.[14] The memorandum of the prisoners in the residence of Richard des Poulies, read by

Jean de Montréal, was explicit: 'The said brothers ask you, Lords, the leave and the opportunity to come to the council that you are to convene to support their rights as reason demands.' [15]

The pope's promise was dated 1308; in 1310 the commissioners had prudently evaded the issue. At the opening of the Council, Pope Clement acted as though he had forgotten it and did not mention it. It was abruptly and unexpectedly recalled around the end of October, when seven Templars burst into the room where the commission was meeting and insisted on defending the Order; the next day, or the day after that, two others did the same. This is how Pope Clement himself presented the facts in a letter he sent to the king of France on 4 (or 11) November 1311:

> To inform your royal greatness of the truth of all the events that are occurring in the Templar Affair, I must not keep back the following fact: whereas the information made against the Order of the Templars was read before the prelates and other ecclesiastical men who have come to the present holy Council and were gathered to deliberate, one day seven brothers of the Order of the Templars and the next day two others, appeared, in our absence before those same prelates and ecclesiastical men and offered to defend the Order; they asserted that one thousand five hundred or two thousand brothers of the Order who lived in Lyon or in its environs joined them for that defence. Although they appeared spontaneously, we did however arrest them and placed them in detention. And now we have taken precautions to reinforce our security. We announce these events to your highness so that it will advise us to what is necessary to be done to guard your person. [16]

Did the Templars who were free really number 'one thousand five hundred to two thousand', as the pope said? There is probably some exaggeration here, but we have counted more than the nine arrested during the session. The theologian Jean de Pouilly, present at the Council, indicated 'that he had seen and heard many Templars who offered to defend the Order'. [17] We can in any case ask where they came from, and why they were able to circulate freely near Vienne (admittedly outside the kingdom of France). In truth, the issue is not so much the number of Templars who were around Vienne as the attitude of the priests of the Council, the very great majority of whom were favourable to their appearance. Pope Clement was able to verify this during the secret meeting of the large commission that he convened at the beginning of December: the priests were

> individually summoned for that purpose by the pope, who asked them if they should hear the Templars or grant them a defence. All the prelates from Italy except one, those from Spain, Germany, Sweden, England, Scotland, and Ireland answered in the affirmative. Those of France did so too, with the exception of the three archbishops of Reims, Sens and Rouen.[18]

Let's look at what the English procurator at the court in Rome, Henry Ffykers, who was also present in Vienne, wrote on 27 December:

> A great argument has occurred regarding the Templar Affair to know if one should legally allow them to present a defence. The majority of prelates, or rather all of them except five or six belonging to the king of France's royal council, held that belief. Because of that the pope is very irritated with the prelates.[19]

For the opposing view the pope could resort to the written memoranda he had received. Guillaume Le Maire, for example, was in favour of a radical solution: they should eliminate the Order as fast as possible and reject 'futile and irritating claims of a defence'.[20] The problem is that we have only this one memorandum in the archives. This tells us very little about the opinions of the prelates in attendance.

The announcement of the imminent arrival of the king of France, who on 30 December had convened a meeting of the Estates of the kingdom (still the same old formula!) in Lyon for 16 February, did nothing to calm the debate.

The pope was eager to be done with the affair, but following the position of the Council would do the opposite and drag it out. Faced with the determination of most of the Council, he procrastinated and left things hanging (while waiting for the king of France to arrive, as the ambassador of the king of Aragon said). And so they would go on to other things: the commission would discuss what should be done with the Temple property: that is, the property of an Order that had not yet been suppressed, since the Council had postponed a decision on its fate.

The suppression of the Order of the Temple

The importance of the debate over whether the Order should be defended at the Council is highlighted by the place it was given in the bull *Vox in excelso*, through which the Order was suppressed on 22 March 1312. In it, the pope recalls the investigations carried out on individuals, the synthesis of those investigations that was carried out at the priory of Groseau in Malaucène, the opening of the Council and the establishment of the large commission, the days spent reading the summaries of the investigations before the commission and, finally, the secret consistory of the members of the commission during which the intrusion of the nine Templars is mentioned. Then, following that exposition, he adds:

> The greater part of the cardinals and nearly the whole council, that is those who were elected by the whole council and were representing the whole council on this question, in short the great majority, indeed four-fifths among every nation taking part, were firmly convinced, and the said prelates and procurators advised accordingly, that the Order should be given an opportunity to defend itself and that it could not be condemned, on the basis of the proof provided thus far, for the heresies that had been the subject of the investigation, without offence to God and injustice. Certain others on the contrary said that the brothers should not be allowed to make a defence of their Order [...] the Order up to now does not permit its canonical condemnation [...] the good name of the Order has been largely taken away the heresies attributed to it.

And finally came the decision:

> After long and mature deliberation, having in mind God alone and the good of the Holy Land without turning aside to right or to left, we elected to proceed by way of provision and ordinance; in this way scandal will be removed, perils avoided and property saved for the help of the Holy Land.

The pope adds that the Council is in agreement with this position and that the Church had already suppressed the religious Orders in that way before concluding that, 'not by definitive sentence, but by apostolic provision or ordinance, we suppress, with the approval of the sacred council, the Order of Templars, and its rule, habit and name'.[21]

Suppressed but not condemned.

The pressure Pope Clement put on the Council, as well as that which the king put on the pope and that Council, caused this compromise to be accepted by the great majority of priests, who were nonetheless against it. The bishop of Valencia in Spain was, however, not convinced and said so, outside the Council, asking the members to see things clearly: there were good and bad Templars, and 'the Order of the Temple continues to exist within the good ones; as such, it has not sinned, it is holy and just in its composition'.[22]

On 3 April, in the presence of Philip the Fair and the French court, the bull *Vox in excelso* was solemnly promulgated during the Council's second plenary session. It took another month of bitter negotiations to convince the king of France and the Council to accept the devolution of the Temple property to the Order of the Hospital, which was decided on by the bull *Ad providam*, promulgated on 6 May, during the Council's closing session.

That same day, the bull *Considerantes dudum* sealed the fate of the Templars.[23] Not surprisingly, three scenarios were set out:

- Templars who had been absolved and reconciled by the bishops (those who had confessed and stuck with their confessions) were allowed to live according to their status on the income from the property of the suppressed Order;
- non-reconciled Templars, who had refused to recognise their sins, would be judged according to the law;
- as for the truly incorrigible – that is, those who after having first confessed recanted their confessions – they too would be judged according to the law and canonical sanctions. Relapse into heresy wasn't mentioned; it seems that the issue was not brought up or, if it was (which Jean de Pouilly's position on the issue suggests, since he participated in the Council), it was not recorded. *Considerantes dudum* did not open the door to new burnings at the stake.

However, the chroniclers who wrote about this bull do mention relapse and burning. There was Jean de Saint-Victor:

Those among the Templars who confessed said errors and persisted in their confession, would be forced to do penance; the others who continued to deny would be held in prison; the third group, those who first confessed and who then said they had lied because of strong torture were condemned to the stake.[24]

It seems indeed that Jean de Saint-Victor was mistaken because of the individual cases of the Grand Master and Geoffroy de Charney in 1314. *Considerantes dudum* offered a framework: on the one hand, those who had told the truth (they had confessed) would, after a light penance, be freed; on the other, those who had denied (the truth), continually or after straying, would be sentenced to life imprisonment.

In fact, not all the proceedings had come to an end. Furthermore, the pope, in his conclusion of the bull *Vox in excelso*, recognised this: 'through this decree [the suppression of the Order], however, we do not wish to derogate from any processes made or to be made concerning individual Templars by diocesan bishops and provincial councils.'[25]

In Nîmes, on the fifth day before the Ides of November, or 9 November, Guillaume de Saint-Laurent stated that he had received from the bishop Bertrand de Languissel a letter dated the preceding 28 October reproducing a missive from the cardinal of Tusculum – Beranger Frédol – sent from Avignon on 25 October. The cardinal granted absolution and authorised the administration of the sacraments to the Templars of the diocese of Nîmes being held in the castle of Alès. Guillaume de Saint-Laurent was to carry out the instructions in that letter which was given to him by a notary on 8 November. On the 9th he then gathered all the Templars into the great hall of the castle of Alès. There were only twenty-two of them. He asked them to confirm the confessions they had made the year before (after the use of torture, let's remember), then absolved them of the sentence of excommunication that they had been given, reconciled them with the Church and reintegrated them into the communion of the saints.[26] We can assume that those twenty-two Templars were treated like all the reconciled brothers: 'benignly'. But there is no trace of them after November 1312.

This was the end of the episcopal proceedings. Judgement still had to be pronounced, following the criteria defined in the bull *Considerantes dudum*, within the framework of the council of the province of Narbonne, which – this document is indeed the proof – had not yet been convened. It would not meet until 1315, and even then it still could not settle every case. In September 1315, in fact, the archbishop of Narbonne, Bernard de Farges, a nephew of Pope Clement, asked his suffragan bishop of Elne, in Roussillon, to present before the provincial council the Templars of his diocese whom he had questioned in 1310.[27] Roussillon was not in the kingdom of France; it was a possession of the king of Majorca. King Sancho refused to turn over 'his' Templars to the archbishop. A letter from the king of France on this subject had no effect. The new pope, John XXII, wrote to the archbishop of Narbonne on 13 January 1317 asking him to wrap things up and pronounce judgement on the Templars of Elne in their absence.[28] Either the provincial council had still not met by that date, or it had met but had temporarily set aside the case of the Templars from Roussillon. This indeed seems to have been the case since it was not until 1319, in another provincial council of Narbonne held in Béziers, that the affair was concluded. The Templars still had not appeared; only the reports of the investigations of 1310 had been sent for consideration. The men were not considered *in absentia*; they had simply been judged from the files.[29]

What became of the Templars?

Let's be clear: it was outside France, in Aragon-Catalonia and in England, that we have the most information about what became of the Templars after the Council of Vienne.[30] For the kingdom of France there are very few documents that tell us anything about the reconciled Templars who received pensions from the Templar property that was transferred to the Order of the Hospital.

In 1319 an investigation into the revenue of the bailiwick of Bertaignemont, a former Temple house in the diocese of Beauvais, reveals that Adam, *dit* Torchon, and Gautier de Sommereux, formerly Templars, received 17 *sous* 6 *deniers* per week for their expenses and 6 *livres* 5 *sous* per year for their clothing.[31] We know nothing about them before this date. There is also mention of two sisters of the Temple who received a pension. The fate of the sisters of the Order at the time of the trial is an interesting question (the fact that there were sisters is proved by this mention). Unfortunately, we know nothing more about them. The same investigation also informs us about Thoni, a dependence of the house of Bertaignemont: two Temple sisters – Hermengarde called La Pregace, and Oedea de Haute-Avesnes – each received 10 *sous tournois* per week for expenses and 75 *sous* per year for their clothing, whereas Pierre de Bresle received the same sums as Adam Torchon. We know of Pierre de Bresle, from the diocese of Beauvais, since he had been arrested in Paris in 1307 but not interrogated; he was transferred to Dammartin-en-Goële in February 1308, and it was from there that he went to Paris on 16 February 1310 to defend the Temple before the papal commission; he was held in the Blavot residence.[32] It would be tempting to connect him with the person of the same name who was received into the Order before June 1294 and who on that date was commander of Sommereux, but if we believe Baudouin de Saint-Just, who was received by him on that date, he was dead.[33]

In 1313 in Toulouse two knights and six sergeants received a pension of 18 *deniers* per day (the knights) and 9 *deniers* per day (the sergeants). They were still being held, which was perhaps due to the fact that at that time the bishopric of Toulouse was still a suffragan of the archbishopric of Narbonne and the provincial council had not yet met.[34] Narbonne, again, was a problem: twenty-two Templars from that province were incarcerated in Sens. In 1318 Pope John XXII wrote to the archbishop of Narbonne to ask him to release from the Temple property in his archbishopric the money necessary for their pensions.[35] As for examples of Templars sentenced to life imprisonment, they are, apart from the six cases mentioned in the records of the papal commission, and which we've already seen (Renaud de Provins and the others), extremely rare.[36] The myth that Templars were imprisoned in the guardhouse of the gate towers in Domme and scratched out their despair and hatred of the king and the pope on the walls there must be discarded. An ongoing study being undertaken by the Atemporelle agency and the Ministry of Culture at the request of the mayor's office in Domme has revealed that the supposed documentary evidence was falsified – in addition to the fact that it has been proved elsewhere that no Templars were ever held in Domme.

Then there is the case of Pons de Bure, a priest brother from the diocese of Langres, present in Paris on 10 February 1310 to defend the Order, whom we know of from a letter written by the pope dated 1 May 1321. He had been in prison in Sens for twelve years, having been sentenced for life, but Pope John XXII allowed him to celebrate a Mass at that time. Had he been freed on that occasion?[37]

There is another interesting case: that of the priest Gilles de Rotangi. He was a chaplain brother of the Temple and also curate of the parish church of Oisemont, for which the Temple was the patron: that is, it had the right to name the incumbent. He appears often in the trial records, because in many testimonies he is cited under the names of Rotangi-Rontangi or Rotengi-Rotengi, Botengy, Rotengny but also Gilles d'Oisemont or simply Gilles. He was from the diocese of Amiens where Oisemont was also located, and was born around 1250. He entered the Temple on 2 February 1285 in Sommereux, another commandery of the diocese of Amiens, and, as receptor or as a simple assistant, participated in a dozen receptions into the Order between 1291 and 1307. He did not appear in person in the documentation before 9 February 1310, the date when he appeared as a Temple defender with a group of Templars being held in the Paris abbey of Saint-Martin-des-Champs;[38] he presented a memorandum on behalf of his co-detainees. He appeared before the provincial council of Reims in May or June 1310, where he was released from the sentence of excommunication but condemned to prison without being defrocked. He was fortunate to have his sentence shortened, an adjustment made by Philippe de Voët, provost of Poitiers, and Jean de Janville, the Templars' guard, 'for certain reasons'.[39] He wore the mantle of the Order when he was called to testify before the papal commission on 28 January 1311.[40] By then he had been held in Asnières-sur-Oise, in the bailiwick of Senlis, since July 1310 with seven other reconciled Templars. He was taken to Paris for that interrogation, then went back to Asnières, where he appears to have stayed from February to June 1311, at least.[41]

Despite his tribulations, it seems that Gilles de Rotangi was able to keep the benefice of being curate of Oisemont. On 21 January 1311, in fact, even though Gilles was getting ready to appear before the commission, Pope Clement was dealing with a complaint from Oudard de Bellement, rector of the church Saint-Martin d'Oisemont, who could not take possession of it because it was still held by the Templar brother Gilles d'Amiens (who was none other than Gilles de Rotangi). According to the plaintiff, Gilles d'Amiens had been sentenced for heresy, which was not mentioned in the letter granting the benefice to Oudard de Bellement. Officially, Gilles de Rotangi, although sentenced and imprisoned, remained the curate of Oisemont.[42] We don't know what happened to him afterwards, whether he managed to leave his prison or not or (even less likely) whether he was able to retain the parish of Oisemont.

From these examples we must come to the conclusion that, before and after the decisions of the Council of Vienne, there was no automatic application of the principles set out regarding sanctions. Renaud de Cugnières, Pierre de Clermont, Bernard de Sornay and Renaud de Provins were sentenced by the Council of Sens to life in prison 'in some form'; this could be interpreted as a reduction of their sentence.

Finally, there is the case of Renaud de la Folie, who in 1307 was included on the list of the royal chancellery as a fugitive. On 27 November 1309 he was cited by Ponsard de Gizy for having denounced Gérard de Villers, Master of France, during a general chapter in February 1307, for his part in the loss of the isle of Ruad in 1302.[43] On the run, Renaud de la Folie sought refuge in the hospital of Saint-Mammès in Langres, a place designated to offer asylum. He spent five years there until the day, at the end of 1312, when the Templar Affair seemed to have definitely ended, and the king of France sent two equerries, Richard and Jean, called Perceval, to retrieve the fugitive Templar. A letter from the king dated 26 November 1312 sent from Paris informs us of this; the king of France, in fact, having openly violated the right to asylum at the hospital of Saint-Mammès, had to provide the dean and the cathedral chapter of Langres, of which the hospital was a dependence, letters assuring them of their legal and jurisdictional rights.[44] He promised; he swore he would never do it again.

The burning of Jacques de Molay (March 1314)[45]

In Poitiers the pope had reserved judgement on the Order dignitaries for himself; he reiterated this on several occasions and again on 6 May 1312 in Vienne, when he pronounced the closing of the Council. In August 1308 in Chinon he had proceeded to investigate those individuals through the intermediary of three cardinals. He had only to pronounce judgement on them, which could happen only after the Council had reached its decisions.

In the meantime Jacques de Molay and Hugues de Pairaud appeared on three occasions before the commission responsible for investigating the Order and refused to participate in the proceedings. Therefore they took no part in the Templars' revolt of 1310, or in the attempts they made at that time to defend their Order. On 2 March 1310, the date of his last appearance, Jacques de Molay simply repeated that he wanted to be taken before the pope, the only person before whom he would talk.[46] On 13 March, Hugues de Pairaud and Geoffroy de Gonneville did the same.[47] Geoffroy de Charney never appeared before the commission; as for Raimbaud de Caromb, there was no more mention of him after Chinon: he probably died.

Where were the dignitaries being held at this time? Arrested in Paris and imprisoned in the Temple in 1307, they were transferred on 25 January 1308: Jacques de Molay to Corbeil, Hugues de Pairaud to Rochefort-en-Yvelines, Raimbaud de Caromb to Montlhéry, and Geoffroy de Charnay to Montereau-fault-d'Yonne. On 2 February Geoffroy de Gonneville, who was being held in

Gisors, was transferred to Vernon.[48] They must have all gone together to Poitiers in June/July 1308, but they stopped in Chinon, where they were imprisoned in the royal castle; it was there that, in August, the cardinals sent by the pope interrogated them. From there, on an unknown date, they went back to the prisons of Île-de-France, perhaps even to the prisons where they had been transferred in January 1308, unless it was to the Temple in Paris. Ordered on the morning of 26 November 1309 to bring Jacques de Molay before the papal commission as soon as possible, the bishop of Paris did so that afternoon. So de Molay was not far away. After March 1310 there was silence. When in March 1314 the four surviving dignitaries were brought to Paris to hear the judgement to be handed down against them, they may have come from Gisors: 'The four prisoners were taken from the dungeon of Gisors', we are told by Georges Bordonove.[49] Gisors is in the diocese of Rouen. A group of fifty-eight Templars was still being held there in March 1310.[50] According to Andreas Beck, who refers to Konrad Schottmüller, Jacques de Molay and his cohort would have been in prison in Gisors from March 1311 to March 1314. But Schottmüller says only this: 'Until March 1310, when he was again interrogated in Paris, the Grand Master remained in Paris. Later, he was taken to Gisors and we don't hear anything about him until 11 March 1314 when he was brought to Paris.'[51] Unfortunately, this assertion does not rest on any documentation. A mention, tenuous, suggests something different: Hugues de Pairaud, who did not support Jacques de Molay in 1314, was sentenced to life imprisonment and then imprisoned in Montlhéry, as we will see; wasn't he already there earlier? Why wouldn't Jacques de Molay have been taken back to Corbeil?

Pope Clement took his time. After the Council of Vienne, he had a lot to do with matters concerning the devolution of the Temple property to the Hospital, and it wasn't until 22 December 1313 that he finally dealt with the dignitaries. On that day he decided to send three cardinals to Paris to inform them of the judgement.[52] He chose his nephew Arnaud de Farges, archbishop of Auch, Arnaud Novelli and Nicolas de Fréauville. There was no question of having the dignitaries appear before the pope, no question of a trial or a debate; as the pontiff recalled in his letter, the investigation had been carried out by three cardinals whom he had assigned for that in Chinon in 1308. All that remained was to impose a salutary punishment, the carrying out of which he assigned to his envoys. Granted, they would once again hear the accused before pronouncing their judgement, but this was purely a formality.

The cardinals arrived in Paris in March 1314 and had the four dignitaries brought before the bishop's 'scales of justice' located on the plaza in front of the cathedral of Notre-Dame, opposite the north portal.[53] This is the account by the continuator of the chronicle of Guillaume de Nangis:

> The Grand Master of the Order of Templars and three other Templars, namely the Visitor of the Order in France, and the masters from Aquitaine and Normandy, on whom the pope had reserved pronouncing judgement, all four openly and publicly admitted the crimes of which they were accused in the presence of the archbishop of Sens [Philippe de Marigny] and of a few other prelates and men learned in canon law and in divine law, assembled especially for this purpose by order of the pope, by the bishop of Albano and two other cardinals, and to whom were given communication of the advice of the counsel of the accused. Since they persisted in their confessions, and appeared to want to persist until the end, after mature deliberation, on the advice of said counsel, said assembly sentenced them, the day after the feast of Saint Gregory, on the public square of the plaza of the church of Paris to perpetual imprisonment. But then, although the cardinals believed they had definitely concluded this affair, suddenly two Templars, the Grand Master of Outremer and the Grand Master of Normandy, defended themselves vociferously against a cardinal who was then speaking and against the archbishop of Sens and, without any respect began to deny all that they had confessed, which caused great surprise to many people.
>
> When the cardinals had handed them over to the provost of Paris [a royal agent], who was present, only so that he could keep them under guard until they could deliberate more fully over them the next day, as soon as these things reached the king's ears in the royal palace, he consulted with his own advisers and, without speaking of it with the clergy, made a prudent decision to have the two Templars consigned to the flames towards evening on that very day, on a little island in the Seine, situated between the royal garden and the church of the Hermit Brethren. They appeared to endure this torture with such indifference and calm that their firmness and their final denials were for all witnesses a subject of admiration and stupor. The two other Templars were locked in a dungeon, according to the terms of their arrest.[54]

As another chronicler of the time, the Dominican Bernard Gui, pointed out, the king 'waited for no other judgement from the Church since two cardinals were still present in Paris'.[55]

The date given in the chronicle of Guillaume de Nangis was the day after the Feast of Saint Gregory, or Monday 18 March (the feast day fell on 12 March); this is the date most often retained by historians of the Temple trial. But other chroniclers, such as Bernard Gui, have proposed the Monday before the Feast of Saint Gregory, or 11 March. We tend to agree with Bernard, since the chronology he proposes is most often very accurate.[56] The king must have been present in Paris, because it was he who decided to deliver the two rebels to the stake without further ado. Nothing in Philip the Fair's itinerary enables us to confirm one or the other of those two dates, 11 or 18 March, since no specific dates are mentioned for the month of March. The king was in Paris in March, that's all.[57]

As for the place where the stake was erected, it was on an island which in the fourteenth century was called the 'Island of the Jews', located below the gardens of the royal palace on the southern branch of the Seine, opposite the left bank and the church of the Hermits of Saint-Augustin; neither the Pont-Neuf nor the tip of the place du Vert-Galant existed at that time. The islet belonged to the abbey of Saint-Germain-des-Prés, which in the days that followed received a letter of no prejudice from the Paris parliament. The king, as stated in the letter, had not wanted to infringe on the jurisdiction of the abbot by 'having two men who were formerly Templars burned on the isle in the Seine adjoining the point of our garden, between our said garden on one side of the river and the religious house of the brothers of the Order of Saint-Augustin of Paris, on the other side of the river, over which he [the abbot of Saint-Germain] had full legal jurisdiction'.[58]

Hugues de Pairaud and Geoffroy de Gonneville, who had not argued against the pope's judgement, saved their skins but at the price of life in prison. An accounting document confirms that Hugues de Pairaud was in prison in Montlhéry on the date of 31 August 1321:

On that day there came [to the Chamber of accounts] monsieur Guillaume Clignet, to take care of several commissions to be done there, and said Sir Guillaume, through a text, told the things that follow: that is, that brother Hugue de Peraut, once visitor of the Temple, from Montlhéry where he was being guarded, told him that he had entrusted the safe-keeping of a small chest to a brother named Pierre Gaude, once commander of the houses of Dormelles and Beauvoir, near Moret, in which chest there were 1,189 pieces of gold and 5,010 pieces of silver worth 20 *livres* 17 *sous* and 6 *deniers tournois*.[59]

Hugues de Pairaud's treasure, actually not very great, did not stay hidden for long. The commander, Pierre Gaude, was worried and gave it to a poor fisherman, who, once all the Templars were arrested, gave it to the bailiff of Sens so as not to get into trouble. And so it was returned to the king's treasury, which is why we know about it: like it or not, bureaucracy can have its advantages.

Post-scriptum: on 21 July 1773, through the papal brief *Dominus ac redemptor*, Pope Clement XIV suppressed the Order of the Jesuits, and justified his decision in these terms:

> The other Roman pontiffs, our predecessors, followed the same steps, as circumstances required. Among others, Pope Clement by a letter *sub plumbo*, expedited the 3rd of May in the year 1312, induced thereto by the general discredit into which the order of Templars was fallen, did entirely suppress and abolish the said Order, though it had been legally approved, and though, on account of the services it had rendered to the Christian republic, the Holy See had heretofore bestowed on it many and important privileges, faculties and exemptions; and though the General Council of Vienne, to whom the examination of this affair had been committed, had not thought proper to pronounce a formal and definitive sentence.[60]

CONCLUSION

We have reached the end of this voyage through time and space, during which I have attempted to follow the Templars from the kingdom of France as they confronted various forms of adversity. I believe I have revealed some facts that have not always been taken into account in the histories of the trial of the Temple, probably because, since the trial has been situated within the context of the confrontation between the papacy and the French monarchy, the temptation has been great to focus exclusively on those two powers and see the Templars merely as pawns or 'punchbags'. I believe that my approach – starting with the Templars and their reactions as they confronted those two powers – has been beneficial insofar as it has shown that during this affair they were engaged as fully fledged players in a game in which there were ultimately three teams. If the Templar Affair lasted five years – actually, seven – instead of moving along quickly in a few weeks the way Philip the Fair wanted it to, it is of course because the pope didn't see things the way the king did, but also because the Templars resisted. The dual question 'What did the king want, what did the pope want?' was answered differently depending on whether it was asked in 1307 or 1312. Because the Templars did not just sit back and passively allow their fate to be sealed.

Philip the Fair

In 1307–8 the king and his advisers harassed the pope. They asked him these questions: when are you going to act, when are you going to decide to purge Christendom of that 'Templar heresy'? Pope Clement was prevaricating, said all those who thought that that was all he was capable of. No, in fact he was resisting, in his own way. The Templars, except for the brief period during which the Grand Master retracted his confession at the end of December 1307, seemed completely paralysed and, it's true, out of commission at that time. However, at the end of June 1308 the king gave in and agreed to a compromise on the Templar Affair; he agreed that it could be prolonged; he agreed to the pope's timetable, accepting the time it would take for dual proceedings to be carried out as they should be: several months, or several years, since they were to meet again in October 1310 at the General Council. If the king complied, it is because he was placing the Templar Affair within the larger context not only of the French monarchy's relations with the papacy but also of the role of the French monarchy and its 'Very Christian king' within the world order as desired by God.[1]

In Poitiers, between 5 and 13 July, the king mounted a fresh attack, but it went largely beyond the framework of just the Templar Affair. I have already discussed the demands he presented to the pope 'on the Saturday following the translation of the blessed martyr Saint Thomas': that is, on 7 July.[2] Guillaume de Plaisians was assigned to present these demands to the pope, which he did on 13 July during a consistory: 1) that the pope and the Curia remain in France; 2) that the pope condemn the Templars following their confessions; 3) that, if there must be a General Council, it be held in France; 4) that the pope canonise Celestine V, Boniface VIII's predecessor; 5) that the pope order the burning of the remains of Boniface VIII; and 6) that the pope absolve and release Guillaume de Nogaret from his sentence of excommunication.

Only one demand related to the Templars: the routine matter of condemning them as soon as possible, once the pope had heard them. Three demands involved Boniface VIII and the aftermath of Anagni, and two dealt with the power of the French monarchy over the papacy. In the two years following the trial the memory of Boniface VIII essentially took precedence over the Templar Affair. The king of France, so eager up to then to suppress the Order, would now let things drag on.

The pope responded to all the demands in the negative.

Clement V

We must not misunderstand Pope Clement's attitude to the Templars: it was much more complex than it may seem. Why not believe him when he said, in his letter of 24 August 1307, which opened the door to an investigation into the Order, that he did not want to believe the accusations being brought against it? And why not also accept that, after he vehemently protested against the king's initiative of 13 October 1307, he would then be 'shattered' by the confessions obtained by that same king? He was well aware of the conditions under which those confessions had been obtained, but even so, they did exist. This explains his obstinacy in wanting to interrogate the Templars himself, which he finally did at the end of June 1308. Essentially, his doubts could only be reinforced: the Templars whom he interrogated all pleaded guilty, and the five dignitaries questioned two months later in Chinon did the same. There was no plan for saving the Temple then; Pope Clement did not clear the Order and the brothers of all suspicion: he simply absolved and reconciled with the Church any penitent who recognised his errors (and who would later be sanctioned for his actions[3]).

For Pope Clement form mattered more than substance; otherwise he would have been able to follow Philip the Fair's lead. He did not set up (dual) proceedings in Poitiers to save the Temple and the Templars; rather, their purpose was to allow the Church to control the unfolding of the affair and, more generally, of all Church affairs. The 'Poitiers compromise' was Pope Clement's agreement to honour Philip the Fair's wishes by announcing the imminent opening of an investigation into Boniface VIII, while specifying that he didn't believe he was a heretic, but that an investigation would be carried out by the Church under the control of the pope, as henceforth the Templar Affair would be. This was the issue at stake during the consistory of 13 July 1308. Pope Clement's responses, as reported through our English document and by the chronicler Ptolemy of Lucca, are unambiguous:[4] 1) he would not stay in France, as he wanted to return to Rome, a much more practical and central location for managing the affairs of Christendom; 2) he would zealously oversee the Templar Affair, but without departing from the rules he had set forth; 3) regarding the location of a possible council, he had no preference; 4) to canonise someone, miracles had to have been performed; he was waiting for these; 5) Boniface VIII had shown that he was a good and Catholic man; Pope Clement was thus stupefied by the king's demands and he asked him not to insist further on that point, although he agreed to open an investigation; and 6) he flatly refused to lift the excommunication of Guillaume de Nogaret.

This was in 1308. What was left of the king's plans in 1312, following the Council of Vienne? The pope was in Avignon, outside the kingdom of France; the Templar Affair had been settled, but clearly not entirely to the satisfaction of the king; the council was held in Vienne and not in Lyon, as the king had wanted; Vienne was not in the kingdom, even if Lyon just barely was; Pierre de Morrone, and not Celestine V, had been canonised; Boniface VIII would not be condemned; Nogaret's excommunication was lifted on the condition that he spend five years in the Holy Land. Which he did not do, of course, but, since he died in 1313, it hardly mattered any more.[5]

If Pope Clement's attitude to the king was clear, it was much less clear, much more ambiguous, where the Temple was concerned.

The compromise in Poitiers specified placing individual Templars and Temple property under the guardianship of the Church. This was carried out formally, but the men and the property remained *de facto* under the control of the king and his agents, even if those agents were sometimes accompanied by representatives of the bishops. Pope Clement did, however, differentiate between individuals and the property. Difficulties were indeed foreseeable as far as individuals were concerned (and in fact there were some), but they seemed more easily overcome than those that involved the control of Temple property. Following Poitiers, the pope dealt first with his return to Rome. In fact, taking his time during the move, during the autumn of 1308 and the winter of 1309, he went to Avignon, where he decided to establish the papal see while waiting for the conditions that would enable him to go to Rome (which never occurred). He had less time to devote to the Templars, and, for the most part, it was the transfer of their property to the Church that demanded his attention. He wanted to make sure that the property would not be misappropriated. He had many exchanges with the king on that subject, especially since he knew the king did not like the solution he envisioned if the Temple was suppressed: the devolution of its property to the Order of the Hospital.

The diocesan commissions responsible for investigating individuals did not begin their work until the spring of 1309. Many did not start until 1310; some (such as that of Nîmes) would continue meeting until 1312. As for the setting up of the papal commissions, and in particular the one involving the kingdom of France, this occurred even later.

The papal commission

While examining the work of the papal commission in Paris, as seen in the preceding chapters, I wondered what the commissioners were really looking for, what they hoped to obtain from the Templars they had summoned to testify, and thus what the pope expected of the commission. The commissioners were appointed by the pope, and even though the king had approved their appointments, they were not under his control; they were the pope's representatives, which they made known on several occasions – and this was not a mere formality. Was the commission assigned to exonerate the Templars? Listening to the brothers' denials and the rigour of their defence of the Order in February–May 1310, it could well have done so. After all, the papal commissions of Ravenna and Tarragona did.[6] At the beginning the Paris commission did, however, encourage the Templars' 'revolt', and the brothers were allowed to reject *en bloc* the accusations brought against their Order, to extol its qualities and merits and to glorify its work in service to the Holy Land, the Church and Christendom. The commissioners agreed to listen to their speeches, but did they hear them? There was something else preoccupying them: they wanted the Templars present in Paris to choose proxies to represent them and to respond to the 127 articles of accusation brought against the Order within the framework of the proceedings decided by Pope Clement in the bull *Faciens misericordiam* of 2 August 1308.

Those proceedings were designed to find out not whether the Templars were guilty or innocent but, rather, whether the Order was guilty or not. Its purpose was to verify whether the Order was guilty of having, through the bad practices of which it was accused – practices which the commissioners seemed convinced did exist – encouraged and covered up the crime of heresy. And so the commissioners expected the Templars to help them, by responding honestly and truthfully to the 127 articles, to verify whether the Order was guilty of heresy.

The papal commission was the pope's commission and not the king's. The two men had agreed on a compromise in Poitiers, and so the commission was an instrument of that compromise. There was no question that the pope would thwart the king by recognising the innocence of the Order and the brothers, but nor would he justify the action undertaken by the king and his agents against the Order by acknowledging any heresy on the part of the Templars. Substance and form!

In the end, the papal commission of Paris worked to provide arguments to support the solution that the pope planned to set out at the Council of Vienne: the Order of the Temple could not be condemned for heresy because it was not heretical; but the errors of its members sullied its reputation (its *fama*) and rendered it useless. And so it would be suppressed. The king of France certainly believed, through his inopportune initiative, that he had acted for the good of the Church; he can be forgiven, but nevertheless he was wrong.

Individual Templars may have been guilty of erring. If they humbly acknowledged their errors, they would be pardoned after a light penance. If they continued to deny, they were not innocent but stubborn, which merited not death but a just and severe punishment. Finally, if after having acknowledged their errors, they retracted their confessions because they had been obtained through torture, pressure and ill treatment, they would not be considered relapsed: the archbishop of Sens was thwarted; but the Templars deserved a just punishment following canon law. What would it be? Life in prison, probably, as in the preceding case. There were no burnings at the stake following the decisions of Vienne.[7] The fires ignited in 1314 for Jacques de Molay and Geoffroy de Charney were by order of the king, even if Elizabeth Brown has recently presented a contrary view on this point.[8]

Henri de Harcigny, or the Templar resistance

With their defensive position of February–May 1310, the Templars who came to testify before the papal commission seriously upset the ongoing proceedings and damaged the compromise of Poitiers. They had come to proclaim their innocence and to defend the purity of their Order. They requested that they be able to do so at the Council of Vienne, and some actually appeared, counting on their allies, the support of priests of the Council and even of French bishops.

In short, the Templars resisted and not only during the three months in the spring of 1310. Before. Afterwards. There was a broader resistance, which lasted some time. We cannot escape our sources. On 13 September 1307 the royal order of arrest set out the Templars' main crimes; the following year those crimes were embellished, sorted and reorganised into two lists of 88 and 127 articles. The instructions attached to that arrest order instructed the royal agents and inquisitors to investigate to obtain the truth – that is, a confession of those crimes – through torture, if necessary: 'and if [the Templars] confess the truth, they [the king's agents, the inquisitors] will put their depositions in writing after having called witnesses.'[9] On 22 September the inquisitor of France asked his colleagues in the Midi to hear the depositions of the Templars there and, if it appeared that the crimes were true, 'to send without delay the depositions to the lord king and to us, in France'.[10]

On 23 November 1307, Raoul de Ligny, inquisitor in the bishoprics of Metz, Toul and Verdun, wrote to the king to tell him that the preceding 25 October he had interrogated two German Templars arrested in the bailiwick of Chaumont while they were returning to their country. Conrad de Mayence and brother Henri categorically denied the accusations. Raoul released the two Templars, who continued their journey to Germany. He waited for several weeks before sending the report of the interrogations to the king: the two Templars having confessed nothing, their testimony was useless and did not merit an official record. He created one, however, at the request of the bailiff of Chaumont, but the letter was sealed only with his seal, and the record did not become a public instrument bearing the seal of a notary.[11]

In the following months the king, in order to find support for his actions against the Templars, revealed the number of them who had confessed: 500 in January 1308, he wrote to the king of Aragon.[12] There was not a word, of course, about those who did not admit anything. And Guillaume de Plaisians, in his speech in Poitiers on 29 May, relied on the hundreds of confessions obtained to force the pope's hand.[13] We know that four Templars (out of 138) interrogated by the inquisitors in Paris did not confess; we also know that not all the Templars who were prisoners at the Temple of Paris at the time were interrogated or, if they were, that they did not all have the honour of seeing their depositions recorded by the notaries. Perhaps they did not tell the truth? The continuator of Guillaume de Nangis writes 'that a large number [of Templars] denied absolutely everything and several, who had at first confessed, then denied and continued their denials to the end'.[14] Guillaume de Plaisians, still in May 1308 in Poitiers, hinted that the pope, through his hesitations, was favouring the Templars' retractions of their confessions.

The proceedings against individuals undertaken by the bishop of Clermont in 1309 show two things: the large number of Templars who were on the run in that diocese, hidden and protected by relatives or friends; and that the bishops were not royal agents or inquisitors – the bishop of Clermont interrogated everyone and recorded all the depositions, though more briefly, it is true, for those of the Templars who denied. In Clermont, twenty-nine denied while forty confessed.[15]

I won't look again in detail at the true revolt of the Templars in February–May 1310, and will mention only some significant figures: 659 Templars were present at the time in Paris, the vast majority of whom were there to defend the Order. One hundred succumbed to fear after the shocking actions of the archbishop of Sens on 11 May 1310, and renewed the confessions they had made earlier.[16] And what about the other 500? Were they non-reconciled, like the 70 who were held in prisons in the bailiwick of Senlis between June 1310 and 1312?[17] None of them gave depositions before the commission in 1311, whereas 37 of the 52 other reconciled Templars, also detained in the bailiwick, did.

Let's add the attempts made by the Templars at the end of 1311 to defend the Order before the Council of Vienne; there were probably not fifteen hundred or two thousand of them, but there must have been more than the nine who dared to appear before the large commission and who were arrested. We should also take into account what Jean de Pouilly, the theologian who was very hostile to the Templar cause, present at the Council, said: 'that he had seen and heard many Templars who appeared in order to defend the Order'.[18]

Thus it was not only in February–May 1310 that the Templars resisted. Given the size of their revolt, we might call it a rebellion, but it must in any case be placed within a continuous movement of resistance throughout the years 1307–12. Deprived of leaders, as Jacques de Molay and the other dignitaries of the Order proved not to be up to the task – the sacrifice of the Grand Master and Geoffroy de Charney in 1314 only partially made up for a position that must certainly be attributed not to a lack of courage but rather to a lack of discernment in their choice of defence strategy – betrayed by the pope, even though they might have seen that he was dealing with extenuating circumstances, the Templars created a united front.

The problem is that we don't know – or have only a very sketchy idea of – who the resisters were. They existed outside of the interrogation records to which historians rush to 'pull out the true from the false'. There is, of course, a lot of 'truth' in those records, but not where scholars like to 'dig around': not in the 'confessions' but alongside them, in the thousand and one pieces of information we glean through asides, small (and sometimes larger) paragraphs describing everyday life during the proceedings, through those masses of Templar names, consciously (and sometimes 'fancifully') recorded by the commission notaries and destined for the most part to remain only names whose silence says more and delivers more truth than the lamentable confessions obtained through torture.

Shall we look at one example of this?

Who will ever know who Henri de Harcigny, the Templar with seven names, really was: his name is written Hercigni (10 November 1307), Arsigni (5 February 1308), Li Abès (10 February 1310), Antinhi (13 March 1310), Archeim (28 March 1310), Hentingentis (4 April 1310) and Arsegny (January 1312). A native of the diocese of Laon, he owed his name to the village of Harcigny, canton of Vervins, in the Aisne. Henricus de Hercigni was forty years old when he was interrogated in Paris on 10 November 1307 and had just been received into the Order, shortly before the Feast of the Purification of the Virgin (2 February 1307), by Jean de Celle, commander of the house of Seraincourt, in the diocese of Reims. His deposition was briefly recorded (twelve lines), and for good reason: 'He said through his oath that he made many promises to observe the statutes and secrets of the Order, and nothing else dishonest was asked of or said to him; and he said that he knew of nothing dishonest about the Order.' [19] Was there pressure, violence, torture? We'll never know. Refusing to accuse the Order, he was of no interest to his judges.

Imprisoned in the Temple, Henri de Arsigni was transferred on 5 February 1308 with nine other Templars to Peiners or Peavers in the diocese of Sens, a non-identified place, but which could be Pers-en-Gâtinais, canton of Ferrières in the Loiret. [20] Out of his nine fellow detainees, seven confessed before the inquisitors, but Jean de Paris, like him, did not give in; the ninth, Gilles de Valenciennes, was not interrogated. This group of ten Templars stayed in this detention site for two years. All ten of them, including Anricus Li Abès, went to Paris to defend the Order on 10 February 1310. [21] They were present at the meeting of ninety Templars on 13 March (Henricus de Antinhi) and on 28 March in the orchard of the bishopric (Anricus de Archeim). [22] The ten, including Henricus de Hentingentis, were held in the residence of Penne Vayrié on rue de Lieudelle, with thirteen other Templars who had come from Trappes on 23 February; they were registered there on 4 April 1310. [23] The group was later dispersed.

We lose sight of Jean de Paris, who had not confessed, and several others. Jean de Nivelles or de Borletta did not persevere in his defence of the Temple and went back to his initial confession before the papal commission on 15 February 1311. [24] Henri de Arsegny, Gilles de Valenciennes and Nicolas d'Amiens were taken to Senlis to be detained, in the residence of Pierre de la Cloche, where their presence was noted in April 1311 and January 1312 in a group of ten non-reconciled Templars. [25] Nicolas d'Amiens had confessed in November 1307; he must have appeared before a diocesan commission before which he retracted his initial confession and then held to that latter position, which would explain why he wasn't reconciled.

Henri de Harcigny, who entered the Temple at forty, eight months before the arrests, proved to be very consistent: from 1307 to 1312 he never admitted anything. After that he must have been sentenced to life in prison. No one would imagine, I think, that he had an easy time of it. His was a path that, far from being unique, wonderfully illustrates the obstinate resistance of not a negligible number of Templars.

APPENDICES

A PROBLEM OF IDENTIFICATION: THIERS-SUR-THÈVE (DIOCESE OF SENLIS)

Beginning on 6 February 1310 and until 2 May of the same year, forty-three groups of Templars appeared in Paris to defend the Order, having come from various places in the kingdom. Only one place is difficult to identify, and thus to locate on a map.[1]

On 14 February 1310 eleven Templars brought from Tyers in the diocese of Sens appeared before the commission. I have not been able to identify this place in the localities included in the diocese of Sens at that time, unless it was Turri, or Thoury in the *département* of the Loiret, which is an arbitrary guess. A careful examination of the make-up of the group suggests a different location. Eight of the eleven Templars from this group were natives of the Picardy and Champagne dioceses: Tournai, Laon, Beauvais, Troyes, Langres (two) and Reims (two); another man, indicated as being a native of the diocese of Vienne, was in reality from Châlons-en-Champagne (see Appendix 2). The last two were natives of the dioceses of Paris and Sens, but Jean de Montmélian (Johannes de Monte Meliandi), also called Jean Lochan, Loychon, Louton or Lozon, came from Montmélian, in the Oise, located to the south of Senlis (and belonging to the royal bailiwick of Senlis) but in the diocese of Paris.

We find these Templars, divided into two groups, in other documents dating from 1308 and 1310–11. Five of them were transferred on 31 January 1308 from the Temple of Paris to Montmélian: these were Jean Lochon or de Montmélian, Jean Malvenu (or Malip, Malvo), Pierre de Landres, Bertrand de Saint-Paul and Pierre Mambresis (or Maubretis).[2] They were still imprisoned there as non-reconciled Templars after they went to Paris in February 1310, and are noted as being there between July 1310 and 1311.[3] As for the six others, also non-reconciled, they were held during the same period in Thiers-sur-Thève, in the bailiwick of Senlis:[4] they were Jean Poitevin (or Peytavin), Bertrand de Bissy (or Bernard de Bissy), Laurent de Provins, Hugues de Villers, Jacques de Saci and one other, whom we are unable to identify with certainty. The two locations of Montmélian, which belonged to the commune of Plailly, and Thiers-sur-Thève were in the canton of Senlis, in the Oise. In 1310–11 they were both part of the bailiwick of Senlis, but Thiers was part of the diocese of Senlis, and Plailly and Montmélian in the diocese of Paris.

Would the Tyers of the diocese of Sens be the Thiers-sur-Thève of the diocese of Senlis? In which case the scribe who wrote down the names of the group of 14 February would have been mistaken about the identification and the location of the place, confusing Sens and Senlis.[5] This is a hypothesis that another document corroborates and reinforces. Again on Tuesday 31 January a group of six Templars, whose names are unfortunately not provided, was transferred from the Temple of Paris to Thiais, which was soon identified as Thiais, commune of Val-de-Marne, near Paris; the sergeant responsible for moving and guarding these six Templars was 'Jehan Le Chervoisier'. Now in 1310–11 the guard of the Templars of Thiers-sur-Thève was 'Jehan Le Sernoizier', sergeant on horseback from Châtelet of Paris. Le Chervoisier and Le Sernoizier were clearly the same person. Just like Tyers, Thiais was a mistake; it was Thiers-sur-Thève.

The eleven Templars of 14 February 1310 had been transferred in 1308 from Paris to two locations next to the bailiwick of Senlis, one in the diocese of Senlis (Thiers-sur-Thève), the other in the diocese of Paris (Montmélian). Brought together, they travelled from Thiers-sur-Thève to Paris before 14 February. When at the end of May 1310 the papal commission adjourned until 3 November, they were taken back to their respective prisons, where, as records show, they remained from July 1310 to the middle of 1311. They either did not confess or had recanted their confessions and maintained their positions because they were not reconciled.

THE STRANGE DIOCESE OF VIENNE, ON THE BORDERS OF THE ARGONNE FOREST

The diocese of Vienne, of the ecclesiastical province of the same name, belonged not to the kingdom of France but to the Dauphiné, which was at that time a territory of the Empire. Because of that, the Templars arrested in that diocese were not summoned before the papal commission based in Paris. It is, however, possible that the Templars who came from the diocese, arrested in the kingdom of France, may have appeared before the commission in Paris. So it would not be surprising if in the lists compiled by the commission notaries or from among the interrogated Templars we find a few of them who were natives of the diocese of Vienne. Yet there is something suspicious about the Templars from that diocese appearing on the lists and at the interrogations in the trial records. Seven are cited in the publication by Michelet and another in the records of the trial in Cyprus.

In Michelet one finds cited:

- Petrus de sancto Maniero or Mamerto, interrogated, Michelet, vol. I, pp. 71, 566, 586–8;
- Humbertus de Torbone, interrogated in 1307 and 1310, Michelet, vol. I, pp. 65, 107, 114, 282, 377, 406–9; Michelet, vol. II, p. 366;
- Petrus de Moydies, Modies, interrogated, Michelet, vol. II, pp. 263, 265–7;
- Johannes de Chali, interrogated, Michelet, vol. II, pp. 263, 263–5;
- Bertrandus (or Bernardus) de sancto Paulo, defender of the Order, who came from Thiers-sur-Thève, not interrogated, Michelet, vol. I, pp. 69, 104, 129, 130;

- Petrus de Symeyo, Surref, Sivref, Syare, not interrogated, Michelet, vol. I, pp. 65, 108, 114, 282;
- Ancherius de Suete, Sivré, Syare, not interrogated, Michelet, vol. I, pp. 70, 137, 282.

Cited in Schottmüller, *Untergang*, vol. II, p. 81, one finds Aymo de Gala or de Claramonte, interrogated in Cyprus in 1310.

Let's add to our dossier a sizeable but enlightening geographical blunder: Gérard de Passage, of the diocese of Metz, interrogated on 27 April 1310, indicated that he accompanied the commander of Trêves who was going to Paris for the chapter and that he had been sent to the residence of Valloysia (this was Avalleur, Aube) of the diocese of Vienne at the time when he says he had gone to a reception held in Chalon (sur Saône) (Michelet, vol. I, p. 216).

This is what should lead us to question the 'Vienne' origin of those Templars.

Interrogated on 20 February 1311, Pierre de Saint-Mamert, a sergeant brother, was received in Mormant, diocese of Langres, around Easter 1305.

Humbert de Torbone was interrogated on 9 November 1307 in Paris, then on 15 January 1311; he was a knight, was received in La Neuville near Châlons, on the Feast of Saint John the Baptist 1290 or 1292 and occupied the function of commander of the *baillie* of Châlons at the time of his arrest. A defender of the Temple, he appeared before the papal commission on 10 February 1310, but withheld his support of the Order on 19 May 1310. His name appeared in various spellings and forms: Torbone (Michelet, vol. I, p. 65), Torvono, sancto Jocro (Michelet, vol. I, p. 114), sancto Jorio (Michelet, vol. I, p. 406), sancto Jorre (Michelet, vol. I, p. 377), sancto Jorgio (Michelet, vol. I, p. 282) and even Lambertus de Tornon (Michelet, vol. I, p. 107).

Jean de Chali, interrogated on 26 May 1311 was received in Bure, diocese of Langres, on Christmas 1301 (Michelet, vol. II, pp. 263–5).

Pierre de Modies, interrogated the same day as Jean de Chali, was received in Thors, in the diocese of Langres as well, on Christmas 1303 (Michelet, vol. I, pp. 265–7).

Aymon de Gala, or de Clermont (in Argonne), interrogated in Cyprus in 1310, was received in La Neuville on Christmas 1304 or 1305 by Gaucher de Liancourt, commander of the *baillie* of Reims, in the presence of Humbert de Torbone and of Andrea, chaplain of La Neuville (Schottmüller, *Untergang*, vol. II, p. 181).

These five Templars were thus received in the dioceses of Reims, Châlons-en-Champagne and Langres: that is, in a geographical sector that had nothing to do with the diocese of Vienne and the Dauphiné.

Humbert de Torbone or Saint-Joire was the uncle of Aymo de Gala-Clermont and of a Pierre de Torbone or Tolvo, knight, who had entered the Temple around 1303 in La Neuville; Humbert attended the second reception conducted by Aymon d'Oiselay, future marshal of the Temple in Cyprus, in the following months. Another Pierre de Torbone, also a knight, and who had died before the date of the testimony, is cited by Pierre de Janz, sergeant of the diocese of Beauvais (Michelet, vol. II, pp. 32–4): Pierre de Janz and Gérard de La Chape (from the diocese of Châlons) were received together by that Pierre de Torbone in La Neuville 'it will have been twenty-eight years on the next Feast of Saint John the Baptist', or in 1283; and among those present at that reception were a Jacques de Vienne, sergeant, and brother Andrea, chaplain of the house of La Neuville cited several times in the records by the names of Andrea, Andrea de Roche or Andrea de Vienne (Michelet, vol. II, pp. 32–4; Michelet, vol. I, pp. 406–7; Schottmüller, *Untergang*, vol. II, p. 207).

A look at a simple Michelin map may clear up the confusion about that curious diocese of Vienne. On the border of what was once called 'flea-ridden' Champagne and the forest of Argonne flows the Tourbe, whose source is at Somme-Tourbe and which flows to the north, where it irrigates Ville-sur-Tourbe before joining the Aisne, while parallel to it is the Brionne, which originates in Somme-Brionne, which also flows north, passing through Vienne-la-Ville where it connects with a stream that comes from Vienne-le-Château. A bit farther to the east, on the other side of the forest of Argonne, is Clermont-en-Argonne. The commandery of La Neuville-au-Temple was located some 40 kilometres to the west of these places, 10 kilometres to the north of Châlons-en-Champagne; today it is the commune of Dampierre-au-Temple.

The scribes and notaries of 1310–11 did not have a Michelin map. The Templars in question, when they stated their identities, perhaps told them that they came from Vienne, which was probably correct. On their registers they turned that into the diocese of Vienne, which was not correct.

It wouldn't surprise me if the same type of error was also committed on the subject of Amblard de Vienne, listed as a knight of Vienne, active in the Order before 1283 to 1295 at least, and who spent his entire career in Poitou-Aquitaine, of which he was the master during that period. The River Vienne flows through there.

THE ARTICLES OF ACCUSATION AGAINST THE TEMPLARS

The list below shows the 88 articles brought against individual Templars and the 127 articles against the Order. The articles found in both sets of proceedings are indicated in Roman script, and those that were brought only against the Order are in italics. Article 61 was divided for the two sets of proceedings, causing the list of 88 articles to be renumbered; the new numbers are given in parentheses.

Even though the Templars insisted that their Order responded exclusively to a holy cause, and that it had been approved by the apostolic see, it was still true that during their reception brothers of that Order had observed the following rites:

1. When he was first received into the Order, or at some time afterwards, or as soon as an opportunity arose, the postulant was induced or admonished by those who had received him within the bosom of the fraternity, to renounce Christ or Jesus, or the crucifixion, or at one time God and at another time the blessed virgin and sometimes all the saints.
2. The brothers carried out these rites as a group.
3. The majority of them did this.
4. Sometimes even after their reception.
5. Those who received them taught that Christ was not the true God (or Jesus, or the Crucified One).
6. That he had been a false prophet.
7. That he had suffered his Passion and his suffering not for the redemption of mankind but as punishment for the crimes he had committed.

8.   That neither the receiver nor those who had been received could hope to be saved by Jesus; the former told this to the latter (or the equivalent of it).

9.   Postulants were induced to spit on the cross, on an image of the cross, on a carved cross or on an image of Christ (except that, sometimes, postulants spat next to it).

10.   They were sometimes ordered to trample on the cross.

11.   The brothers who were received sometimes trampled on the cross of their own volition.

12.   They urinated on the cross, while stepping on it, and made others urinate: this would happen on Good Friday.

13.   Some of them, on that day or throughout Holy Week, met together to perform such acts.

14.   They worshipped a cat, which from time to time appeared during their meetings.

15.   They performed this ceremony in contempt of Christ and the Catholic faith.

16.   They did not believe in the sacrament of the altar.

17.   Some of them.

18.   The majority of them.

19.   Nor in the other sacraments of the Church.

20.   The priests of the Order did not utter the words by which the body of Christ is consecrated in the canon of the Mass.

21.   Some of them.

22.   The majority.

23.   Those who received them ordered them to do so.

24.   They believed, or at least they were told, that the Grand Master could absolve them of their sins.

25.   The Visitor, as well.

26.   The commanders as well, many of whom were lay brothers.

27.   And so they absolved them.

28.   At least some of them.

29.   The Grand Master of the Order had confessed, before eminent persons, even before his arrest.[6]

30.   During the reception of the brothers or around that time, the one who received and the one who was received sometimes kissed each

other on the mouth, the navel or the naked stomach, as well as on the anus or the backbone.

31. Only on the navel.
32. On the lower back.
33. On the penis.
34. During this ceremony postulants were made to swear that they would not leave the Order.
35. They were immediately ordered to swear this.
36. Receptions occurred clandestinely.
37. Only brothers of the Order attended.
38. This is why there has long been a strong suspicion against the Order.
39. The suspicion is widespread.
40. Newly received brothers were told they could have carnal relations with one another.
41. That it was allowed for them to do so.
42. That they should allow it and receive it reciprocally.
43. That to do so was not a sin for them.
44. They did it themselves, or a large number of them.
45. A few did.
46. In every province they had idols, meaning heads, some of which had three faces, others only one, others in the shape of a human skull.
47. These idols, or idol, were worshipped, especially in their great Chapters and gatherings.
48. They venerated them.
49. Like God.
50. As their saviour.
51. A few did.
52. The majority of the members of the Chapter did.
53. They claimed that the head could save them.
54. That it made them rich.
55. That it gave them all the wealth of the Order.
56. That it made trees blossom.
57. Made the earth to bring forth seed.

58. They bound or touched the head of the idols with cords, with which they bound themselves around their shirts or next to their skin.

59. These small cords were given to every brother during his reception, or a piece of cord.

60. They did this in worshipping the idol.

61. They were ordered to wear the cords constantly, even at night.

(62) Even at night.

62 (63) This was the usual way brothers were received.

63 (64) Everywhere.

64 (65) The majority of them.

65 (66) Those who refused to carry out these rites during their reception or afterwards were killed or thrown in prison.

66 (67) Some of them.

67 (68) The majority of them.

68 (69) They were ordered, under oath, to reveal nothing of these ceremonies.

69 (70) Under penalty of death or prison.

70 (70) They were forbidden to reveal the way they were received.

71 (72) They did not dare to talk about it among themselves.

72 (73) If one of them were discovered revealing it, he was punished by death or prison.

73 (74) They were ordered to confess only to brothers of the Order.

74 (75) The brothers told of these sins did not correct them.

75 (76) Or denounce them to our Holy Mother Church.

76 (77) They did not break with the observance, nor with the communion of brothers, though they were able to do so.

77. *All of this was observed Outremer, in the places where depending on the time the Grand Master and the convent of the Order resided.*

78. *Sometimes the denial of Christ was carried out in the presence of the Grand Master or the convent.*

79. *It was usually observed in Cyprus.*

80. *As well as overseas, in all the kingdoms and places where brothers were received into the Order.*

81. *It was observed in the entire Order, in a general and common way.*

82. *For a long time.*

83. *Following an old custom.*

84. *Following the statutes of the Order.*

85. *These observances, customs, ordonnances and statutes ruled the entire Order, here and beyond the seas.*

86. *They were part of the rules of the Order introduced after the approval of the apostolic see.*

87. *The receptions of the brothers were conducted, in a general way, throughout the Order in this way.*

88. *The Grand Master ordered its observation.*

89. *As did the Visitors.*

90. *As did the commanders.*

91. *As did other dignitaries of the Order.*

92. *They observed them themselves, and saw that they were observed.*

93. *Some of them did.*

94. *No other way of reception into the Order was observed.*

95. *In the memory of any member of the Order still alive, there was never in his time another way of being received.*

96. *The Grand Master, the Visitors, the commanders, and other masters of the Order severely punished those who didn't observe or refused to observe these rites and the rest.*

97. *In this Order, neither alms nor hospitality were observed as was appropriate.*

98 (79). In this Order it was not considered a sin to acquire the goods of others legally or illegally.

99 (78). In this Order they swore an oath to work to enrich the Order using all means, both legal and illegal.

100. *It was not considered a sin to perjure oneself in this area.*

101. *Chapters were held in secret.*

102. *In secret, either at the hour of the first sleep, or during the first awakening in the night.*

103. *In secret when all the people outside the Order were out of the residence and its grounds.*

104. *In secret, given that the Templars withdrew to hold their Chapter, and locked the doors of the residence and the church so tightly that it was no longer possible to have the slightest access, or to see or hear what went on inside.*

105. *In such secret they placed guards on the roof of the residence or the church where they held their Chapter, in order to prevent anyone from approaching.*

106. *This secret they observed especially during the reception of brothers.*

107. *For a long time there persisted in the Order the depraved opinion that the Grand Master could absolve the brothers of their sins.*

108. *Even more serious: the Grand Master could absolve the brothers of their sins, even not confessed, if they did not confess them, through shame or fear of the penance that would be inflicted upon them.*

109. *These errors, the Grand Master recognised them before his arrest, spontaneously, before trustworthy clerics and laymen.*

110. *In the presence of great dignitaries of the Order.*

111. *Those who committed these errors, got them and continue to get them, not only from the Grand Master, but even from other commanders and above all from visitors of the Order.*

112. *All that the Grand Master, especially with his General Chapter did and decided, was to be observed by the entire Order.*

113. *He demanded this power and had appropriated it for some time.*

114. *These perverse customs and depravity lasted for so long that the Order could have been reformed once, twice or several times, by individuals, since they were introduced.*

115. *All those who, in the Order, in its two parts (in the Orient and in the Occident) knew about these depravities refused to correct them.*

116. *Or to denounce them to our Holy Mother Church.*

117. *Still did not break with the observance of these sins nor with the communion of the sinning brothers, even though they could have done so.*

118. *A large number of brothers left the Order because of the ignominy and the depravity, some to enter into another house, others to remain in the world.*

119. *For all these reasons, a profound indignation has shaken against the Order the hearts of high personages, kings and princes, and has extended to almost all the Christian people.*

120 (80). All these facts are well known by the brothers of the Order.

121 (81). They are of public knowledge and common opinion both among the brothers of the Order and outside it.

122. *Of the majority of them, at least.*

123. *Of some.*

124. *The Grand Master of the Order, the Visitor, the grand masters of Cyprus, Normandy, and Poitou, as well as many other commanders* (82) and some of the brothers of the Order have acknowledged these facts, both in judgement as elsewhere, before solemn people, in several places and before several public people.

125 (83). Some of the brothers of the Order, knights and priests, and others in the presence of our lords the pope and the cardinals have acknowledged the facts, at least in large part.

126 (84). Under oath.

127 (85). Even some in a consistory.

(86). We will also investigate the brothers as individuals, about their reception, the place it occurred, the time of their reception and those in attendance, as well as the way in which they were received.

(87). Item, if they knew or heard when and by whom the alleged sins began and where they took root; and the causes and circumstances
. . .

(88). Item, it will be asked of brothers if they knew where alleged heads or idols or others were, and by what means they were carried and kept and by whom?

Appendix 4

ORIGINAL DIOCESES OF TEMPLARS WHO APPEARED IN PARIS FROM 6 FEBRUARY TO 2 MAY 1310

Province of Reims

Reims	14
Châlons-en-Champagne	9
Laon	25
Noyon	12
Amiens	40
Soissons	25
Senlis	2
Beauvais	26
Thérouanne	5
Cambrai	8
Arras	4
Tournai	13
Total	*183*

Province of Sens

Sens	22
Auxerre	7
Nevers	4
Troyes	19
Meaux	11
Paris	36
Chartres	18
Orléans	7
Total	*124*

Province of Rouen[7]

Rouen	13
Évreux	10
Lisieux	1
Sées	2
Bayeux	6
Coutances	5
Total	*37*

Province of Tours[8]

Tours	14
Le Mans	1
Saint-Brieuc	1
Total	*16*

Province of Lyon

Lyon	3
Mâcon	1
Chalon-sur-Saône	3
Autun	19
Langres	74
Total	*100*

Province of Bordeaux[9]	
Bordeaux	0
Poitiers	10
Angoulême	3
Périgueux	3
Total	16

Province of Bourges[10]	
Bourges	15
Limoges	33
Clermont	29
Le Puy	2
Cahors	15
Rodez	6
Albi	4
Total	104

Province of Auch[11]	
Auch	3
Lectoure	1
Tarbes	3
Couserans	6
Total	13

Province of Narbonne[12]	
Narbonne	5
Toulouse	5
Carcassonne	3
Pamiers	2
Béziers	3
Agde	6
Maguelonne	4
Nîmes	3
Uzès	2
Total	33

Distribution by large geographical groupings

North (archbishoprics of Reims, Rouen, Sens, plus Langres and Autun)	437
West (Tours)	16
Centre (Bordeaux, Bourges, Lyon, minus Langres and Autun)	127
South (Auch, Narbonne)	46

Dioceses of other ecclesiastical provinces

Viviers:[13] 1; Geneva: 1; Besançon: 5;
Elne: 1; Aix-en-Provence: 1; Asti: 1; Bologna: 1;
Salisbury: 1; Liège: 4;
Toul: 1; Verdun: 1; Mayence: 1; Magdebourg: 1;
Trèves: 1

Trajenctensis (Utrecht?): 1
The so-called diocese of Vienne:[14] 5

TEMPLARS PRESENT AT THE PROVINCIAL COUNCILS OF SENS AND REIMS

Templars who participated in the council of the province of Sens in Paris:
(* = did not participate in the defence of the Order on 19 May 1310)

Gautier de Bure (Michelet, vol. I, p. 296)

Odo de Dona Petra (Michelet, vol. I, p. 306)

Garnier de Venesi (Michelet, vol. I, p. 311)

Aimeri de Burez (Michelet, vol. I, p. 316)

Jean Quentin (Michelet, vol. I, p. 334)

Jean de Branlis (Michelet, vol. I, 337)

Jean de Saint-Quest (Michelet, vol. I, p. 338)

Simon de Corbon (Michelet, vol. I, p. 350)

Jean de Viviers (Michelet, vol. I, p. 355)

Simon de Lyons-en-Santerre (Lechuno) (Michelet, vol. I, p. 364)

Gérard de Causse (Michelet, vol. I, p. 379)

Humbert de Torbone or Saint-Joire (Michelet, vol. I, p. 406)*

Guy Dauphin (Michelet, vol. I, p. 415)

Renaud de Tremblay (Michelet, vol. I, p. 421)*

Philippe Agate (Michelet, vol. I, p. 428)

Jean de Saint-Leu (Michelet, vol. I, p. 431)*

Barthélemy de Troyes (Michelet, vol. I, p. 433)*

Othon de Anone (Michelet, vol. I, p. 436)

Lambert de Cormeilles (Michelet, vol. I, p. 439)

Robert de Cormeilles (Michelet, vol. I, p. 441)

Raynier de Larchant (Michelet, vol. I, p. 494)*

Pierre d'Herblay (Michelet, vol. I, p. 496)*

Guillaume d'Herblay (Michelet, vol. I, p. 498)

Jacques Le Verjus (Michelet, vol. I, p. 503)*

Jean de Romprey (Michelet, vol. I, p. 506)

Jean de Buffavent (Michelet, vol. I, p. 509)

Robert Vigier (Michelet, vol. I, p. 512)

Pierre de Blois (Michelet, vol. I, p. 514)*

Simon de Commercy (Michelet, vol. I, p. 517)*

Jean de Cormele (Michelet, vol. I, p. 520)*

Pierre Picard (Michelet, vol. I, p. 522)*

Christian de Bicey (Michelet, vol. I, p. 524)*

Pons de Benèvre (Michelet, vol. I, p. 538)*

Jean de Bessu St-Germain (Michelet, vol. I, p. 541)*

Thibaud de Basimont (Michelet, vol. I, p. 543)*

Thomas Quentin (Michelet, vol. I, p. 554)*

Humbert de Germila (Michelet, vol. I, p. 560)*

Nicolas de Troyes (Michelet, vol. I, p. 571)*

Pierre de Cercellis (Michelet, vol. I, p. 574)*

Gilles de Chevru (Michelet, vol. I, p. 578)*

Jean de Nici (Michelet, vol. I, p. 581)

Raoul de Saulx (Michelet, vol. I, p. 583)*

Jean de l'Aumône (Michelet, vol. I, p. 588)

Jean de Tour, treasurer (Michelet, vol. I, p. 595)

Renaud de Provins (Michelet, vol. II, pp. 3–4)

Jean de Mortefontaine (Michelet, vol. II, p. 3)

Guillaume de Hoymont (Michelet, vol. II, p. 3)

Renaud de Cugnières (Michelet, vol. II, p. 4)

Pierre de Clermont-en-Beauvaisis (Michelet, vol. II, p. 4)

Bernard de Sornay (Michelet, vol. II, p. 4)

Pierre de Grumesnil (Michelet, vol. II, p. 23)*

Guillaume Boncelli (Michelet, vol. II, p. 26)*

Baudouin de Gisa (Michelet, vol. II, p. 28)

Jean de Pont-l'Évêque (Michelet, vol. II, p. 30)*

Pierre de Janz (Michelet, vol. II, p. 32)*

Étienne de Tour (Michelet, vol. II, p. 35)*

Jean de Frégeville (Michelet, vol. II, p. 37)

Eudes de Bure (Michelet, vol. II, p. 109)

Jean de Noyon (Michelet, vol. II, p. 261)*

Templars who participated in the council of the province of Reims in Senlis (May/June 1310):

Thomas de Jamvalle (Michelet, vol. I, p. 443)

Robert Le Brioys (Michelet, vol. I, p. 447)

Guillaume de la Place (Michelet, vol. I, p. 450)

Gilles de Rotengi (Michelet, vol. I, p. 463)

Foulques de Neuilly (Michelet, vol. I, p. 477)

Alliaume (Adelinus) de Lignières (Michelet, vol. I, p. 479)

Nicolas de Meanny (Michelet, vol. I, p. 482)

Thomas de Rochancourt (Boncourt) (Michelet, vol. I, p. 485)

Jean de Grèz (Gressibus) (Michelet, vol. I, p. 487)

Hugues d'Oisemont (Michelet, vol. I, p. 490)

Mathieu de Cressonessart (Michelet, vol. I, p. 535)

Pierre de Sainte-Maxence (Michelet, vol. I, p. 621)

Raoul de Taverny (Michelet, vol. I, p. 626)

Bono de Voulaines (Vollenis) (Michelet, vol. I, p. 630)

Dominique de Dijon (Michelet, vol. I, p. 632)

Henri de Faverolles (Michelet, vol. I, p. 634)

Virmundus de Sanconi (Michelet, vol. I, p. 637)

Nicolas de Compiègne (Michelet, vol. I, p. 639)

Pierre de Lagny (Michelet, vol. II, p. 1)

Robert Le Verrier (Michelet, vol. II, p. 41)

Jean Peynet (Pernet) (Michelet, vol. II, p. 71)

Robert de Ramboval (Reinheval, alias Preposito) (Michelet, vol. II, p. 74)

Jean Bocher de Grandvillers (Michelet, vol. II, p. 77)

Gilles de Lovencourt (Lana Curia) (Michelet, vol. II, p. 112)

Guy de Belleville (Michelet, vol. II, p. 114)

Jean de Canes (Michelet, vol. II, p. 116)

Henri de Compiègne (Michelet, vol. II, p. 118)

LIST OF TEMPLARS WHO REFUSED TO DEFEND THE ORDER ON 19 MAY 1310

After that, the following Tuesday which was the 19th day of May, there gathered in the chapel of the aforementioned Saint-Éloi, said lord commissioners, with the exception of the lords of Narbonne and Bayeux, excused as was mentioned above, and were brought to the presence of said lord commissioners the brothers named below who, ordered individually (*sigillatim*) by the above-mentioned lord commissioners to say why they had come, each responded for them that, as once they had been offered before said lord commissioners to defend the Order of the Temple, in the same way they wished to withdraw and withdrew said defence and renounced their defence. The names of said brothers are:

Names	*Diocese*	*Date of presentation before the commission*
Humbertus de sancto Jorgio	Vienne (*sic*)	16 Jan. 1311 (Michelet, vol. I, p. 402)
Ancherius and	Vienne (*sic*)	
Petrus de Syare knights	Vienne (*sic*)	
Petrus de sancta Gressa	Amiens	
Johannes de Ponte Episcopi	Noyon	11 Mar. 1311 (Michelet, vol. II, p. 30)
P. de Jans	Beauvais	11 Mar. 1311 (Michelet, vol. II, p. 32)
Philippus de Villa Selva	Noyon	
Egidius de Cheruto	Sens	19 Feb. 1311 (Michelet, vol. I, p. 578)
Otho de Anona	Langres	22 Jan. 1311 (Michelet, vol. I, p. 436)
P. de Cheruto	Sens	11 Feb. 1311 (Michelet, vol. I, p. 529)
Aymo de Perbona	Troyes	
Robertus de Monboin	Sens	

Names	Diocese	Date of presentation before the commission
Thomas de Martinhiaco, priest	Laon	
Symon de Cormissiaco	Reims	9 Feb. 1311 (Michelet, vol. I, p. 517)
Poncius de Bono Opere	Langres	12 Feb. 1311 (Michelet, vol. I, p. 538)
Johannes de Noviomo	Soissons	22 May 1311 (Michelet, vol. II, p. 261)
Nicolaus de Trecis	Soissons	18 Feb. 1311 (Michelet, vol. I, p. 571)
Johannes de Bersi de sancto Germano	Soissons	12 Feb. 1311 (Michelet, vol. I, p. 541)
Guillelmus Ardoini	Orléans	
Thomas Quintini	Bayeux	16 Feb. 1311 (Michelet, vol. I, p. 554)
P. de Sarcellis	Paris	19 Feb. 1311 (Michelet, vol. I, p. 574)
Johannes de sancta Genefa	Liège	
P. de Grumenilio, priest	Beauvais	10 Mar. 1311 (Michelet, vol. II, p. 23)
P. de Blesis, priest	Chartres	8 Feb. 1311 (Michelet, vol. I, p. 154)
Christianus de Bice	Langres	10 Feb. 1311 (Michelet, vol. I, p. 524)
P. le Picart de Buris	Langres	9 Feb. 1311 (Michelet, vol. I, p. 522)
Jacobus dit Vergus	Meaux	5 Feb. 1311 (Michelet, vol. I, p. 503)
Gerardus de Belna	Autun	
Johannes de Corvella Cormelle	Soissons	9 Feb. 1311 (Michelet, vol. I, p. 520)
Abertus de Corvella	Châlons-en-Champagne	17 Feb. 1311 (Michelet, vol. I, p. 560)
Bartholomaeus de Trecis	Besançon	22 Jan. 1311 (Michelet, vol. I, p. 433)
Guillelmus de Gi	Besançon	17 Feb. 1311 (Michelet, vol. I, p. 564)
Theobaldus de Basmonte	Chartres	13 Feb. 1311 (Michelet, vol. I, p. 543)
Tonzsanus de Lenhivilla	Beauvais	
Johannes de Ellemosina	Paris	20 Feb. 1311 (Michelet, vol. I, p. 588)
Radulphus de Salicibus	Laon	20 Feb. 1311 (Michelet, vol. I, p. 583)
Nicolaus de la Gella	Laon	
Raynerius de Larchamp	Sens	4 Feb. 1311 (Michelet, vol. I, p. 494)
Raynaudus de Tremplayo, priest	Paris	20 Jan. 1311 (Michelet, vol. I, p. 421)
Stephanus de Turno	Paris	12 Mar. 1311 (Michelet, vol. II, p. 35)
Guillelmus Becelli	Évreux	10 Mar. 1311 (Michelet, vol. II, p. 26)
Richardus de Caprosia	Paris	
Johannes de sancto Lupo and	Paris	21 Jan. 1311 (Michelet, vol. I, p. 431)
P. de Arbleya	Paris	4 Feb. 1311 (Michelet, vol. I, p. 496)

Thus it was done on the aforesaid day and place, by said lord commissioners, present myself, Floriamonte Dondedei, Hugone Nicolai, Guillelmo Radulpho and other notaries already named.

Appendix 7

TEMPLARS INTERROGATED IN PARIS IN OCTOBER/NOVEMBER 1307 AND BEFORE THE PAPAL COMMISSION IN 1311

Thibaud de Basemont (Michelet, vol. II, p. 288; vol. I, p. 542)

Pons de Benèvre (Bono Opere) (Michelet, vol. II, p. 408; vol. I, p. 538)

Pierre de Blois (Michelet, vol. II, p. 333; vol. I, p. 514)

Gautier de Bure (Michelet, vol. II, p. 344; vol. I, p. 296)

Gérard de Causse (Gauche, Cancer) (Michelet, vol. II, p. 290, vol. I, p. 379)

Gilles de Chevru (Cantuco, Chamino) (Michelet, vol. II, p. 387; vol. I, p. 578)

Nicolas de Compiègne (Michelet, vol. II, p. 417; vol. I, p. 639)

Jacques de Crumellis (Michelet, vol. II, p. 351; vol. I, p. 545)

Guy Dauphin (Michelet, vol. II, p. 280; vol. I, p. 415)

Dominique de Dijon (Michelet, vol. II, p. 368; vol. I, p. 632)

Étienne de Domont (Michelet, vol. II, p. 323; vol. I, p. 566)

Jean de *Elemosina* (l'Aumône) (Michelet, vol. II, p. 308; vol. I, p. 588)

Gilles *de Encreyo*, de Ecci (Michelet, vol. II, p. 373; vol. I, p. 249)

Guillaume de Gii (*Giaco*) (Michelet, vol. II, p. 289; vol. I, p. 564)

Jean de Gizy (Michelet, vol. II, p. 414; vol. I, p. 566)

Raoul de Gizy (Michelet, vol. II, p. 363; vol. I, p. 394)

Pierre de Grumesnil (Michelet, vol. II, p. 318; vol. II, p. 23)

Guillaume d'Herblay (Arramblay) (Michelet, vol. II, p. 299; vol. I, p. 498)

Pierre d'Herblay (Michelet, vol. II, p. 307; vol. I, p. 496)

Hélie de Jocro (Michelet, vol. II, p. 389; vol. I, p. 531)

Humbaud de Laboyssade (Besseyta) (Michelet, vol. II, p. 303; vol. II, p. 85)

Renier de Larchant (Michelet, vol. II, p. 278; vol. I, p. 494)

Jacques Le Verjus (Michelet, vol. II, p. 397; vol. I, p. 503)

Jean de Nivelle (Borletta) (Michelet, vol. II, p. 281; vol. I, p. 548)

Jean de Pont-l'Évêque (Michelet, vol. II, p. 378; vol. II, p. 30)

Humbert de Saint-Joire (Torbone) (Michelet, vol. II, p. 366; vol. I, p. 406)

Jean de Saint-Leu (Michelet, vol. II, p. 287; vol. I, p. 431)

Raoul de Saulx (*Salicibus*) (Michelet, vol. II, p. 406; vol. I, p. 583)

Raoul de Taverny (Michelet, vol. II, p. 375; vol. I, p. 626)

Jean de Tour (Michelet, vol. II, p. 315; vol. I, p. 595)

Renaud de Tremblay (Michelet, vol. II, p. 279; vol. I, p. 421)

Nicolas de Troyes (Michelet, vol. II, p. 405; vol. I, p. 571)

Jean de Valbellent (Michelet, vol. II, p. 558; vol. I, p. 550)

Guillaume de Vernège (Varnage) (Michelet, vol. II, p. 302; vol. II, p. 178)

Bono de Voulaines (*Vollenis*) (Michelet, vol. II, p. 402; vol. I, p. 630)

Appendix 8

LIST OF TEMPLARS DETAINED IN THE BAILIWICK OF SENLIS
(1310–1312)

Places of detention:

V: residence of the abbey of Achy in Villers-Saint-Paul, Oise. 12 reconciled (r) Templars.

A: residence of Guiart d'Asnières, Asnières-sur-Oise. 8 Templars (r).

B: tower or residence of the bishop of Beauvais, Beauvais, Oise. 12 non-reconciled (nr) Templars.

C: castle (or dungeon) of Saint-Aubin de Crépy. 10 Templars (r).

L: castle of la Mote de Luzarches, Luzarches, Val-d'Oise. 10 Templars (r).

M: castle of Montméliant, Plailly, Oise. 11 Templars (nr).

P: residence of Pierre de Plailly, Plailly, Oise. 11 Templars (nr) (16 at the beginning, 5 escaped, 1 recaptured).

Po: city and castle of Pont, Compiègne, Oise. 9 Templars (nr).

S1: residence or manor that belonged to Jean Le Gagneur, Senlis, Oise. 12 Templars (r).

S2: residence of Pierre de la Cloche, de Crépy, Senlis, Oise. 10 Templars (nr).

(S3 another residence, Senlis, Oise). See Beauvais.

T: residence of the bishop of Beauvais or castle of Thiers, Thiers-sur-Thève, Oise. 12 Templars (nr).

Documents:

BnF, MS fr. 20334

BnF, MS lat. 9800

BnF, Clairambault 1313

AN, K 37 C, no. 40 ter and K 38 no. 8/2

r: reconciled

nr: non-reconciled

D: defender (Feb.–April 1310)

ND: non-defender (Feb.–April 1310)

117 identified plus 5 unnamed escapees

52 reconciled

65 non-reconciled (plus 5 escapees)

Residence: Abbey of Achy in Villers-Saint-Paul (V)

Name	Dates	r/nr	D/ND	Michelet ref.	Int.	Michelet ref.
Thomas de Janvalle	7/10–3/11	r	D	vol. I, p. 64	yes	vol. I, p. 460
Jean de Bollencourt	7/10–3/11	r	D	vol. I, p. 63	yes	vol. I, p. 461
Robert Le Brioys	7/10–3/11	r	D	vol. I, p. 68	yes	vol. I, p. 447
Henri de Compiègne	7/10–3/11	r	D	vol. I, p. 63	yes	vol. II, p. 118
Robert de Gorrenflos	7/10–3/11	r	D	vol. I, p. 62	yes	vol. II, p. 56
Adam d'Inferno	7/10–3/11	r	D	vol. I, p. 68	yes	vol. II, p. 61
Philippe de Lavercines	7/10–3/11	r	D	vol. I, p. 68	yes	vol. II, p. 63
Martin de Marselhes	7/10–3/11	r	D	vol. I, p. 63	yes	vol. II, p. 69
Philippe de Manin	7/10–3/11	r	D	vol. I, p. 63	yes	vol. II, p. 66
Guillaume de la Place	7/10–3/11	r	D	vol. I, p. 63	yes	vol. I, p. 450
Jean Canes (des Quesnes)	7/10–3/11	r	D	vol. I, p. 68	yes	vol. II, p. 116
Bertrand de Sommereux	7/10–3/11	r	D	vol. I, p. 63	yes	vol. II, p. 59

Residence: Asnières (A)

Name	Dates	r/nr	D/ND	Michelet ref.	Int.	Michelet ref.
Hugues d'Alli	7/10–12/10	r	D	vol. I, p. 83	no	
Colart de Bornel, Le Monnier	7/10–6/11	r	ND			
Jean Bras-de-Fer	7/10–1/12	r	D	vol. I, p. 64	no	
Guill. du Mesnil-Aubry	7/10–1/12	r	D	vol. I, p. 68	no	
Michel Musset	7/10–1/12	r	D	vol. I, p. 63	no	
Gilles de Rotangi	7/10–6/11	r	D	vol. I, p. 62	yes	vol. I, p. 463
Jean de Saint-Just	7/10–1/12	r	D	vol. I, p. 63	yes	vol. I, p. 468
Pierre de Saint-Leu	7/10–6/11	r	D	vol. I, p. 77	no	

Residence: Beauvais (September 1310 to June 1311), then Senlis (Oct./Nov. 1311), then Asnières (April 1312) (B)

Name	Dates	r/nr	D/ND	Michelet ref.	Int.	Michelet ref.
Arnoul Arbia (Lambre)	9/10–4/12	nr	D	vol. I, p. 60	no	
Henri d'Ardenbourt (Erden.)	9/10–4/12	nr	D	vol. I, p. 60	no	
Henri de Brabant*	9/10–3/11	nr	D	vol. I, p. 60	no	
Pierre Capoin	9/10–4/12	nr	D	vol. I, p. 60	no	
Bernard de Castres	9/10–4/12	nr	D	vol. I, p. 60	no	
Jacques Candebur (Cadibeuf)	9/10–4/12	nr	D	vol. I, p. 60	no	
Philippe de Douai (Vignes)	9/10–4/12	nr	D	vol. I, p. 60	no	
Gilles de Perbone	9/10–4/12	nr	D	vol. I, p. 60	no	

Name	Dates	r/nr	D/ND	Michelet ref.	Int.	Michelet ref.
Henri de la Plache**	9/10–11/11	nr	D	vol. I, p. 60	no	
Hélie de Templemars	9/10–4/12	nr	D	vol. I, p. 60	no	
Jean de Vercinare	9/10–4/12	nr	D	vol. I, p. 60	no	
Nicolas de Versequin	9/10–4/12	nr	D	vol. I, p. 60	no	

* Henri de Brabant was transferred neither to Senlis nor to Asnières.
** Disappeared in November 1311, although a Jean du Sac appears in the group when it was transferred to Asnières.
All, except Henri de Brabant, were held in Paris in the residence of the abbey of Saint-Magloire, Michelet, vol. I, p. 136.

Residence: Crépy (C)

Name	Dates	r/nr	D/ND	Michelet ref.	Int.	Michelet ref.
Nicolas de Compiègne	8/10–4/11	r	D	vol. I, p. 77	no*	
Mathieu de Cressonessart	8/10–4/11	r	D	vol. I, p. 74	yes	vol. I, p. 535
Renaud de Cugnières	8/10–4/11	r**	D	vol. I, p. 63	no	
Dominique de Dijon	8/10–4/11	r	D	vol. I, p. 68	yes	vol. I, p. 632*
Henri de Faverolles	8/10–4/11	r	D	vol. I, p. 68	yes	vol. I, p. 634
Hélie de Jouarre (Jocro)	8/10–4/11	r	D	vol. I, p. 77	yes	vol. I, p. 531*
Pierre de Lagny	8/10–4/11	r	D	vol. I, p. 74	yes?	vol. II, p. 1
Virmundus de Sanconi	8/10–4/11	r	D	vol. I, p. 60	yes	vol. I, p. 637
Raoul de Taverny	8/10–4/11	r	D	vol. I, p. 77	yes	vol. I, p. 626*
Bono de Vollenis	8/10–4/11	r	D	vol. I, p. 77	yes	vol. I, p. 630

* But interrogated in 1307 (Michelin, vol. II, pp. 417, 368, 389, 374).

** Is said to have been reconciled at the Council of Senlis, but condemned to life in prison by the Council of Sens (Michelin, vol. II, pp. 3–4).

Residence: Luzarches (L)

Name	Dates	r/nr	D/ND	Michelet ref.	Int.	Michelet ref.
Jean Le Bouchier (Bocherii)	8/10–10/11	r	D	vol. I, p. 74	yes	vol. II, p. 77
Jean Fort de Vin	8/10–10/11	r	D	vol. I, p. 68	no	
Jean Le Ganbier	8/10–6/11	r	D	vol. I, p. 65	yes	vol. I, p. 471
Gilles de Lana curia (Louvencourt, Louvaincourt)	8/10–6/11	r	D	vol. I, p. 74	yes	vol. II, p. 112
Pierre de Maison Vignier	8/10–10/11	r	D	vol. I, p. 60	no	
Gaubert de Marle	8/10–10/11	r	ND	vol. I, p. 79	no	
Jean Pernet (Peynet)	8/10–10/11	r	D	vol. I, p. 74	yes	vol. II, pp. 69–71
Robert de Rabanval	8/10–10/11	r	D	vol. I, p. 74	yes	vol. II, p. 74
P. de Saint-Just	8/10–5/11	r	D	vol. I, p. 74	yes	vol. I, p. 474
Barthélemy de Voulaine	8/10–10/11	r	D	vol. I, p. 68	no	

Residence: Montmélian (M)

Name	Dates	r/nr	D/ND	Michelet ref.	Int.	Michelet ref.
Pierre d'Acies	7/10–3/11	nr	D	vol. I, p. 86	no	
Guillaume de Beauvais	7/10–3/11	nr	D	vol. I, p. 74	no	
Pierre de Landres	7/10–3/11	nr	D	vol. I, p. 69	no	
Jean Lochon	7/10–3/11	nr	D	vol. I, p. 69	no	
Pierre de Mambressis	7/10–3/11	nr	D	vol. I, p. 69	no	

Name	Dates	r/nr	D/ND	Michelet ref.	Int.	Michelet ref.
Jean de Mannen (Malip)	7/10–3/11	nr	D	vol. I, p. 69	no	
André Mederarii (Le Mortier)	7/10–3/11	nr	D	vol. I, p. 74	no	
Raoul Morant (Grandivilliers)	7/10–3/11	nr	?	?	no	
Bertrand de Saint-Paul	7/10–3/11	nr	D	vol. I, p. 69	no	
Gérard de Songeons	7/10–3/11	nr	D	vol. I, p. 64	no	
Thierry de Valle Bellant	7/10–3/11	nr	D	vol. I, p. 60	no	

Residence: Plailly (P)

Name	Dates	r/nr	D/ND	Michelet ref.	Int.	Michelet ref.
Gossoyn de Bruges	7/10–11/11	nr	D	vol. I, p. 64	no	
Thomas d'Escamps (Cames)	7/10–3/12	nr	D	vol. I, p. 64	no	
Eudes Coclarius (Le Culherier)	7/10–3/12	nr	D	vol. I, p. 83	no	
Nicolas de Marra	7/10–3/12	nr	D	vol. I, p. 68	no	
Pierre de Monte Goyni	7/10–3/12	nr	D	vol. I, p. 68	no	
Eudes de Nanteuil	7/10–3/12	nr	D	vol. I, p. 60	no	
Pierre Le Picart	7/10–3/12	nr	D	vol. I, p. 71	no	
Pierre Le Prévot (Prepositi)	7/10–3/12	nr	D	vol. I, p. 83	no	
Philippe de Troisfon (Crespen)	7/10–3/12	nr	D	vol. I, p. 68	no	

| Gautier de Villesavoir | 7/10–11/11 | nr | D | vol. I, p. 83 | no | |
| Jean Waubert (Vomberti) | 7/10–3/12 | nr | D | vol. I, p. 64 | no | |

Residence: Compiègne, castle of Pont (Po)

Name	Dates	r/nr	D/ND	Michelet ref.	Int.	Michelet ref.
Dreux de Chevru	7/10–5/11	nr	D	vol. I, p. 85	no	
Henri Zelot (Chapelins)	7/10–5/11	nr	D	vol. I, p. 85	no	
Geoffroy de la Fère	7/10–5/11	nr	D	vol. I, p. 85	no	
Robert Harlé (Ermenonville)	7/10–5/11	nr	D	vol. I, p. 85?	no	
Robert de Monts-de-Soissons	7/10–5/11	nr	D	vol. I, p. 85?	no	
Robert de Mortefontaine	7/10–5/11	nr	D	vol. I, p. 85?	no	
Anceaux de la Rochelle	7/10–5/11	nr	D	vol. I, p. 85	no	
Guillaume de Roy	7/10–5/11	nr	D	vol. I, p. 85	no	
Evrard de Valdencia	7/10–5/11	nr	D	vol. I, p. 85	no	

Residence: Senlis 1, residence of Jean Le Gagneur (S1)

Name	Dates	r/nr	D/ND	Michelet ref.	Int.	Michelet ref.
Guy de Belleville	9/10–10/11	r	D	vol. I, p. 79	yes	vol. II, p. 114
Jean de Grès (Grez?)	9/10–10/11	r	ND		yes	vol. I, p. 487
Nicolas de Ancinimonte	9/10–10/11	r	ND	vol. I, p. 78	no	
Thomas de Roquencourt	9/10–10/11	r	D	vol. I, p. 73	yes	vol. I, p. 485*

Name	Dates	r/nr	D/ND	Michelet ref.	Int.	Michelet ref.
Boncourt, Hennencourt						
Guillaume de Lafons, Clefons	9/10–10/11	r	D?	vol. I, p. 108	yes	vol. I, p. 619
Aliaume de Linières	9/10–10/11	r	ND		yes	vol. I, p. 479
Nicolas de Meannay	9/10–10/11	r	ND		yes	vol. I, p. 482
Gérard de Moineville	9/10–10/11	r	D	vol. I, p. 78	yes	vol. I, p. 624
Foulque de Neuilly	9/10–10/11	r	ND		yes	vol. I, p. 477
Hugues d'Oisemont	9/10–10/11	r	ND		yes	vol. I, p. 490
Étienne de Provins	9/10–10/11	r	D	vol. I, p. 78	no	
Pierre de St-Maxence	9/10–10/11	r	ND		yes	vol. I, p. 621

* Interrogation 1307 (Michelet, vol. II, p. 416)

Residence: Senlis 2, residence of Pierre de la Cloche (S2)

Name	Dates	r/nr	D/ND	Michelet ref.	Int.	Michelet ref.
Nicolas d'Amiens	4/11–1/12	nr	D	vol. I, p. 64	no	
Jean de Cormeles	4/11–10/11	nr	D	vol. I, p. 85	no	
Henri de Harsegni (Li Abès)	4/11–1/12	nr	D	vol. I, p. 63	no*	
Henri de la Place	4/11–10/11	nr	D	vol. I, p. 60	no	
Thibaud de Plomion	4/11–1/12	nr	D	vol. I, p. 64	no	
Henri de Percigny	4/11–1/12	nr	D	vol. I, p. 64	no	

Name	Dates	r/nr	D/ND	Michelet ref.	Int.	Michelet ref.
Jean du Sac (Ausato)	1/11	nr	D	vol. I, p. 59**	no	
Gilles de Valencienne	4/11–1/12	nr	D	vol. I, p. 63	no	
Jean de Verneuil	1/12	nr	D	vol. I, p. 59	no	
Gautier de Villers	4/11–1/12	nr	D	vol. I, p. 59	no	

* Interrogated in 1307 (Michelet, vol. II, p. 375)
** Did not appear with this group in April and October 1311; mentioned in a group of eleven under the guard of Daniel Grant in Senlis, then transferred to Asnières in April 1312.

Residence: Thiers-sur-Thève (I)

Name	Dates	r/nr	D/ND	Michelet ref.	Int.	Michelet ref.
Bernard de Bissi (Bicey)	7/10–10/11	nr	D	vol. I, p. 69	no	
Robert de Charmes	7/10–10/11	nr	D	vol. I, p. 85	no	
Jean de la Haie (Malip?)	7/10–10/11	nr	D	vol. I, p. 69	no	
Robert de Montreuil	7/10–10/11	nr	D	vol. I, p. 84	no	
Jean de Maison Dieu	7/10–10/11	nr	D	vol. I, p. 86	no	
Renaud de Paris	7/10–10/11	nr	D	vol. I, p. 77	no	
Renaud de Ploisy	11/10	nr	D	vol. I, p. 67	no	
Jean Peitavin (Poitevin)	7/10–10/11	nr	D	vol. I, p. 69	no	
Laurent de Provins	7/10–10/11	nr	D	vol. I, p. 69	no	
Pierre Regis (LeRoy)	7/10–10/11	nr	D	vol. I, p. 86	no	
Jacques de Sacy (Sanceyo)	7/10–10/11	nr	D	vol. I, p. 69	no	

Name	Dates	r/nr	D/ND	Michelet ref.	Int.	Michelet ref.
Hugues de Villers	7/10–10/11	nr	D	vol. I, p. 69	no	

TEMPLARS' APPEARANCE BEFORE THE PARIS COMMISSION AND THEIR INTERROGATIONS

(April/May 1310 and 17 December 1310–May 1311)

* interrogated but not present in the group

** present in the group but not interrogated

Italics = not a Templar

NB: In these lists I follow exactly the orthography given by Michelet. So, in this appendix only, I do not distinguish between names given in the vernacular and those given in Latin. For example: Scivriaco is given here in roman, although in my text the name appears in italics.

A. April/May 1310

11 April 1310	25	Michelet, vol. I, p. 174
	Johannes de Scivriaco**	
	Johannes de Fallegio**	
	Johannes de Juvenii**	
	Johannes de Capricordio**	
	Johannes Thaiafer (from Genoa)	Michelet, vol. I, p. 187
	Huguetus de Buris	Michelet, vol. I, p. 205
	Guaufredus (de) Thantan	Michelet, vol. I, p. 222
	Johannes Anglicus	Michelet, vol. I, p. 193
	Nicolaus de Capella**	
	Johannes de Bollena**	
	Johannes de Cathalona**	

	Arnulphus de Marnayo**	
	Robertus de Layme**	
	Johannes de Valle Bruandi**	
	Henricus de Landesi**	
	Galterus de Belna**	
	Johannes de Henesi**	
	Guillelmus de sancto Suppleto**	
	P. de Montaont**	
	Girardus de Passagio	Michelet, vol. I, p. 212
	Radulphus de Praellis	Michelet, vol. I, p. 175
	Guichardus de Marciaco	Michelet, vol. I, pp. 182, 186
	*Johannes de Vassegio***	
	Nicolaus Symonis	Michelet, vol. I, p. 176
11–13 April 1310	Johannes de sancto Benedicto	Michelet, vol. I, pp. 177, 178
5 May 1310	8	Michelet, vol. I, p., 232
	Raymundus de Versinacho	Michelet, vol. I, p. 233
	Baudoynus de S. Justo	Michelet, vol. I, p. 241
	Thomas de Chamino**	
	Johannes Buchandi (Bertaldi)	Michelet, vol. I, p. 270
	Ancherius (Amerius) de Villa Ducis	Michelet, vol. I, p. 275
	Ambertus de Ros (Humbertus de Podio)	Michelet, vol. I, p. 264
	Jacobus de Trecis	Michelet, vol. I, p. 254
	Giletus de Encreyo	Michelet, vol. I, p. 249

B. 17 December 1310–26 May 1311

17 December 1310	12	Michelet, vol. I, p. 287
	Galterus de Buris	Michelet, vol. I, p. 296
	Stephanus de Doimont (Divione)	Michelet, vol. I, p. 301
	Odo de Doura Petra (Dona Petra)	Michelet, vol. I, p. 306
	Enricus (Aimericus) de Buris	Michelet, vol. I, p. 316
	Johannes (de) Thara	Michelet, vol. I, p. 290
	Garnerius de Vernefraaco (Venesi)	Michelet, vol. I, p. 311

	Albertus de Columbis (Arbertus De Columpnis)	Michelet, vol. I, p. 320
	Theobaldus Tavernarii (de Taverniaco)	Michelet, vol. I, p. 324
	P(etrus) de Loyson	Michelet, vol. I, p. 328
	P(etrus) de Bello Monte	Michelet, vol. I, p. 331
	Johannes Quintini (Quentini) de Benna	Michelet, vol. I, p. 334
	Johannes de S. Questo	Michelet, vol. I, p. 338
31 December 1310	8	Michelet, vol. I, p. 337–8
	Johannes de Branlis	Michelet, vol. I, p. 341
	Bartholomeus de Glevon (de Glano)	Michelet, vol. I, p. 344
	Reginaldus de la Lopière (Renandus de Villa Mostrue)	Michelet, vol. I, p. 348
	Symon de Corbon(e)	Michelet, vol. I, p. 350
	Gaubertus de Silli (de Silhi)	Michelet, vol. I, p. 353
	Johannes de Vivariis (Viveriis)	Michelet, vol. I, p. 355
	Matheus de Tille (de Tilleyo)	Michelet, vol. I, p. 358
	Symon de Lions (de Lechuno)	Michelet, vol. I, p. 364
9 January 1311	3	Michelet, vol. I, pp. 367–8
	Johannes de Boilhencort (Pollencourt)	Michelet, vol. I, p. 368
	Petrus de Bolhencourt (Poignencort, Polheicourt)	Michelet, vol. I, pp. 371, 377
	Petrus (de) Boucheures	Michelet, vol. I, p. 374
11 January 1311	7	Michelet, vol. I, p. 377
	Guido Delphini	Michelet, vol. I, p. 415
	Addam de Valamanut (Vollencourt)	Michelet, vol. I, p. 409
	Humbertus de s. Jorre (Jorio)	Michelet, vol. I, p. 406
	Gerardus de Causo (Causso)	Michelet, vol. I, p. 379
	Petrus de Boneli (Bocli)	Michelet, vol. I, p. 412
	Hugo de Gamone (Calmonte)	Michelet, vol. I, p. 402
	Radulphus de Enesi (Gisi)	Michelet, vol. I, p. 394
20 January 1311	7	Michelet, vol. I, p. 421
	Raynardus (Raynaudus) de Tremplayo (Tremplaio)	Michelet, vol. I, p. 421
	Albertus de Canellis	Michelet, vol. I, p. 424
	Philippus Agate	Michelet, vol. I, p. 428
	Johannes de s. Lupo	Michelet, vol. I, p. 431

	Bartholomeus de Trecis	Michelet, vol. I, p. 433
	Otho de Ayrone (Anone)	Michelet, vol. I, p. 436
	Robertus de Cormelhes (Cormeliis)	Michelet, vol. I, p. 441
	(Lambertus de Cormellis*)	Michelet, vol. I, p. 439[15]
26 January 1311	6	Michelet, vol. I, p. 443
	Egidius d'Oysimont (Rotangi)	Michelet, vol. I, p. 463, vol. II, p. 132
	Guillelmus de Platea	Michelet, vol. I, p. 450
	Thomas de Jemville (Jamvalle, Janvalle)	Michelet, vol. I, p. 443, 460
	Robertus de Brioys (le Brioys)	Michelet, vol. I, p. 447
	Johannes de Bolencourt (Bollencourt)	Michelet, vol. I, p. 461
	Johannes de s. Justo	Michelet, vol. I, p. 468

Interrogations of the members of this group were interrupted by the appearance, on the same day, of the eight Templars on the following list, and then on the next day, 27 January, by the interrogation of Stephanus de Nereaco, a Minor brother from Lyon.

26 January 1311	8	Michelet, vol. I, p. 446
	Johannes le Gambier de Grandi Villarii	Michelet, vol. I, p. 471
	Thomas de Bonnencourt (Boncourt)	Michelet, vol. I, p. 485
	Allemanus de Ligneriis (Alelinus de Lineriis)	Michelet, vol. I, p. 479
	Nicolaus de Meanvoy (Meannay)	Michelet, vol. I, p. 482
	Hugo d'Oysemont (Oysimont)	Michelet, vol. I, p. 490
	Petrus de S. Justo	Michelet, vol. I, p. 474
	Johannes de Gressibus	Michelet, vol. I, p. 487
	Fulco de Nulliaco	Michelet, vol. I, p. 477
27 January 1311	*Stephanus de Nereaco*	Michelet, vol. I, pp. 454–9
27 January 1311	7	Michelet, vol. I, p. 459
	Guillelmus de Aramblay (Arreblayo)	Michelet, vol. I, p. 498
	Johannes de Turno jr (treasurer)	Michelet, vol. I, p. 595
	Petrus de Reblay (Arbleyo)	Michelet, vol. I, p. 496
	Renerius (Raynerius) de Larchant	Michelet, vol. I, p. 494
	Jacobus de Vernis (Le Vergus)	Michelet, vol. I, p. 503

	Johannes Ruffemont (Buffavent)	Michelet, vol. I, p. 509
	Johannes de Rompre (Rumpreyo)	Michelet, vol. I, p. 506
8 February 1311	10	Michelet, vol. I, p. 511
	Petrus de Blesis	Michelet, vol. I, p. 514
	Robertus Vigerii	Michelet, vol. I, p. 512
	Christianus de Biceyo	Michelet, vol. I, p. 524
	Petrus Picardi de Buris	Michelet, vol. I, p. 522
	Poncius de Bono Opere	Michelet, vol. I, p. 538
	Symon de Cormersci (Cormessi)	Michelet, vol. I, p. 517
	Helias de Jotro	Michelet, vol. I, p. 531
	Johannes de Conriucle (de Cormele)	Michelet, vol. I, pp. 520, 527
	Matheus de Cresson Essart	Michelet, vol. I, p. 535
	Petrus de Chevruto (Cherruto)	Michelet, vol. I, p. 529
11 February 1311	10	Michelet, vol. I, p. 540
	Jacobus (de) Cormele	Michelet, vol. I, p. 545
	Johannes de Valbellant (Vanbellant)	Michelet, vol. I, p. 550
	Johannes de Besu s. Germani (Bessu)	Michelet, vol. I, p. 541
	Odo de Castroduni	Michelet, vol. I, p. 558
	Theobaldus de Basimont(e)	Michelet, vol. I, p. 542
	Stephanus d'Omont (de Domont)	Michelet, vol. I, p. 556
	Guillelmus de Gi(i)	Michelet, vol. I, p. 564
	Johannes de Barleta (Nivella)	Michelet, vol. I, p. 548
	Albertus de Grevilla (Humbertus de Germilla)	Michelet, vol. I, p. 560
	Thomas Gancin (Quintini)	Michelet, vol. I, p. 554
17 February 1311	9	Michelet, vol. I, p. 566
	Johannes de Gisi	Michelet, vol. I, p. 566
	Radulphus de Salicibus	Michelet, vol. I, p. 583
	Petrus de S. Mamerto	Michelet, vol. I, p. 586
	Reginaldus le Bergerot (Raynandus Bergeron)	Michelet, vol. I, p. 591
	Johannes de Niciaco (de Nici)	Michelet, vol. I, p. 581
	Gilo de Cheruto (Egidius de Cheuruto)	Michelet, vol. I, p. 578
	Nicolaus de Trecis	Michelet, vol. I, p. 571
	Petrus de Cercellis	Michelet, vol. I, p. 574
	Johannes de Elemosina	Michelet, vol. I, p. 588

25 February 1311	6	Michelet, vol. I, p. 601
	Gerardus de Rupe Amatoris	Michelet, vol. I, p. 602
	Stephanus de (las) Gorsolas	Michelet, vol. I, pp. 604, 614
	Ahimericus (Aymericus) de Premi	Michelet, vol. I, p. 608
	Petrus Maysorilier (Poncius de Masualier)	Michelet, vol. I, p. 611
	Johannes Fabri	Michelet, vol. I, p. 614
	Hugo la Hugonia	Michelet, vol. I, p. 616
27 February 1311	3 + 1	Michelet, vol. I, p. 619
	Anthonius Syci (Sici) de Vercellis	Michelet, vol. I, p. 641
	Guillelmus de Fonte	Michelet, vol. I, p. 619
	Petrus de S. Mayencio (Maxencio)	Michelet, vol. I, p. 621
	Girardus de Monachivilla (Manachivilla)	Michelet, vol. I, p. 624
1 March 1311	7	Michelet, vol. I, p. 624
	Radulphus de T(h)averniaco	Michelet, vol. I, p. 626
	Bono de Vollenis	Michelet, vol. I, p. 630
	Dominicus de Divione	Michelet, vol. I, p. 632
	Enricus (Anricus) de Faverolis	Michelet, vol. I, p. 634
	Gyronundus de Saccommin (Virmudus de Sanconi)	Michelet, vol. I, p. 637
	Nicolaus de Compendio	Michelet, vol. I, p. 639
	Petrus de Latinhiaco	Michelet, vol. II, p. 1
8 March 1311	6	Michelet, vol. II, p. 6
	Guillelmus de Torrage	Michelet, vol. II, p. 11
	Guillelmus deu Liege	Michelet, vol. II, p. 6
	Petrus Theobaldi	Michelet, vol. II, p. 18
	Helias Raynaudi	Michelet, vol. II, p. 21
	Guillelmus Terice (d'Errée)	Michelet, vol. II, p. 13
	Thomas de Panpalona	Michelet, vol. II, p. 15
10 March 1311	5	Michelet, vol. II, p. 23
	Petrus de Grimenilio (Grumenil)	Michelet, vol. II, p. 23
	Petrus Janz	Michelet, vol. II, p. 32
	Guillelmus Boncelli	Michelet, vol. II, p. 26
	Baudoynus de Gisi (Gisa)	Michelet, vol. II, p. 28
	Johannes de Ponte Episcopi	Michelet, vol. II, p. 30

11 March 1311	5	Michelet, vol. II, p. 35
	Robertus Le Verrier	Michelet, vol. II, p. 41
	Johannes de Bali (Baali)	Michelet, vol. II, p. 44
	Stephanus de Turno	Michelet, vol. II, p. 35
	Jacobus de villa Parisia	Michelet, vol. II, p. 39
	Johannes de Fregevilla	Michelet, vol. II, p. 37
13 March 1311	4	Michelet, vol. II, p. 47
	Symon lo Begue	Michelet, vol. II, p. 50
	Garinus de Corbon	Michelet, vol. II, p. 53
	Stephanus de Brolio	Michelet, vol. II, p. 54
	Adam de sancto Johanne in Brocuria	Michelet, vol. II, p. 47
15 March 1311	19	Michelet, vol. II, p. 52
	Robertus de Correnflos	Michelet, vol. II, p. 56
	Bertrandus de Somorens	Michelet, vol. II, p. 59
	Johannes Rocherii de Grandi Villarii	Michelet, vol. II, p. 77
	Adam de Inferno	Michelet, vol. II, p. 61
	Philippus de Manin (Manni)	Michelet, vol. II, pp. 66, 77
	Robertus de Rambeval (Reinheval alias dictus prepositus)	Michelet, vol. II, p. 74
	Philippus de Lavercines	Michelet, vol. II, p. 63
	Martinus de Marselhes	Michelet, vol. II, p. 69
	Johannes Peynet	Michelet, vol. II, p. 71
	Petrus de Siven (Siveu)	Michelet, vol. II, p. 80
	Geraldus Judicis (de Augnihaco)	Michelet, vol. II, p. 82
	Martinus de Monte Trichardi	Michelet, vol. II, p. 88, 107
	Johannes Durandi	Michelet, vol. II, p. 91, 108
	Johannes de Raans (de Ruivans)	Michelet, vol. II, p. 94, 109
	Bartholomeus de Podio Revelli	Michelet, vol. II, p. 101
	Petrus de sancto Benedicto	Michelet, vol. II, p. 96
	Petrus de Monte Chalveti	Michelet, vol. II, p. 99
	Andreas de Monte Laudato	Michelet, vol. II, p. 103
	Raynaudus Larchier	Michelet, vol. II, p. 105
	(Humbaudus de la Boyssada*)	Michelet, vol. II, p. 85
26 March 1311	6	Michelet, vol. II, p. 109
	Egidius de Lovencort	Michelet, vol. II, p. 112
	Johannes de Gaenes (de Canes)	Michelet, vol. II, p. 116

	Guido de Bellavilla (Bella Villa)	Michelet, vol. II, p. 114
	Anricus de Compendio (Conpendio)	Michelet, vol. II, p. 118
	Oddo de Buris	Michelet, vol. II, p. 109
	Philippus Griselli (Grisselli)	Michelet, vol. II, p. 119
29 March 1311	9	Michelet, vol. II, p. 121
	Bertrandus de Villaribus	Michelet, vol. II, p. 122
	Guillelmus Textoris	Michelet, vol. II, p. 129
	Guillelmus de Mazayas (Masayas)	Michelet, vol. II, p. 125
	Guido (de) la Chastaneda	Michelet, vol. II, p. 127
	Johannes de Mendaco (de Menat)	Michelet, vol. II, p. 133
	Johannes Senandi	Michelet, vol. II, p. 136
	Johannes Adam	Michelet, vol. II, p. 141
	Hugo Charnerii	Michelet, vol. II, p. 143
	Rogerius La Rocha (de Rupe)	Michelet, vol. II, p. 148
	Bertrandus de Ansonio (Bernardus de Alsonio)	Michelet, vol. II, p. 146
2 April 1311	9	Michelet, vol. II, p. 151
	Renardus de Bort	Michelet, vol. II, p. 151
	Bernardus Ademari	Michelet, vol. II, p. 156
	Durandus Passerion (Passarion)	Michelet, vol. II, p. 160
	Petrus Almavini (Amalini)	Michelet, vol. II, p. 165
	Raymundus Amalini (Amalvini)	Michelet, vol. II, p. 167
	Guigo de Rupe Talhada (Ruppe Talhata)	Michelet, vol. II, p. 154
	Petrus Gontandi	Michelet, vol. II, p. 158
	Bertrandus (Bernardus) Boni Hominis	Michelet, vol. II, p. 162
	Guibertus Rogerii	Michelet, vol. II, p. 169
4 April 1311	11	Michelet, vol. II, p. 165
	Petrus de Turonis	Michelet, vol. II, p. 172
	Matheus de Montelupello	Michelet, vol. II, p. 175
	Petrus de Lanneis (de Lanoys)	Michelet, vol. II, p. 188
	Bartholomeus Bartholeti	Michelet, vol. II, p. 186
	Guillelmus de Plexeyo	Michelet, vol. II, p. 184
	Guillelmus Talheboys	Michelet, vol. II, p. 182
	Gaufredus de Monchanson (Montchausit)	Michelet, vol. II, p. 181

	Arnaudus Brucgeon (Breion de Goerta)	Michelet, vol. II, p. 189
	Johannes Picardi**	
	Audebertus de Porta	Michelet, vol. II, p. 171
	Parisius de Buris	Michelet, vol. II, p. 177
6 April 1311	1	
	Guillelmus de Vernegia	Michelet, vol. II, p. 178
19 April 1311	2	Michelet, vol. II, p. 191
	Bartholomeus Bocherii	Michelet, vol. II, p. 191
	Radulphus Louveti	Michelet, vol. II, p. 196
19 April 1311	*Pierre de La Palud, preaching brother*	Michelet, vol. II, pp. 195–6
7 May 1311	7	Michelet, vol. II, p. 198
	Hugo de Narzac (Narsac)	Michelet, vol. II, p. 205
	Guillelmus de Sermoya (Soromina)	Michelet, vol. II, p. 199
	Petrus de Nobiliaco	Michelet, vol. II, p. 214
	Guillelmus Audeberti (Audenbon)	Michelet, vol. II, p. 202
	Helias de Chasac, dictus Cotati (Costati)	Michelet, vol. II, p. 209
	Petrus de Vernhia (la Vernha)	Michelet, vol. II, p. 216
	Petrus Geraldi alias dictus de Meleduno (de Mursac)	Michelet, vol. II, p. 211
11 May 1311	6	Michelet, vol. II, p. 217
	Guido de Rupe	Michelet, vol. II, p. 219
	Hugo de Fauro	Michelet, vol. II, p. 220
	Guido Las Chassandas (las Chaussandas)	Michelet, vol. II, p. 225
	Jordanus Pauta	Michelet, vol. II, p. 227
	Boso de Masualier	Michelet, vol. II, p. 228
	Petrus Piffandi (Pufandi)	Michelet, vol. II, p. 231
19 May 1311	10	Michelet, vol. II, p. 233
	Hugo de Janzac	Michelet, vol. II, p. 234
	Guillelmus Aprilis	Michelet, vol. II, p. 236
	Petrus Maurini	Michelet, vol. II, p. 238
	Durandus Charnerii	Michelet, vol. II, p. 241
	Petrus Blavi	Michelet, vol. II, p. 245
	Stephanus de Cellario	Michelet, vol. II, p. 243
	Michael de Podio	Michelet, vol. II, p. 252

	Petrus Bonafont, Bono Fonte	Michelet, vol. II, p. 248
	Johannes Sarraceni	Michelet, vol. II, p. 250
	Stephanus Glotonis	Michelet, vol. II, p. 254
22 May 1311	3	Michelet, vol. II, p. 256
	Johannes de Noviomo	Michelet, vol. II, p. 261
	Bertrandus Guasc	Michelet, vol. II, p. 258
	Guillelmus de Cardalhac	Michelet, vol. II, p. 256
26 May 1311	3	Michelet, vol. II, p. 263
	Johannes de Chali	Michelet, vol. II, p. 263
	Petrus de Moydies (Modies)	Michelet, vol. II, p. 265
	Raynaldus Belli Pili de Capella	Michelet, vol. II, p. 267
	De Daminhie	

6 Templars interrogated before 11 April 1310
7 Templars (out of the 8 who appeared on 5 May) before the adjournment of 31 May 1310
211 Templars interrogated beginning on 17 December[16]
Total: 6 + 7 + 211 = 224
6 non-Templars interrogated, 3 before 12 May 1310 (out of the 4 who appeared) and 3 after 17 December.

NOTES

Epigraph

1. Translated by George Gordon-Lennox; found at http://www.societe-voltaire.org/voltaire-conspiracies.pdf

Introduction

1. J. Loiseau, *Les Mamelouks, XIIIe-XVIe siècle*, Paris, Seuil, 2014.

2. M. Barber, *The Trial of the Templars*. First published in 1978, the work has been continually revised since then; 2nd edn, Cambridge, Cambridge University Press, 2006.

3. Jules Michelet published these investigations from a manuscript in Paris (BnF); this isn't a copy of a manuscript from the Vatican, but also an original version. See Chapter 14, p. 216, and n.3.

4. Pierre Dupuy, *Traittez concernant l'histoire de France: sçavoir la condamnation des Templiers, avec quelques actes; l'histoire du schisme, les papes tenans le siege en Avignon et quelques procez criminels*, Paris, 1654; reprinted a century later under the title *Histoire de l'ordre militaire des Templiers ou chevalerie du Temple de Jérusalem depuis son établissement jusqu'à sa décadence et sa suppression*, Brussels, 1751; an anastatic reprint has been published (Nîmes, Rediviva, 2002); J. R. Strayer, *The Reign of Philip the Fair*, Princeton, Princeton University Press, 1980; J. Favier, *Philippe le Bel*, Paris, Fayard, repr. 1999; paperback edn, 2013.

5. J. Riley-Smith, 'Were the Templars Guilty?' and 'The Structures of the Orders of the Temple and the Hospital in *c.*1291', in Susan J. Ridyard (ed.) *The Medieval Crusade*, Woodbridge, Boydell Press, 2004.

6. A. Luttrell, 'Observations on the Fall of the Temple', in P. Josserand, L. F. de Oliveira and D. Carraz (eds), *Élites et Ordre militaires au Moyen Âge*, Madrid, Casa de Velázquez, 2015, pp. 365–72.

7. See P. Partner, *The Murdered Magicians. The Templars and their Myths*, Oxford, Oxford University Press, 1981; R. and A.-M. Sève, *Le procès des Templiers d'Auvergne 1309–1311*, Paris, CTHS, 1986, p. 88; A. Demurger, *Les Templiers*, Paris, Seuil, 2005.

8. Sève, *Templiers d'Auvergne*, p. 88.

9. A. Forey, 'Could Alleged Templar Malpractices Have Remained Undetected for Decades?', in J. Burgtorf, P. Crawford and H. Nicholson (eds), *The Debate on the Trial of the Templars (1307–1314)*, Farnham, Ashgate, 2010, pp.11–20.

10. J. Théry, 'Une hérésie d'État. Philippe le Bel, le procès des "perfides templiers" et la pontificalisation de la royauté française', in M.-A. Chevalier, *La Fin de l'ordre du Temple*, Paris, P. Geuthner, 2012, p. 80.

11. S. L. Field, 'La fin de l'ordre du Temple à Paris: le cas de Mathieu de Cressonessart', in Chevalier, *La Fin*, p. 108.

12. J. Théry, 'Procès des templiers', in N. Beriou and P. Josserand (eds), *Prier et combattre: Dictionnaire européen des Ordres religieux militaires*, Paris, Fayard, 2009, p. 743.

13. A. Demurger, *Les Templiers*, p. 494–9.

14. R. H. Bautier, 'Diplomatique et histoire politique: ce que la critique diplomatique nous apprend sur la personnalité de Philippe le Bel', *Revue historique*, CCLIX (1978); M. Barber, 'The World Picture of Philip the Fair', *Journal of Medieval History*, 8 (1982).

15. Research undertaken by Julien Théry, Sébastien Nadiras and others into royal ideology at the turn of the fourteenth century has unearthed new material, which reinforces this explanation. Théry, 'Une hérésie d'État'; S. Nadiras 'Guillaume de Nogaret en ses dossiers: Méthodes de travail et de gouvernement d'un conseiller royal au début du XIVe siècle', doctoral thesis from the Université Paris-1 (2012); A. Provost, *Domus Diaboli. Un évêque en procès au temps de Philippe le Bel*, Paris, Belin, 2010.

1 Prelude (1305–1307)

1. Gizy, in the Aisne, near Laon.

2. Jules Michelet, *Le Procès des templiers*, Collections des documents inédits sur l'Histoire de France, 1841–51, repr. Paris, CTHS, 1987, vol. I, pp. 36–7. We don't know if he appeared during the inquisitorial investigation or during the proceedings investigating individuals led by Pope Clement (see Chapter 7).

3. *Ce sont le treytour, li quel ont proposé fauseté et délauté contra este de la religion deu Temple: Guillalmes Roberts moynes, qui les mitoyet à geine, Esquius de Floyrac de Biterris, cumprior de Montfaucon, Bernardus Peleti, prieus de Maso de Genois, et Geraues de Boyzol, cehalier, veneus à Gisors*; Michelet, vol. I, pp. 36–7; Georges Lizerand, *Le Dossier de l'affaire des templiers*, Paris, Les Belles-Lettres, 1923, p. 157.

4. D. Bryson, 'Three (*sic*) Traitors of the Temple. Was Their Truth the Whole Truth?', in J. Burgtorf, P. Crawford and H. Nicholson, *The Debate on the Trial of the Templars (1307 –1314)*, Aldershot, Ashgate, 2010, pp. 97–103.

5. More precisely, from Brulhois: *Biterris*, a hamlet in Marmont-Pachas, canton of Laplume, Lot-et-Garonne; see J. Clémens, 'La rumeur agenaise de l'enfermement templier au début du XIVe siècle', *Revue de l'Agenais*, 123 (1996), pp. 219–235, and 124 (1997), pp. 23–40.

6. Heinrich Finke, *Papsttum und Untergang des Temperorden*, Münster, 1907, vol. II, pp. 318–19; Clémens, 'La rumeur agenaise', pp. 230–32; C. V. Langlois, 'L'affaire des templiers', *Journal des savants* (1908), pp. 423–5.

7. Michelet, vol. I, p. 28.

8. AN, J 413, no. 28.

9. *Regestum Clementis papae V ex Vaticanis archetypis, editio, cura et studio monachorum ordinis sancti Benedicti*, 9 vols, Rome, 1885–92, vol. VI, no. 7183; see A. Demurger, *The Last Templar: The Tragedy of Jacques de Molay*, new updated edn, London, Profile Books, 2009, pp. 164 and 255, n. 32.

10. E. Boutaric, 'Documents relatifs à l'histoire de Philippe le Bel', *Notices et extraits des manuscrits de la Bibliothèque impériale*, vol. XX, 1861, pp. 161–2.

11. C. R. Cheney, 'The Downfall of the Templars and a Letter in Their Defence', in *Medieval Miscellany Presented to Eugène Vinaver*, Oxford, Medieval Texts and Studies, 1973, p. 71.

12. Finke, *Papsttum*, vol. II, pp. 83–4; Malcolm Barber, *The Trial of the Templars*, 2nd edn, Cambridge, Cambridge University Press, 2006, p. 66. English translation of the letter in M. Barber and K. Bate, *The Templars: Selected Sources Translated and Annotated*, Manchester, Manchester University Press, 2002, pp. 256–7.

13. Elisabeth Lalou, *Itinéraire de Philippe IV le Bel (1285–1314)*, vol. II, *Routes et résidences*, Mémoires de l'Académie des inscriptions et belles-lettres, Paris, De Boccard, 2007, p. 305.

14. A. Demurger, 'Clément V', in P. Levillain, *Dictionnaire historique de la papauté*, Paris, Fayard, 2006, pp. 367–9; S. Menache, *Clement V*, Cambridge, Cambridge University Press, 1998; A. Paravicini Bagliani, *Boniface VIII, un pape hérétique?*, Paris, Payot, 2003.

15. S. Menache, 'Chronicles and Historiography: The Interrelationship of Fact and Fiction', *Journal of Medieval History*, 32 (2006), pp. 333–45; Menache, *Clement V*, pp. 18–19.

16. E. Boutaric, 'Clément V, Philippe le Bel et les Templiers', *Revue des questions historiques*, vol. X (1871) and vol. XI (1872), pp. 3–4.

17. Lalou, *Itinéraire*, vol. II, pp. 265–6.

18. E. Baluze, *Vitae paparum avenionensium*, rev. edn by G. Mollat, Paris, 1913–22, vol. 3, p. 60; and Barber and Bate, *The Templars*, p. 243.

19. Michelet, vol. I, pp. 2–3.

20. Finke, *Papsttum*, vol. II, p. 46.

21. Michelet, vol. I, p. 192.

22. Finke, *Papsttum*, vol. II, p. 145; Barber, *Trial*, p. 66.

23. Michelet, vol. I, p. 168; Lizerand, *Le dossier de l'affaire des templiers*, Paris, Les Belles-Lettres, 1923, new edn, 2006, p. 185.

24. Michelet, vol. II, p. 192.

25. Michelet, vol. II, p. 200.

26. Michelet, vol. II, p. 358; Michelet, vol. I, pp. 550–54.

27. R. Oursel, *Le Procès des templiers*, Paris, Denoël, 1955, p. 194, and n. 105, pp. 250–51, presents him as an example of one of these 'moles' introduced into the Order by Nogaret. This is not true; he was simply an apostate Templar.

28. Michelet, vol. II, pp. 277–8; Konrad Schottmüller, *Der Untergang des Templer-Ordens*, 2 vols, Berlin, 1887, vol. II, *Urkunden*, pp. 35–6; Barber, *Trial*, p. 66.

29. Michelet, vol. II, pp. 253–9; it should read 'fifty' years.

30. C. Vogel, 'Templar Runaways and Renegades before, during and after the Trial', in Burgtorf, Crawford and Nicholson, *The Debate*, pp. 317–26.

31. Michelet, vol. I, p. 76.

32. J. Riley-Smith, 'Were the Templars Guilty?', in Susan J. Ridyard (ed.), *The Medieval Crusade*, Woodbridge, Boydell Press, 2004.

33. Michelet, vol. I, p. 254.

34. The numbers are precise, but are nonetheless out by a few dozen units. A certain number of uncertainties, appearing when the data were cross-checked, have not yet been resolved: homonymy, doubling, confusions and memory lapses of the witnesses and so forth. I would say that, today, they are the most accurate of all the wrong numbers.

35. The number 231, provided by the papal commission itself, is generally used by historians. Having counted and recounted, I arrive at 230, from which one must subtract six depositions given by non-Templars. See Chapter 13, pp. 202–3.

36. J. Favier, *Philippe le Bel*, Paris, Fayard, repr. 1999; paperback edn, Paris, 2013, p. 9.

37. One hundred and thirty-eight Templars were interrogated in 1307, and 224 in 1310–11; 35 were deposed during the two procedures. Therefore: $138 + 224 - 35 = 327$ Templars.

38. Michelet, vol. I, pp. 564–5. Guillaume de Gy, received in Marseille in 1303 in the company of Jacques de Coublans, Richard and Jean de Montclar and several others who 'made the passage'. See Demurger, *The Last Templar*, Chapter 8, pp. 95–110; A. Demurger, 'Outre-mer. Le passage des templiers en Orient d'après les dépositions du procès', in *Chemins d'outre-mer. Études sur la Méditerranée médiévale offertes à Michel Balard*, 2 vols, Paris, Publications de la Sorbonne, 2004, pp. 217–230; A. Demurger, 'Between Barcelona and Cyprus: The Travels of Berenguer of Cardona, Templar Master of Aragon and Catalonia (1300–1301)', in Jorgen Burgtorf and Helen Nicholson (eds), *International Mobility in the Military Orders (Twelfth to Fifteenth Centuries): Travelling on Christ's Business*, Cardiff, University of Wales Press, 2006, pp. 65–74.

39. X. Hélary, *La Bataille de Courtrai*, Paris, Tallandier, 2012.

40. See Demurger, *The Last Templar*, Chapter 8, pp. 140–49.

41. Finke, *Papsttum*, vol. II, p. 35.

42. Finke, *Papsttum*, vol. II, p. 36 and n. 23.

43. Finke, *Papsttum*, vol. II, p. 38 and n. 25.

44. Guillaume de Nangis, *Chronique latine de Guillaume de Nangis de 1113 à 1300 avec les continuations de cette chronique de 1300 à 1368*, ed. Hercule Géraud, 2 vols, Paris, SHF, 1843, p. 358; Géraud de Frachet, *Chronicon Girardi de Fracheto*, RHGF, vol. XXI, p. 28.

45. Finke, *Papsttum*, vol. II, p. 149; See Barber, *Trial*, pp. 107–12, who gives a detailed analysis of Jean Bourgogne's text. The English translation of Jean Bourgogne's text is from Barber and Bate, *The Templars*, pp. 263–71.

46. *Regestum Clementis papae*, vol. VI, pp. 280–88; this letter is included in a letter from Pope Clement dated 1 July 1311, cited in Demurger, *The Last Templar*, p. 164, n. 32.

47. See A. J. Forey, 'Letters of the Last Two Masters', *Nottingham Medieval Studies*, XLV (2001), pp. 166–7.

48. Finke, *Papsttum*, vol. II, p. 143; and Lizerand, *Dossier*, p. 117; Barber and Bate, *The Templars*, pp. 265–6.

49. This is still the testimony of Jean Bourgogne. Baluze, *Vitae paparum* (n. 18), vol. 3, p. 60; Barber and Bate, *The Templars*, pp. 243–5.

50. Finke, *Papsttum*, vol. II, p. 149.

51. Baluze, *Vitae paparum*, vol. 3, p. 60; Boutaric, 'Clément V', pp. 24–5, gives a French translation of this letter. English translation in Barber and Bate, *The Templars*, p. 243.

52. Michelet, vol. II, p. 373; A. Demurger, *The Last Templar*, p. 172.

53. According to B. Frale, *L'Ultima Battaglia dei Templari*, Rome, Viella, 2001, pp. 77–8, who provides no proof of this.

54. Finke, *Papsttum*, vol. II, p. 58, no. 39; A. J. Forey, 'Were the Templars Guilty even if They Were Not Heretics or Apostates?', *Viator*, 42 (2011), pp. 130–31.

55. G. Bordonove, *La Tragédie des Templiers*, Paris, Pygamalion, 1993, p. 21, mentions this fact without comment.

2 The Arrests (13 October 1307)

1. AN, J 413, no. 22; the two texts have been translated and published in Lizerand, *Le Dossier*, pp. 16–29.

2. Let's recall that bailiffs and seneschals were the direct representatives of the king in a bailiwick (most often in the northern part of the kingdom) or a seneschalsy (most often in southern regions).

3. AD Nord, B 1458 (4590); Léon Ménard, *Nîmes, Histoire civile, ecclésiastique et littéraire de la ville de Nismes*, 7 vols, Paris, 1750, vol. I, *Preuves* no. 136, pp. 195–7; AN, J 413, no. 22: this is the text published in Lizerand, *Le Dossier*, pp. 19–29.

4. AD Nord, B 1458 (4589); mentioned in Lalou, *Itinéraire*, p. 298.

5. AN, JJ 44, fol. 3; Lalou, *Itinéraire*, p. 297; J. A. MacNamara, *Gilles Aycelin, the Servant of Two Masters*, Syracuse, NY, Syracuse University Press, 1973, pp. 171–2, indicates that on 22 September Pierre de Belleperche resigned the post of keeper of the seal, following which Guillaume de Nogaret was named. Belleperche was ill; in fact he died on 17 January 1308. Gilles Aycelin later kept the seal on several occasions, filling in for Guillaume de Nogaret; perhaps he also filled in for Belleperche in 1307?

6. On Bernard Gui see B. Guenée, *Entre l'Église et l'État. Quatre vies de prélats français à la fin du Moyen Âge*, Paris, Gallimard, pp. 49–86, here p. 62.

7. A. Palès-Gobilliard (ed.), *L'Inquisiteur Geoffroy d'Ablis et les cathares du comté de Foix (1308–1309)*, Paris, éditions du CNRS, 1984.

8. BnF, MS Lat. 10919, fol. 52; Finke, *Papsttum*, vol. II, no. 29, pp. 44–6.

9. Guillaume de Nangis, *Chronique latine*, p. 360.

10. M. Bertrand, 'Les templiers en Normandie', *Heimdal, Revue d'art et d'histoire de Normandie*, 26 (1978), gives the date of 6 October for this operation, but without giving any proof.

11. L. Delisle, *Étude sur la condition de la classe agricole et l'état de l'agriculture en Normandie au Moyen Âge*, Paris, 1851, pp. 721–8. The commandery of Frémeaux 'falls within the seigneury of Monseigneur Charles in the county of Alençon'; the king thus did not have direct sovereignty, and his agents probably had to be diplomatic with the count.

12. Abbé Petel, *Templiers et hospitaliers dans le diocèse de Troyes*, 1908, p. 12 (cited in Lizerand, *Le Dossier*, p. 26).

13. A. Trudon des Ormes, *Étude sur les possessions de l'ordre du Temple en Picardie*, Amiens, 1892, p. 197.

14. M. Miguet, *Templiers et hospitaliers en Normandie*, Paris, CTHS, 1995, p. 49.

15. Miguet, *Templiers et hospitaliers*, p. 44.

16. Miguet, *Templiers et hospitaliers*, pp. 44–5.

17. A. Higounet-Nadal, 'L'inventaire des biens de la commanderie du Temple de Sainte-Eulalie du Larzac en 1308', *Annales du Midi*, 68 (1956), pp. 255–62.

18. M. Wilmart, 'Salariés, journaliers et artisans au service d'une exploitation agricole templière: la commanderie de Payns au début du XIVe siècle', in A. Baudin, G. Brunel and N. Dohrmann (eds), *L'Économie templière en Occident*, Troyes, 2013, p. 279.

19. J. Burgtorf, 'The Trial Inventories of the Templars' Houses in France. Select Aspects', in Burgtorf, Crawford and Nicholson, *The Debate*, pp. 105–15; A. du Bourg, *Histoire du Grand Prieuré de Toulouse*, Toulouse, 1883, supporting documents, pp. xv–xvii.

20. Michelet, vol. I, pp. 320, 324, 331.

21. Michelet, vol. II, pp. 180.

22. Michelet, vol. I, pp. 223.

23. Michelet, vol. I, pp. 458.

24. Schottmüller, *Untergang*, vol. II, pp. 44–5.

25. L. Esquieu, 'Les Templiers de Cahors', in *Bulletin de la Société des Études du Lot*, 23 (1898), pp. 167–8 (the excerpt concerning the arrest of the Templars). The complete document *Te Igitur, 1232–1655*, located in the Bibliothèque Municipale de Cahors, was published by M. Lacombe and M. Combarieu, Cahors, 1888. The place cited is La Capelle-Livron (Capella), commune of Caylus, Tarn-et-Garonne, diocese of Cahors.

26. P. Josserand, 'Les templiers en Bretagne au Moyen Âge: mythe et réalité', *Annales de Bretagne et des Pays de l'Ouest*, 119 (2012), p. 15.

27. Michelet, vol. I, p. 301.

28. E. Boutaric, *Notices et extraits des documents inédits relatifs à l'histoire de France sous Philippe le Bel*, Paris, 1861, no. XXIV.

29. F. Hooghe, 'The Trial of the Templars in the County of Flanders', in Burgtorf, Crawford and Nicholson, *The Debate*, pp. 292–3, citing P. Rogghe, *De orde van de Tempelridders en haar geschiedenis in het oude graafschap Vlaanderen*, Ghent, 1973, p. 148.

30. AN, J 413, no. 23; reproduced in facsimile and transcribed in Miguet, *Templiers et Hospitaliers*, p. 138 (he omits brother Thomas).

31. Jean de Saint-Victor, 'Excerpta e memoriali historiarum auctore Johanne Parisiensi Sancti Victoris Parisiensis canonico regulari', *Recueil des historiens des Gaules et de la France*, vol. XXI, Paris, 1855, p. 649.

32. AN, J 413, no. 28.

33. Ménard, *Nîmes*, vol. I, pp. 195–209.

34. Michelet, vol. I, pp. 250, 369, 71–2, 350, 353, 364–5, 328; Michelet, vol. II, p. 181; Michelet, vol. I, p. 264; Michelet, vol. II, pp. 185, 202, 186.

35. Michelet, vol. I, p. 334.

36. Michelet, vol. II, p. 23.

37. *Chronographia Regum Francorum*, ed. H. de Moranvillé, Paris, SHF, 1891, vol. I, p. 180, n. 1.

38. Finke, *Papsttum*, vol. II, p. 114.

39. Michelet, vol. I, pp. 223–4.

40. Schottmüller, *Untergang*, vol. II, p. 67.

41. BnF, MS 10919, fol. 84; edited by Finke, *Papsttum*, vol. II, pp. 74–5.

42. His flight is also mentioned in the depositions of Jean de Buffavent (Michelet, vol. II, p. 509) and Eudes de Bure (Michelet, vol. II, p. 110).

43. Probably Barralus de Grasilhano, knight and commander of Puy from 1300 to 1307; D. Carraz, unpublished typewritten appendices to his thesis, 'L'ordre du Temple dans la basse vallée du Rhône', vol. IV, p. 111.

44. Grignan, in the Comtat Venaissin.

45. Michelet, vol. I, p. 409. He was caught, although we do not know in what circumstances. Indeed, interrogated on 18 January 1311, Adam de Vollencourt (the same one) says he had taken off his mantle and shaved his beard before he was arrested when he learned that the others had been arrested and that he was in the Empire, where anyone could come and go freely and secretly.

46. Michelet, vol. I, p. 412. He was caught, as he says in his deposition of 18 January 1311; he took off his mantle and shaved his beard so that he would not be recognised before his arrest, which occurred after that of others.

47. Michelet, vol. I, pp. 30–31; see Chapter 8, p. 126.

48. See Chapter 14, p. 229.

49. Barber, *Trial*, p. 61, n. 8.

50. Sève, *Templiers d'Auvergne*, p. 99; see the detail in Chapter 7, p. 109.

51. Finke, *Papsttum*, vol. II, p. 339.

52. P.-V. Claverie, *L'ordre du Temple en Terre sainte et à Chypre*, Nicosia, Centre de Recherche Scientifique, 2005, vol. II, p. 281, which refers to *Chroniques d'Amadi et de Strambaldi*, ed. L. de Mas-Latrie, Collection des documents inédits sur l'histoire de France, 2 vols, Paris, 1891–3, vol. I, pp. 290–91. Amadi is not as precise and indicates that the marshal of the Order on Cyprus (Aymé d'Oiselay) made contact with his friends in Genoa to solicit their help.

53. See n. 41.

54. See Chapter 14, pp. 232–3.

55. See Chapter 4, pp. 59–60.

3 The King and the Inquisition (October–November 1307)

1. A. Baudin and G. Brunel, 'Les templiers en Champagne. Archives inédites, patrimoines et destin des hommes', in *Les Templiers dans l'Aube*, Troyes, La Vie en Champagne, 2013, pp. 63–9.
2. Michelet, vol. II, p. 4.
3. H. Prutz has also published a very incomplete record of an interrogation in Bayeux, dated 28 October; but the names of the six Templars that he indicates also appear among the thirteen in the record from Caen. In fact, there has been some confusion between the two versions of the Caen interrogation, one of which is in Latin, the other in French; the Latin version (AN, J 413, no. 17) corresponds to the one pointed out by H. Prutz under the name of Bayeux; the second (AN, J 413, no. 20) is the one published, but not in its entirety, by H. Finke. See the clarification provided by Sean L. Field in 'Torture and Confession in the Templar Interrogations at Caen, 28–29 October 1307', *Speculum*, 91 (2016), pp. 297–327, who publishes both versions.
4. Forty-five were announced, forty-four were present, but forty-three were interrogated.
5. AN, J 413, no. 15; S. L. Field, 'The Inquisitor Ralph of Ligny, two German Templars and Marguerite Porète', *Journal of Medieval Religious Cultures*, 39 (2013), pp. 1–22.
6. Michelet, vol. II, p. 304.
7. Michelet, vol. II, pp. 398–400.
8. Michelet, vol. II, pp. 279, 299–300.
9. Michelet, vol. II, pp. 363–4.
10. Michelet, vol. II, p. 369, *Castro Villari*.
11. Michelet, vol. II, p. 375.
12. Michelet, vol. I, p. 501; Michelet, vol. II, p. 386.
13. Michelet, vol. I, pp. 64, 103, 561; Michelet, vol. II, pp. 388, 394–5; AN, J 413, no. 28.
14. AN, J 413, no. 28 and K 38, no. 8/2; Michelet, vol. I, p. 64.
15. D. Carraz, *L'Ordre du Temple dans la basse vallée du Rhône*, Lyon, Presses Universitaires de Lyon, 2005, pp. 523–8; V. Challet, 'Entre expansionisme capétien et relents d'hérésie: le procès des templiers du Midi', *Les Ordres religieux militaires dans le Midi (XIIe-XIVe siècle)*, Cahiers de Fanjeaux, no. 41, Toulouse, 2006, pp. 139–43; T. Kramer, 'Terror, Torture and the Truth: The Testimonies of the Templars Revisited', *The Debate*, pp. 71–85.
16. Ménard, *Nîmes*, vol. I, p. 195.
17. *Sine comissariis inquisitoris domini pape.*
18. Ménard, *Nîmes*, vol. I, pp. 197–205.
19. Ménard, *Nîmes*, vol. I, p. 206.
20. Ménard, *Nîmes*, vol. I, pp. 207–8.
21. AN, J 413B, no. 23; Miguet, *Templiers et hospitaliers*, p. 138.

22. AN, J 413, no. 20; A Gilbert-Dony, 'Les derniers templiers du bailliage de Caen', *Bulletin de la Société des Antiquaires de Normandie*, LXII (1994–7), Caen, 2003, pp. 190–93.

23. This was Hugues Morel; was he the successor of Esquieu de Floyrac from Biterris?

24. Finke, *Papsttum*, vol. II, pp. 316–21.

25. AN, J 413, no. 21.

26. Michelet, vol. I, pp. 69–70, 106–7, 130–31.

27. AN, J 413, no. 25; A. Nicolotti, 'L'interrogatorio dei Templari imprigionati a Carcassonne', *Studi Medievali*, 52 (2011), pp. 703–12.

28. Michelet, vol. I, p. 241.

29. Michelet, vol. II, p. 4.

30. Michelet, vol. I, pp. 225, 296.

31. Michelet, vol. I, p. 224.

32. Michelet, vol. I, pp. 270 and 262. I have not been able to identify this monastery in Poitiers (or more widely in Poitou): was it the priory of Montreuil-Bonnin perhaps, of the diocese of Poitiers, a dependence of the abbey of Saint-Cyprien de Poitiers? See Dom H. L. Cottineau, *Répertoire topo-bibliographique des abbayes et prieurés*, 3 vols, Mâcon, 1935, vol. II, p. 1973.

33. Finke, *Papsttum*, vol. II, p. 332 (interrogation in Poitiers, 30 June 1308).

34. Schottmüller, *Untergang*, vol. II, pp. 31–2.

35. Michelet, vol. I, p. 276, and vol. II, p. 86.

36. H. C. Lea, *The History of the Inquisition of the Middle Ages*, 3 vols, New York, Harper & Brothers, Franklin Square, 1888.

37. Lizerand, *Le Dossier*, pp. 26–7.

38. Barber, *Trial*, p. 71.

39. J.-M. Carbasse, *Introduction historique au droit pénal*, Paris, Presses Universitaires de France, 1990, p. 138.

40. Carbasse, *Introduction historique*, p. 163.

41. Their first depositions were sometimes reread to them when they were called to testify again: this was the case with Pons de Castelbon in Nîmes in 1308 (see Chapter 5, pp. 82–3).

42. Michelet, vol. II, p. 373; Michelet, vol. I, p. 249.

43. The following were tortured: Ademar d'Esparre in Toulouse; Jean de Cugy in Paris; Itier de Rochefort in Cahors; Raymond Étienne in Carcassonne; Géraud de Saint-Martial; Déodat Jafet; Raymond Massol (Schottmüller, *Untergang*, vol. II, p. 31–2, 40–42, 47–8, 48–50, 65, 68, 71); Humbert de Comborn (Finke, *Papsttum*, vol. II, p. 332–3). The following gave in before being tortured: Jean de Juvigny, Pierre de Conders, Pierre de Montsoult (or *Monte Seudi*), Pierre de Broce (Schottmüller, *Untergang*, vol. II, p. 42–4, 48–50, 59–61, 61–2). The following underwent harsh treatment: Simon Chrétien of Provins, Guillaume Haynueies, Atho de Sauvagnac (Schottmüller, *Untergang*, vol. II. pp. 39, 63, 69).

44. Schottmüller, *Untergang*, vol. II, pp. 52–3.

45. Schottmüller, *Untergang*, vol. II, pp. 40–42.

46. Schottmüller, *Untergang*, vol. II, pp. 47–8.

47. Schottmüller, *Untergang*, vol. II, p. 68.

48. Finke, *Papsttum*, vol. II, p. 332.

49. At the time of the arrests: Gérard de Passage, Bernard de Vado, Baudouin de Saint-Just, Gillet de *Encreyo*, Humbert du Puits, Jean Bertaud, Jean de Villiers-le-Duc and Jean de Cormele. Before the bishop: Ponsard de Gizy, Aymon de Barbone, Jean de Furno or Tortavilla, Consolin de Jorio and seventeen Templars from Périgueux, Raymond de Vassignac, Jean de Pollencourt, Raynier de Larchant, Robert Vigier, Étienne Las Gorsolas, Guillaume d'Errée, Thomas de Pampelune, Pierre Thibaud, Hélie Raynaud and Audebert de Porte. For a few others, there is no specific information.

50. Michelet, vol. I, pp. 40, 67, 230, 240, 264.

51. Michelet, vol. I, pp. 218, 75, 40.

52. Michelet, vol. I, pp. 527, 42.

53. Michelet, vol. I, pp. 69, 512–14.

54. Guillaume de Nangis, *Chronique latine*, p. 362.

4 At Notre-Dame de Paris (?), 24 or 26 December 1307

1. Finke, *Papsttum*, vol. II, pp. 58–9.

2. Barber, *Trial*, p. 78, n. 83.

3. H. Finke, *Papsttum*, vol. II, pp. 60–61.

4. Michelet, vol. II, pp. 295–6.

5. A. Demurger, *Jacques de Molay*, Paris, 2014 (English edition: *The Last Templar*, London, Profile Books, 2009).

6. Jean de Saint-Victor, 'Excerpta', p. 649.

7. Guillaume de Nangis, *Chronique latine*, p. 362.

8. Finke, *Papsttum*, vol. II, pp. 32–3.

9. J. Burgtorf, *The Central Convent of Hospitallers and Templars: History, Organization and Personnel (1099/1120–1310)*, Leiden, Brill, 2008, pp. 529–32 (Charnay), pp. 668–70 (Liancourt); P.-V. Claverie, *L'ordre du Temple en Terre sainte*, vol. I, p. 326; letter from Jacques de Molay, dated Poitiers, 9 June 1307, and included in a letter from Pope Clement of 1 July 1311 in *Regestum Clementis papae*, vol. VI, pp. 280–88, no. 7183.

10. As opposed to B. Frale, *Il papato e il processo ai Templari*, Rome, Viella, 2003, pp. 159–66, which does not take into account the fact that the other dignitaries of the Temple imprisoned in Paris had not yet been interrogated.

11. Finke, *Papsttum*, vol. II, pp. 307–8.

12. Finke, *Papsttum*, vol. II, pp. 309–13.

13. And not thirty-eight, see Barber, *Trial*, p. 80.

14. Finke, *Papsttum*, vol. II, pp. 47–8.

15. Finke, *Papsttum*, vol. II, pp. 48–9.

16. See note 3.

17. Jean de Saint-Victor, 'Excerpta', p. 651; Guillaume de Nangis, *Chronique latine*, p. 362.

18. Jean de Saint-Victor, 'Excerpta', p. 651; cited in G. Lizerand, 'Les dépositions du grand maître Jacques de Molay', *Le Moyen Âge*, XXVI (1913), pp. 85–6.

19. E. Boutaric, 'Clément V, Philippe le Bel et les templiers', pp. 32–3. Boutaric has published this letter and its translation from the original (AN, J 416, no. 2), stressing that Baluze did not publish it or mention it in his publication (Baluze, vol. 3), 'thereby betraying the rights of truth and history'. English translation of 27 October 1307 letter in Barber and Bate, *The Templars*, pp. 249–50.

20. Barber, *Trial*, p. 91. English translation found at: http://www.osmth.it/files/ PASTORALIS-PRAEMINENTIAE---Il-documento-papale-che-segno-..---Versione-in-inglese-1-sett-2013.pdf, p. 22.

21. Baluze, *Vitae*, vol. 3, p. 90; Barber, *Trial*, p. 91.

22. Baluze, *Vitae*, vol. 3, p. 91–4, and vol. 2 (notes), p. 113.

23. Finke, *Papsttum*, vol. II, respectively pp. 110–11 and 115–19.

24. Finke, *Papsttum*, vol. II, p. 115.

25. Frale, *Il papato e il processo ai Templari*, p. 86 and n. 76.

26. Finke, *Papsttum*, vol. II, p. 111.

27. It is difficult to believe them, given that four of them were related to the pope.

28. Baluze, *Vitae*, vol. 3, pp. 91–2.

29. Frale, *Il papato e il processo ai Templari*, p. 97.

30. Frale, *Il papato e il processo ai Templari*, p. 98. The author says on the day after 22 November; it could only have been after 1 December, the date of the pope's letter, which they were supposed to take to the king.

31. Finke, *Papsttum*, vol. II, p. 116; Lizerand, 'Les dépositions', pp. 87–8.

32. Baluze, *Vitae*, vol. 3, pp. 92–4; Bordonove, *La Tragédie des Templiers*, pp. 167–8.

33. Frale, *Il papato e il processo ai Templari*, pp. 97–8.

34. P. Dupuy, *Traitez concernant l'histoire de France*, Bruxelles, 1685, Preuves, pp. 91–2, no. 34.

35. Schottmüller, *Untergang*, vol. II, p. 37.

36. Finke, *Papsttum*, vol. II, pp. 338–9.

37. Finke, *Papsttum*, vol. II, p. 144; a comparison with the 'rough draft' of the text, published in Lizerand, *Le Dossier*, pp. 118–19, is a good example of the hardening of the king's advisers' tone during his intervention on 29 May.

38. Finke, *Papsttum*, vol. II, pp. 116–17; Lizerand, 'Les dépositions', p. 88.

39. Finke, *Papsttum*, vol. II, p. 102; the entire document is cited and translated into French in Bordonove, *La Tragédie des templiers*, p. 179; I will return to this text in the next chapter.

40. AN, J 413, no. 28: 'On this same day [Friday 3 February], Monseignor H. de la Celle put outside the Temple all the sergeants who had been guards there, except for fourteen who lived there and R. Toroelle and his companions, and brother G. Robert and his household.' On the identity of this last person see the recent study by P. Florentin, *Guillaume Robert et le secret des templiers. Un moine limousin contre l'ordre du Temple*, Limoges, 2017.

41. AN, J 413, no. 28; a document that I have already cited regarding the arrest of the Templars.

42. Therefore Jacques de Molay could not have been imprisoned in Corbeil before that date; many accounts of the Temple trial have him living in that city earlier. Jean de Saint-Victor confirms this transfer of Jacques de Molay and three other Templars: Jean de Saint-Victor, 'Excerpta', p. 649.

43. The text says Peauers in Gâtinais. I identify it as Pers-en-Gâtinais, commune of Ferrières, Loiret.

44. The text says Thieis; for the reasons that lead me to identify it as Thiers-sur-Thève, in the diocese of Senlis, see Appendix 1.

45. This may be Conflans-Sainte-Honorine or Conflans, near Vincennes, where the Countess Mahaut of Artois had a lovely manor house: P. Hartmann, 'Conflans près Paris', *Mémoires de la Société de l'histoire de Paris et de l'Île-de-France*, 35 (1908), pp. 1–188.

46. It was from Gisors that Jean de Tour, the treasurer, and Geoffroy de Gonneville, the master of Aquitaine, were taken respectively to the nearby castles of Goulet and Vernon.

47. Twenty-nine, in fact, because in Saint-Martin-des-Champs the first man in charge of the prison, Jean de Senlis, was fairly quickly replaced by Geoffroy de Reims.

48. See Chapter 12.

5 Power Struggle (January–June 1308)

1. H. Finke, *Acta aragonensia, Quellen zur Kirchen und Kulturgeschichte aus der diplomatischen Korrespondenz Jaymes II (1291–1327)*, Berlin, 1908, vol. III, p. 173.

2. See Chapter 2, p. 42.

3. Finke, *Papsttum*, vol. II, pp. 58–60.

4. Finke, *Papsttum*, vol. II, p. 114; J. Théry, 'La fuite du commandeur des templiers de Lombardie (nuit du 13 février 1308)', in *Les trente nuits qui ont fait l'Histoire*, Paris, Belin, 2014, pp. 105–15; E. Bellomo, *The Templar Order in North-West Italy (1142–c. 1330)*, Leiden, Brill, 2008, pp. 204–6.

5. Finke, *Papsttum*, vol. II, p. 114. The letter from the bishop of Lleida is dated 10 March 1308.

6. C. Port, *Le Livre de Guillaume Le Maire, Mélanges historiques*. 'Choix de documents', in 'Collection de documents inédits sur l'histoire de France', Paris 1877, vol. 2, pp. 418–23 and 424.

7. Boutaric, 'Clément V, Philippe le Bel et les templiers', pp. 41–2.

8. Lizerand, *Le Dossier*, p. 57.

9. An English translation of the questions can be found in Barber and Bate, *The Templars*, pp. 258–60.

10. Lizerand, *Le Dossier*, pp. 56–71; Barber and Bate, *The Templars*, p. 262.

11. See Chapter 11, pp. 187–8.

12. A third, written in the same format – questions, responses – as the consultation at the university, cannot be dated to the beginning of 1308, as Georges Lizerand, who published it, proposes (pp. 71–83), since it alludes to the Grand Master's recanting of his initial confession in Chinon in August 1308; it was written later, perhaps even in 1310 and, in any case, in a different context. *L'Affaire*, pp. 71–83. See also Chapter 11, pp. 187–8 below.

13. Lizerand, *Le Dossier*, pp. 84–95 and 96–101.

14. P. Dubois, *De recuperatione Terrae sanctae*, ed. Angelo Diotti, Florence, Leo Olschki, 1977. In this text Dubois develops many questions to which he provides sometimes very original answers; he also discusses the Templar Affair.

15. Barber, *Trial*, p. 97.

16. Bordonove, *La Tragédie des templiers*, p. 187, already proposes this chronology.

17. C. R. Cheney, 'The Downfall of the Templars and a Letter in Their Defence', *Medieval Miscellany Presented to Eugene Vinaver*, Medieval Texts and Studies, Oxford, 1973, pp. 65–79; the date is proposed by P. F. Crawford in 'The University of Paris and the Trial of the Templars', *Military Orders*, 3, History and Heritage, Ashgate, 2008, p. 116.

18. Thus it cannot have come from the masters of the university; see Barber, *Trial*, p. 96, n. 17.

19. Michelet, vol. I, p. 40.

20. Cheney, 'The Downfall of the Templars', p. 74.

21. If one accepts, of course, this new dating.

22. The documentation is gathered in G. Picot, *Documents relatifs aux états généraux et assemblées réunis sous Philippe le Bel*, in 'Collection de documents inédits sur l'histoire de France', Paris, 1901.

23. Picot, *Documents relatifs*, pp. 490–91; Lizerand, *Le Dossier*, pp. 102–7: letter of convocation dated from Melun 25 March 1308.

24. Lizerand, *Le Dossier*, pp. 106–9.

25. Barber, *Trial*, pp. 102–6; M. Satora, 'The Social Reception of the Templar Trial in Early Fourteenth Century France: The Transmission of Information', in *The Debate*, pp. 161–8.

26. S. Menache, 'The Templar Order: A Failed Ideal?' *The Catholic Historical Review*, 79 (1993), p. 16.

27. Lizerand, *Le Dossier*, pp. 108–9.

28. Lalou, *Itinéraire*, p. 311; John Burgunyó also mentions this date in a letter of the same day, 26 May: Finke, *Papsttum*, vol. II, p. 134.

29. Ménard, *Histoire de Nîmes*, pp. 181–2: this interrogation of April 1308, in which the interrogation of November 1307 is inserted, is itself inserted in the interrogations of 1310.

30. Challet, 'Entre expansionnisme capétien et relents d'hérésie', p. 145.

31. Picot, *Documents relatifs*, p. 540, no. 734.

32. See Chapter 7.

33. Sève, *Templiers d'Auvergne*, pp. 44 and 117.

34. Michelet, vol. I, pp. 264, 270.

35. Michelet, vol. I, p. 212.

36. Michelet, vol. I, p. 249.

37. *Itinéraire*, p. 311; Finke, *Papsttum*, vol. II, p. 134; Barber, *Trial*, p. 106, which indicates that the king returned to Paris before going to Poitiers, something the 'Itinerary' does not confirm.

38. Finke, *Papsttum*, vol. II, pp. 140–50. French translation in C. V. Langlois, 'L'affaire des templiers', *Journal des savants*, 1908, p. 426; English translation in Barber and Bate, *The Templars*, pp. 263–71.

39. Lizerand, *Le Dossier*, pp. 110–24.

40. Lizerand, *Le Dossier*, pp. 124–37.

41. Barber, *Trial*, pp. 114–15.

42. 'Documents relatifs au procès des Templiers en Angleterre rapportés par L. Blancard', *Revue des sociétés savantes*, VI (1867), pp. 418–19.

6 Compromise: Poitiers–Chinon (June–August 1308)

1. G. Lizerand, *Clément V et Philippe le Bel*, Paris, 1910, documentary evidence no. 10 and 11, pp. 440, 442 (the originals are in the AN, J 413, no. 6 and 7).

2. 'Documents relatifs au procès des Templiers en Angleterre rapportés par L. Blancard', p. 418 (British Library [BL], Harley MS, no. 247, fol. 144).

3. B. Frale, 'The Chinon Chart. Papal Absolution of the Last Templar Master Jacques de Molay', *Journal of Medieval History*, 30 (2004), pp. 109–34 and especially pp. 110–12.

4. Schottmüller, *Untergang*, vol. II, pp. 14–71; Finke, *Papsttum*, vol. II, pp. 329–40.

5. Michelet, vol. I, p. 70.

6. Michelet, vol. I, pp. 73–4.

7. Michelet, vol. I, p. 271.

8. Michelet, vol. I, pp. 231–2, 232.

9. Barber, *Trial*, says there are fifty-four identified Templars; I don't know how he arrives at this number.

10. Schottmüller, *Untergang*, vol. II, pp. 44–5.

11. Michelet, vol. I, p. 76.

12. See n. 2.

13. Frale, *Il papato e il processo ai Templari*, pp. 114, 130.

14. Schottmüller, *Untergang*, vol. II, p. 45–6.

15. Schottmüller, *Untergang*, vol. II, pp. 35–8; Finke, *Papsttum*, vol. II, p. 330.

16. Pierre de Brana, Robertus de Gay, Déodat Jafet, Raymond Mossel, Itier de Rochefort, Géraud de Saint-Martial, Adémar d'Esparre and Raymond Étienne stated they had been tortured.

17. Michelet, vol. I, p. 73.

18. Michelet, vol. I, p. 70.

19. Finke, *Papsttum*, vol. II, p. 152.

20. 'Documents relatifs au procès des Templiers en Angleterre rapportés par L. Blancard', p. 419.

21. Michelet, vol. I, p. 174.
22. Michelet, vol. I, p. 229.
23. Michelet, vol. I, p. 70.
24. Michelet, vol. I, pp. 76.
25. Michelet, vol. II, pp. 123, 127.
26. Boutaric, 'Clément V, Philippe le Bel et les Templiers', pp. 46–9, citing BnF, MS lat. 10919, fols 11 and 112.
27. AN, JJ 43, xxix–xl; C. Port, *Le Livre de Guillaume Le Maire, évêque d'Angers*, Collection des documents inédits sur l'histoire de France, Mélanges historiques, vol. 2, Paris, 1877, pp. 418–23.
28. Port, *Le Livre de Guillaume Le Maire*, pp. 423–4.
29. Port, *Le Livre de Guillaume Le Maire*, pp. 423–4.
30. See 'Documents relatifs au procès des Templiers en Angleterre rapportés par L. Blancard', pp. 419–20. The document quoted is BL, Harley MS, no. 252, fol. 113.
31. The date of the feast is 3 July, which in 1308 fell on a Tuesday.
32. Ptolemy da Lucca, *Vita Clementis papae V*, 2d. Baluze, vol. I, p. 130; see the chapter in J. Coste (ed.), *Boniface VIII en procès. Articles d'accusation et déposition des témoins (1303–1311)*, critical edition, introduction and notes, Rome, 'L'Erma', 1995, pp. 368–70.
33. Lizerand, *Clément V et Philippe le Bel*, no. 12, pp. 443 and 444.
34. Boutaric, 'Clément V, Philippe le Bel et les Templiers', pp. 53–4, citing AN, J 415, no. 10.
35. Finke, *Papsttum*, vol. II, p. 155.
36. Port, *Le Livre de Guillaume Le Maire*, pp. 398–416; on this Hospitaller project, see A. Demurger, *Les Hospitaliers; de Jérusalem à Rhodes (vers 1050–1317)*, Paris, Tallandier, 2013, pp. 470–75.
37. Port, *Le Livre de Guillaume Le Maire*, pp. 428–32 (*Regnans in coelis*) and 435–41 (*Faciens misericordiam*).
38. In this form, the text of *Faciens misericordiam* is published by Port, *Le Livre de Guillaume Le Maire*, pp. 435–41 (this is the copy addressed to the archbishop of Tours), and in Sève, *Templiers d'Auvergne*, pp. 93–8 (a copy addressed to the archbishop of Bourges). See the list of articles in Appendix 3.
39. This version is published in Michelet, vol. I, pp. 2–7; it has been translated into French by R. Oursel, *Le Procès des Templiers*, pp. 47–50.
40. See the list in Appendix 3.
41. Frale, *Il papato e il processo ai Templari*, p. 147, citing *Regestum Clementis Papae V*, no. 3584.
42. Finke, *Papsttum*, vol. II, p. 155.
43. Frale, 'The Chinon Chart', pp. 109–33.
44. Finke, *Papsttum*, vol. II, pp. 324–9.
45. Frale, *Il papato e il processo ai Templari*, pp. 198–215.
46. The Vatican Archives contain the archives of the papacy; among them, the Archivio segreto contains the personal archives of the popes, which are 'secret' only by virtue of

the fact that they were sealed with the seal of 'secret' (whence the word 'secretary'). In truth, the 'secret' archives have been open to researchers for quite some time.

47. See the latest developments of this vain media euphoria: B. Frale, '1308: il piano di Clement V per salvaguardare l'ordine dei Templari', strongly countered by M. Heiduk, 'Die Chinon-charta von 1308 – die Wende im Templerprozess? Ein archivalischer Fund und sein publizistisches Echo', both in A. Speer and D. Wirmer (eds), *1308: Eine Topographie historischen Gleichzeitigkeit*, Berlin and New York, De Gruyter, 2010, respectively pp. 125–39 and 140–60.

48. A. Demurger, '" Manuscrit de Chinon" or "Moment Chinon?"' Quelques remarques sur l'attitude du pape Clément V envers les templiers à l'été 1308', in M. Montesano (ed.), *'Come l'orco della Fabia.' Studi per Franco Cardini*, Florence, Sismel, Edizione del Galuzzo, 2010, pp. 111–21. This article contains a few errors in the examination of the papal bulls; they are corrected in this work.

49. Frale, *Il papato e il processo ai Templari*, pp. 144–50.

50. And not Annecy, as Frale writes in *Il papato e il processo ai Templari*, p. 213.

51. Published in Frale, *Il papato e il processo ai Templari*, pp. 216–19.

52. P. Viollet, 'Les interrogatoires de Jacques de Molay, grand maître du Temple. Conjectures', *Mémoires de l'Académie des inscriptions et belles lettres*, vol. XXXVIII, (1909); to explain these silences, the author has constructed a sophisticated explanation. He didn't need to go to such lengths.

53. Hypothesis made by Frale, *Il papato e il processo ai Templari*, pp. 154–8.

54. See Chapter 8, pp. 130–32.

55. Coste (ed.), *Boniface VIII en process*, p. 368, citing the letter of 19 August 1308 of Jean Bourgogne: Finke, *Papsttum*, vol. II, p. 157. Pope Clement must have decided not to go to Rome. He stopped in Avignon.

7 Clermont: The Diocesan Commissions (June 1309)

1. C. Port, *Le Livre de Guillaume Le Maire, évêque d'Angers*, Collection des documents inédits sur l'histoire de France, Mélanges historiques, vol. 2, Paris, 1877, p. 418.

2. AN, J 416, no. 17, repr. in Lizerand, *Clément V et Philippe IV le Bel*, p. 450; see also J. M. Roger, 'Le Prieuré de Champagne des "chevaliers de Rhodes", 1317–1522', unpublished thesis from the University Paris-IV-Sorbonne, 2001, p. 204, n. 8–9.

3. Roger, 'Le Prieuré de Champagne', pp. 213–20.

4. That is, a concession for the working and the yield of an estate, granted to an overseer for a fixed rent of pre-determined length (one year or three years).

5. A. Demurger, 'Dal Tempio all'Ospedale. Il destino delle commande templari nella contea di Auxerre (sec. XIV)' in F. Tommasi (ed.), *Acri 1291. La fine della presenza degli ordini militari in Terra Santa e i nuovi orientamenti nel XIV secolo*, Perugia, Quattroemme, 1996, pp. 93–6.

6. Demurger, *Jacques de Molay*, pp. 127–8.

7. AN, JJ 40, no. 64 for the king's letter; *Regestum Clementis papae V*, vol. III, no. 2938, pp. 137–8, for the pope's letter; interspersed in this letter from the pope is the letter of Jacques de Molay's donation; it is reprinted in J.-B. de Vaivre, *La Commanderie d'Epailly et sa chapelle templière*, Mémoires de l'Académie des inscriptions et belles lettres, Paris, De Boccard, 2005, pp. 197–8.

8. See A. Demurger, 'Les ordres religieux-militaires et l'argent: sources et pratiques', in K. Borchardt, K. Döring and P. Josserand and H. Nicholson (eds), *The Templars and Their Sources*, London and New York, Routledge, 2017, pp. 166–83.

9. Finke, *Papsttum*, vol. II, p. 183.

10. Finke, *Papsttum*, vol. II, pp. 189–201.

11. Frale, *Il papato e il processo ai Templari*, p. 116.

12. Port, *Le Livre de Guillaume Le Maire*, pp. 446–8.

13. Lizerand, *Dossier*, reprints the document, pp. 138–45; his proposed date is on p. 145, n. 1.

14. There are also the records from the diocese of Elne, in Roussillon, outside the kingdom; there is also a truncated record, and thus undatable and non-localisable, of twenty-five Templars from the Rhone Valley and the Dauphiné, again, outside the kingdom. That of Elne was reprinted by Michelet, following the records from Paris 1309–11 and from Paris 1307; the second, reprinted in Finke, *Papsttum*, vol. II, pp. 342–64, has been the focus of a new publication by Barbara Frale, 'L'interrogatorio ai Templari nella provincia di Bernardo Gui: un'ipotesi per il frammento del registo Avignonese 305', in *Dall'Archivio segreto vaticano. Miscellanea di testi, saggi e inventari*, Città del Vaticano, Archivio Segreto I (2006), pp. 199–272.

15. Sève, *Templiers d'Auvergne*, pp. 34–5.

16. See Chapter 9, pp. 135–7.

17. Sève, *Templiers d'Auvergne*, pp. 98–106.

18. Michelet, vol. I, p. 144: 'Many wanted to defend the Order, but they were not permitted to do so, which was said expressly by the brothers held in Clermont'; Michelet, vol. II, pp. 125, 134, 138, 147 (Riom).

19. Sève, *Templiers d'Auvergne*, p. 99.

20. Sève, *Templiers d'Auvergne*, pp. 105–6.

21. Sève, *Templiers d'Auvergne*, pp. 38–9.

22. See Appendix 3.

23. According to the numbering system adopted by A.-M. Chagny-Sève: Bertrand de Sartiges (no. 41); Bertrand Amblard (no. 43); Pierre Rose (no. 46), who was, however, a priest; Guillaume de Puy-Minaud (no. 49); Jean de Bellefaye (no. 50); Jean de Sornac (no. 52); Guillaume de Chamborand (no. 53), in *romana lingua expositis*; Jean Limousin (no 54); Durand Aldebalt (no. 57); Boson Coheta (no. 58); Pierre de Brion (no. 60); Audin de Vendat (no. 61); Jean de l'Orto (no. 62); Étienne Lajarousse (no. 63), also a priest; Jean de Malemort (no. 65); Andrea Jacob (no. 67); Étienne de la Roussille (no. 69).

24. Jean de Saint-Victor, pp. 654–5.

25. I do not provide the references (which are in Michelet, vols I and II), as there are far too many of them.

26. Michelet, vol. I, p. 499.
27. Michelet, vol. I, p. 241. In 1309 Easter was on 30 March; Quadragesima began on the first Sunday of Lent, six weeks earlier, on 16 February; the third Thursday of Lent, middle of Quadragesima, was on Sunday 9 March.
28. Michelet, vol. I, p. 402.
29. Michelet, vol. I, p. 556.
30. Michelet, vol. II, p. 323.
31. Michelet, vol. I, pp. 229–30.
32. Michelet, vol. I, pp. 368, 371, 374, 461, 477, 479, 482, 485, 487, 490; Michelet, vol. II, pp. 41, 44, 47.
33. P. Desportes, *Diocèse d'Amiens, Fasti ecclesiae gallicanae*, 1, Turnhout, Brepols, 1996, pp. 58–60. Michelet, vol. I, p. 443, Michelet, vol. II, p. 69.
34. Michelet, vol. I, p. 303.
35. Michelet, vol. I, p. 517.
36. Michelet, vol. I, pp. 254, 296, 316.
37. Michelet, vol. I, p. 334.
38. V. Tabbagh, *L'Archevêché de Sens, Fasti Ecclesiae gallicanae*, 11, Turnhout, Brepols, 2009, pp. 122–6.
39. Ménard, *Nîmes*, pp. 171–81 and 183–94, for the interrogations before the diocesan commissioners of Nîmes; see V. Challet, 'Entre expansionnisme capétien et relents d'hérésie', p. 146.
40. Michelet, vol. I, pp. 63, 98, 106.
41. Ménard, *Nîmes*, pp. 173–4, 176, 177.
42. Ménard, *Nîmes*, pp. 173–4, 176, 177. This deposition of November 1307 is reproduced twice in Ménard's book: at p. 207, in the course of the interrogations of 16 November 1307; and at p. 182, 1st column and 2nd column, top, interpolated in the deposition of 1308, itself interpolated in that of June 1310.
43. Ménard, *Nîmes*, p. 183, 1st column.
44. See Chapter 14, pp. 17–18 and 225–6.
45. Michelet, vol. II, p. 172: *quod fuerat ante tortus*.
46. Michelet, vol. I, pp. 37, 42.
47. Michelet, vol. I, pp. 229–30; Finke, *Papsttum*, vol. II, pp. 319–21.
48. Michelet, vol. I, pp. 71–2; Lizerand, *Le Dossier*, pp. 170–75.
49. Michelet, vol. I, p. 591.
50. Michelet, vol. I, pp. 70, 71, 72.

8 The Papal Commission Gets Off to a Slow Start (August– November 1309)

1. Letter reproduced in Michelet, vol. I, pp. 8–9; Finke, *Papsttum*, vol. II, pp. 189–201; Barber, *Trial*, p. 132.

2. Michelet, vol. I, p. 6.

3. Michelet, vol. I, p. 7.

4. Michelet, vol. I, p. 10.

5. Michelet, vol. I, pp. 14–15.

6. Michelet, vol. I, p. 15.

7. B. Galland, *Deux archevêchés entre la France et l'Empire. Les archevêques de Lyon et les archevêques de Vienne du milieu du XIIe siècle au milieu du XIVe siècle*, Rome, École française de Rome, 1994.

8. All of the texts are published in A. Demurger, 'Encore le procès des templiers. A propos d'un ouvrage récent', *Le Moyen Âge*, 97 (1991), pp. 35–9; commentary on this case in J.-B. Marquette, 'A propos d'un document bazadais inédit concernant le procès des templiers', *Les Cahiers du Bazadais*, 94 (1991), pp. 35–40.

9. Michelet, vol. I, p. 23.

10. Michelet, vol. I, p. 46.

11. Michelet, vol. I, pp. 24–5.

12. Michelet, vol. I, pp. 25–6.

13. Michelet, vol. I, p. 27.

14. AN, J 413, no. 28 (where Gérard de Causse is called Gérard du Cancer); see Chapter 4, pp. 70–73.

15. He is named *Cretis*, but this is probably a mis-spelling of *Trecis*.

16. Michelet, vol. II, pp. 290, 288, 278–9, 279–80, 406, 405.

17. Michelet, vol. I, pp. 77–8 (Tremblay, Larchant, Saulx), 80 (Troyes), 81 (Basemont, Caus).

18. Michelet, vol. I, p. 28.

19. Michelet, vol. I, pp. 28–9.

20. Michelet, vol. I, pp. 30–32.

21. See Chapter 1, pp. 12–14.

22. Michelet, vol. I, pp. 36–9. In this paragraph and the following, which are devoted to the declarations of Jacques de Molay, the narrative that I give, from the depositions of these two men, is similar, but shorter, to the two excellent chapters in Bordonove, *La Tragédie des templiers*, pp. 235–40 and 227–34.

23. Michelet, vol. II, pp. 363–4, 397, 285, 408.

24. AN, J 413B, no. 23; Miguet, *Templiers et hospitaliers*, p. 138.

25. Michelet, vol. I, p. 78.

26. Michelet, vol. I, p. 80.

27. A translation and publication of these two depositions are found in Lizerand, *Le Dossier*, pp. 146–55 and 162–71, and in Bordonove, *La Tragédie des Templiers*; P. Viollet, *Les interrogatoires de Jacques de Molay, grand maître du Temple. Conjectures*, Paris, 1901; Lizerand, 'Les dépositions', pp. 81–106.

28. Michelet, vol. I, pp. 32–5.

29. He would say similar things at the stake in 1314.

30. There is nothing of the sort in the *Chroniques de Saint-Denis*.

31. Michelet, vol. I, p. 46.

32. Michelet, vol. I, p. 47.

33. Michelet, vol. I, pp. 52–3.

34. Coste (ed.), *Boniface VIII en process,* p. 370.

35. Boutaric, 'Clément V, Philippe le Bel et les templiers', pp. 59–77; the text is translated in its entirety by the author. However, he is mistaken about the date; it was December 1310, and not December 1309, as is proven by the presence of the bishop of Bayeux in that delegation. The bishop of Bayeux, Guillaume Bonnet, a member of the papal commission, in fact excused himself to his colleagues in the commission for his absence in November/December 1310; see P. Viollet, 'Beranger Frédol, canoniste', HLF, vol. 34, Paris, 1915, p. 87.

9 The Papal Commission at Work (1309–1311)

1.   Thus very recently, D. R. Streeter, 'The Templars Face the Inquisition: The Papal Commission and the Diocesan Tribunals in France, 1308–1311', in *The Debate,* pp. 87–95.

2.   Barber, *Trial,* p. 137.

3.   Streeter, 'The Templars Face the Inquisition', p. 90: 'G. A. was totally the creature of the king.'

4.   McNamara, *Gilles Aycelin,* pp. 160 and 171–2. See Chapter 2, p. 32, n. 5.

5.   Favier, *Philippe le Bel,* pp. 28–9. F. Pegues, *The Lawyers of the Last Capetians,* Princeton, NJ, Princeton University Press, 1962, shares this point of view, unlike McNamara, who writes: 'Aycelin was not acting as an intimidated or naive man, but as a very competent judge who knew exactly what the king wanted' (*Gilles Aycelin,* p. 173).

6.   Barber, *Trial,* p. 139; P. Maurice, *Fasti Ecclesiae Gallicanae,* no. 8, *Le diocèse de Mende,* Brepols, 2004, p. 92; Streeter, 'The Templars Face the Inquisition', p. 93.

7.   A rule edicted by Clement IV in 1265 (bull *Licet ecclesiarum*).

8.   J. K. Bulman, *The Court Book of Mende and the Secular Lordship of the Bishop,* Toronto, University of Toronto Press, 2008.

9.   Cited by J. Théry, 'Une hérésie d'État', in *La Fin des Templiers,* p. 88, n. 55.

10. This is according to P. Maurice, *Le diocèse de Mende;* but, as we will see, the solution was also proposed by an anonymous author, in 1310 perhaps.

11. S. Menache, *Clément V,* Cambridge, Cambridge University Press, 1998, p. 81.

12. Boutaric, 'Clément V, Philippe le Bel et les Templiers', which wrongly indicates a date of 1309; see P. Viollet, 'Beranger Frédol, canoniste', *HLF,* vol. 34, p. 87.

13. B. Gams, *Series episcoporum, archiepisicoporum eccesiae catholicae,* Ratisbonne, 1873, p. 565.

14. A *camera post aula,* or *propinqua aula* or *adherente aule episcopali.*

15. Michelet, vol. I, pp. 89–97.

16. Michelet, vol. I, pp. 99–111.

17. Michelet, vol. I, p. 178.

18. Michelet, vol. I, p. 217.

19. Michelet, vol. I, p. 277.

20. Michelet, vol. I, pp. 285–6.

21. Michelet, vol. I, p. 443.

22. Michelet, vol. II, p. 88.

23. See Chapter 13, pp. 205–8, on these movements from the places of detention from the bailiwick of Senlis.

24. *Regestum Clementis papae V*, vol. 3, no. 3524 and 3531 for the bishops of Limoges and Mende; no. 3517 and 3527 for Jean de Montlaur and Jean de Mantoue; no. 3523 for Guillaume Agarni.

25. At each daily session a general overview is given: in the presence of the said lord commissioners. The absence of any other details signifies, I think, that the record referred to the preceding session and not that all the commissioners (that is, seven) were present, because when that was the case it was made clear in one way or another, and it was most often stressed by the use of *omnes* ('all'). Let's look at this sequence of sessions as an example: 2 January 1311: in the presence of the bishops of Mende and Limoges, of Mathieu de Naples and Jean de Mantua, archdeacon of Trente – thus the archbishop of Narbonne, the bishop of Bayeux and Jean de Montlaur are absent; on 4 January: in the presence of the commissioners except the archbishop of Narbonne – the bishop of Bayeux and Jean de Montlaur had thus returned, among the four others cited on 2 January; 5 January and the following days up to 11 January: in the presence of the said commissioners; this refers to those present on 4 January, thus without the archbishop of Narbonne because on 11 January the archbishop of Narbonne and the other commissioners were gathered; then on 12 January: in the presence of the said commissioners ...

26. Michelet, vol. I, p. 284.

27. Michelet, vol. I, p. 485.

28. Michelet, vol. II, p. 252.

29. Michelet, vol. II, p. 198; see also Michelet, vol. I, pp. 371, 443, 459.

30. Michelet, vol. I, p. 560: *coram eisdem commassiriis, hoc salvo quod, cum dictus frater Odo deposuit de abnegacione Jhesu Christi, dictus dominus Matheus ex causa recessit.*

31. Michelet, vol. I, pp. 82, 277, 443, 459; Michelet, vol. II, p. 198.

32. Michelet, vol. I, pp. 73, 86.

33. Michelet, vol. I, p. 82.

34. Michelet, vol. I, pp. 63, 68; Michelet, vol. II, p. 252.

35. Michelet, vol. I, pp. 68, 84.

36. Michelet, vol. I, pp. 314, 377, 554–8; Michelet, vol. II, p. 74.

37. Michelet, vol. I, p. 20.

38. Michelet, vol. I, pp. 289–90, 344–50.

39. Michelet, vol. I, p. 484.

40. Michelet, vol. I, p. 485.

41. Michelet, vol. I, pp. 59, 87.

42. Michelet, vol. I, p. 197.

43. Michelet, vol. I, p. 288.

44. Michelet, vol. I, p. 344.
45. Michelet, vol. I, p. 7: *vel tres, duo videlicet de prelate predictis, cum altero saltem de aliis …*
46. Michelet, vol. I, p. 285.
47. There is a problem with the chronology here: 'Opening of the next parliament the day before the Feast of Saint-Vincent.' This fell on 22 January.
48. Michelet, vol. II, pp. 74 and 77.
49. Michelet, vol. I, p. 41.
50. Michelet, vol. I, p. 82.
51. Michelet, vol. I, p. 87.
52. Michelet, vol. I, pp. 229, 232.
53. Michelet, vol. I, p. 39.
54. Michelet, vol. I, p. 88.

10 The Templars' Revolt (February–May 1310)

1. Michelet, vol. I, pp. 144–5.
2. Michelet, vol. I, pp. 57–8.
3. Michelet, vol. I, pp. 59; Sève, *Templiers d'Auvergne*, pp. 65–6 and 175–18, 160–63 and 154–7.
4. In this group ten Templars are named, but one of them, Jean de Mamberchin, ill and dying, was not present.
5. Tyers, diocese of Sens: there is an error by the scribe: in reality, it is Thiers-sur-Thève, diocese of Senlis. See Appendix 1.
6. Michelet, vol. I, pp. 70, 105, 136.
7. See a detailed analysis of this process of drawing up lists in A. Demurger, 'Eléments pour une prosopographie du "peuple templier": la comparution des templiers devant la commission pontificale de Paris (février–mai 1310)', in Josserand, Oliveira and Carraz, *Élites et Ordres militaires au Moyen-Age*, pp. 17–36.
8. Michelet, vol. I, pp. 96–8.
9. Michelet, vol. I, pp. 67 and 110.
10. Michelet, vol. I, pp. 105, 136, 150; Pierre de Cortemple is registered with the group from Sens on 14 February, Michelet, vol. I, p. 70.
11. Michelet, vol. I, p. 57.
12. Michelet, vol. I, pp. 85–6.
13. Michelet, vol. I, pp. 77–8.
14. Michelet, vol. I, pp. 79–80.
15. Michelet, vol. I, pp. 5–7, 111.
16. AN, J 413, no. 28; Michelet, vol. I, pp. 63, 97, 107, 153.
17. See Appendix 8 (Senlis); F. Hooghe, 'The Trial of the Templars in the County of Flanders (1307–1312)', in *The Debate*, p. 297.
18. See Chapter 8, p. 128.

19. Or Stephanus Le Bergonho de Serena, rue de la Cithare.

20. Or Leuragé, Rabiosse, de la Ragera, Henregea; in vico Calino (rue de Chaume).

21. Richard des Poulies, a rich Parisian clothier in possession since 1282 of 3,000m² of land at the corner of the rue du Temple and the rue Richard des Poulies in the recently endowed new city of the Temple. *Poulies*: ledges on which laundry was hung. See Geneviève Étienne, 'La Villeneuve du Temple aux XIIIᵉ et XIVᵉ siècle', *Actes du 100ᵉ Congrès National des Sociétés Savantes* (Paris, 1975), *Études sur l'histoire de Paris et de l'Île-de-France*, vol. 2, Paris, Bibliothèque nationale de France, 1978, pp. 87–99.

22. Cistercian abbey of Preuilly in the diocese of Sens (today diocese of Meaux, commune of Égligny, Seine-et-Marne).

23. Rue Lieudelle, not identified.

24. Or Guilleri, rue de la Coutellerie.

25. J. Hillairet, *Dictionnaire historique des rues de Paris*, 2 vols, Paris, Éditions de Minuit, 1963; H. Géraud, *Paris sous Philippe le Bel*, repr. Tubingen 1991; P. Lorentz and D. Sauchon, *Atlas de Paris au Moyen Âge*, Paris, Parigrame Éditions, 2006.

26. Michelet, vol. I, p. 145.

27. Michelet, vol. I, p. 128. Is this the owner of the house of Guillaume de Latigny where the Templars were held?

28. Michelet, vol. I, pp. 128–9.

29. Michelet, vol. I, p. 151.

30. Michelet, vol. I, p. 101.

31. Michelet, vol. I, p. 102.

32. Michelet, vol. I, p. 112.

33. Michelet, vol. I, pp. 112, 75.

34. Michelet, vol. I, p. 124.

35. Michelet, vol. I, p. 114.

36. Michelet, vol. I, p. 118.

37. Michelet, vol. I, p. 124.

38. Michelet, vol. I, p. 126.

39. Michelet, vol. I, p. 138.

40. Michelet, vol. I, p. 113.

41. Michelet, vol. I, pp. 113–14.

42. Michelet, vol. I, p. 137.

43. Michelet, vol. I, pp. 117, 134, 135.

44. Michelet, vol. I, pp. 129–30.

45. Michelet, vol. I, p. 120.

46. Michelet, vol. I, p. 75.

47. Michelet, vol. I, p. 139.

48. Michelet, vol. I, pp. 139–44.

49. Michelet, vol. I, pp. 145–6.

50. Michelet, vol. I, pp. 147–9.

51. Michelet, vol. I, pp. 149–50.

52. Michelet, vol. I, pp. 162–3.

53. Michelet, vol. I, pp. 130, 147.

54. Michelet, vol. I, pp. 152–3.

55. Michelet, vol. I, p. 154.

56. Michelet, vol. I, p. 154.

57. Michelet, vol. I, p. 157.

58. Michelet, vol. I, pp. 115–16, 120–24, 128–9, 145, 150–51, 152, 170–71.

59. Michelet, vol. I, pp. 139–44.

60. Michelet, vol. I, pp. 126–8 and 165–9.

61. Michelet, vol. I, p. 150.

62. Michelet, vol. I, p. 130.

63. Michelet, vol. I, pp. 133, 134, 153, 154.

64. Michelet, vol. I, p. 170.

65. An allusion to Saint Bernard, who sometimes, wrongly, appears as the writer of the Rule of the Order.

66. Michelet, vol. I, pp. 120–24. See Bordonove, *La Tragédie des templiers*, who cites and translates it in its entirety, pp. 251–4. I might add that he cites and translates many texts produced in this short period of the defence of the Order and that I made extensive use of his work for this chapter.

67. Jean de Montréal also presented the treatises (in the *langue d'oc*) of the Templars held in the residence of Richard des Poulies.

68. Very few in reality, but not because the Order was suspect.

69. Here we can see an allusion to the famous Guillaume le Maréchal, who took vows to enter the Temple during the Third Crusade and who carried out his vows on his deathbed, thirty years later, while wearing the mantle of the Temple which he had had made on purpose. See G. Duby, *Guillaume le Maréchal, ou le meilleur chevalier du monde*, Paris, Fayard, 1984, pp. 17–22.

70. Michelet, vol. I, pp. 126–8.

71. Michelet, vol. I, pp. 165–9.

72. See an analysis of this text in T. Burrows, 'The Templars' Case for their Defense in 1310', *The Journal of Religious History* (Sydney University Press), 13 (1984–5), pp. 248–60.

73. Michelet, vol. I, pp. 169–71.

74. Michelet, vol. I, pp. 172–3.

75. Bordonove, *La Tragédie des templiers*, p. 266, points this out well: the commissioners were simple investigators who gathered depositions and documents to build a case which they submitted for the judgement of the pope and the Council.

76. Michelet, vol. I, p.286.

77. Donato Calvi, *Effemeride sagro-profana di quando memorabile sia successo in Bergamo*, 3 vols, Milan, vol. 2, 1676, p. 22; E. Bellomo, *The Templar Order in North-West Italy (1142–c. 1330)*, Leiden, Brill, 2008, pp. 206–7.

11 The Council of Sens: The Revolt is Quelled (11–12 May 1310)

1. Also known as *Johannes Anglicus* de Hinquemate.
2. Michelet, vol. I, p. 174.
3. Michelet, vol. I, p. 182.
4. Michelet, vol. I, pp. 182–5.
5. Michelet, vol. I, pp. 193–201.
6. Michelet, vol. I, pp. 205–28.
7. Michelet, vol. I, pp. 233–59.
8. Michelet, vol. I, pp. 259–64.
9. Michelet, vol. I, p. 76; came with a group from Poitiers.
10. Michelet, vol. I, p. 87; second group from the Temple of Paris.
11. Michelet, vol. I, pp. 101–2; came alone.
12. Michelet, vol. I, p. 204.
13. Michelet, vol. I, p. 409.
14. Michelet, vol. I, p. 233.
15. Michelet, vol. I, p. 263.
16. Michelet, vol. I, pp. 263–4.
17. *Fasti Ecclesiae gallicanae*, vol. 11, *Diocèse de Sens*, by V. Tabbagh, Paris, 2009, pp. 126–8.
18. Michelet, vol. I, p. 197.
19. Michelet, vol. I, pp. 264–8.
20. Michelet, vol. I, pp. 268–74.
21. Michelet, vol. I, pp. 274–5.
22. Michelet, vol. I, pp. 275–6.
23. According to Jean de Pouilly, *Quodlibet V*, question 15, cited by K. Ubl, 'Haeretici Relapsi. Jean de Pouilly und die juristischen Grundlagen für die Hinrichtung der Tempelritter', in Speer and Wirmer (eds), *1308: Eine Topographie historischen Gleichzeitigkeit*, p. 165.
24. Michelet, vol. I, p. 60.
25. Jean de Saint-Victor, 'Excerpta', p. 654; Guillaume de Nangis, *Chronique latine*, pp. 377–8.
26. C. Guyon, *Les Écoliers du Christ. L'ordre canonial du Val des Écoliers, 1201–1539*, Saint-Étienne, Université de Saint-Étienne, 1998, p. 208.
27. By giving the number of fifty-nine who were burned, the chronicler in fact adds to the fifty-four that were burned on 12 May the five who were burned on 27 May.
28. Guillaume de Nangis, *Chronique latine*, pp. 377–8. The other detailed narratives are, *Les Grandes Chroniques de France*, J. Viard (ed.), vol. VIII, Paris, Société de l'Histoire de France, 1934, p. 272, and Bernard Gui, *Des Gestes glorieux des Français de l'an 1202 à l'an 1311*, Collection des mémoires relatifs à l'histoire de France, ed. F. Guizot, vol. 15, Paris, 1824, pp. 406–7.
29. L. Delisle, 'Guillaume d'Ercuis, précepteur de Philippe le Bel', HLF, vol. XXXII, Paris, 1898, p. 166.

30. *Grandes chroniques de France*, vol. VIII, p. 273: 'After which occurred, the day before the Ascension of Our Lord Jesus Christ [27 May], other Templars, in the same place were burned. One of them was chaplain of the king of France.'

31. Bernard Gui, *Des Gestes glorieux*, p. 406; *Chronique et annales de Gilles Le Muisit (1276–1352)*, ed. H. Lemaître, Société de l'Histoire de France, Paris, 1906, p. 79; Gilles Le Muisit is mistaken about the dating: he gives the date of 1309 for the Council of Senlis as well as for that of Sens.

32. F. J. M. Raynouard, *Monumens historiques relatifs à la condamnation des chevaliers du Temple et à l'abolition de leur ordre*, Paris, 1813, pp. 109–11. Raynouard gives the names attested by the testimony of other Templars: eight names, one of which, Gaucerand of Bures, is not on this list. But he omits Lucho de Sernoy, burned in Senlis. He then gives a list of thirty-eight names, Templars who, according to him, were presented as defenders of the Order and were then mentioned in various testimonies of Templars as deceased ('*quondam*' etc.). But the Templars indicated as dying during the years 1310–11 did not necessarily all die at the stake.

33. Delisle, 'Guillaume d'Ercuis', p. 166; *Grandes chroniques de France*, vol. VIII, p. 273. Jean de Taverny or Jean de Tour? We know that, besides the two Jean de Tours who were treasurer of the Temple of Paris and treasurer of the king, another Jean de Tour was royal chaplain. In documents that deal with the transfer of Templars from the Temple of Paris to detention sites scattered throughout Île-de-France in January/February 1308 there was 'the young chaplain' transferred to Moret on 25 January, and the 'old chaplain' transferred to Beaumont-sur-Oise on 3 February 1308. The first was Raoul d'Herblay, the second was Jean de Tour; AN, J 413, no. 28. Confusion between Tour/Taverny is possible, since the seigneurie of Tour was not very far from Taverny.

34. Michelet, vol. I, p. 70.

35. Guillaume de Nangis, *Chronique latine*, p. 381. This is Jean de Tour the Elder.

36. Bernard Gui, *Des gestes glorieux*, p. 406.

37. Guillaume de Nangis, *Chronique latine*, p. 378.

38. *Grandes chroniques de France*, vol. VIII, pp. 272–3.

39. Lizerand, *Le Dossier*, pp. 71–83; Barber *Trial*, pp. 170–71.

40. BnF, MS lat. 15372, fols 181–185; N. Valois, 'Jean de Pouilly, théologien', *HLF*, vol. 34, Paris, 1915, pp. 224ff.; N. Valois, 'Deux nouveaux témoignages sur le procès des templiers', *Compte-rendus des séances de l'année 1910 de l'Académie des Inscriptions et Belles Lettres*, Paris, 1910, pp. 230–38.

41. Ubl, 'Haeretici Relapsi', pp. 163–4; W. J. Courtenay, 'The Role of the University Masters and Bachelors at Paris in the Templar Affair, 1307–1308', in Speer and Wirmer (eds), *1308: Eine Topographie*, pp. 179–80. Between 24 or 26 December 1307 (the date of Jacques de Molay's retraction) and 18 April 1308, the beginning of the year 1308, as per the calendar beginning with Easter, which was followed at the time in France.

42. Jean de Pouilly's arguments are developed in question 15 of the fifth collection of *Quodlibet* by the author: BnF, MS lat. 15372, fol. 181r: *Utrum, si aliquis sit confessus haeresim et postea revocet in facie Ecclesiae dicendo se falsum dixisse, talis debeat dici relapsis.*

See Noël Valois, 'Jean de Pouilly, théologien', p. 265. The text, as well as other texts by Jean de Pouilly concerning the heresy, is published in W. J. Courtenay and K. Ubl, *Gelehrte Gutachten und königliche Politik im Templerprozess*, Hanover, 2010, pp. 85–146.

43. Barber, *Trial*, pp. 173–4; see Valois, 'Jean de Pouilly, théologien', and Courtenay and Ubl, *Gelehrte Gutachten*.

44. Another author, Paul F. Crawford, compares the list of fourteen of 1308 with the twenty-one theologians who condemned Marguerite Porète for heresy in 1310 (she was burned on 1 June), and develops an entire argument on the interferences between the Templar Affair and the recurrent conflicts in the University of Paris between the secular masters and the regular masters on the subject of the privilege of exemption. This is a separate issue: P. F. Crawford, 'The University of Paris and the Trial of the Templars', *Military Orders* 3, History and Heritage, Ashgate, 2008, pp. 115–22.

45. Ubl, 'Haeretici Relapsi', p. 163.

46. Guillaume de Nangis, *Chronique latine*, p. 378.

47. Michelet, vol. I, p. 278.

48. Michelet, vol. I, p. 281.

49. Michelet, vol. I, p. 281.

50. Bellomo, *The Templar Order in North-West Italy*, pp. 206–7.

51. Michelet, vol. I, pp. 282–3.

52. This was Pierre de sancta Gressa (Michelet, vol. I, p. 65) and Renaud de Tremblay (Michelet, vol. I, p. 77).

53. Michelet, vol. I, pp. 286–7.

54. *Fasti Ecclesiae gallicanae*, vol. 11, *Diocèse de Sens*, pp. 126–8. The session of August 1311 of the Council of Sens is announced in the letter of convocation (for 18 August) addressed to the bishops and reproduced in abbot Lebeuf, *Mémoires concernant l'histoire civile et ecclésiastique d'Auxerre et de son ancien diocèse*, Édition A. Challe et M. Quantin, 4 vols, Auxerre, 1855, vol. IV, p. 156, no. 258. The act is dated the Thursday before the Feast of Saint-Arnoul (which falls on 18 July).

55. Michelet, vol. II, pp. 3–4. Besides Renaud de Provins, there were Jean de Mortefontaine and Guillaume de Hoymont, priests, and Renaud de Cugnières, knight, Pierre de Clermont-en-Beauvaisis and Bernard de Cernay (in the diocese of Paris).

12 Interlude: In the Prisons of Senlis (June 1310–1312)

1. See Appendix 8.

2. Michelet, vol. I, pp. 85–6.

3. Michelet, vol. I, pp. 132–3.

4. BnF, MS fr. 20334, no. 58.

5. The farmer is the one who leased, for a fixed rent paid to the king, the management of the Templar property in a demesne, a lordship or a town.

6. BnF, MS fr. 20334, no. 54.

7. BnF, Clair. 1313, no. 28; Michelet, vol. I, pp. 84–6.

8. BnF, MS fr. 20334 (69 acts); MS lat. 9800 (12 acts); Clairambault 1313 (40 acts); AN, K 37C no. 40 ter; K 38 no. 8/2; Prutz, *Entwicklung,* publishes twelve in part; Raynouard, *Monumens*, p. 107, makes a brief reference to these documents, which have not been of much interest to historians of the trial of the Temple.

9. BnF, Clairambault 1313, no. 24.

10. BnF, Clairambault 1313, no. 37; MS fr. 20334, nos. 56 and 57.

11. BnF, MS lat. 9800, no. 10, 11, 12.

12. BnF, MS lat. 9800, no. 13. This Guillaume de Gisors is the one who had decided to confer the nine Templars from Gisors on Pierre Proventel in Compiègne.

13. BnF, MS fr. 203354, nos. 28 and 30.

14. Raoul Morant, of the group imprisoned in Montmélian.

15. Michelet, vol. I, p. 151.

16. BnF, Clairambault 1303, no. 36.

17. BnF, MS fr. 20334, no. 7.

18. BnF, Clairambault 1313, no. 46.

19. BnF, Clairambault 1313, no. 39.

20. BnF, Clairambault 1313, no. 45.

21. BnF, Clairambault 1313. no. 14.

22. BnF, MS fr. 20334, no. 49.

23. BnF, MS fr. 20334, nos. 26, 68, 70; MS lat. 9800, no. 9.

24. This is Henri de Brabant, who disappears from the lists in April 1311.

25. In the residence of Jean Le Gagneur one fewer, but the document does not reproduce the list of Templars detained at the time (October 1311), BnF, MS fr. 20334, no. 67.

26. Pierre de Saint-Just in June 1311 and Jean Gambier in October 1311.

27. BnF, MS lat. 9800, no. 7.

28. Hughes d'Ailly, then Gilles d'Oisemont, Pierre de Saint-Leu and Nicolas Le Monnier.

29. BnF, MS fr. 20334, no. 80.

30. Michelet, vol. I, p. 622.

31. Michelet, vol. I, pp. 443, 459; Michelet, vol. II, p. 132.

32. Michelet, vol. I, pp. 443, 468.

33. Michelet, vol. I, pp. 446, 471, 474.

34. BnF, MS lat. 9800, no. 15, and MS fr. 20334, no. 47.

35. BnF, MS lat., 9800, no. 11.

36. BnF, MS fr. 20334, no. 50; Clairambault 1313, no. 45.

37. BnF, MS lat. 9800, no. 18.

38. BnF, MS lat. 9800 no. 10.

39. BnF, MS lat. 9800, no. 7.

13 The Second Phase of Interrogations (Paris, 1311)

1. Michelet, vol. I, pp. 286–90.
2. Michelet, vol. II, p. 165; he was a member of the group that appeared on 4 April 1311.
3. Michelet, vol. I, p. 439; Michelet, vol. II, p. 85.
4. Antonio Sicci da Vercelli (Michelet, vol. I, pp. 641–8), Étienne de Nérac, Minor brother from Lyon (Michelet, vol. I, p. 454), and Pierre de la Palud, Preaching brother, also from Lyon (Michelet, vol. II, p. 195).
5. The number of Templars usually quoted, 231, covers all the individual interrogations of the period from April 1310 to 26 May 1311; there were, in fact, only 230, including the depositions of six non-Templars.
6. Michelet, vol. I, p. 433.
7. I am not aware of a judgement pronounced by the council of the ecclesiastical province of Bourges (of which Clermont was a suffragan) in the years 1309–12; there was one in 1315, whose object was not specified; it is possible to imagine that it may have dealt with the Templars, as happened with a provincial council gathered in Narbonne the same year, 1315. On all of this see Sève, *Templiers d'Auvergne*, pp. 71–86.
8. The three 'admitters' are Guillaume d'Espinasse, Gilbert Laporte and Guillaume Brughat.
9. Michelet, vol. II, pp. 151–4.
10. Michelet, vol. II, pp. 121, 233.
11. Michelet, vol. II, p. 198.
12. A. Trudon des Ormes, *Liste des maisons et de quelques dignitaires de l'Ordre du Temple en Syrie, en Chypre et en France d'après les pièces du procès*, Paris, 1900, p. 202.
13. Michelet, vol. II, pp. 199–217.
14. Michelet, vol. II, pp. 6–23.
15. By contrast, we don't have any information about the 'transport' of the Templars being held in Paris and in its surrounding area between their prison (the Paris Temple, for example) and the place where the commission was meeting.
16. BnF, MS fr. 20334, no. 56 and 57.
17. Michelet, vol. I, p. 468: *in domo fratrum Minorum quam juxta eorum ecclesiam consuevit inhabitare dominus episcopus Laudunensis* (testimony of Jean de Saint-Just of 29 January 1311).
18. Michelet, vol. I, p. 619.
19. Michelet, vol. I, pp. 619, 621, 624.
20. Before directing the council of the province of Reims in Senlis in May 1310, the archbishop of Reims officiated over the investigation into individuals in his diocese of Reims probably in 1309.
21. Michelet, vol. I, p. 461.
22. BnF, MS fr., 20334, no 63.
23. BnF, MS fr., 20334, no. 64.

24. Michelet, vol. II, pp. 446, 477, 479, 482, 485, 487, 490. It is difficult to accept that the Hue d'Oisemont indicated as housing the seven Templars from Senlis was the same as the Templar Hugues d'Oisemont interrogated on 4 February.

25. Michelet, vol. I, pp. 446, 471, 474.

26. BnF, Clairambault 1313, no. 37.

27. Sève, *Templiers d'Auvergne*, pp. 72–85.

28. Michelet, vol. I, pp. 379–84; Michelet, vol. II, pp. 290–91.

29. Michelet, vol. I, p. 377.

30. Michelet, vol. I, p. 460; see also Michelet, vol. I, p. 511, and vol. II, p. 151.

31. S. L. Field, 'La fin de l'ordre du Temple à Paris: le cas de Mathieu de Cressonessart', in Chevalier, *La Fin des Templiers*, pp. 101–32.

32. Cressonsacq, canton of Estrées-Saint-Denis, Oise.

33. Bellinval, commune of Brailly-Cornehotte, canton of Crécy, Somme; diocese of Amiens.

34. This is what Sean L. Field conjectures; he specifies that Mathieu knew Latin. But Mathieu may equally well not have had any ties with that family and simply have been from Cressonessart (Cressonsacq).

35. The identification proposed by Sean L. Field is not correct.

36. Michelet, vol. I, pp. 145–6.

37. Michelet, vol. I, pp. 165–7.

38. Michelet, vol. I, pp. 511 and 535–8.

39. Michelet, vol. I, pp. 367, 368–70. He should not be confused with an almost homonymous Jean de Bolencourt or Bollencourt, from the diocese of Beauvais, interrogated on 27 January; Michelet, vol. I, pp. 443, 461–3.

40. La Ronzière: Les Rosières, commune of Neuville-Coppegueule, canton of Oisemont, in the Somme, diocese of Amiens.

41. Michelet, vol. I, pp. 377–9.

42. Michelet, vol. II, pp. 15–18, 18–21.

43. Michelet, vol. II, pp. 88–96, 107–9.

44. Michelet, vol. II, pp. 3–4.

45. Michelet, vol. I, p. 174.

46. The distinctive garb for the brothers of the Temple was a mantle, white for the knights, dark for the sergeants and chaplain brothers, upon which was a cross – red – on the left shoulder. See A. Demurger, 'Habit', in N. Beriou and P. Josserand (eds), *Prier et combattre: dictionnaire européen des Ordres religieux militaires*, Paris, Fayard, 2009, p. 421.

47. This was a short thick beard; the long beard in the illustrations of the eighteenth and nineteenth centuries is imaginary: such ferocious warriors would have found them a hindrance.

48. Michelet, vol. I, p. 187.

49. I go into the question of the wearing of the habit and the beard in the records of the Temple trial in A. Demurger, 'La barbe et l'habit dans l'affaire du Temple: adhésion, rupture, résistance', forthcoming, in a collection of writings in honour of Alan Forey.

50. Michelet, vol. I, pp. 368, 371, 374, 447, 461, 479, 532, 535, 619, 624, 632; Michelet, vol.
     II, pp. 39, 44, 56, 74, 105, 112, 182, 218, 220, 225, 227, 228, 231; except for the four that I
     pointed out above, the explanation is simple, and one need not make too much of it.
51. Michelet, vol. I, p. 344.
52. Michelet, vol. I, p. 634.
53. Michelet, vol. II, p. 220.
54. Michelet, vol. I, p. 301.
55. Michelet, vol. I, pp. 320, 324, 331.
56. Michelet, vol. I, pp. 334, 348, 353, 358, 364.
57. Michelet, vol. I, p. 586.
58. Michelet, vol. I, pp. 461, 548; 402, 424, 591.
59. Michelet, vol. I, p. 348.
60. Michelet, vol. I, p. 402.
61. Michelet, vol. I, pp. 424–5.
62. Michelet, vol. I, p. 112.
63. Michelet, vol. I, p. 67.
64. Michelet, vol. I, p. 137.
65. Finke, *Papsttum*, vol. II, p. 152.
66. Michelet, vol. II, pp. 3–4.
67. G. Alberigo (ed.), *Les Conciles oecuméniques*, vol. 2: *Les décrets*, I, *De Nicée à Latran V*,
     Paris, Éditions du Cerf, 1994, p. 711.

14 The Council of Vienne and the Burning of Jacques de Molay (1311–1314)

1. Michelet, vol. II, pp. 263, 265, 267.
2. Michelet, vol. II, p. 269.
3. Michelet, vol. II, pp. 272–3. An introductory note retraces the path of this document to its
    depositing in the Bibliothèque nationale in 1793: BnF, MS lat. 11796. This note specifies
    that the document on paper deposited in Notre-Dame could not be communicated to
    anyone without the express permission of the pope. This document is often considered to
    be a copy, not very carefully done, of the original on parchment deposited in the Vatican
    Archives; this is not true. The use of paper was probably less prestigious than parchment;
    the Bibliothèque nationale de France does not possess the (usurped) mystery of the
    'Archivio secreto' of the Vatican Archives. Nonetheless, it is indeed an original copy.
    Still, the two documents can be distinguished by this: the copy in the Vatican Archives,
    sent to Pope Clement, served as a working document for the special commission which
    synthetised the investigations for the work of the Council of Vienne. Because of this it
    includes marginal annotations that make it certainly precious but no more original than
    the document that remained in Paris. The notations provided at the end of the report by
    the notaries are in my opinion unambiguous. See: Field, 'La fin de l'ordre du Temple à

Paris', p. 109; A. Luttrell, 'The Election of the Templar Master James de Molay', in *The Debate*, p. 23, no. 18; Frale, *Il papato e il processo ai Templari*, p. 141.

4. Outside France the sessions of the papal commissions were still held in August.

5. See Chapter 7.

6. Ménard, *Nîmes*, p. 215: *Et est sciendum quod quidam de predictis fratribus fuerunt questionate moderate, tres septimane et plus sunt elapse, et ex tunc citra questionati non fuerunt.*

7. AN, J 490, no. 778: in this letter of 14 February 1311 (not sent, but we have the copy sent to the Vatican Archives), the king stops his pursuit of Boniface VIII; see J. Coste, *Boniface VIII en procès*, p. 754, nos. 5–7.

8. *Regestum Clementis papae V*, vol. VII, 1, nos. 7493–7498; 7523–7529; 7595; Raynouard, *Monumens*, p. 167.

9. *Regestum Clementis papae V*, vol. VII, 1, no. 7517.

10. *Regestum Clementis papae V*, vol. VII, 1, no. 7521.

11. J. Lecler, *Le Concile de Vienne, 1311–1312*, Paris, Fayard, 2005; E. Müller, *Das Konzil von Vienne*, Munster, 1934; R. Lauxerois (ed.), *Vienne au crépuscule des Templiers*, Grenoble, Presses Universitaires de Grenoble, 2014.

12. Frale, *Il papato e il processo ai Templari*, pp. 147–8, citing *Regestum Clementis papae V*, vol. III, no. 3584; Barber, *Trial*, pp. 248–9.

13. Michelet, vol. I, p. 115.

14. Michelet, vol. I, p. 157; see also Michelet, vol. I, pp. 164, 165.

15. Michelet, vol. I, p. 171.

16. Raynouard, *Monumens*, pp. 176–7; G. Lizerand, *Clément V et Philippe le Bel*, Appendix, no. 30, pp. 472–3.

17. BnF, MS lat. 15372, fol. 185; it concerns question 15 of the *Quodlibet* V already mentioned (Chapter 11) and mentioned by N. Valois, 'Jean de Pouilly, théologien', pp. 230–31.

18. Ptolemy da Lucca, '*Seconda vitae Clementis V*', in Baluze, *Vitae paparum Avinionensium*, ed. G. Mollat, vol. I, Paris, 1928, p. 42. The three French prelates are Pierre de Courtenay, archbishop of Reims, Philippe de Marigny, archbishop of Sens, and Gilles Aycelin, archbishop of Rouen. Their attitude is not a surprise, but it is surprising that they were so isolated from the other French prelates present in Vienne. Who said that Philip the Fair ruled the French episcopate with an iron fist?

19. C.-V. Langlois, 'Notices et documents relatifs à l'histoire des XIIIe et XIVe siècles', *Revue historique*, 87 (1905), pp. 75–6.

20. Port, *Le livre de Guillaume Le Maire*, pp. 471–4.

21. G. Alberigo, *Les Conciles oecuméniques*, vol. 2, 1, *Les décrets*, pp. 709–13. English translation in Barber and Bate, *The Templars*, pp. 309–18.

22. Finke, *Papsttum*, vol. II, pp. 287–8.

23. The two bulls are published and translated in Alberigo, *Les Conciles oecuméniques*, pp. 712–19 for the first, pp. 720–25 for the second.

24. Jean de Saint-Victor, 'Excerpta', p. 658.

25. Alberigo, *Les Conciles oecuméniques*, p. 713. English translation in Barber and Bate, *The Templars*, p. 318.

26. Ménard, *Nîmes*, pp. 212–16.

27. The reports of the investigations were published by Jules Michelet following the reports of the papal commission of Paris of 1310 and the interrogations in Paris of 1307: Michelet, vol. II, pp. 421–515. See R. Vinas, *Le Procès des templiers en Roussillon*, Perpignan, Tdo Éditions, 2009.

28. John XXII, *Lettres communes*, ed. G. Mollat, Paris 1904–46, vol. 1, no. 2510.

29. R. Vinas, *Le procès des templiers*, p. 153.

30. G. Mollat, 'La dispersion définitive des templiers après leur suppression', *Compte-rendus des séances de l'Académie des inscriptions et belles-lettres*, 96 (1952), pp. 376–80. A. J. Forey, *The Fall of the Templars in the Crown of Aragon*, Aldershot, Ashgate, 2001, Chapter 6; A. J. Forey, 'The ex-Templars in England', *Journal of Ecclesiastical History*, 53 (2002), p. 18–37; A. J. Forey, 'Templars after the Trial: Further Evidence', *Revue Mabillon*, 84 (2012), p. 89–110.

31. AN, S 4951A, I, 42 no. 6; published in V. Bessey, *Les commanderies de l'Hôpital en Picardie au temps des chevaliers de Rhodes 1309–1522*, Millau, Éditions Conservatoire Larzac, 2005, p. 316.

32. Bessey, *Les commanderies de l'Hôpital en Picardie*, p. 323; Michelet, vol. I, pp. 73, 104, 135; AN, J 413, no. 28.

33. Michelet, vol. I, p. 242.

34. A. du Bourg, *Ordre de Malte. Histoire du Grand Prieuré de Toulouse*, Toulouse, 1883, p. 74. The see of Toulouse was turned into an archbishopric in 1317.

35. John XXII, *Lettres secrètes et curiales relatives à la France*, ed. A. Coulon and S. Clémencet, Paris, 1906–67, vol. I, no. 236; Forey, 'Templars after the Trial', p. 95, n. 41.

36. F. Boisserie and A.-S. Brun, *Domme (24). Porte des Tours. Étude documentaire et expertise archéologique des graffiti.* Rapport intermédiaire, Parthenay, July 2017, which condemns as fraudulent P. M. Tonnelier, 'A Domme en Périgord, le message des prisonniers', *Archéologia* 32 (January–February 1970), p. 24.

37. John XXII, *Lettres communes*, vol. 3, no. 13307; Forey, 'Templars after the Trial', p. 102.

38. Michelet, vol. I, pp. 62, 97, 107, 128.

39. Michelet, vol. I, p. 463.

40. Michelet, vol. I, pp. 463–8.

41. See Appendix 8; BnF, MS fr. 20334 (9–16); Clairambault 1313 (17, 28, 42).

42. *Regestum Clementis papae V*, vol. VI, no. 6493.

43. Michelet, vol. I, p. 39.

44. Musée des Archives Départementales, Collection of facsimiles, documents taken from the archives of prefectures, town halls and hospices, Paris, Imprimerie nationale, 1878, p. 221, no. 104 of the Haute-Saône.

45. See Demurger, *The Last Templar*.

46. Michelet, vol. I, pp. 87–8.

47. Michelet, vol. I, p. 88.

48. AN, J 413, no. 28; see Chapter 4, pp. 70–73.

49. Bordonove, *La Tragédie des templiers*, p. 343.

50. Michelet, vol. I, pp. 84–6.

51. A. Beck, *La fine dei Templari*, Casale Monferrato, Edizioni Piemme, 1994, p. 159; Schottmüller, *Untergang*, vol. I, p. 623.

52. *Regestum Clementis papae V*, vol. VIII, no. 10337.

53. J. Hillairet, *Dictionnaire historique des rues de Paris*, vol. II, p. 232.

54. Guillaume de Nangis, *Chronique latine*, p. 402–3. English translation of the second paragraph in Demurger, *The Last Templar*, p. 196.

55. B. Gui, *Flores Chronicorum*, French translation of 1316, BnF, MS fr. 1409, fol. 157.

56. See the unpublished work by G. Delépinay: 'Le 11 mars 1314, sur l'île aux Juifs'.

57. *Itinéraire*, p. 417.

58. E. Boutaric, *Actes du Parlement de Paris*, Paris, 1863, vol. II, p. 122, no. 4272; Demurger, *The Last Templar*, p. 199.

59. C. V. Langlois, 'Extrait du 2ᵉ journal de la chambre des comptes', *Notices et extraits des manuscrits de la Bibliothèque nationale*, Paris, vol. 40 (1917), p. 258; M. Bompaire, 'Trésor de Templiers et trésors de Juifs au XIVᵉ siècle', *Bulletin de la Société française de numismatique*, September 1998, pp. 185–6; J.-B. de Vaivre, *La Commanderie d'Épailly et sa chapelle templière*, Paris, 2005, publishes the document in appendices, pp. 188–9, no. XXXI. It was the 5,010 pieces of silver that were worth 20 *livres* 17 *sous* and 6 *deniers tournois* in money of account.

60. Raynouard, *Monumens*, p. 196–7; P. Boutry, 'Clément XIV', in P. Levillain, ed, *Dictionnaire historique de la papauté*, Paris, Fayard, 1994, pp. 394–7. English translation found at https://archive.org/details/bullsofpopesclemoocath.

Conclusion

1. I remind the reader of the already dated, but at the time pioneering, article by Malcolm Barber, 'The World Picture of Philip the Fair', *Journal of Medieval History*, 8 (1982), which announces the research and studies undertaken by, among others, Julien Théry in 'Une hérésie d'État, Philippe Le Bel, le procès des "perfides templiers" et la pontificalisation de la monarchie française', in Chevalier, *La Fin des Templiers*, pp. 63–100.

2. The date of the Feast is 3 July, which in 1308 fell on a Tuesday. See 'Documents relatifs au procès des Templiers en Angleterre rapportés par L. Blancard', *Revue des sociétés savantes*, VI (1867), pp. 419–20. It involves the document in the British Museum, MS Harley, no. 252, fol. 113.

3. B. Frale, '1308. Il piano di Clement V per salvaguardare l'ordine dei Templari', and, in contrast, M. Heiduk, 'Die Chinon-Charta von 1308 – die Wende im Templer prozess? Ein archivalischer Fund und sein publizistisches Echo', in Speer and Wirmer (eds), 1308: *Eine Topographie historischen Gleichzeitigkeit*, pp. 125–39 and 140–60.

4. Ptolemy da Lucca, *Vita Clementis papae V*, 2d. Baluze, vol. I, p. 130; see the chapter by J. Coste, *Boniface VIII en procès*, pp. 368–70.

5. A Norman chronicle from the fourteenth century relates the death of Guillaume de Nogaret: 'Then it happened that Guillaume de Longaret died, and died most hideously, his tongue discoloured, by which the king was most amazed, and several others who had been against the pope Boniface.' *Chronique normande du XIVe siècle*, ed. A. and E. Molinier, Société de l'Histoire de France, Paris, 1872, p. 29.

6. R. Caravita, *Rinaldo da Concorezzo, arcivescovo di Ravenna (1303–1321) al tempo di Dante*, Florence, Leo Olschky, 1964, and later articles by this author; J.-M. Sans i Travé, *La fi dels Templers catalans*, Barcelona, Pagés, 2008, pp. 316–23.

7. We still find all too often, in historical literature little concerned with delving into sources, that two thousand Templars were burned after Vienne. Even when one wants to sell paper, one mustn't play with fire.

8. A final show of strength. Let us not, however, be under any illusions. If the rules had been respected, the cardinals would have taken up the affair the day after the protest of Jacques de Molay; and if as henceforth could have been anticipated, Jacques de Molay and Geoffroy de Charnay had confirmed their last words, they would this time have been judged relapsed and delivered to the 'secular arm' (i.e., the king and his agents) and burned. Refusing to follow the narrative of the chronicle of Guillaume de Nangis on this point, Elizabeth Brown goes further in this direction in saying that, the case of relapse being perfectly clear, the cardinals themselves decided to 'return' to the 'secular arm' the guilty men – de Molay and Charny – so that they could be led off to the stake. E. A. R. Brown, 'Philip the Fair, Clement V and the End of the Knights Templar: The Execution of Jacques de Molay and Geoffroi de Charny in March 1314', *Viator* 47 (2016), pp. 285–8.

9. Lizerand, *Le Dossier*, pp. 26–7.

10. Finke, *Papsttum*, vol. II, pp. 45–6.

11. S. L. Field, 'The Inquisitor Ralph of Ligny, two German Templars and Marguerite Porète', *Journal of Medieval Religious Cultures*, 39 (2013), pp. 12–22.

12. Finke, *Acta aragonensia*, vol. III, p. 173.

13. See Chapter 5, pp. 85–6.

14. Guillaume de Nangis, *Chronique latine*, vol. I, p. 362.

15. See Chapter 7, pp. 109–11.

16. Out of these 659, 44 publicly withdrew their defence of the Order on 19 May (31 of them were interrogated later by the commission and confirmed their previous confessions) and 56 others also did so without announcing it publicly.

17. See Appendix 8.

18. See Chapter 14, pp. 221–2 and n. 17.

19. Michelet, vol. II, p. 375.

20. AN, J 413, no. 28.

21. Michelet, vol. I, p. 63.

22. Michelet, vol. I, pp. 97, 107. Thierry of Reims, however, is not mentioned on 28 March.

23. Michelet, vol. I, p. 153.

24. Michelet, vol. I, pp. 548–50; from the diocese of Liège, he is also called Borletta, or de Barletta, because he spent part of his career in southern Italy.

25. BnF, MS fr. 20334 (65, 69); see Appendix 8.

Appendices

1. Michelet, vol. I, p. 69.
2. AN, J 413, no. 28.
3. BnF, MS fr. 20334 (41–5); see Appendix 8.
4. BnF, MS fr. 20334 (41–5).
5. Having verified the original, BnF, MS lat. No. 11796, we cannot attribute an erroneous reading to Jules Michelet, who published the document. The error is indeed that of the scribe, who confused Sens and Senlis.
6. An allusion to the fact that Jacques de Molay, in a meeting with the king before the arrests, would have admitted this practice. Guillaume de Plaisians, in the speeches he gave in Poitiers in May and June 1308, mentioned this fact.
7. The diocese of Avranche is missing.
8. The dioceses of Angers, Nantes, Rennes, Dol, Saint-Malo, Tréguier, Saint-Pol-de-Léon, Quimper and Vannes are missing.
9. The diocese of Saintes is missing.
10. The diocese of Mende is missing.
11. The dioceses of Bazas, Dax, Aire, Lescar, Bayonne, Oloron and Comminges are missing.
12. The diocese of Lodève is missing.
13. The diocese of Viviers was in the kingdom of France, but it was a suffragan of the archbishopric of Vienne, like the diocese of Geneva.
14. See Appendix 2.
15. Indicated as a *supra juratus* witness, although absent from the above list.
16. Two were interrogated although they do not appear in the groups: Lambert de Cormeilles, of the diocese of Paris (Michelet, vol. I, p. 439), and Humbaud de la Boyssade (Michelet, vol. II, p. 85); one appears in a group but was not interrogated: Johannes Picardi (Michelet, vol. II, p. 165). Thus a total of interrogated Templars: 210 (-1 + 2) = 211.

SOURCES AND BIBLIOGRAPHY

Trial records

This study is based primarily on the records from the trials brought against the Templars in the kingdom of France. Below is a list of the trial records with archive references and relevant publications.

Troyes (1307), AN, J 413, no. 16; publication: Arnaud Baudin and Ghislain Brunel, 'Les Templiers en Champagne. Archives inédites, patrimoines et destins des hommes', in *Les Templiers dans l'Aube*, texts collected and published by *La vie en Champagne*, Troyes, 2013, pp. 62–9.

Pont de l'Arche et Roche d'Orival (1307), AN, J 413 no. 23; publication: Michel Miguet, *Templiers et hospitaliers en Normandie*, Paris, CTHS p. 138; S. L. Field, 'Royal Agents and Templar Confessions in the *bailliage* of Rouen', *French Historical Studies*, 39 (2016), pp. 35–70.

Paris (1307), AN, J 413, no. 18; publication: Jules Michelet, *Le Procès des templiers*, vol. II, Paris, 1851, pp. 275–20.

Caen (1307), AN, J 413, no. 17 (Latin version) and 20 (French version); publication: S. L. Field, 'Torture and Confession in the Templar Interrogations at Caen, 28–29 October 1307', *Speculum*, 91 (2016), pp. 297–327.

Cahors (1307) Barcelona, ACA, Pergamenos, no. 2486; partial publication: Finke, *Papsttum*, vol. II, pp. 316–21.

Cahors (2–3 January 1308), AN, J 413, no. 21; Prutz, *Entwicklung*, p. 327.

Carcassonne, AN, J 413, no. 25; publication: A. Nicolotti, 'L'interrogatorio dei Templari imprigionati a Carcassonne,' *Studi Medievali*, 52 (2011), pp. 703–12.

Aigues-Mortes-Alès-Nîmes (1307–1312), BnF, Baluze, 396, nos. 6 and 7; Ménard, *Histoire de Nîmes*, vol. 1, pp. 166–216.

Poitiers (1308), Vatican, Reg. Aven. no. 48, Benedict XII, vol. I, fols 438–451; publication: Schottmüller, *Untergang*, vol. II, pp. 1–71 (fols 438–448); Finke, *Papsttum*, vol. II, pp. 329–40 (fols 448–51).

Chinon, original version: Vatican, Archivio Segreto, *Archivum Arcis, Armarium* D 217; publication: Frale, *Il papato e il processo ai Templari*, pp. 198–220.

Chinon, traditional version: Vatican, Reg. Aven no. 48 Benedict XII, fols 437—438; publication: Finke, *Papsttum*, vol. II, pp. 320—29.

Clermont (June 1309), BnF, Baluze, 395, no. 5; publication: Sève and Chagny-Sève, *Le Procès des Templiers d'Auvergne, 1309—1311*.

Paris (1310—11), BnF, Latin manuscript 11796; Vatican, Archivio Segreto; publication: Michelet, vol. I, pp. 1—681; vol. II, pp. 1—276.

Other sources

Alberigo, G. (ed.), *Les Conciles œcuméniques*, vol. 1: *L'Histoire*; vol. 2: *Les décrets*, 1, *De Nicée à Latran V*, Paris, Éditions du Cerf, 1994 (trans. from the Italian edn, Bologna, 1972).

Baluze, E., *Vitae paparum avenionensium*, 4 vols, rev. edn by G. Mollat, Paris, 1913—22.

Blancard, L., 'Documents relatifs au procès des Templiers en Angleterre', *Revue des sociétés savantes*, 4th ser., VI (1867), pp. 416—20.

Chronique et annales de Gilles Le Muisit (1276—1352), ed. H. Lemaître, Paris, SHF, 1906.

Chronique latine de Guillaume de Nangis de 1113 à 1300 avec les continuations de cette chronique de 1300 à 1368, ed. Hercule Géraud, 2 vols, Paris, SHF, 1843.

Chronique métrique attribuée à Geoffroi de Paris, 1312—1316, ed. A. Diverres, Paris, 1950.

Chronique normande du XIVe siècle, ed. A. and E. Molinier, Paris, SHF, 1872.

Chronographia regum francorum, ed. H. de Moranvillé, Paris, SHF, 1891.

Coste, J. (ed.), *Boniface VIII en procès. Articles d'accusation et depositions des témoins (1303—1311)*, annotated edn, ed. and notes by Jean Coste, Rome, L'Erma, 1995.

Finke, H., *Acta aragonensia, Quellen zur Kirchen und Kulturgeschichte aus der diplomatischen Korrespondenz Jaymes II (1291—1327)*, Berlin, 1908.

——, *Papsttum und Untergang des Templerorden*, 2 vols, Munster, 1907.

Les Grandes Chroniques de France, ed. J. Viard, 10 vols, Paris, SHF, 1932, vols 7 and 8.

Gui, B., *Fleur des chroniques RHGF*, vol. 21; translation in F. Guizot, *Collection des mémoires relatifs à l'histoire de France*, Paris, 1824, vol. 15, pp. 333—410, under the title 'Des gestes glorieux des Français de l'an 1202 à l'an 1311'.

John XXII (1316—1324), *Lettres communes analysées d'après les registres dits d'Avignon et du Vatican*, ed. Guillaume Mollat, 16 vols, Paris, Bibliothèque des Écoles françaises d'Athènes et de Rome, 1904—46.

John XXII, *Lettres secrètes et curiales relatives à la France extraites des registres du Vatican*, ed. A. Coulon and S. Clémencet, 3 vols, Paris, Bibliothèque des Écoles françaises d'Athènes et de Rome 1906—67.

Jean de Saint-Victor, 'Excerpta e memoriali historiarum auctore Johanne Parisiensi Sancti Victoris Parisiensis canonico regulari', *Recueil des historiens des Gaules et de la France*, vol. XXI, Paris, 1855.

Lizerand, G., *Le Dossier de l'affaire des templiers*, Paris, Les Belles-Lettres, 1923, new edn, 2006.

Ménard, L., *Histoire civile, ecclésiastique et littéraire de la ville de Nismes*, 7 vols, Paris, 1750, vol. I, *Preuves* (interrogation of the Templars from the diocese of Nîmes), pp. 166–219.

Michelet, J., *Le Procès des templiers*, Collections des documents inédits sur l'Histoire de France, 1841–51; new edn, Paris, CTHS, 1987.

Musée des Archives départementales. Collection of facsimiles, documents taken from the archives of prefectures, town halls and hospices, Paris, Imprimerie nationale, 1878.

Nicolotti, A., 'L'interrogatorio di Templari imprigionati a Carcassonne', *Studi Medievali*, 52 (2011), pp. 697–729.

Oursel, R., *Le Procès des templiers*, Paris, 1955.

Picot, G. (ed.), *Documents relatifs aux États généraux et assemblées réunis sous Philippe le Bel*, Paris, 1903.

Port, C., *Le Livre de Guillaume Le Maire, évêque d'Angers*, in *Mélanges historiques*, vol. 2, Collection de documents inédits sur l'histoire de France, Paris, 1877.

Prutz, H., *Entwicklung und Untergang des Tempelherrenordens, mit Benutzung bisher ungedruckter Materialien*, Berlin, 1888.

Ptolemy da Lucca, *Vita Clementis papae V*, in Baluze, *Vitae paparum Avenionensium*, vol. I.

Regestum Clementis papae V ex Vaticanis archetypis, [...] *editio, cura et studio monachorum ordinis sancti Benedicti*, 9 vols, Rome, 1885–92.

Schottmüller, K., *Der Untergang des Templer-Ordens*, 2 vols, Berlin, 1887; vol. II, *Urkunden*.

Collections of essays

Bériou, N., and Josserand, P. (eds.), *Prier et combattre. Dictionnaire européen des ordres religieux-militaires*, Paris, Fayard, 2009.

Burgtorf, J., Crawford, P., and Nicholson, H. (eds), *The Debate on the Trial of the Templars (1307–1314)*, Farnham, Ashgate, 2010.

Chevalier, M.-A. (ed.), *La Fin de l'ordre du Temple*, Paris, Geuthner, 2012.

Josserand, P., de Oliveira, L. F., and Carraz, D. (eds), *Élites et ordres militaires au Moyen Âge, Rencontres autour d'Alain Demurger*, Madrid, Casa de Velázquez, 2015.

Individual works

Barber, M., *The Trial of the Templars*, Cambridge, Cambridge University Press, 1978; 2nd edn, 2006.

——, 'The World Picture of Philip the Fair', *Journal of Medieval History*, 8 (1982), pp. 13–27.

——, and Bate, K., *The Templars: Selected Sources Translated and Annotated*, Manchester, Manchester University Press, 2002.

Bautier, R. H., 'Diplomatique et histoire politique. Ce que la critique diplomatique nous apprend sur la personnalité de Philippe le Bel', *Revue historique*, CCLIX (1978), pp. 3–27.

Beck, A., *La fine dei Templari*, Casale Monferrato, 1994; trans. from the German (*Der Untergang der Templer*), Freiburg im Breisgau, 1992.

Bellomo, E., *The Templar Order in North-West Italy (1142–c. 1330)*, Leiden, Brill, 2008.

Bertrand, M., 'Les templiers en Normandie', *Heimdal, Revue d'art et d'histoire de Normandie*, 26 (1978).

Bessey, V., *Les Commanderies de l'Hôpital en Picardie au temps des chevaliers de Rhodes (1309–1522)*, Millau, Conservatoire Larzac templier et hospitalier, Bez-et-Esparon, Études et Communications, 2005.

Bompaire, M., 'Trésor de Templiers et trésors de Juifs au XIVe siècle', *Bulletin de la Société française de numismatique*, 52, 1998, pp. 185–8.

Bordonove, G., *La Tragédie des templiers*, Paris, Pygmalion, 1993.

Boutaric, E., *Actes du Parlement de Paris*, Paris, 1863.

——, 'Clément V, Philippe le Bel et les Templiers', *Revue des questions historiques*, vols 10 and 11 (1871–2).

——, 'Documents relatifs à l'histoire de Philippe le Bel', *Notices et extraits des manuscrits de la Bibliothèque impériale*, vol. XX, 1861, pp. 161–2.

Boutry, P. 'Clément XIV', in P. Levillain (ed.), *Dictionnaire historique de la papauté*, Paris, Fayard, 1994, pp. 394–7.

Brown, E. A. R., 'Philip the Fair, Clement V and the End of the Knights Templar: The Execution of Jacques de Molay and Geoffroi de Charny in March 1314', *Viator* 47 (2016), pp. 229–92.

Bryson, D., 'Three (*sic*) Traitors of the Temple. Was Their Truth the Whole Truth?' in Burgtorf, Crawford and Nicholson (eds), *The Debate*, pp. 97–103.

Bulman, J. K., *The Court Book of Mende and the Secular Lordship of the Bishop*, Toronto, University of Toronto Press, 2008.

Burgtorf, J., *The Central Convent of Hospitallers and Templars: History, Organization and Personnel (1099/1120–1310)*, Leiden, Brill, 2008.

——, 'The Trial Inventories of the Templars' Houses in France: Select Aspects', in Burgtorf, Crawford and Nicholson (eds), *The Debate*, pp. 105–15.

Burrows, T., 'The Templars' Case for their Defence in 1310', *The Journal of Religious History* (Sydney University Press), 13 (1984–5), pp. 248–60.

Calvi, D., *Effemeride sagro-profana di quando memorabile sia successo in Bergamo*, 3 vols, Milan, vol. 2, 1676.

Caravita, R., *Rinaldo da Concorezzo, arcivescovo di Ravenna (1303–1321) al tempo di Dante*, Florence, Leo Olschki, 1964.

Carbasse, J.-M., *Introduction historique au droit pénal*, Paris, Presses universitaires de France, 1990.

Carraz, D., *L'Ordre du Temple dans la basse vallée du Rhône. Ordres militaires, croisades et sociétés méridionales*, Lyon, Presses universitaires de Lyon, 2005.

Cazelles, R., *Nouvelle histoire de Paris*, vol. 3: *De la fin du règne de Philippe Auguste à la mort de Charles V*, Paris, 1972.

Cerrini, S., *La Passione dei Templari*, Milan, Mondadori, 2016.

Challet, V., 'Entre expansionnisme capétien et relents d'hérésie: le procès des templiers du Midi', *Les Ordres religieux militaires dans le Midi (XIIe-XIVe siècle)*, Cahiers de Fanjeaux, no. 41, Toulouse, 2006, pp. 139–61.

Cheney, C. R., 'The Downfall of the Templars and a Letter in Their Defence', in F. Whitehead, A. M. Diverès and F. E. Sutcliffe (eds), *Medieval Miscellany Presented to Eugene Vinaver*, Manchester, Manchester University Press, 1965, pp. 65–79.

Claverie, P.-V., *L'Ordre du Temple en Terre sainte et à Chypre au XIIIe siècle*, 3 vols, Nicosia, Centre de recherche scientifique, 2005.

Clemens, J., 'La rumeur agenaise de l'enfermement templier au début du XIVe siècle', *Revue de l'Agenais*, 123 (1996), pp. 219–33, and 124 (1997), pp. 23–40.

Cottineau, Dom H. L., *Répertoire topo-bibliographique des abbayes et prieurés*, 3 vols, Mâcon, 1935, vol. 2, p. 1973.

Courtenay, W. J., 'Marguerite's Judges: The University of Paris in 1310', in S. L. Field, R. E. Lerner and S. Piron (eds), *Marguerite Porète et le 'Miroir des simples âmes': Perspectives historiographiques, philosophiques et littéraires*, Paris, Vrin, 2013, pp. 215–31.

———, 'The Role of University Masters and Bachelors at Paris in the Templar Affair, 1307–1308', in A. Speer and D. Wirmer (eds), *1308: Eine Topographie historischen Gleichzeitigkeit*, Berlin and New York, De Gruyter, 2010, pp. 171–81.

———, and Ubl, K., *Gelehrte Gutachten und königliche Politik im Templerprozess*, Hanover, Hahnsche Buchhandlung, 2010 (with the publication of texts regarding the relapse of the theologian Jean de Pouilly).

Crawford, P., 'The Involvement of the University of Paris in the Trials of Marguerite Porète and of the Templars, 1308–1310', in Burgtorf, Crawford and Nicholson (eds), *The Debate*, pp. 129–43.

———, 'The University of Paris and the Trial of the Templars', in V. Mallia-Milanes (ed.), *History and Heritage*, vol. 3 of *The Military Orders*, Aldershot, Ashgate, 2008, pp. 115–22.

Delisle, L., *Étude sur la condition de la classe agricole et l'état de l'agriculture en Normandie au Moyen Âge*, Paris, 1851.

———, 'Guillaume d'Ercuis, précepteur de Philippe le Bel', HLF, vol. XXXII, Paris, 1898.

Demurger, A., *Les Hospitaliers; de Jérusalem à Rhodes (vers 1050–1317)*, Paris, Tallandier, 2013.

———, *Jacques de Molay. Le crépuscule des templiers*, Paris, Payot, 2002, 2007; rev. edn, Petite Bibliothèque Payot, 2014. [English-language edition: *The Last Templar: The Tragedy of Jacques de Molay*, new updated version, London, Profile, 2009.]

———, *Les Templiers, Une chevalerie chrétienne au Moyen Âge*, Paris, Éditions du Seuil, 2005; new edition with postface: Point-Seuil, 2014.

———, 'Between Barcelona and Cyprus: The Travels of Berenguer of Cardona, Templar Master of Aragon and Catalonia (1300–1301)', in Jorgen Burgtorf and Helen Nicholson (eds), *International Mobility in the Military Orders (Twelfth to Fifteenth Centuries): Travelling on Christ's Business*, Cardiff, University of Wales Press, 2006, pp. 65–74.

———, 'Clément V', in P. Levillain, *Dictionnaire historique de la papauté*, Paris, Fayard, 2006, pp. 367–9.

——, 'Dal Tempio all'Ospedale: Il destino delle commande templari nella contea di Auxerre (sec. XIV)', in F. Tommasi (ed.), *Acri 1291. La fine della presenza degli ordini militari in Terra Santa e i nuovi orientamenti nel XIV secolo*, Perugia, Quattroemme, 1996, pp. 93–8.

——, 'Éléments pour une prosopographie du "peuple templier": la comparution des templiers devant la commission pontificale de Paris (février-mai 1310)', in P. Josserand, L. F. de Oliveira and D. Carraz, *Élites et ordres militaires au Moyen Âge*, Madrid, 2015, pp. 17–36.

——, 'Encore le procès des templiers. A propos d'un ouvrage récent', *Le Moyen Âge*, 97 (1991), pp. 25–39.

——, 'Habit', in N. Beriou and P. Josserand (eds), *Prier et combattre: Dictionnaire européen des Ordres religieux militaires*, Paris, Fayard, 2009.

——, '" Manuscrit de Chinon" or "Moment Chinon"? Quelques remarques sur l'attitude du pape Clément V envers les templiers à l'été 1308', in M. Montesano (ed.), *'Come l'orco della Fabia'. Studi per Franco Cardini*, Florence, Sismel, Edizione del Galuzzo, 2010, pp. 111–21.

——, 'Les ordres religieux-militaires et l'argent: sources et pratiques', in K. Borchardt, K. Döring, P. Josserand and H. Nicholson (eds), *The Templars and Their Sources*, London and New York, Routledge, 2017, pp. 166–83.

——, 'Outre-mer: Le passage des templiers en Orient d'après les dépositions du procès', *Chemins d'outre-mer: Études sur la Méditerranée médiévale offertes à Michel Balard*, 2 vols, Paris, Publications de la Sorbonne, 2004, pp. 217–30.

Du Bourg, A., *Ordre de Malte: Histoire du Grand Prieuré de Toulouse*, Toulouse, 1883.

Duby, G., *Guillaume le Maréchal, ou le meilleur chevalier du monde*, Paris, Fayard, 1984.

Dupuy, P., *Histoire du différend d'entre le pape Boniface VIII et Philippe le Bel, roy de France*, Paris, 1685.

——, *Traittez concernant l'histoire de France: sçavoir la condamnation des Templiers, avec quelques actes; l'histoire du schisme, les papes tenans le siege en Avignon et quelques procez criminels*, Paris 1654; repr. a century later as *Histoire de l'ordre militaire des Templiers ou chevalerie du Temple de Jérusalem depuis son établissement jusqu'à sa décadence et sa suppression*, Brussels, 1751; an anastatic reprint was published (Nîmes, Rediviva) in 2002.

Étienne, G., 'La Villeneuve du Temple aux XIIIᵉ et XIVᵉ siècle', in *Études sur l'histoire de Paris et de l'Île-de-France*, Actes du 100e congrès national des sociétés savantes (Paris, 1975), vol. 2, Paris, BnF, 1978, pp. 87–9.

Fasti Ecclesiae Gallicanae, Turnhout, Brepols:
  1: Diocese of Amiens, by P. Desportes, 1996.
  2: Diocese of Rouen, by V. Tabbagh, 1998.
  3: Diocese of Reims, by P. Desportes, 1998.
  8: Diocese of Mende, by P. Maurice, 2008.
  11: Diocese of Sens, by V. Tabbagh, 2009.

Favier, J, *Philippe le Bel*, Paris, Fayard, 1978, repr. 1998; paperback 'Texto' edn, 2013.

Field, S. L., 'La fin de l'ordre du Temple à Paris: le cas de Mathieu de Cressonessart', in Chevalier (ed.), *La Fin de l'ordre du Temple*, pp. 101–32.

——, 'The Inquisitor Ralph of Ligny, Two German Templars and Marguerite Porète', *Journal of Medieval Religious Cultures*, 39 (2013), pp. 1–22.

———, 'Royal Agents and Templar Confessions in the *Bailliage* of Rouen', *French Historical Studies*, 39 (2016), p. 35–70.

———, 'Torture and Confession in the Templar Interrogations at Caen, 28–29 October 1307', *Speculum*, 91 (2016), pp. 297–327.

Forey, A. J., *The Fall of the Templars in the Crown of Aragon*, Aldershot, Ashgate, 2001.

———, 'Could Alleged Templar Malpractices Have Remained Undetected for Decades', in Burgtorf, Crawford and Nicholson (eds), *The Debate*, pp. 11–20.

———, 'The ex-Templars in England', *Journal of Ecclesiastical History*, 53 (2002), pp. 18–37.

———, 'Letters of the Last Two Masters', *Nottingham Medieval Studies*, XLV (2001), pp. 166–7.

———, 'Towards a Profile of the Templars in the Early Fourteenth Century', in *The Military Orders*, vol. I, M. Barber (ed.), *Fighting for the Faith and Caring for the Sick*, Aldershot, Routledge, 1994, pp. 196–204.

———, 'Were the Templars Guilty, Even if They Were Not Heretics or Apostates?', *Viator*, 42 (2011), pp. 115–41.

———, 'Templars after the Trial: Further Evidence', *Revue Mabillon*, 84 (2012), pp. 89–110.

Frale, B., *L'ultima battaglia dei Templari. Dal codice ombra d'obbedienza militare alla costruzione del processo per eresia*, Rome, Viella, 2001.

———, *Il papato e il processo ai Templari: l'inedita assoluzione di Chinon alla luce della diplomatica pontifica*, Rome, Viella, 2003.

———, 'The Chinon Chart: Papal Absolution of the Last Templar, Master Jacques de Molay', *Journal of Medieval History*, 30 (2004), pp. 109–34.

———, 'Du catharisme à la sorcellerie: les inquisiteurs du Midi dans le procès des templiers', in *Les Ordres religieux-militaires dans le Midi (XIIe-XIVe siècle)*, Cahiers de Fanjeaux, no. 41, Toulouse, 2006, pp. 169–86.

———, 'L'interrogatorio ai Templari nella provincia di Bernardo Gui: un'ipotesi per il frammento del registo Avignonese 305', in *Dall'Archivio segreto vaticano. Miscellanea di testi, saggi e inventari*, Vatican City, Archivio Segreto I (2006), pp. 199–272.

———, '1308: Il piano di Clement V per salvaguardare l'ordine dei Templari', in Speer and Wirmer (eds), *1308: Eine Topographie historischen Gleichzeitigkeit*, pp. 125–39.

Galland, B., *Deux archevêchés entre la France et l'Empire. Les archevêques de Lyon et les archevêques de Vienne du milieu du XIIe siècle au milieu du XIVe siècle*, Rome, École française de Rome, 1994.

Gams, B., *Series episcoporum, archiepiscoporum ecclesiae catholicae*, Ratisbonne, 1873.

Géraud, H., *Paris sous Philippe le Bel*, Tübingen, 1991 (reprint of the 1887 edn).

Gilbert Dony, A., 'Les derniers templiers du bailliage de Caen', *Bulletin de la Société des antiquaires de Normandie*, LXII [1994–7], (2003), pp. 175–96.

Guyon, C., *Les Écoliers du Christ: l'ordre canonial du Val des Écoliers, 1201–1539*, Saint-Étienne, Université de Saint-Étienne, 1998.

Hartmann, P., 'Conflans près Paris', *Mémoires de la Société de l'histoire de Paris et de l'Île-de-France*, 35 (1908), pp. 1–188.

Heiduk, M., 'Die Chinon Charta von 1308 – die Wende im Templerprozess? Ein archivilischer Fund und sein publizistisches Echo', in Speer and Wirmer (eds), *1308: Eine Topographie historischen Gleichzeitigkeit*, pp. 140–60.

Hélary, X., *La Bataille de Courtrai*, Paris, Tallandier, 2012.

Higounet-Nadal, A., 'L'inventaire des biens de la commanderie des templiers de Sainte-Eulalie du Larzac en 1308', *Annales du Midi*, 68 (1956), pp. 255–62.

Hillairet, J., *Dictionnaire historique des rues de Paris*, 2 vols, Paris, Éditions de Minuit, 1963.

Hooghe, F., 'The Trial of the Templars in the County of Flanders', in Burgtorf, Crawford and Nicholson (eds), *The Debate*, pp. 285–300.

Josserand, P., 'Les templiers en Bretagne au Moyen Âge: mythe et réalité', *Annales de Bretagne et des Pays de l'Ouest*, 119 (2012), pp. 7–33.

Juillet, J., *Templiers et Hospitaliers du Quercy*, Cahors, Éditions du Laquet, 1999.

Kramer, T., 'Terror, Torture and the Truth: The Testimonies of the Templars Revisited', in Burgtorf, Crawford and Nicholson (eds), *The Debate*, pp. 71–85.

Lalou, É., *Itinéraire de Philippe IV le Bel (1285–1314)*, 2 vols, vol. 1, *Introduction*; vol. 2, *Routes et résidences, mémoires de l'Académie des inscriptions et belles-lettres*, Paris, De Boccard, 2007.

Langlois, C.-V., 'L'affaire des templiers', *Journal des savants* (1908), pp. 417–35.

——, 'Extrait du 2ᵉ journal de la chambre des comptes', *Notices et extraits des manuscrits de la Bibliothèque nationale*, Paris, vol. 40 (1917).

——, 'Notices et documents relatifs à l'histoire des XIIIᵉ et XIVᵉ siècles: Nova Curie', *Revue historique*, 87 (1905), pp. 55–79.

——, 'Le procès des templiers', *Revue des Deux Mondes*, 103 (1891), pp. 382–421.

Lauxerois, R. (ed.), *Vienne au crépuscule des templiers*, Grenoble, Presses universitaires de Grenoble, 2014.

Lea, H. C., *The History of the Inquisition of the Middle Ages*, 3 vols, New York, Harper & Brothers, 1888.

Lebeuf, Abbot, *Mémoires concernant l'histoire civile et ecclésiastique d'Auxerre et de son ancien diocèse*, Édition A. Challe et M. Quantin, 4 vols, Auxerre, 1855.

Lecler, J., *Le Concile de Vienne, 1311–1312*, Paris, Fayard, 2005.

Lizerand, G., *Clément V et Philippe IV le Bel*, Paris, 1910.

——, 'Les dépositions du grand maître Jacques de Molay', *Le Moyen Âge*, XXVI (1913), pp. 81–106.

Loiseau, J., *Les Mamelouks, XIIIᵉ–XVIᵉ siècle*, Paris, Seuil, 2014.

Lorentz, P., and Sauchon, D., *Atlas de Paris au Moyen Age*, Paris, Parigrame Éditions, 2006.

Luttrell, A., 'The Election of the Templar Master James de Molay', in Burgtorf, Crawford and Nicholson (eds), *The Debate*, pp. 21–31.

——, 'Observations on the Fall of the Temple', in P. Josserand, L. F. de Oliveira and D. Carraz (eds), *Élites et Ordre militaires au Moyen Âge*, Madrid, Casa de Velázquez, 2015, pp. 365–72.

McNamara, J. A., *Gilles Aycelin, the Servant of Two Masters*, Syracuse, NY, Syracuse University Press, 1973.

Marquette, J.-B., 'À propos d'un document bazadais inédit concernant le procès des templiers', *Cahiers du Bazadais*, 94 (1991).

Menache, S., *Clement V*, Cambridge, Cambridge University Press, 1998.

——, 'Chronicles and Historiography: The Interrelationship of Fact and Fiction', *Journal of Medieval History*, 32 (2006), pp. 333–45.

——, 'The Templar Order: A Failed Ideal?', *The Catholic Historical Review*, 79 (1993), pp. 1–21.

Miguet, M., *Templiers et hospitaliers en Normandie*, Paris, CTHS, 1995.

Mollat, G., 'La dispersion définitive des templiers après leur suppression', *Compte-rendus des séances de l'Académie des inscriptions et belles-lettres*, 96 (1952), pp. 376–80.

Müller, E., *Das Konzil von Vienne*, Munster, 1934.

Nadiras, S., 'Guillaume de Nogaret en ses dossiers: méthodes de travail et de gouvernement d'un conseiller royal au début du XIVe siècle', doctoral thesis from Université Paris-1 (14 March 2012).

Nicolotti, A., 'L'interrogatorio dei Templari imprigionati a Carcassonne', *Studi Medievali*, 52 (2011), pp. 703–12.

Palès-Gobilliard, A., (ed.), *L'Inquisiteur Geoffroy d'Ablis et les cathares du comté de Foix (1308–1309)*, Paris, CNRS, 1984.

Paravicini Bagliani, A., *Boniface VIII, un pape hérétique?*, Paris, Payot, 2003.

Partner, P., *The Murdered Magicians: The Templars and Their Myths*, Oxford, Oxford University Press, 1981.

Pegues, F. J., *The Lawyers of the Last Capetians*, Princeton, Princeton University Press, 1962.

Provost, A., *Domus Diaboli: Un évêque en procès au temps de Philippe le Bel*, Paris, Belin, 2010.

Raynouard, F. J. M., *Monumens historiques relatifs à la condamnation des chevaliers du Temple et à l'abolition de leur ordre*, Paris, 1813.

Riley-Smith, J., 'The Structures of the Orders of the Temple and the Hospital in c.1291', in S. J. Ridyard (ed.) *The Medieval Crusade*, Woodbridge, Boydell Press, 2004, pp. 125–43.

——, 'Were the Templars Guilty?,' in S. J. Ridyard (ed.), *The Medieval Crusade*, Woodbridge, Boydell Press, 2004, pp. 107–24.

Rogozinski, J., 'The Counsellors of the Senescal of Beaucaire', *Speculum*, vol. 44, no. 3 (July 1969), pp. 421–39.

Sans i Travé, J.-M., *La fi dels Templers catalans*, Barcelona, Pagés, 2008.

Satora, M., 'The Social Reception of the Templar Trial in Early Fourteenth Century France: The Transmission of Information', in Burgtorf, Crawford and Nicholson (eds), *The Debate*, pp. 161–8.

Schmidt, T., *Der Bonifaz Prozess*, Cologne and Vienna, 1989.

Sève, R., and A.-M., *Le Procès des Templiers d'Auvergne, 1309–1311*, Paris, CTHS, 1986.

Speer, A., and Wirmer, D. (eds), *1308: Eine Topographie historischen Gleichzeitigkeit*, Berlin and New York, De Gruyter, 2010.

Strayer, J. R., *The Reign of Philip the Fair*, Princeton, Princeton University Press, 1980.

Streeter, D. R., 'The Templars Face the Inquisition: The Papal Commission and the Diocesan Tribunals in France, 1308–1311', in Burgtorf, Crawford and Nicholson (eds), *The Debate*, pp. 87–95.

Théry, J., 'La fuite du commandeur des templiers de Lombardie (nuit du 13 février 1308)', in *Les trente nuits qui ont fait l'Histoire*, Paris, Belin, 2014, pp. 105–15.

——, 'Une hérésie d'état: Philippe le Bel, le procès des "perfides templiers" et la pontificalisation de la royauté française', *Médiévales*, 60 (2011), pp. 157–86. Repr. and modified in Chevalier (ed.), *La fin de l'ordre du Temple*.

——, 'Procès des templiers', in N. Bériou and P. Josserand (eds), *Prier et combattre*, pp. 743–50.

Tonnelier, P.-M., 'À Domme en Périgord: le message des prisonniers,' *Archeologia*, 32 (1970), pp. 25–37.

Trudon des Ormes, A., *Étude sur les possessions de l'ordre du Temple en Picardie*, Amiens, 1892.

——, *Liste des maisons et de quelques dignitaries de l'Ordre du Temple en Syrie, en Chypre et en France d'après les pièces du procès*, Paris, 1900.

Ubl, K., 'Haeretici Relapsi. Jean de Pouilly und die juristischen Grunedlagen für die Hinrichtung der Tempelritter', in Speer and Wirmer (eds), *1308: Eine Topographie historischen Gleichzeitigkeit*, pp. 161–70.

Vaivre, J.-B. de, *La Commanderie d'Epailly et sa chapelle templière*, Mémoires de l'Académie des inscriptions et belles lettres, Paris, De Boccard, 2005.

Valois, N., 'Deux nouveaux témoignages sur le procès des templiers', *Compte-rendus des séances de l'année 1910 de l'Académie des Inscriptions et Belles Lettres*, Paris, 1910, pp. 230–38.

——, 'Jean de Pouilly, théologien', *Histoire littéraire de la France*, vol. 34, Paris, 1914, pp. 220–81.

Vinas, R., *Le Procès des templiers en Roussillon*, Perpignan, Tdo Éditions, 2009.

Viollet, P., 'Beranger Frédol, canoniste', HLF, vol. 34, Paris, 1915.

——, 'Les interrogatoires de Jacques de Molay, grand maître du Temple: conjectures', *Mémoires de l'Académie des inscriptions et belles-lettres*, XXXVIII (1909).

Vogel, C., 'Templar Runaways and Renegades before, during and after the Trial', in Burgtorf, Crawford and Nicholson (eds), *The Debate*, pp. 317–26.

Wilmart, M., 'Salariés, journaliers et artisans au service d'une exploitation agricole templière: la commanderie de Payns au début du XIVᵉ siècle', in A. Baudin, G. Brunel and N. Dohrmann (eds), *L'Économie templière en Occident*, Troyes, 2013, pp. 273–93.

INDEX OF PLACES

[T] = Temple house or commandery

INDEX OF PEOPLE

[T] = Templar
dit/dite = also known as